Religion and Politics
in the U

SECOND EDIT

Withdrawn

Religion and Politics in the United States

SECOND EDITION

Kenneth D. Wald
University of Florida, Gainesville

PRESS

A Division of Congressional Quarterly Inc.
Washington, D.C.

To Robin, Dara, and Jaina

Book and cover design by Kachergis Book Design

Printed in the United States of America

Library of Congress Cataloging-in-Publication Data
Wald, Kenneth D.
    Religion and politics in the United States / Kenneth D. Wald.
—2nd ed.
        p.   cm.
    Includes bibliographical references and index.
    ISBN 0-87187-604-3
    1. Religion and politics—United States—History—20th
century.   2. United States—Religion—1960–   3. United
States—Politics and government—1981–1989.   I. Title.
BL2525.W35   1989
322'.1'097309048—dc20   91-2777

Contents

Figures

Preface to the First Edition

There is a sense, of course, in which religion is a subjective and personal matter but there is also a sense in which it is an objective fact and can be dealt with as such. It is a fact that there is such a thing as Christianity and that it has exerted a profound influence upon our thinking and institutions. To understand this influence is essential whether one is . . . a Christian or not.

—John H. Hallowell, *Religious Perspectives of College Teaching in Political Science*

I have written this book to show that religion is more important in American politics than most Americans realize but in different ways than they commonly imagine.

From reading the typical textbook on American government, one might think that religion has political relevance only on those rare occasions when church and state collide over issues like prayer in the public schools, abortion policy, or public observance of religious holidays. With only brief mention of such controversies, most textbooks imply that religious issues are at best secondary, that government's more serious tasks are such things as economic growth, public safety, world peace, and social justice. As I hope to show in the following pages, one cannot fully understand how America discharges the task of governing itself without recognizing the profound influence of religion.

Religion has penetrated public life in many ways. Not only has the American religious tradition contributed to some of the enduring principles that undergird the political system, but also religious values and interests have helped to shape the political perspectives of individuals, probably affecting their reactions to both candidates and issues. Religious communities have entered the political process itself, in an organized effort to influence public policy on a wide range of issues. There is much more to the religious factor in American politics than just the church-state debate, as important as that is.

Of course, any time one highlights a particular factor in politics there is a risk of crediting that factor with too much influence. Even though religion is important in American politics and has been overlooked in the past, it is important to recognize at the outset that it is only one of many influences upon American political values, institutions, and policies. Thus, just as I will attempt to identify the conditions that enhance religious influence upon government and politics, so also will I note circumstances that limit the political impact of religious forces.

Although political observers are finally coming to recognize the political significance of religion in the United States, they have yet to give up another durable stereotype about religion in politics—namely, that religion is inevitably a force for conservatism and preservation of the existing social order. Recent attempts to enlist some religious denominations in conservative movements have reinforced the image of religion as a pillar of tradition. But, in fact, the political implications of religion have been much too ambiguous to justify the image of uniformity among believers. Today, as always, deeply religious people can be found on different sides of most issues and at all points along the political spectrum. Around the globe, religion has inspired fervent loyalty to some governments and revolution against others. In the United States, the liberal Jesse Jackson and the conservative Jerry Falwell both draw upon a common theological tradition of evangelical Protestantism. I hope the reader will come away from the book with greater awareness of the political diversity associated with American religion.

Recognizing the political role of religion is not the same thing as judging it. Classroom experience makes me vividly aware that people reach different verdicts about the connection between religion and politics. Some people applaud it as necessary and proper; others denounce it as the root of mischief and evil. In this book I have tried to inform readers about both the noble and the unfortunate sides of the religious element in politics. In the intellectual minefield that is religion and politics, no one book can satisfy everyone or would be of much value if it did. This book is offered on the principle that good teaching prompts believers to question a faith and encourages skeptics to appreciate its value. In that sense, I hope to educate people who believe deeply in a religious faith as well as those who reject or do not care much about religion.

The reader should also know that this text takes a social scientific perspective on the subject of religion and politics. After trying to explain that thought in many different ways, I find that I cannot improve on the words of a scholar who began a book on the same topic by warning readers that "to be a historian is to seek to explain in human terms. If God speaks, it is not through him. If He speaks to others, the historian cannot vouch for it. In this sense the historian is necessarily secularist" (Strout 1974, xiv). As that comment suggests, the social scientific approach refuses to explain religion in terms of supernatural forces, insisting instead on finding human causes for patterns of human behavior. Likewise, most social scientists resist the opposite tendency to reduce religion to a biological or genetic trait. Supernaturalists may explain the survival of religion as God's will while some natural scientists might attribute the persistence of religion in society to the sound dietary principles and healthy life-styles of believers (see National Research Council 1982, 6–10). While both these explanations may be true and useful, the social scientist prefers to emphasize the operation of human consciousness and choice. Thus Chapter 1 invokes neither the hand of God nor the principles of evolution to explain why religion prospers in America. Instead, consistent with the social scientific outlook, it calls attention to cognitive factors—humanity's apparent need to reduce uncertainty about its place in the universe—and elements of the social and political structure that encourage religious observance. The rest of the book follows suit.

The book begins with two chapters that establish the framework for studying the relationship between religion and politics in the United States. Chapter 1 demonstrates the continuing significance of religion in American life, and Chapter 2 identifies the features of religion and the American political system that promote regular interaction between the two spheres. In ensuing chapters I examine the potential political impact of religion on different levels of political life. Separate chapters are devoted to the influence of religion on fundamental American beliefs about politics and governance (Chapter 3); mass partisan and ideological orientations (Chapter 4); views about church/state relations (Chapter 5); and specific policy debates and issues on the public agenda

(Chapter 6). The next two chapters explain the often puzzling changes that have taken place in the political behavior of major religious groups in the United States—Chapter 7 explores the theologically conservative Protestant churches, and Chapter 8 similarly analyzes the other major religious traditions, groups whose interesting patterns of stability and change have sometimes been lost in the glare of publicity devoted to the evangelical Protestants. I conclude with a chapter that weighs the positive and negative contributions of religion to politics and governance in the United States.

Because religion's role in politics is the subject of strong feeling, readers may want to know something more about the author's background and beliefs. Without revealing more than is necessary, I am Jewish, the child of Holocaust survivors and the grandchild of Holocaust victims. That heritage, which has shaped me in many ways I can only dimly comprehend, has certainly contributed to an abiding interest in the topic being examined and to a keen appreciation for the potential political consequences of religious belief. It may also account for my belief that religion should speak to public affairs. Though well aware that churches perform an important spiritual mission that might suffer from excessive political involvement, I nonetheless believe that religious institutions have a responsibility to remind the state of its ethical obligations. Accordingly, I am more comfortable when churches challenge the government than when they vest the state with a holy aura. Readers of different backgrounds may spot other assumptions that seem natural to me but are perhaps contentious to them.

Although I cannot be certain of all the ways my personal background has influenced the book, a good memory permits me to identify persons in the foreground who helped prepare the author for writing it. I owe a great debt to scholars who paved the way for this project with pioneering studies of religion and politics, and to contemporary investigators scattered among the academic disciplines of political science, history, sociology, anthropology, and religion. On a more individual level, some of the thoughts expressed here were forged in the heat of collaborative teaching and research with Mike Lupfer and Bill Marty of Memphis State University and with Sam Hill and Dennis Owen at the University of Florida. The manuscript benefited from the close reading and incisive suggestions of Clarke Cochran of Texas Tech, Jim Guth of Furman University, Corwin Smidt of Calvin College, and Robert Wuthnow of Princeton University and from the careful assessments of Marilyn Moller, Anne McCoy, and Dan Flanagan of St. Martin's Press. There was a manuscript to review only because Michael Weber and Peter Dougherty of St. Martin's showed a willingness to invest in a project with the potential of high intellectual payoffs but uncertain market prospects. Their confidence can never fully be repaid, but it will certainly help if lots of people buy the book.

I only wish my father had lived long enough to see the book and appreciate his influence on it. The values that were planted at home were further nurtured by teachers and clergy who continued my education, often without knowing it. My wife, Robin, and my daughters, Dara and Jaina, shared my life (and word processor) during the writing of the book, alternately helping me to keep going and distracting me from the task with various pleasant alternatives. The book was completed, on schedule, while Robin was writing a book of her own, one child was beginning school, and the other was teething. That should convince even the most skeptical person that supernatural forces work in the universe.

K.D.W.

REFERENCES

Hallowell, John H. 1951. *Religious Perspectives of College Teaching in Political Science*. New Haven, Conn.: Edward W. Hazen Foundation.

National Research Council. 1982. *Diet, Nutrition, and Cancer.* Washington, D.C.: National Academy Press.

Strout, Cushing. 1974. *The New Heavens and the New Earth*. New York: Harper and Row.

Preface to the Second Edition

Like its predecessor, this edition stresses the importance of religion in American public life and the diversity that religion imparts to politics. I revised the text chiefly to take account of recent developments, to incorporate new research findings, and, in a few cases, to clarify arguments left ambiguous or underdeveloped in the first edition. This new edition still maintains a social scientific perspective on issues seldom treated from that vantage point. As before, the book is consecrated in the hope of subverting the state of mind represented by the epigram, "For believers, there are no questions, and for unbelievers there are no answers."

I completed my revisions of the text during a sabbatical in Jerusalem. As a firm believer in comparative study, I went to Israel to observe the interaction of religion and politics in a very different environment. The year yielded much more data than expected; the crisis in the Persian Gulf, the intensification of the Palestinian uprising, an outbreak of Islamic fundamentalism, and the renewal of hostilities between Israel's secular and religious populations all added to the already rich atmosphere of the region.

All this comparative study has not changed my views about religion in politics; it has only deepened them. For example, the public outrage in Israel generated by attempts to compel observance of the Sabbath and other commandments brought to mind Jefferson's and Madison's prescient warnings about the dangers to both church and state from government-sponsored religious coercion. The occasional tendency of both Jewish and Islamic activists to claim God as a cheerleader in tribal conflicts reminded me of a similar tendency that surfaces periodically in American political conflict. During my stay in Israel, some religious leaders were the source of moral inspiration, others the source of moral bewilderment—as if to reinforce my belief about the divergent political tendencies inherent in religion. Similarly, the anger I felt when terrorists knifed civilians in the name of Allah was offset somewhat by reading about other Muslims whose religious convictions prompted them to disarm bombs and to save a deranged Israeli soldier who had wandered off into the desert. Rarely have both the constructive and destructive political implications of religion been so manifest. The net effect of this experience lends urgency to the conclusion reached in the book.

In revising the first edition, I benefited greatly from collaborative work with the intrepid band of scholars active in the APSA Section on Religion and Politics. They know who they are, and readers will guess their identities by looking for names that recur with great frequency in the references. I appreciate the hospitality extended to me during my Israeli stay by Avraham Diskin and the Department of Political Science at the Hebrew University of Jerusalem. Hazel Pridgen, the only truly indispensable member of the political science department at the University of Florida, bravely tackled BITNET so that she could respond to my incessant trans-Atlantic requests for information, references, and reprints.

The staff of CQ Press—especially David Tarr, Brenda Carter, Kathryn Suarez and Ann O'Malley—provided wonderful guidance and support; I know of no other publisher that would create a housing referral service for a displaced author. Kristen Carpenter Stoever edited the manuscript with sensitivity and grace, never once complaining about my inability to distinguish between "upon" and "on." I regret that Joanne Daniels, who spent three years apologizing for not publishing the first edition, didn't hang around CQ Press quite long enough to see the results of her persistence.

On the home front, I continue to receive a sublime mixture of encouragement and distraction from the members of my family. Even though their situations have changed somewhat since the first edition, I am happy to rededicate the volume to them.

K.D.W.

Religion and Politics in the United States

SECOND EDITION

1. A Secular Society?

When you introduce religion into politics, you're playing with fire.
—Senator Lowell P. Weicker, Jr., *New York Times*, March 21, 1984

Religion and politics are necessarily related.
—President Ronald W. Reagan, *Church & State*

People are usually taught that it is impolite to argue religion or politics with strangers and dangerous to do so with friends. These topics are treated with such delicacy because they evoke strong passions; men and women have been known to discuss, debate, argue, organize, demonstrate, resist, fight, and kill—or be killed—on behalf of their religious or political beliefs. What, then, could possibly justify violating both taboos by writing a book about religion *and* politics?

The answer is simply that religion has reemerged as an important political factor in the United States. The increasing religious overtones in recent presidential campaigns are one sign of the trend. The election of a Catholic president by a predominantly Protestant electorate in 1960 was widely celebrated as marking the end of religious appeals in politics.[1] But in 1976, candidate Jimmy Carter's strong profession of religious faith drew close attention from a national media largely unfamiliar with the phenomenon of "born-again" Christianity. Four years later, all three candidates on the November ballot claimed to be evangelical Protestants, and several ministers with large television audiences drew national headlines for their organized efforts on behalf of the Republican nominee. In 1984, many conservative Protestant ministers again drummed up support for Ronald Reagan, and the Democrats chose among three major contenders with strong religious credentials: a Baptist minister (Jesse Jackson), a former divinity student (Gary Hart), and the son of a Methodist minister (Walter Mondale). The evidence of a religious motif in 1988 included the candidacies of two ministers (Democrat Jesse Jackson and Republican Pat Robertson), widespread public concern about the "character" of several candidates, and the overriding emphasis on "traditional values" during the campaign. In America's single most important political ritual, the selection of a president, the religious emphasis has been plain to see.

In recent years, moreover, the national agenda has included a host of controversial questions that touch upon deeply held religious beliefs and outlooks—issues such as abortion, women's role in society, pornography, homosexuality, and the arms race. Contemporary controversies about prayer and religious clubs in public schools and government recognition of religious holidays exemplify the continuing debate over church-state relations. Even economic policy questions, traditionally deemed beyond the sphere of religious concern, are increasingly looked at from a "moral" perspective (Pasquariello 1985). During 1985, for example, the Roman Catholic bishops in the United States released a searching theological critique of the U.S. economy, and the Reagan administration proposed changes in tax laws that, it was claimed, would strengthen the biblically ordained institution of the family.

The growth of religious controversy around the globe has also reverberated in American political life. In response to a powerful resurgence of Islamic fundamentalism during the 1980s, the United States tried to act as peacekeeper in Lebanon, was held hostage in Iran, and supplied weapons to Moslem rebels in Afghanistan. As the Islamic resurgence dominated U.S. foreign policy considerations in the 1980s, the collapse of European communism will probably recast international relations in the 1990s. The uprisings that toppled the governments of Eastern Europe and threatened Soviet unity were championed by religious groups. In several countries allied with the United States, notably Korea and the Philippines, churches played a similar role by undercutting repressive regimes. American churches and religious groups have been eager to shape the government's response to these new developments. The long tradition of support for anti-Communist governments and movements has given way in many churches to preoccupation with human rights abuses (Livezey 1989). Some churches have pressed the government to negotiate reductions in nuclear weapons, to admit more political refugees from Central America, and to cut economic ties with the government of South Africa. Remaining true to their traditions, some conservative churches raised funds to combat left-wing movements in Latin America.

On the basis of this evidence, a strong case can be made for studying the impact of religion in national political life. We may applaud it, deplore it, be repelled or fascinated by it—but the first imperative is to understand how and why religion has been such an important factor in American politics. Despite the evidence, scholars and citizens alike were slow to recognize the political impact of religion in the United States. The underestimation stemmed in large part from a mistaken belief in the inevitable "secularization" of modern life. As the next section shows, the widespread belief that religion was destined to recede from the mind of humanity prepared observers to discount religious influences in the political realm.

The Puzzle of Religious Vitality

Textbooks on American government send a message that "religion is not and never has been a significant factor either in the development of our political institutions or in their operations" (Carey 1982, 7). Critics blame this "secular" prejudice on authors' supposed indifference or outright hostility toward religion. For the most part, however, the neglect of religion as a political force stems from widespread acceptance of certain social theories that guide academic research away from religion (Warner 1979). A novelist who wrote that "a man's eyes can only see what they're learnt to see" understood well that expectations can become blinders, prompting us to overlook important information and developments. In the case of religion, most scholars "learnt to see" *secularization*, broadly understood as the decline of religious influence in advanced industrial societies, and that expectation drew their attention away from religion in the political realm.

The concept of secularization encompasses a variety of processes as complex as the phenomenon of religion itself (Glasner 1977, chap. 2). In its most neutral sense, secularization refers only to changes in religion as society develops. One process, *differentiation*, means the development of religion as a specialized institution with its own sphere of competence. When religion is differentiated, it retreats from a privileged position in such fields as the law, education, and medicine and restricts its operations to other realms. The unique task of religion in modern society, according to this view, is providing individuals with consolation and comfort. Under modern conditions, religion also experiences *privatization*. That term refers to the evolution of religion into a matter of personal judgment and choice that exerts its profoundest impact on individuals. A privatized faith is reluctant to tell society how it ought to behave. A third process associated with secularization, *desacralization*, refers to changes in thought rather than to the transformation of religious organizations. Desacralization is the tendency to explain the everyday world in terms of material reality rather than supernatural forces. Modern societies often treat as ordinary what more traditional civilizations may imbue with a divine character. Finally, secularization is often equated with *liberalization* of religious doctrine, the lowering of barriers between religious groups, and the relaxation of orthodoxy. Together, these processes constitute the *neutral* definition of secularization.

If secularization is understood simply as religious change of this sort, it leaves room for religion—modified, adapted, and adjusted to new circumstances—as a significant force in contemporary society. None of the trends described above would necessarily remove religion from the political universe and some might even strengthen its relevance to political conflict. But many scholars have raised secularization into an iron law that boldly predicts the virtual extinction of organized religion and points to the consequent elimination of religious influences in contemporary culture. This particular understanding of secularization, the "naive" version that predicts diminishing significance for religion in politics, is associated with two of the most influential theories of social change, the *modernization* approach and the *class conflict* model.

The modernization approach predicts transformations in life and thought because of the rapid growth of cities; the rise of factory production; the spread of education, communication, and technology; and the emergence of vast administrative apparatuses, or bureaucracies. Sociological observers of the late nineteenth and early twentieth centuries believed that these developments, which define what we mean by "modern," had wrought massive changes in the place of religion in society. Before the onset of modernization, most people lived in small, geographically isolated settlements and were preoccupied by the daily task of producing life's necessities. With limited exposure to external influences, people living in the settlements shared a stable set of beliefs, customs, and traditions. Subject to forces beyond their control, particularly weather and disease, people were receptive to supernatural outlooks. The myths and folk religions of primitive cultures are commonly thought to have originated in fear of the unknown, in dread and awe (Goodenough 1972). This description may conjure up images of a Stone Age pygmy tribe in a rain forest, but the portrait would be just as appropriate for the Irish villages, Norwegian communes, and East European *shtetls* whose migrants eventually populated much of the United States.

According to modernization theory, the forces of modernity shatter such cultures. Migration to a city in search of work removes the villagers from traditional influences and brings them into regular contact with persons from different backgrounds. When the villages are penetrated by new means of communication, even those who stay put are subject to new influences. Traditional values, particularly the emphasis on fate and the supernatural, are undermined by the doctrine of scientific cause-and-effect taught in school, factory, and mass media (Inkeles 1983). When held up to scientific standards of proof and evidence, religious claims and, therefore, religious faith may falter. Individuals further discover that relations between people, formerly governed by traditions of deference and obedience in conformity to divine will, change under the impact of modernity. Exchange, bargaining, and negotiation become the accepted mode of interaction, with law and reason (not religion) determining the framework. Loyalty is given not out of reverence but as repayment for services rendered. As a consequence, people come to define their personal identity and political interests not in terms of religion but as a function of their standing in the marketplace—as owners, workers, proprietors of small businesses, and so forth.

According to the predictions of modernization theory, societies that have been fully exposed to the currents of modern life will accord religion a minor role (Halebsky 1976, chaps. 1–4). Except among the elderly, raised in a more devout age, and the residents of cultural backwaters, the practice of religion will diminish. The institutions of religion will suffer a similar fate unless they are transformed into agencies of social welfare and service centers—and even then churches must compete with the state to perform these tasks. An even more telling sign of religious decay is the erosion of religious thought:

Men act less and less in response to religious motivation: they assess the world in empirical and rational terms, and find themselves involved in rational organizations and rationally determined roles which allow small scope for such religious predilections as they might privately entertain. Even if . . . non-logical behaviour continues in unabated measure in human society, then at least the terms of non-rationality have changed. It is no longer the dogmas of the Christian Church which dictate behaviour, but other quite irrational and arbitrary assumptions about life, society and the laws which govern the physical universe. (Wilson 1966, 10)

The change in the terms of thought, from a God-centered to a human-centered world, is the most dramatic testament to the victory of secularization in the modern world. This understanding of modern society leaves little room for religion as a social or political factor.

The forecast of religious decline in the modern world has been reinforced by another influential theory of social change—Marxism. Like modernization theorists, Marx and Engels believed that religious sentiments reflected a human response to forces that defied understanding, and that faith in the supernatural was likely to be a casualty of economic development (Aptheker 1968). Writing in the middle of the nineteenth century, Marx began with the paradox that the human conquest of nature, which ought to have put an end to hunger and oppression, seemed instead to have intensified inequality. The sources of wealth, differing from one era to the next, had always been monopolized by and used to enrich the few at the expense of the many. But with the coming of industrialization and factory-based economies, he argued, the process of exploitation became more severe. Once subordinate to the forces of nature, workers now found themselves subordinate to economic elites. Unemployment replaced natural calamity as the scourge of human existence.

In this setting, Marx suggested, religion appealed most strongly to the oppressed who desperately needed some explanation for their plight. Christianity found its pioneers among slave populations because it promised them the solace of a better life to come; psychologically, the Christian religion was a balm, an alternative to despair. Subsequently, the growth of Christianity was encouraged by the dominant groups in society because it might teach the "lower orders"—be they slaves, serfs, or industrial workers—to accept their condition as God's will and to look for solace in the afterlife. In this way, Marx argued in a famous passage, religion became the "opiate" of the people.

In Marx's view, a society built on exploitation could not long endure because the oppressed majority would eventually recognize its exploitation. As conditions worsened, the working class would realize the inequity of prevailing economic arrangements and their source in man-made doctrines and practices. When this occurred, Marx expected an uprising, the seizure of power on behalf of the previously oppressed majority and the creation of a new, more just and humane social order. In this new world, the mass of humankind would reclaim its proper place as the maker of its own destiny and all the artificial doctrines developed to support the dethroned system—including religion—would be consigned to the dustbin of history. Religion, which had persisted because of intolerable social conditions, would simply evaporate with these social transformations.

Bolstered by theories that confidently forecast the demise of religion, many students of politics predicted that religious controversy would eventually disappear from the political agenda, to be replaced by disputes rooted primarily in economics. Students of political behavior similarly anticipated a shift in the basis of political loyalty from "premodern" factors such as religion, ethnicity, and region to more modern factors like social class, occupational standing, and socioeconomic status (Epstein 1967, 88; Hechter 1975). In "mature" political systems, it was said, political campaigns no longer resembled emotional religious crusades but instead took on the flavor of slick exercises in public relations; sober appeals to self-interest replaced passionate calls for national salvation. What most political observers never expected to find was an advanced industrial society in which religion exercised a tenacious hold on the public mind and strongly influenced the conduct of political life. Yet that is precisely what we find in the contemporary United States.

The Persistence of Religion

By most conventional yardsticks, the United States was one of the first nations to achieve modernization, and it continues to lead the way in many aspects of social development. If modernization leads inevitably to the decline of religious institutions, practices and feelings—what I have called the "naive" understanding of secularization—then the erosion of religion ought to show up first in such a mobile, affluent, urban, and expansive society. Yet American religion, like Mark Twain, has obstinately refused to go along with reports of its imminent death.

American religion has certainly experienced the processes associated with the neutral definition of secularization. Religion is a specialized institution with a limited public role and religious affiliation is a matter of personal choice. Consistent with the experience of desacralization, Americans generally interpret events from a scientific and naturalist perspective. Many orthodox doctrines and forms of devotion have been abandoned or modified by church authorities. But these changes do not add up to the global decline in faith predicted by naive secularization theory. It cannot be denied that some religions have lost intensity, esteem, and membership or that many Americans are indifferent or antagonistic toward religion. Yet even these elements of decline have been offset by spectacular growth in some religions, the flowering of new faiths, periodic revivals of religious enthusiasm, and the spread of religious sentiment to some of the most "secularized" segments of the population (Hastings and Hoge 1986; Hadden 1987). The naive model of secularization cannot withstand the facts.

Just how poorly modernization and Marxist theories of religion fit the United States is demonstrated graphically in Figure 1.1, which reflects information from fifteen different countries. The diagonal line shows the relationship between level of economic development and the proportion of a representative national sample who told interviewers that religious beliefs were "very important" to them.[2] The downward slope of the line as the level of "modernization" increases generally confirms the prediction that economic development goes hand in hand with a decline in traditional religious sentiment. The United States is a conspicuous exception, however, to the generalization. With by far the highest score on the index of economic development, this country was also among the most "religious" of countries as shown by the answers its citizens gave to interviewers. The magnitude of American "exceptionalism" can best be gauged by comparing the proportion of Americans that valued religious beliefs very highly—51 percent—with the proportion that should have done so on the basis of the pattern in all countries—a mere 5 percent.

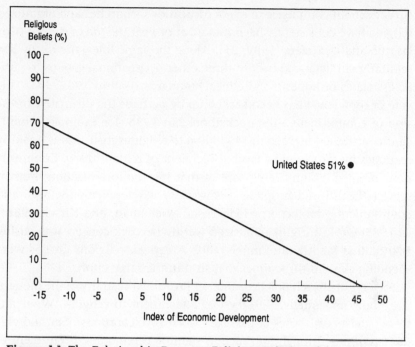

Figure 1.1 The Relationship Between Religious Beliefs and Economic Development

By all the normal yardsticks of religious commitment—the strength of religious institutions, practices, and belief—the United States has resisted the pressures toward secularity. Institutionally, churches are probably the most vital voluntary organization in a country that puts a premium on "joining up." A tabulation by the National Council of Churches lists approximately 340,000 churches in the United States with a total membership of about 135,000,000 (Jacquet 1983, 238).[3] Depending on how "membership" is defined, the 135,000,000 church members amount to somewhere between three-fifths and three-fourths of the adult population. Despite all the talk about "decline," the proportion of church members among persons aged fifteen and older is virtually the same today (76.9 percent) as it was in 1950 (78.5 percent) and, with due allowance for the raggedness of historical data, actually seems to be higher now than recorded by the first official census of churches in 1890.[4]

Support for organized religion shows up in other ways. In annual surveys about confidence in major institutions, churches and organized religion have consistently been ranked at or near the top of the list (Colasanto and DeStefano 1989, 21). Along the same lines, the clergy has regularly outdistanced twenty-three other occupational groups in public estimates of honesty and ethical standards (Gallup 1982, 14). This vote of confidence has been backed up by perhaps the ultimate expression of commitment—the pocketbook. In 1986, for example, Americans contributed more than $40 billion to religious institutions, making churches by far the most favored recipient of philanthropy. Congregations devoted a significant share of that income to education, human service, health and hospitals, community development, the arts, and environmental protection (Hodgkinson, Weitzman, and Kirsch 1988). In 1985, while a highly publicized worldwide rock concert was raising $70 million for African famine relief, American religious groups were spending close to three times that sum in the same effort.[5]

Surveys of church practice, another presumed casualty of the modern age, show an equally high level of attachment to religion. What anthropologists call "rites of passage" (formal celebrations of an individual's progress through life, such as naming ceremonies, attainment of adulthood, marriage, and funerals) are still monopolized by the churches in the United States, as they are in many other cultures. But as national data reveal, devotion is hardly limited to such occasions (Figure 1.2). At one extreme, about one-third of the population claims never to attend church outside of weddings and funerals. The "unchurched" comprise the self-defined irreligious (9 percent of the entire population), another 7 percent who consider themselves religious but who have no denominational commitment, and the remaining 15 percent who identify personally with a religious group but do not participate. Slightly more than one-third of the population maintains a moderate association with churches. Though the moderate category includes those who attend church only a few times a year (10 percent), most people in this category (25 percent) attend at least once a month. The most intensely religious third of the population includes people who are in church every week (19 percent) and those who attend even more than once a week (16 percent).

Churchgoing is but one form of religious behavior; Americans engage in a wide range of other public and private devotional acts (Figure 1.3). More than three-quarters of all Americans identify with a religion and

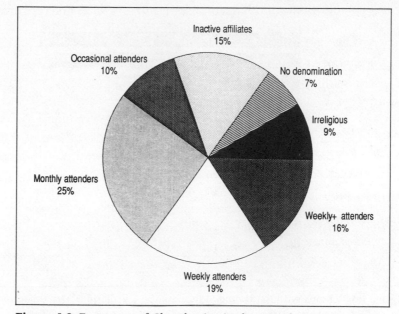

Figure 1.2 Frequency of Churchgoing in the United States (Source: Calculated by the author from the 1989 pilot study, American National Election Study, Center for Political Studies)

consider it important in their lives. Substantial majorities report formal membership in a church and daily prayers. Approximately one-third of the population claims to get a "great deal" of daily guidance from religion and to monitor religious television and radio programs weekly. Almost 20 percent say they read the Bible on a daily basis. One in ten claims membership in independent religious organizations and daily reading about religion in newspapers and magazines. About one in twenty report attempting to convince someone else to accept their faith each day. Based on questions from the same survey, religious involvement appears far more widespread than many forms of political participation. More Americans identify with a denomination than a political party, and the typical citizen is much more likely to attend church than a political meeting. The proportion of citizens who claim to evangelize on behalf of their faith exceeds the percentage who report having tried to influence another person's vote.

Cynics may regard these statistics as superficial, a tribute more to habit and conformity than to deep-seated faith. In truth, it is much

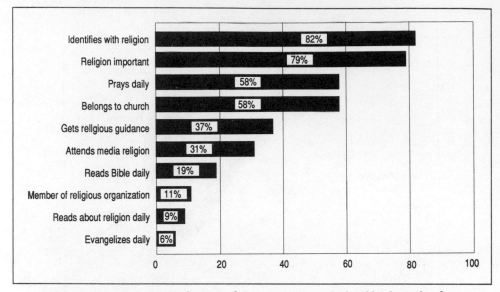

Figure 1.3 Religiosity in the United States (Source: Calculated by the author from the 1989 pilot study, American National Election Study, Center for Political Studies)

more challenging to prove the persistence of religious feeling. Precisely that aspect of religion—its capacity to keep people's minds focused on questions of ultimate value, on heaven, hell, right, wrong, judgment, justice—supposedly should have declined with the triumph of modern culture. Because "feelings" of any sort are notoriously slippery things to measure, perhaps the best that can be done here is to note that major studies of contemporary values have repeatedly asserted the underlying importance of religion. For example, a major life insurance company commissioned a report to assess what Americans believed and how those beliefs were related to factors such as age, social standing, place of residence, and so forth. Despite this secular orientation, the authors found that the religious factor emerged as a kind of superstar among all the other pieces of information:

In investigating major aspects of American life—community involvement, political and moral beliefs, personal relationships, and work—time and again, systematic analysis led to the one factor that consistently and dramatically affects the values and behavior of Americans. This factor is level of religious commitment. The initial intention of this study was not to prepare a report on the impact of religion on American life, but the pattern of responses was compelling. (Research and Forecasts 1981, 6)

Detailed findings from a host of surveys have borne out this conclusion. By overwhelming majorities, Americans have continued to endorse the core assumptions of Christianity—the existence of God, the divinity of Jesus, the reality of an afterlife—and to insist on the importance of these values in their own lives (Gallup 1982, 112–127). When Americans think about God, they conceive of a creator and healer; the image of heaven carried in the minds of modern Americans depicts a place of union with God and reunion with loved ones (Davis 1984, 114–126). "Two centuries after the intellectual world has said that these kinds of things do not happen," reported a scholar who interviewed 2,000 small-town Midwesterners, many people reported mystical experiences such as visions, prophetic dreams, voices from heaven, and visits from spirits.[6]

To the extent that such things can be measured, religious feeling, like religious institutions and practices, has survived intact in probably the most "modern" society known in history. Statistics have been used to make the point because numbers are the currency of argument in a scientific culture. But because national statistics often have a numbing effect, they should be supplemented with a local example. The stability of a religious texture in American life has been demonstrated forcefully by a continuing study of a small industrial town in eastern Indiana. In the 1920s, a pair of gifted social observers decided to put "Middletown," a pseudonym for Muncie, under the microscope of social analysis (Lynd and Lynd 1929). Curious about the changes wrought by the passage of fifty years, a team of social scientists set out in the 1970s to repeat the study of Muncie (Caplow, Bahr, and Chadwick 1983). In the half-century since the first study, Muncie had experienced all the changes that are supposed to encourage secularization—rapid population growth, relentless technological advance, the spread of education, increasing bureaucracy, the penetration of mass media, an expanded governmental presence. Could the vibrant religious tradition of the town possibly survive the corrosive effects of these changes?

Despite the odds against it, traditional religion was found to be doing quite nicely in modern Muncie. In the words of the most recent study of the town, "The Reverend Rip Van Winkle, Methodist minister, awakening in Middletown after a 60-year sleep, would hardly know he had been away" (ibid., 280). He might be surprised by the growth of tolerance among religious groups, but little else had changed since the

1920s. The "Middletown" residents of the 1970s seemed every bit as pious as their grandparents and great-grandparents. Most people still subscribed to the core beliefs of Christianity and, whether measured by the numbers of clergy and buildings, by financial contributions, or by attendance at worship, the churches flourished. But surely, it may be argued, the survival of religion was purchased at a high price—by sacrificing the traditional emphasis on the emotional and spiritual for a more modern style stressing reason and social reform. This plausible suggestion collapses under the evidence of growth in the most theologically conservative churches, a renewed emphasis on emotional forms of worship in all denominations, and the continuing priority placed by the clergy on the spiritual well-being of their flocks. Against all expectations, the most recent study of Muncie uncovered a community with reverence for the sacred and faith in religion as a source of strength and guidance.

Because I have been trying to counter the widespread myth that religion is dead or declining in the United States, I have deployed the arguments for persistence in the starkest possible way. By making the case so emphatically, I do not want to suggest that American religion is altogether immune to the forces of modernity. We know, for example, that the appeal of the "old time" religion remains strongest among certain population groups: housewives, the elderly, inhabitants of rural areas and small towns, Southerners, and persons with low levels of education. These groups share limited exposure to such major institutions of modernization as the marketplace, cities, industry, and schools. People who are deeply embedded in those institutions are less likely to have maintained commitment to religious orthodoxy. We also know that religion has adapted to modern thought by recasting God. In the vision of some religious authorities, God now appears not only as the almighty power of the universe and source of redemption but also as a psychologist, economic adviser, athletic trainer, and friend (Hunter 1983, chaps. 4, 6).

It is one thing to acknowledge these changes, quite another to "overinterpret" them as signs of the imminent extinction of religious sentiment in American life. Religion has certainly been touched and influenced by the modern world, but it is more accurate to speak of secularization as adjustment and adaptation than to employ the image of decline and fall. The United States has managed to modernize without casting off religion in the process. As we shall see throughout the remainder of the book, religious change has not meant the removal of religious concern from the public agenda. In some instances, the process of secularization has enhanced the relevance of religion to political life.

Possible Explanations

Where did modernization theorists and Marxists go wrong in predicting that religion would disappear from the highly developed United States? Both types of social theory appear to have underestimated both the need for religion, even in the most advanced societies, and the capacity of American religious institutions to adapt to changing circumstances.

Some students of religion cite the durability of beliefs about the supernatural as proof that religion meets a basic human need, much like food and shelter (Bell 1977; Greeley and Baum 1973; Prozesky 1984; Stark and Bainbridge 1985). Alone among creatures on earth, human beings possess the capacity to think in a sophisticated way about their place in the universe. They wonder about the meaning of life, the reality of death, the basis of ethical behavior and human cooperation. They ask, among other questions, why some people commit evil; why the good and innocent should suffer from it; and how, apart from instinct, they can even think to know what is good and what is evil. To answer these questions about life—to give meaning to human existence—they develop systems of belief that include religion. So long as the world requires some explanation, it is argued, human beings will create faiths to live by. Nothing about this notion would bother most modernization theorists or Marxists. They would argue, merely, that the need for a system of meaning will eventually be satisfied fully by science or by a comprehensive body of political ideas, making religion unnecessary.

Science seems inadequate, however, as a religious substitute. The assumption that scientific understanding eliminates a need for religious explanation falters because of persistent questions about life on this planet that no scientific advance can ever settle. It is hard to see how familiarity with, for example, the third law of thermodynamics can ever comfort troubled people or improve upon religious faith in enabling them to cope with the inevitability of mortality.[7] Science is simply irrelevant to such questions. In other cases, the progress of science may reinforce concern for spirituality. The more Albert Einstein learned about the beauty and symmetry of nature, the more he appreciated what he saw as God's hidden hand; he is not the only scientist to have been so moved (Tracy 1973). Finally, science may actually intensify concern about questions of value. The spectacular growth of medical technology has raised agonizing moral dilemmas about the nature and conditions of life, dilemmas that appear on the political agenda in the form of issues such as abortion, euthanasia, organ transplantation, in vitro fertilization, genetic engineering, embryo experimentation, life extension, and "living wills." Progress in weapons development has underlined dramatically the problem of human evil and the necessity for cooperation. To the extent science liberates humanity from human misery and economic insecurity, it gives us freedom to ponder questions of ultimate value.

In advanced technological societies, paradoxically, there has been a striking loss of faith in reason as a solution to all human problems. Consider this assessment of the current mood:

These are gloomy times. People are fatalistic and death possessed. There is a conviction that we have been collectively asleep at the wheel, that the path of so-called reason has taken us far along the road to hell, probably past the point of no return. More and more, the feeling is taking hold that we are on the edge of a volcano that is about to explode. (Frankel 1984, 162)

This comment, all the more remarkable because its author is a man described as "a business consultant who specializes in information and telecommunications technologies," illustrates how a society built on science may generate profound discontent with the consequences of scientific activity. For some people, the reaction to a technological society apparently run amok is a return to spirituality, a renewed respect for the religious values that science once seemed to render unnecessary.

If not science, will politics perhaps substitute for religious faith? The quest for justice through political movements may well take on the form of a religious crusade. But in the end, when political movements have triumphed, the perennial problems remain, and the perennial solutions, including religion, offer themselves. Well before the collapse of Communist regimes in Eastern Europe, some Marxist intellectuals were prompted by the abuses and inadequacies of the system to consider traditional religious dogma as a source of reform (Machovec 1976). More fundamentally, the efforts of many of these regimes to replace religious faith with a new "Socialist consciousness" must now be regarded as spectacular failures. Poland is only the most vivid illustration of how Marxism was no match for the power of religious orthodoxy (Szajkowski 1983).

In the United States, political faith has not yet managed to supplant religious commitment. While some political activists discard their religious faith as an impediment to social change, others see no necessity to choose between them. When religious and political loyalties do appear to collide, the choice may actually favor the former. During the turbulent political era of the late 1960s and early 1970s, the extremes of the American political spectrum were symbolized by Eldridge Cleaver, an eloquent and angry spokesman for black nationalism, and his opposite number, a conservative political operative named Charles Colson who once boasted that he would have sacrificed his own grandmother to gain political advantage. In the 1980s, disillusioned with the consequences of their political activism, these two firebrands shared public platforms to preach for a return to biblical Christianity. With less publicity, other intellectuals have traveled the same path from political activism to religious commitment (Schumer 1984). A few conversions may not indicate a social trend, but they do illustrate that politics may prove to be an ineffective alternative to religion.

Why the United States?

The inadequacy of science and politics only partly explains the persistence of religion in the United States. Theories about intrinsic human needs and failed alternatives are global concepts that do not resolve questions about why the United States, in particular, has remained so much more deeply tied to religion than other modern societies. American exceptionalism in religion, amply documented in Figure 1.1, has usually been attributed to cultural compatibility, a need for social identity, the independence of religion from the state, and a competitive religious environment.

Cultural Compatibility

Early American churches emphasized self-government for congregations and voluntary affiliation for individuals. Organized religion thus helped shape American society to value the autonomy of individuals and to distrust hierarchy (Lipset 1967, 180–192). To this day, Americans find religion "comfortable" because it fits in well with deep-seated cultural values about freedom of choice and individual initiative. Religion may also reinforce the larger culture by supplying what individuals find lacking in society. Robert Booth Fowler (1989) argues that churches thrive in the United States because they provide an antidote to the extremes of individualism and relativism. People join churches, he argues, because they want a sense of community absent from other parts of their lives. They also turn to religion for rules and guidelines, something sorely missing from a society that makes every individual the arbiter of right and wrong.

Social Identity

Religion has also flourished because it meets a continuing need for social identity that is particularly important in the United States. Physical mobility, economic change, and immigration have constantly threatened people with a loss of roots, of a sense that they belong to any meaningful group or tradition. Confronted with chaos, individuals find much-needed stability in religion. In what John F. Kennedy called "a nation of immigrants," the church helped newcomers adjust to life in a new and confusing environment. Churches still fill that role for newcomers who migrate from abroad or simply move around frequently from place to place.

Political Independence

The "wall of separation" between church and state, Thomas Jefferson's metaphor for the independence of churches from government support and patronage, may well have strengthened the position of religion in the United States (Caplow 1985). In the long run, churches closely associated with worldly power risk guilt by association. If a repressive regime endorses a state religion, the church may be perceived as a barrier to justice. Marx had expected religion to collapse when the workers recognized it as a prop of capitalism, justifying exploitation as God's will and conveniently postponing justice until the next life. In truth, state religions have often defended corrupt governments in order to maintain a privileged position.

But American religion has not always served the purpose of the dominant economic powers. Slaveowners found support for servitude in the

Bible, but the slaves could and did read the Old Testament as a call to resistance and revolt. The religious impulse that could be used to justify the worst abuses of capitalism could also fuel movements against the oppression of industrial workers. Even today, when many Roman Catholics have joined the ranks of the wealthy and powerful, their church continues to speak out against poverty and to remind Americans about the plight of the oppressed.

Unlike the churches in many other societies, those in the United States appear to have avoided an exclusive association with any particular political affiliation. This conclusion has been supported by a study of public opinion in eight West European societies. In countries with a tradition of state-supported religion, surveys revealed moderately strong statistical associations between individual religiosity and political ideology (McDonough, Barnes, and Pina 1984, 661–663). Political conflict pitted a "secular" left wing against a "religious" right. In the United States, by contrast, a much weaker relationship was found between personal religious attachment and self-described ideological position. This suggests that the tie between religion and ideology is not natural but rooted in history. By remaining independent of the state, reserving the right to pass judgment, American religion has avoided becoming an adjunct of the political system and, so, can remain unscathed when the political system itself is in disrepute. The high regard for churches in the United States may owe something to their avoidance of too close an identification with any political party or administration.

Religious Pluralism

Signifying the remarkable diversity of denominations in the country, religious pluralism contributes to the persistence of religion in the United States (Salisbury 1983). The early settlers subscribed to a variety of faiths, and Americans have since taken advantage of the freedom of religion to found literally hundreds of new sects (Marty 1984). The diversity among the early settlers was compounded by the importation of new faiths through the global population migration to America. To an extent possibly unparalleled in the modern world, the American citizen is confronted with a vast range of denominational options. As a result, no single denomination today comprises more than about 40 percent of the church membership (Quinn et al., 1982, 1–3); thus, it is correct to say that all Americans belong to minority religions. This conclusion holds at the local level: nearly half the U.S. population resides in counties in which no single denomination has majority status (Salisbury, Sprague, and Weiher 1984).

Pluralism has forced the churches to compete for members and, so, encouraged them to adapt to new social realities. In religion, like in politics and economics, competition in an open market has stimulated the participants to bid for support with all manner of incentives. Denominations have had to master the very latest techniques in persuasion and recruitment as they reach out to potential "consumers"—hence, the churches' use of sophisticated means of communication, marketing skills, and information technology (McDaniel 1989; Stewart 1989). The emphasis on attracting members from the religious marketplace has also prompted the churches to offer attractive benefit packages and services that in other countries might be provided by government.[8] As noted above, even the message of religion has been tailored to modern times, through an emphasis on the relevance of religion to worldly pursuits as diverse as sports, the stock market, and mental health. In countries lacking religious diversity, churches may well remain attached to symbols, rituals, and patterns of behavior that cannot withstand the social forces that promote secularity. Not having the luxury of a monopoly, the American churches have deliberately cultivated skills and qualities that almost certainly have contributed to the persistence of religious attachment.

I have gone to such lengths to stress the staying power of religion for a reason. Religious conflict in politics is commonly treated as a throwback, an interesting diversion from the "real" issues of the modern era. But if religion remains a vital force in this day and age, then one cannot claim to understand the contemporary era without appreciating the religious factor, especially in the realm of politics. The remainder of the book delineates the many ways religion intersects political life in the United States.

NOTES

1. In fact, as we subsequently learned, a substantial proportion of the electorate was moved by the religious issue in 1960 (Dawidowicz and Goldstein 1974).
2. Figure 1.1 is an ordinary, least-squares regression equation with data for fifteen countries: Canada, Britain, France, West Germany, Italy, Brazil, Mexico, India,

Japan, Australia, Holland, Belgium, Finland, Norway, and Denmark. The independent variable was Cole's (1979, 209–210) economic development index based on twenty-two separate statistics. The dependent variable, the proportion of the national sample who described religious beliefs as "very important," was obtained from Hastings and Hastings (1979, 333). The aggregate values Gallup reported for Scandinavia and the Benelux nations were assigned to the individual countries. This approach was first suggested by Walter Dean Burnham.

3. Another recent survey estimates the number of congregations at just under 300,000 (Hodgkinson, Weitzman, and Kirsch 1988).

4. For a summary of church membership over the years, see Jacquet (1983, 242), but note that the entry for 1890 should be 21.7 rather than the 41.7 million printed erroneously. Survey-based estimates of church membership among adults, dating back only half a century, also show remarkable stability (Colasanto and DeStefano 1989, 19).

5. "Churches Act in Concert for African Aid," *Miami Herald*, July 26, 1985, 1-C, 5-C.

6. "Mystical Experiences Abound in Culture That Spurns Them, Studies Say," *Tallahassee Democrat*, Feb. 14, 1987, 1-D.

7. For a fascinating account of how religious values may fill a void where science appears to fail, see the *Manchester Guardian*'s story on a British hospice ("In the Midst of Death We Are in Life," Mar. 4, 1984, 4). It reports:

Religion plays a central part in the life of St. Christopher's. It is not compulsory, nor is it thrust upon patients. "But I don't think anyone could work here for long without the support of some faith," she [the founder] says firmly. The pressure and intensity of the work, the great demands of the dying and their relatives means that those who work there need answers, or at least partial answers in order to sustain themselves.

8. One anecdote may illustrate how the churches outperform "secular" authorities. A Gainesville, Florida, newspaper reports that after a storm blew a tree onto an elderly woman's property, cutting off electricity, she contacted the local utility to restore service. Because the damage occurred on private property to equipment that was legally the responsibility of the woman, the company had no authority to fix the problem. Over the course of the next day and a half, the woman's problem was brought to the attention of a dispatcher for the utility company, a representative from the Older Americans Council, several officials from the local office of the responsible state agency, a citizen advocate, and her church. By the time the public officials had begun to investigate the situation, the church had sent over volunteers to repair the damage and to look after the woman until family members could arrive to help. Theologians used to refer to a "God of the gaps," a deity that was invoked when other resources had failed; this example illustrates how a "church of the gaps" can act when secular authorities fail.

REFERENCES

Aptheker, Herbert, ed. 1968. *Marxism and Christianity.* New York: Humanities Press.
Bell, Daniel. 1977. "Return of the Sacred? Argument on the Future of Religion." *British Journal of Sociology* 28:419–449.

Caplow, Theodore. 1985. "Contrasting Trends in European and American Religion." *Sociological Analysis* 46:101–108.

Caplow, Theodore, Howard M. Bahr, and Bruce A. Chadwick. 1983. *All Faithful People: Change and Continuity in Middletown's Religion*. Minneapolis: University of Minnesota Press.

Carey, George W. 1982. "Religion and American Government Textbooks." *Teaching Political Science* 10:7–19.

Center for Political Studies. 1989. *American National Election Study: 1989 Pilot Study Codebook*. Ann Arbor, Mich.: Institute for Social Research.

Colasanto, Diane, and Linda DeStefano. 1989. "Public Image of TV Evangelists Deteriorates." *Gallup Report* 288:16–21.

Cole, J. P. 1979. *Geography of World Affairs*. Fifth edition. Harmondsworth, Middlesex, England: Penguin.

Davis, James A. 1984. *General Social Surveys, 1972–1984: Cumulative Codebook*. Chicago: National Opinion Research Center.

Dawidowicz, Lucy S., and Leon J. Goldstein, eds. 1974. *Politics in a Pluralist Democracy: Studies of Voting in the 1960 Election*. Westport, Conn.: Greenwood.

Epstein, Leon D. 1967. *Political Parties in Western Democracies*. New York: Praeger.

Fowler, Robert Booth. 1989. *Unconventional Partners: Religion and Liberal Culture in the United States*. Grand Rapids, Mich.: Eerdmans.

Frankel, Carl. 1984. "A Legacy." *American Scholar* 52:159–166.

Gallup Organization. 1982. "Religion in America." *Gallup Report*, no. 201–202.

Glasner, Peter E. 1977. *The Sociology of Secularisation: A Critique of a Concept*. London: Routledge & Kegan Paul.

Goodenough, Erwin R. 1972. "Religion as Man's Adjustment to the Tremendum." In *Ways of Understanding Religion*, edited by Walter H. Capps, 45–48. New York: Macmillan.

Greeley, Andrew, and Gregory Baum, eds. 1973. *The Persistence of Religion*. Concilium Series on Religion in the Seventies, no. 81. New York: Herder and Herder.

Hadden, Jeffrey K. 1987. "Toward Desacralizing Secularization Theory." *Social Forces* 65:587–611.

Halebsky, Sandor. 1976. *Mass Society and Political Conflict: Toward a Reconstruction of Theory*. New York: Cambridge University Press.

Hastings, Elizabeth Hann, and Philip K. Hastings, eds. 1979. *Index to International Public Opinion*. Westport, Conn.: Greenwood.

Hastings, Philip K., and Dean R. Hoge. 1986. "Religious and Moral Attitude Trends Among College Students, 1948–84." *Social Forces* 65:370–376.

Hechter, Michael. 1975. *Internal Colonialism: The Celtic Fringe in British National Development, 1536–1966*. Berkeley and Los Angeles: University of California Press.

Hodgkinson, Virginia A., Murray S. Weitzman, and Arthur D. Kirsch. 1988. *From Belief to Commitment: The Activities and Finances of Religious Congregations in the United States*. Washington, D.C.: Independent Sector.

Hunter, James Davison. 1983. *American Evangelicalism: Conservative Religion and the Quandary of Modernity*. New Brunswick, N.J.: Rutgers University Press.

Inkeles, Alex. 1983. *Exploring Individual Modernity*. Cambridge: Harvard University Press.

Jacquet, Constant H., ed. 1983. *Yearbook of American and Canadian Churches, 1983.* Nashville, Tenn.: Abingdon.

Lipset, Seymour Martin. 1967. *The First New Nation.* Garden City, N.Y.: Doubleday Anchor.

Livezey, Lowell W. 1989. "U.S. Religious Organizations and the International Human Rights Movement." *Human Rights Quarterly* 11:14–81.

Lynd, Robert S., and Helen Merrell Lynd. 1929. *Middletown: A Study in Contemporary American Culture.* New York: Harcourt, Brace.

McDaniel, Stephen W. 1989. "The Use of Marketing Techniques by Churches: A National Survey." *Review of Religious Research* 31:175–182.

McDonough, Peter, Samuel H. Barnes, and Antonio Lopez Pina. 1984. "Authority and Association: Spanish Democracy in Comparative Perspective." *Journal of Politics* 46:652–688.

Machovec, Milan. 1976. *A Marxist Looks At Jesus.* Philadelphia: Fortress.

Marty, Martin E. 1984. *Pilgrims in Their Own Land.* Boston: Little, Brown.

Pasquariello, Ronald D. 1985. *Tax Justice: Social and Moral Aspects of American Tax Policy.* Lanham, Md.: University Press of America.

Prozesky, Martin. 1984. *Religion and Ultimate Well-Being: An Explanatory Theory.* New York: St. Martin's.

Quinn, Bernard, Herman Anderson, Martin Bradley, Paul Goetting, and Peggy Shriver. 1982. *Churches and Church Membership in the United States, 1980.* Atlanta: Glenmary Research Center.

Reagan, Ronald. 1984. "Religion and Politics Are Necessarily Related." *Church & State* 37 (October): 9–11.

Research and Forecasts Inc. 1981. *The Connecticut Mutual Life Report on American Values in the 1980s.* Hartford, Conn.: Connecticut Mutual Life Insurance Company.

Salisbury, Robert H. 1983. "American Politics: Religion and the Welfare State." In *Comparative Social Research,* edited by Richard E. Tomasson, 56–65. Greenwich, Conn.: JAI.

Salisbury, Robert H., John Sprague, and Gregory Weiher. 1984. "Does Religious Pluralism Make a Difference? Interactions Among Context, Attendance, and Beliefs." Paper presented at the annual meeting of the American Political Science Association, Washington, D.C.

Schumer, Franz. 1984. "A Return to Religion." *New York Times Magazine,* April 15, pp. 90–98.

Stark, Rodney, and William Sims Bainbridge. 1985. *The Future of Religion.* Berkeley and Los Angeles: University of California Press.

Stewart, Thomas A. 1989. "Turning Around the Lord's Business." *Fortune,* September 25, pp. 78–84.

Szajkowski, Bogdan. 1983. *Next to God . . . Poland: Politics and Religion in Contemporary Poland.* New York: St. Martin's.

Tracy, David. 1973. "The Religious Dimension of Science." In *The Persistence of Religion,* edited by Andrew Greeley and Gregory Baum, 128–135. New York: Herder and Herder.

Warner, R. Stephen. 1979. "Theoretical Barriers to the Understanding of Evangelical Christianity." *Sociological Analysis* 40:1–9.

Wilson, Bryan. 1966. *Religion in Secular Society.* Baltimore: Penguin.

2. Religion and Politics: Points of Contact

To his followers, who willingly signed over their lives and fortunes, the leader of the cult was a new Messiah, possibly even a God. Under his direction, they would march out of spiritual bondage to achieve harmony and social justice. Even critics who doubted his honesty and regarded him as a manipulator admitted that the leader was a spellbinding orator whose doctrines had a magnetic appeal to poor blacks in urban ghettos. At the height of its popularity, the movement had its own churches, newspapers, schools, and social welfare agencies. Even though he was recognized as a potentially significant political force in America, the leader decided to move his society to the wilds of another continent. The jungle settlement ended in tragedy.

With thousands of their coreligionists dead, the survivors fled across the Atlantic to the United States. Despite the distance, they did not forget the events that had made them refugees. To enlist the American government on behalf of an independent homeland for their persecuted brethren, they organized powerful national associations, raised enormous amounts of money, and tried to pressure public officials by threats of electoral retaliation. Having gained special strength and influence in New York and the Democratic party, the group has nonetheless managed to achieve a national consensus on American support for the beleaguered new nation. Though the cause continues to enjoy considerable sympathy among Americans, the group's single-mindedness occasionally draws the charge that members put the well-being of the foreign homeland above the broader interests of the United States.

A small group of men and women, motivated by intense Christian faith, call on America to mend its evil ways. They are outraged by national policies that deny legal standing to other human beings, policies that have been approved by the U.S. Supreme Court. While willing to try changing the law through normal political activities, some on the fringe of the movement resort to violence against people and institutions committing what they consider the great sin. To their crit-ics, these crusaders for public morality appear narrow-minded, intolerant and uncompromising. The group responds to such accusations by insisting that America return to the religious values that have long sustained the republic.

Another group of American Christians sees the arms race as the paramount threat to world peace and human survival. Persuaded that nations will use weapons if they are available, these activists call on their government to stop its weapons buildup and negotiate treaties of arbitration with its military adversaries. They are also worried about America's growing military involvement in Latin America and urge the government to send teachers, medical supplies and economic assistance instead of troops.

The attentive citizen should have no difficulty attaching names to the groups described in these passages. The cult is obviously the "People's Temple" of Jim Jones, which ended in 1978 with a mass suicide in Guyana. The second vignette, of course, describes the efforts of the American Zionist movement to build public and governmental support for a Jewish homeland in the Middle East. For forty-some years, Zionist leaders have helped to persuade Congress and various presidents to provide strong military and diplomatic assistance to Israel. The third group is immediately recognizable as the "New Christian Right," a label for the religious conservatives who have challenged the liberalization of abortion, changes in long-established sex roles, and other policies regarded as departures from traditional moral values. The final passage clearly deals with the growing support for nuclear disarmament in the Roman Catholic church and other denominations.

Or so it may seem! As closely as the labels appear to fit the facts of each case, the four groups just described are *not* Jim Jones and the People's Temple, the American Zionist movement, the Moral Majority, and the contemporary Catholic peace movement. Whatever the similarities to recent religiously based political actions, the vignettes actually refer to four earlier episodes from American history in which religious enthusiasm fused with political action: the back-to-Africa movement of Marcus Garvey, nationalist political agitation by Irish-American Catholics, the abolitionist crusade against slavery, and the Christian pacifism of William Jennings Bryan.[1] As these examples from the nineteenth and early twentieth centuries make clear, religious activity in politics is neither new nor unprecedented in American experience. To the contrary: a close look at American history reveals a durable tradition of interaction between religious and political activity, arising from and strengthened by several factors.

To understand why religion and politics are so frequently tied together in this country, it is necessary to examine the *incentives* for political activism by religiously committed people and groups, the *opportunities* for involvement, and, finally, the *resources* that enable the religious to participate effectively. Any coherent explanation of the persistent linkage of religion and politics in the United States depends on close examination of all three factors.

The Causes of Religious Intervention in Politics

Visitors to the United States are often struck by the readiness of Americans to enter the political arena in pursuit of moral causes and to interpret complicated public issues in terms of good versus evil (Brogan 1960, chap. 5). Although moral crusades are not unique to the United States, they seem to occur more frequently here than elsewhere. In most other advanced industrial societies, political conflict commonly centers on questions about the distribution of economic resources and burdens. Such issues are not unknown in American political life, but they must share the national agenda with controversies that touch more directly on moral values and religious doctrine. The passion that suffuses such issues as abortion, school prayer, equal rights, pornography, and other moral concerns seems notably lacking when Americans confront questions such as tax rates, national health insurance, labor union rights, or tariff protection. Moreover, at a time when the politics of religious concern seems to be weakening in other advanced societies, it has gained a renewed foothold in American politics.

Why should religion become an element in political controversy in the first place? Part of the answer to this question lies in those forces within religion that encourage political activism. All three aspects, or "faces," of religion are capable of promoting an interest in politics—creed, institution, and social/cultural group (Wald 1983, chap. 5). Although these three elements may not constitute the essence of the concept of religion, they do represent the major "manner and form in which religious phenomena appear in human experience" (Capps 1972, 135), and each provides an incentive for religious groups to enter the political arena.

As used here, *creed* refers to the fundamental beliefs, ideas, ethical codes, and symbols associated with a religious tradition, including what others call a theology or belief system. The emphasis here is on the content of religious teachings and the values that the tradition encourages. As comprehensive systems of belief, religious traditions may provide guidance for believers about appropriate behavior in secular realms, such as politics.

Churches differ in the degree to which they assert a connection between religious faith and political principles. Some, such as the Mennonite congregations, are quite explicit about the political lessons of their faith, announcing that the church is committed to nonviolence, separation of church and state, and mutual service. Other churches transmit political messages through posters and wall hangings, the choice of hymns, the content of sermons and homilies, bumper stickers affixed to the minister's car, announcements during worship services and articles in the church bulletin. In most churches, however, the political orientation has to be inferred from the beliefs and ethical codes of the religious tradition. When a church lacks an authoritative statement of political principles, its members may disagree about how (or even whether) the faith applies to political questions. Whether the cues are direct or indirect, religious belief systems may send messages that influence political outlook and behavior.

Religion and politics can also be linked through the tie of interest. Religious communities are represented in concrete form by specialized *institutions*, the second face of religion pertinent to political activism. In the United States, churches are not merely buildings that provide places for worship; rather, they have become multipurpose agencies providing an astonishing array of services, including formal education, social welfare, pastoral counseling, publishing, charitable fund-raising, recreational facilities, medical care, cemeteries, libraries, and summer camps. Several of the largest churches have become the hubs for worldwide operations, complete with the organizational complexity of a major corporation. Ties to a common denomination and to interchurch movements of various kinds have further enmeshed the churches in a web of formal institutions.

As a result of these extensive responsibilities and activities, churches often acquire a strong and immediate interest in policies determined by the government. A church day school, for example, is subject to governmental regulations on zoning, taxation, health and public safety, professional standards, wages and working conditions, racial integration, curriculum, accreditation, and standardized testing. Religious broadcasting, like its secular counterpart, is regulated by the Federal Communications Commission. A church that offers counseling services or engages heavily in charitable fund-raising may unwittingly expose itself to legal action. Because of the potential impact of governmental decisions on their many activities, religious groups frequently find it valuable—or necessary—to take an active role in the political process.

Religion also denotes a *social group*, a subculture or community of believers. The members of a congregation may share regular social interaction, a common status, and a distinctive way of life. Out of these experiences, a common culture may emerge. Adherents may come to develop a similar way of looking at the world, what is sometimes called a "group mind." Of course, churches differ in the demands they place on members and in the degree to which they constitute genuine communities, as opposed to casual associations. Nonetheless, the communal nature of religion may induce a particular pattern of political activity by members of a congregation. If a church attracts people who experience similar conditions of life, whether poverty or affluence, that shared status may lead congregants to develop a common outlook on politics and social issues. Underlying political tendencies can be brought to the surface by messages from the pulpit and reinforced by continued social interaction with like-minded church members. In some cases— the black churches, for example—political solidarity is virtually imposed on the group members by the hostility of outsiders. The larger the role played by the church in defining the lives of its members, the greater the church's potential impact on their political activities.

A revealing example of how all these incentives can affect the level of political involvement is that of the U.S. Roman Catholic church, which has repeatedly attempted to relate Catholic religious thought to important issues on the national political agenda. Through homilies, sermons, pastoral letters, and the dissemination of papal encyclicals, church leaders have attempted to educate Catholics about how to apply the principles of the faith to diverse public problems such as abortion, national defense, economic policy, and the position of women in society.

The church has also taken a strong public stand on issues that affect the immediate welfare of its institutions. To ease the financial burden of the church's comprehensive system of religious day schools, Catholic leaders have sought public assistance in the form of textbook sharing, public transportation, and tuition tax credits. As individuals, Catholic laypeople have shown a traditional attachment to the Democratic party. This linkage was formed at the turn of the century when the predominantly immigrant and working-class Catholic population found Democrats far more receptive than Republicans to their needs and aspirations. The historical memory of how the Democratic party provided a path of upward mobility for ambitious young Catholics kept the alliance intact even after many Catholics had moved into the social and economic mainstream.

Creed, institutional interest, and social standing have also been responsible for the political actions of other religious groups in American life. To some extent, the Catholic church has only followed in the footsteps of other religious groups (Handy 1984). During the nineteenth century, many Protestant churches took public stands on such vital issues as slavery, tariffs, and imperialism, justifying their preferences as an outgrowth of religious beliefs. In the attempt to defend institutions or public practices that supported Protestant interests, moreover, the churches frequently intervened in the legislative process—trying, for example, to mandate the holy character of the Sunday sabbath or to adjust immigration quotas so as to encourage migration from Protestant nations. Like the Catholics, the Protestants have tended to form alliances with political groups that represent their social and economic interests. For Protestants, no less than for Catholics, creed, institutional self-interest, and social bonds have encouraged political involvement and shaped its form.

In the current period, new or revitalized religious groups have been drawn into political action by the same incentives that have motivated the well-established churches. The forces that encourage an intersection of religion and politics are numerous and diverse. The Mormon church has urged its membership to follow church doctrine in public disputes over abortion, school prayer, pornography, and the like. Evangelical Protestant churches, many of which have become imposing organizations that sponsor broadcast networks, school systems, and major publishing houses, have entered politics to safeguard these institutions from governmental regulation. Because an increasing proportion of the American Roman Catholic community comprises poor and deprived Hispanic immigrants, the Catholic church has become far more aggressive in advocating government spending to address social problems.

How Government Structure Encourages Political Action of Churches

In order for churches to act on the incentives just described, the political system must be open to them. At a minimum, this requires opportunities for participation without legal restriction. Whereas some democratic societies severely limit the political activities of churches and religious leaders, the United States historically has given religious groups relatively free reign to participate in public affairs.[2] The federal tax code does require churches to refrain from endorsing candidates if they want to retain exemption from the income tax, but this provision has not been strictly enforced. The political system is thus open to U.S. churches, in the sense that few formal barriers keep them from political activity.

In another sense, the U.S. political system actually encourages organized groups like churches to compete for influence over public policy (Truman 1962). As political scientists have long recognized, the complex structure of the U.S. government encourages groups to undertake political activity. In this regard, religious groups are no different from the many other organizations that attempt to influence public policy at all levels of society.

Decentralization is fundamental to American political life. Rather than concentrate power in the hands of one institution, the founders of the nation divided political authority among three autonomous branches of government. Advocates of any particular policy thus have three separate routes open to them: they can try to achieve their goals by legislation, by legal action, or through the administrative process. Because political power is further subdivided among at least three separate levels of government (national, state, and local), a group with political goals has additional freedom to choose the ground on which to fight. Governmental fragmentation, accordingly, gives groups multiple points of access to the policy-making process. Such a complex governmental structure may or may not be conducive to good policy making, quick reaction to pressing problems, or clear direction, but it certainly keeps the decision-making process remarkably open to causes that can find an effective advocate.

Decentralization is reinforced by a tradition of popular sovereignty that limits the authority of national party leaders. The American system of political recruitment puts the effective power of nomination in the hands of citizens rather than political parties. Under this system, the elected official always has to attend first to the wishes of the constituents who hold the power to deny nomination. When those citizens are agitated by an issue or problem, the attentive official must pay heed. Responsiveness to the wishes of the voters, even if they conflict with the party platform or the pledges of its leaders, is the highest priority.

The way in which this structure makes a difference for religious groups can be seen in the history of antiabortion movements in the United States and Canada (Schwartz 1981). In Canada, as in the United States, penalties for abortion were reduced or eliminated from the late 1960s to early 1970s. In both countries, liberalization brought forth vociferous objections from Catholics and conservative Protestants. But there the similarities end. The Canadian policy shift has been sustained while liberalized abortion has been significantly curtailed in the United States. The differences are partly due to the religious composition of the two countries but mainly reflect differences in political structure that allowed American opponents of abortion more scope to pursue their agenda.

Organized on the British parliamentary model, the Canadian governmental system offered the opponents of liberalized abortion few opportunities to challenge official policy. Because the criminal code was the exclusive responsibility of the national government, the provincial authorities and local governments could do little to restrict the availability of abortion services. At the national level, the governing Liberal party easily defeated antiabortion efforts originating in the courts or in the Parliament. Political leaders who might have disagreed with the decision to relax restrictions on abortion largely toed the line, lest they endanger their careers in a system that rewards loyalty to party. Thus, despite strong objections from a large Catholic population, the Canadian government was able to persevere in its policy of making abortion more widely available to the population.

The different outcome of the abortion debate in the United States, where antiabortionists have won a number of significant victories, testifies to the many avenues of attack provided by the complex and multifaceted U.S. system of government. When national abortion policy was liberalized through the *Roe v. Wade* decision handed down by the Supreme Court in 1973, critics sought to use the amending power of the Constitution to restore restrictive policies. Failing in that and in attempts to remove abortion from the Court's jurisdiction, they proceeded to chip away at the decision in several other arenas. Congress has been persuaded to reduce or eliminate federal payments for abortion under various programs of health insurance and foreign assistance. Using ordinances, some of which were initiated by petition and approved in public referendums, some states and localities have invoked zoning, the regulation of public health, and parental rights to restrict access to abortion facilities, and several such restrictions have been sustained by the Supreme Court. In 1989, by upholding a Missouri law that placed numerous restrictions on abortion, the Supreme Court conceded to state legislatures much authority to control abortion policy. All the while, abortion opponents have also challenged *Roe* on the ground, so to speak, by organizing demonstrations, parades, pickets, rallies, and other forms of public protest guaranteed by the Bill of Rights. The Supreme Court may yet overturn its 1973 ruling and restore the limits on abortion in effect before *Roe*. Even falling short of that, it is clear that the opponents of abortion have capitalized on the separation of powers and on the federal structure of government to partially offset the Supreme Court's 1973 ruling.

Few of the options used by the religiously motivated opponents of abortion in the United States are available to persons of similar belief in other countries. In most nations, the policy decisions of a national government are not routinely subject to review by an outside agency, nor can they be overturned by appeal to a higher law as embodied in a constitution. Citizens usually lack the tools of direct legislation, the initiative and referendum, which can be used to circumvent the decisions of legislative assemblies. In most circumstances the party in government has a relatively free hand to shape legislation without competition from other national institutions. Similarly, because of concentration of lawmaking authority and administrative power in the central government, provinces and localities are powerless to block the implementation of national policy.

The tradition of popular sovereignty encouraged some American politicians, unlike their Canadian counterparts, to join or at least endorse the antiabortion crusades sponsored by religious groups. As noted above, candidates for public office in the United States are required to develop personal electoral organizations, raise most of their own campaign resources, and emphasize whatever issues resonate most powerfully in the constituency. Once in office, they enjoy considerable leeway from the party line and the freedom to engage in moral advocacy. Where nomination to office, campaign finance, and promotion to higher office depend on the party, as in Canada, ambitious politicians have strong reasons to conform to the party line. The absence of these weapons in American political parties helps to explain why public officials feel free to take up moral causes if they judge that such issues will advance a political standing. For a time, the abortion issue fit that pattern in the United States.

Religion as a Political Resource

Many groups, not just those motivated by religion, have incentives to participate in and opportunities to pursue their goals through political action. Religious groups, however, are especially likely to participate effectively because of their resources: that is, religiously motivated activists possess qualities that can prove valuable in political action. These resources grow out of the three faces of religion already examined in this chapter.

Religious ideas are potentially powerful sources of commitment and motivation. As history has repeatedly taught, human beings will make enormous sacrifices if they believe themselves to be driven by a divine force. When the power of the churches is applied to a political issue, the message is likely to exert substantial influence over attentive parishioners. Until quite recently, the major American churches largely restricted their political preaching to questions involving personal behavior. The "social" message from the pulpit tended to stress public solutions for individual problems such as drinking, gambling, drug use, and licentious sexual behavior. It is precisely on such issues that the attitudes of churchgoers differ most substantially from those of persons who do not regularly encounter church preaching on politics (Hoge and Zulueta 1985).

The potential political strength of religious ideas has been displayed repeatedly in conflict over pornography, homosexual rights ordinances, the Equal Rights Amendment, liberalized abortion laws, and other policies regarding changing social practices. The ability of these issues to ignite political action was nicely demonstrated in a study conducted by political scientists Paul Allen Beck and Suzanne Parker (1985). In interviewing a group of adult Floridians in 1981 and again in 1982, they found that many people shifted their positions on political issues from one interview to the next. This high degree of inconsistency suggested that citizens do not have firm or deep convictions about many of the issues that dominate political conflict. Beck and Parker did find three exceptions to this generalization, all of which involved issues touching on moral values. The members of the sample were most consistent in their views about abortion, school prayer, and the Equal Rights Amendment. Because these issues apparently tap into opinions of great intensity and durability, it is not surprising that the issues have generated sustained political action.

Conflicts over abortion, school prayer and other "social regulatory" issues differ from many items on the political agenda; they center on "community values, moral practices, and norms of interpersonal conduct" rather than allocation of federal funds, redistribution of national resources, or economic regulation (Tatalovich and Daynes 1988, 1). The work of American historians reveals a long history of moral controversies and cultural debates that usually overshadowed economic conflicts (Noll 1990). While it was once thought that the advent of modernity had shifted political debate away from moral concerns to questions about economics, we now recognize the continuing potency of cultural values as a basis for political mobilization (Barone 1990; White 1988; Wildavsky 1987). Astute politicians have capitalized on cultural tensions, crafting political campaigns around appeals to traditional values. During the 1988 presidential campaign, the Republican campaign succeeded in making the Pledge of Allegiance such an issue. Precisely because values and moral practices are their currency, religious groups seem drawn to issues of this nature.

In addition to what might be called their intellectual resources—the capacity to motivate people to action on behalf of moral values—churches also enjoy substantial organizational advantages. Success in politics depends in part on the ability to mobilize citizens behind a common goal, for which purpose it helps greatly to have public credibility, access to citizens, and a means for communicating ideas. The churches, with precisely these traits, are natural political organizations. As observed in the previous chapter, the churches enjoy a very positive image in American society—a level of prestige that can yield political credibility. In terms of access and communication, churches are powerful organizations with formal membership, headquarters, regularly scheduled group meetings, publications, and full-time professional leadership. Because of patterns of association in American society, the church is often the only such well-organized group to which a citizen is likely to belong. If the church wants to transmit political messages, it has the apparatus to do so with great efficiency.

As a social system or subculture, the church has yet other resources that can contribute to a powerful political role. By virtue of participating in a social network, the church member may encounter messages about political issues and interact with fellow members who adhere to the church's line. A person surrounded by church members who participate actively in a campaign is likely to learn about the issues from a religious point of view, to receive encouragement about joining in the activity, and to observe and acquire social skills that may promote political success. Though not intended for that purpose, congregational organizations may serve as leadership training institutes for people who lack other means of exposure to organizational skills.

These social factors help to explain the positive relationship many observers have found between church attendance and voter participation in local and presidential elections (Hill and Cassel 1984; Hougland and Christenson 1983; Hughes and Peek 1986; Macaluso and Wanat 1979; Martinson and Wilkening 1987). These studies infer a connection between religious and political involvement by comparing the attitudes and behavior of people with different levels of exposure to church influence. Political scientists Theodore Macaluso and John Wanat (1979, 160–161) have argued that churches promote a sense of civic responsibility by teaching that civic obligations have a sacred character. This sense of stewardship toward public affairs should translate into higher rates of participation. Treating churches just like other social formations, sociologists (Hougland and Christenson 1983, 406) have contended that participation in associations of any kind provides "the social contacts and organizational skills necessary to understand political action and to exert effective influence." Peterson's (1990) recent finding, that greater levels of involvement in church decision making correlate with political interest, information, and participation, lends support to the notion of a "spillover" effect from religious to political activism. Strate and his colleagues (1989) believe that religious affiliation indicates a high level of community attachment that translates into concern for public affairs. Kim (1985) finds that church membership and attendance promote political interest. It is also possible that participation in a religious community breaks down the individualist tendency in contemporary society and leads people to regard themselves as part of a larger group with legitimate claims on public policy. Whatever the exact factors involved, the churches serve as social networks that seem to draw participants into public affairs.

Although churches possess imposing political resources and the opportunity to participate in politics combined with the incentive to do so, there are three potential limits on religious-group activism.

To begin with, certain types of faith actually depress political involvement. Some religious traditions refuse to get involved with politics, which they see as irrelevant to their primary task of saving souls. A belief about the futility of political action can also be a potent deterrent to political participation (Quinney 1964)—as I once learned when, while I was canvassing for a candidate, a church member slammed a door in my face with the shout, "No politics on Sunday!" Other religious groups have gone even further, insisting that members separate themselves completely from the corrupting influence of all secular institutions and activities. Even if a church does not condemn political participation, it might make such heavy demands on the members' time, energy, and resources that congregants have nothing left to devote to political action. Studies of the impact of religious involvement on a variety of forms of political participation—not just voting—have found no evidence that churchgoing encourages more active forms of political involvement, such as campaign contributions, volunteer work for candidates, or communication with local government officials (Hougland and Christenson 1983; Martinson and Wilkening 1987). British studies also have uncovered a negative relationship between the level of involvement in church life and active participation in political parties and campaigns (Stark 1964; Cheal 1975). There is also evidence from a variety of studies that heavily religious environments discourage women from political careers (Medoff 1986) and generally retard the level of membership in trade unions (Christiano 1988). Hence, the link between religion and participation seems to be restricted to the least demanding form of political action—the casting of a vote.

Another limitation on church political activity is the fear that political clout will be purchased at the expense of spiritual influence. It has long been suspected that churches enjoy such a positive image in the United States because they are regarded as places apart, a refuge from the corruption of other secular institutions. According to polling data, the public generally prefers the churches to remain "above" politics and reacts negatively to clergy who become agents of a particular party or candidate. If the church enters the political world as an active participant, it risks losing some of the prestige and social influence that makes it such a respected institution. That outcome is particularly likely when a church or religious group takes a political position that alienates members who might otherwise remain loyal.

The experience of "liberal" churches in the 1960s, when social activism often produced intense conflict among members, suggests that political involvement inevitably undermines congregational harmony. That conclusion needs to be qualified by recognizing conditions that encourage congregational support for political involvement. Strange as it sounds, support for political involvement may depend on portraying that activism as nonpolitical. That is, church members are likely to accept the legitimacy of political action when it defends religious values or the interests of congregants. In such cases, politics is perceived as an extension of religion rather than as an alien force grafted onto it. That distinction helps to explain how the leader of the American Family Association, an interest group that opposes pornography, abortion, televised sex and violence, and sex education, could blithely attribute the success of his organization to its scrupulous avoidance of politics (People for the American Way 1989. 22). It may also account for the overwhelming level of support that black Americans give to their ministers as political spokespersons. These two examples should serve as a warning not to overestimate the barriers to political activism by churches.

Finally, it is important to remember that churches do not enjoy a monopoly on political resources. Other associations—labor unions, professional groups, service clubs, business networks—possess communications and mobilization capacities. Membership in such organizations also contributes to electoral participation, whether or not there is an explicit political purpose (Hill and Cassel 1984, 24). If church impact is greater than that of other similarly advantaged organizations, that is because church affiliation is so much more widespread than membership in other kinds of associations.

The combination of incentives, opportunities, and resources serves to draw churches into politics at several different levels. Religion may play a role in forming the fundamental assumptions and outlooks that channel public thinking about government and politics. When it operates to affect such basic orientations about politics, religion has an impact on "political culture." At a second level, religion may contribute to political identity and partisan loyalties. The traditional tie between Catholics and the Democratic party illustrates this effect. The third level at which religion interacts with politics involves specific policy debates. The remainder of the book will examine religious influences in those spheres.

It is important to emphasize at this point that the traffic between religion and politics in the United States runs two ways. Religious groups may take the initiative in political action, but they may also react to the decisions of government and other political actors. Roman Catholic doctrine about abortion did not draw the church into political activity until the United States Supreme Court struck down most legal restrictions on the availability of abortion. The politically conservative pastors of the New Christian Right have characterized their entry into politics largely as a response to government actions that left traditional churches aggrieved. Such a reactive posture by the churches may well be more common today because of changes in the scope of governmental authority. The state now claims more regulatory power than it used to—power that may be used to establish policies that affect the major functions of religious groups. If there truly is greater political involvement by religious institutions, that situation may reflect a defensive reaction to an expanded government rather than any desire to impose religious values on a reluctant society.

NOTES

1. For information about these movements, consult the accounts in Burkett 1978; Carroll 1978; and Clements 1982.
2. Many nations prohibit members of the clergy from holding public office. In

Mexico, where the church was identified with the losing side in a civil war, political parties are forbidden to use religious labels and the public role of the church is strictly limited. Trying to keep the lid on simmering religious conflict, Egyptian authorities have even banned bumper stickers with any religious references.

REFERENCES

Barone, Michael. 1990. *Our Country: The Shaping of America from Roosevelt to Reagan.* New York: Free Press.

Beck, Paul Allen, and Suzanne Parker. 1985. "Consistency in Policy Thinking." *Political Behavior* 7:37–56.

Brogan, D. W. 1960. *Politics in America.* Garden City, N.Y.: Doubleday Anchor.

Burkett, Randall K. 1978. *Garveyism as a Religious Movement.* Metuchen, N.J.: Scarecrow.

Capps, Walter H., ed. 1972. *Ways of Understanding Religion.* New York: Macmillan.

Carroll, F. M. 1978. *American Opinion and the Irish Question, 1910–1923: A Study in Opinion and Policy.* Dublin, Ireland: Gill and Macmillan.

Cheal, David. 1975. "Political Radicalism and Religion: Competitors for Commitment." *Social Compass* 22:245–249.

Christiano, Kevin J. 1988. "Religion and Radical Labor Unionism: American States in the 1920's." *Journal for the Scientific Study of Religion* 27:378–388.

Clements, Kendricks. 1982. *William Jennings Bryan: Missionary Isolationist.* Knoxville: University of Tennessee Press.

Handy, Robert T. 1984. *A Christian America?* Second edition. New York: Oxford University Press.

Hill, David B., and Carol Cassel. 1984. "Voting and the Rest of Life: A Social Exchange Theory of Electoral Turnout." Paper presented at the annual meeting of the American Political Science Association, Washington, D.C.

Hoge, Dean R., and Ernesto Zulueta. 1985. "Salience as a Condition for Various Social Consequences of Religious Commitment." *Journal for the Scientific Study of Religion* 24:21–38.

Hougland, J. G., and J. A. Christenson. 1983. "Religion and Politics: The Relationship of Religious Participation to Political Efficacy and Involvement." *Sociology and Social Research* 67:405–420.

Hughes, D. L., and Charles W. Peek. 1986. "Ladies Against Women: Explaining the Political Participation of Traditional and Modern-Role Females." *Political Behavior* 8:158–174.

Kim, Changsu. 1985. "The Influence of the Religious Factor on Political Interest, 1960–1984," Ph.D. diss., University of Cincinnati.

Macaluso, Theodore F., and John Wanat. 1979. "Voting Turnout and Religiosity." *Polity* 12:158–169.

Martinson, Oscar B., and E. A. Wilkening. 1987. "Religious Participation and Involvement in Local Politics Throughout the Life Cycle." *Sociological Focus* 20:309–318.

Medoff, Marshall H. 1986. "Determinants of the Political Participation of Women." *Public Choice* 48:245–253.

Noll, Mark A., ed. 1990. *Religion and American Politics*. New York: Oxford University Press.

People for the American Way. 1989. *Press Clips*. Washington, D.C.: People for the American Way.

Peterson, Steven A. 1990. "Church Participation and Political Participation: The Spillover Effect." Paper presented at the annual meeting of the Midwest Political Science Association, Chicago.

Quinney, Richard. 1964. "Political Conservatism, Alienation, and Fatalism: Contingencies of Social Status and Religious Fundamentalism." *Sociometry* 27:372–381.

Schwartz, Mildred. 1981. "Politics and Moral Causes in Canada and the United States." In *Comparative Social Research*, edited by Richard F. Tomasson, 65–90. Greenwich, Conn.: JAI.

Stark, Rodney. 1964. "Class, Radicalism, and Religious Involvement in Great Britain." *American Sociological Review* 29:698–706.

Strate, J., C. J. Parrish, C. D. Elder, and C. Ford. 1989. "Life-Span Civic Development and Voting Participation." *American Political Science Review* 83:443–464.

Tatalovich, Raymond, and Byron W. Daynes. 1988. "What Is Social Regulatory Policy?" In *Social Regulatory Policy: Moral Controversies in American Politics*, edited by Raymond Tatalovich and Byron W. Daynes, 1–4. Boulder: Westview.

Truman, David. 1962. *The Governmental Process*. New York: Knopf.

Wald, Kenneth D. 1983. *Crosses on the Ballot: Patterns of British Voter Alignment Since 1885*. Princeton, N.J.: Princeton University Press.

White, John Kenneth. 1988. *The New Politics of Old Values*. Hanover, N.H.: University Press of New England.

Wildavsky, Aaron. 1987. "Choosing Preferences by Constructing Institutions: A Cultural Theory of Preference Formation." *American Political Science Review* 81:3–21.

3. Religion and American Political Culture

> People act politically, economically, and socially in keeping with their ultimate beliefs. Their values, mores, and actions, whether in the polling booth, on the job, or at home, are an outgrowth of the god or gods they hold at the center of their being.
>
> —Robert Swierenga, *Religion and American Politics*

In hunting for evidence of religious influence in American political life, most observers examine church-state controversies or search for indications that religious groups vote in solid blocs. Another kind of religious influence is not quite so apparent. As William Lee Miller recognized, religion may contribute to the basic political values that citizens share.

There is also a still more important, if less measurable, *indirect* and long-term effect of the religious tradition upon the nation's politics. This is the impact of ways of thinking, believing, and acting in religious matters upon the shape of the mind, which impact affects the way other fields, like politics, are understood. Such effects, seeping down into the national character, may be discernible not only in clergymen and church people but in members of the society at large. (1961, 83)

By forming an important strand in American culture, religion has helped to define the context of American political life. This chapter will trace connections between the religious ideas and practices prevalent in the American colonies and in subsequent American thought about important political questions.

To assert that religion contributed to the development of national political ideals is not to claim a monopoly for it. In the development of something as complex as a national political creed, secular thought and material interests of many kinds also play vital roles. The modern era has taught us to doubt the purity of motives, especially when they are expressed in terms of idealism, and to look for self-interest as the source of most human action.[1] Recognition that human beings undertake activity for diverse reasons, however, should not mislead a careful observer into ignoring altogether the impact on social conduct of abstract forces such as religion. In the colonial period, when religious creeds, institutions, and communities exerted a major impact on life and work, there was bound to be some spillover into politics. Because the contribution of religion to American political culture covers such important beliefs as obedience, the design of government, and the national mission, the religious roots of American political culture merit close investigation.

The Puritan Imprint on Colonial Thought

Although Americans often think of their country as a "new nation," its history and development largely untouched by the rest of the world, much that appears unique about American culture can be traced to the European heritage of the colonial settlers. For American political thought, the critical element of that heritage was the commitment of the settlers and their descendants to the particular form of Christianity that emerged from the Protestant Reformation (Bercovitch 1975; Niebuhr 1959).

Throughout sixteenth- and seventeenth-century Europe, dissatisfaction with the established churches fueled revolts against ecclesiastical authorities and the civil officials who sustained them. The leaders of the revolt in England, recognized today as the spiritual inspiration of American Protestantism, regarded themselves as nothing less than God's agents, engaged in a desperate struggle for the liberation of the church from "centuries of superstition and error" (Simpson 1955, 17). For their part, the leaders of the Church of England regarded the "Puritan" critics as dangerous heretics who should be suppressed by any means necessary. Eventually convinced that they could not reform or replace the state church, many Dissenters (as critics of the Church of England became known) chose to separate themselves from "an unregenerate government which persisted in maintaining a corrupt church" (ibid., 14–15), leaving England for places where they could practice a religion consistent with their version of Christian faith. Driven by the impulse to create societies that would honor God in what they saw as the one true Christian fashion, the Puritan settlers crossed the Atlantic to found the American colonies. In America, a land without religious traditions, they were free to build a culture in which the Protestant images of God, humanity, and the church became the core assumptions of everyday thought.

The influence of the Puritan outlook on American thought did not depend solely on the weight of numbers. The denominations most closely identified with the Puritan wing of the Protestant Reformation, the Congregationalists and Presbyterians, were dominant only in New England. The Church of England, though a minority faith in most of the settlements, enjoyed official status at one time or another in the southern colonies of Virginia, Georgia, and North and South Carolina. Roman Catholicism was a force to be reckoned with in Maryland. The Middle Atlantic colonies were settled principally by members of the Dutch Reformed church, the Quakers, and adherents of several German Protestant traditions. Even in New England, the dominance of Puritan congregations soon was challenged by the strength of newer sects like the Baptists and the Methodists, and weakened by internal conflicts over questions of theology and politics. Despite this religious diversity, few modern historians would contest the early nineteenth-century judgment of Alexis de Tocqueville (1945, 32) that the Puritan vision suffused the whole of the colonies.

As difficult as it may be for twentieth-century minds to understand one another, the difficulty is compounded many times over when the twentieth-century mind confronts one of the seventeenth and eighteenth centuries. Yet the attempt is essential to any understanding of the perspectives that shaped the early political thought of Americans. In the century and a half that elapsed between the establishment of the first permanent English settlements on the North American continent and the founding of the Republic, the theology of the Reformation was continually adapted and adjusted to the American situation. Though the religious impulse may have waned over time, its preeminence challenged by new intellectual currents and commercial considerations, periodic revivals kept it very much alive in the American mind.

The manner of early American politics bore the imprint of this religious background. For example, the Puritan impulse focused the American mind on the Bible. Under the doctrine that ordinary people needed no intermediary between themselves and the word of God, Puritanism encouraged individuals to look for divine guidance in the Scriptures.

Up to the time of the Revolution and perhaps for sometime thereafter, it is safe to assume, the Bible was the only book familiar to the typical inhabitant of America. To judge from a recent study by Donald Lutz (1984), the biblical tradition seems also to have played a major role in the thought processes of those who led the Revolution and created the Constitution. In an intensive study of nearly one thousand political documents issued to the public from 1760 through 1805, Lutz found that the single most frequent source of citations was the Bible. Though this hardly supports the exaggerated description of the Bible as "the textbook of the fathers of the Republic" (John W. Thornton quoted in Sandoz 1990, 142), it at least suggests an environment of intense scriptural consciousness. That explains why political argument was usually couched in biblical language and biblical analogies were employed to explain the political situation.

Further illustrating the impact of religion, styles of worship were quickly transplanted to the realm of politics. Political campaigning adopted the techniques of mass persuasion invented during the "Great Awakenings," those periodic outbursts of intense religious enthusiasm that swept across the continent. Candidates rallied supporters with torchlight parades, tent meetings, door-to-door canvassing, and public declarations of faith, the same methods pioneered by evangelists seeking religious converts (Jensen 1980). Campaigns appropriated religious hymns for political use or else commissioned campaign songs that drew on sacred music. Daniel Walker Howe (1990, 124–125) traces a prominent American political innovation, the national nominating convention, to the practice of national meetings pioneered by religious associations.

In addition to its impact on the language and techniques of politics, the religious environment was also an important factor in developing national unity among the colonists. In response to the outbreak of hostilities in 1776, an astonished Englishman reported, "From one end of North America to the other, they are FASTING and PRAYING" (quoted in Sandoz 1990, 141). Throughout the revolutionary war, the Protestant clergy built support for the cause by emphasizing the religious nature of the conflict. In a typical sermon preached in 1777, the Reverend Nicholas Street (Cherry 1972) reminded congregants that the people of Israel had grown restive and fearful when led from the security of Egyptian slavery into the unpredictable freedom of the wilderness. In the same manner, he argued, the colonists had thrown off a tyrant only to find themselves apprehensive about the future. They must confront their fears, he said, by recognizing that "God frequently brings his own people into a state of peculiar trials, to discover to them and others what there is in their hearts." In the case at hand, the minister said, God was looking for signs of genuine piety and repentance before delivering the colonies from the hands of their enemies. In addition to providing aid and comfort to the colonial army, the minister advised his audience that it would render a signal duty to the war effort by confessing its wickedness and endeavoring to avoid sin. Some ministers went well beyond this measured tone to equate Britain with the anti-Christ and to treat the republican cause as the pure expression of Christian values (Bloch 1990, 49–52; Noll 1988, chap. 3). Popular support for the revolutionary war owed something to the way the Revolution was "preached to the masses as a religious revival" (Perry Miller quoted in Sandoz 1990, 135).

The imprint of Protestant Christianity on the era of the Founders and, through time, upon contemporary U.S. political life is apparent in several respects. From the body of Puritan thought come three elements that proved especially important for subsequent American political practice: covenant theology, the emphasis on original sin, and the concept of a chosen people. Each of these doctrines was applied by the Puritan thinkers and their successors to the earthly realm of politics. Covenant theology helped Americans decide under what conditions governments deserved obedience. The Puritan image of human sinfulness provided clues about the best design for maintaining stable government. And the idea of "chosenness" encouraged Americans to think about their nation in missionary terms. Despite the passage of two centuries, these ideas continue to cast a long shadow over the conduct of American political life.

Covenant Theology and the Right to Revolt

Most Americans take it for granted that citizens owe allegiance to governments that respect their basic rights and liberties; they also seem to accept without question the assertion in the Declaration of Independence that citizens have a right to revolt against governments that deny fundamental freedoms. The idea of conditional allegiance, of a "contract" between citizens and rulers that can be voided when the government misbehaves, is a cornerstone of American political thought.

This concept of government as a covenant gained such ready acceptance among colonial Americans because it bore a close resemblance to a central element in Puritan theology, the *covenant*. Puritan thinkers gave considerable warrant to this model of association, which appears at several different points in the Bible (Elazar 1980, 12–20). In the most influential of the biblical covenants, Abraham and God were joined together by bonds of mutual obligation as Abraham accepted the promise of God's blessing for himself; his heirs, the people of Israel, in turn pledged to do God's work in the wilderness (Gen. 12:3). This was not an obligation imposed on Abraham by fiat but a "conscious contract with God" in which Abraham "promised to do certain things for God in return for which God pledged Himself to recompense Abraham" (P. Miller 1956, 119). The defining characteristic of a covenant, as the Puritans understood it, was that of a voluntary agreement, sanctified by God, in which individuals freely surrendered autonomy in exchange for something of greater value. God hovered over covenants either as a partner or, in the case of contracts among individuals, as the sanctifier and guarantor in whose name the agreement was forged.

This model of social organization was applied by the Puritans to all manner of human associations. Under the image of the covenant, the "church" was redefined: rather than an institution with authority in a particular geographical area, it was seen as a community of the elect, a gathering of those who received the promise of eternal salvation in exchange for accepting a mission to act as God's agents in this world. Extended to civil societies, the covenant provided a basis for human governance. In crossing the Atlantic, the Puritans envisioned themselves as a latter-day people of Israel, recreating the Hebrew covenant in their pilgrimage to the New World. The most famous reenactment of the covenant ritual was the Mayflower Compact, in which the Pilgrims (a Puritan congregation) aboard the ship pledged to create a holy, Bible-based commonwealth in the wilderness in exchange for God's blessing. This ceremony was repeated after landfall in the famous Plymouth Compact. The settlements that spread throughout the New England colonies during the seventeenth century were founded on similar compacts (Schechter 1980).

The political implications of the covenant idea became especially important when Americans sought to justify their decision to cut all legal ties with Great Britain. The crucial link was forged when the idea of a covenant was extended to encompass an entire nation. If the relationship between colonist and king was a contract sealed by the authority of God—in other words, a covenant—then the terms of that contract bore divine authority. The citizens owed allegiance to the ruler, and the ruler, in turn, was committed to honor the contract by acting within its limits. In the view of the colonists, "Rulers who violate the agreed-upon forms are usurpers and so [are] to be legitimately resisted" (P. Miller 1967, 98).

The implications of this type of reasoning were revolutionary. Whereas others interpreted the Bible as saying that God ordained obedience to government, a view that promoted absolutist rule, the Puritans understood the relationship between people and government as one of mutual obligation. The basis for this revised interpretation was the model of the biblical covenants. Through agreements with Adam, Noah, Abraham and others, God had entered into binding contracts with human beings. Though surely not the equal of the mortals in these partnerships, God nonetheless promised to behave in accordance with the terms of the contract, acting as a kind of constitutional monarch in the universe. If God had agreed to be bound in this manner, how could any earthly monarch presume to claim exemption from limits or obligations?

Fortified by biblical precedent, the colonists insisted that the monarch respect their universal rights as creations of God, along with the specific rights due to them as citizens of the British empire.[2] Because obedience was conditioned on the ruler behaving in conformity with agreed-upon standards, it could justly be withdrawn whenever the standards were violated. Thus, when King George III clearly abridged the rights to which the colonists felt entitled, they claimed that the colonies no longer owed him loyalty. Resistance to a government that violated God's law could even be seen as a religious obligation. The covenanting impulse that prompted their forebears to separate physically from England helped to propel the colonists out of the British empire.

The colonists repeatedly invoked the covenant tradition to justify the breaking of their bonds with Great Britain. Almost a year to the day before the Declaration of Independence was made public, the Continental Congress called on Americans to observe a day of national confession, marked by "publick humiliation, fasting, and prayer." After promising this confession and pledging repentance, the colonists asked God for help in persuading the British to respect the terms of the compact that bound the colonies to the mother country (P. Miller 1967, 90–91). When the British proved resistant to these prayers, the colonists once again stressed the breaking of the covenant as justification for revolt. The Declaration of Independence begins with the assertion that the colonists deserved independence under "the Laws of Nature and Nature's God." Consistent with covenant theory, the colonists asserted that the bond between rulers and ruled was dependent on the ruler's respect for those rights that God granted to men. Once the terms of the compact had been violated by a despotic King George (as the colonists attempted to demonstrate in great detail), the people of America could claim a divine mandate to dissolve their ties. The Declaration concludes with the submission of the purity of the rebels' claim to "the Supreme Judge of the World."

The breaking of the covenant not only entitled the people to withdraw authority from a corrupt government, but also, as the Declaration emphasizes, authorized them to form a new system of rule. Once independence was secured, the colonists went about the task of building a new state on the promise that a new covenant was required. After a false start, they settled on what is sometimes called the American national covenant—the Constitution of the United States. Although the Constitution does not explicitly recognize God as a partner or invoke divine blessing, the document bears the mark of covenant thinking in a number of important respects (Riemer 1980, 138–143; Rothman 1980).

Following the original Hebrew concept of covenant as a voluntary undertaking, the Constitution was a contract freely entered into by the people of the thirteen states. It was presented to them as a document that they were free to accept or reject. The biblical covenant created a "people" who, if they accepted the agreement, were promised God's blessings; similarly, the Constitution was presented in the name of the "People of the United States" to achieve for them such beneficent ends as justice, order, welfare, and liberty. Covenants, as the Puritans understood them, routinely set limits on the power of authorities. The privileges of power were legitimate only insofar as they were carried out with respect for the God-given rights of the contracting parties. Commentators have called attention to the corresponding emphasis on limits in the U.S. Constitution. The document is replete with provisions spelling out what government may *not* do and holding government subject to strict rules and standards in the performance of its duties. Then, too, the Constitution seems to enjoy something of the hallowed status of a covenant. It is treated as a holy relic—encased in a shrine to which citizens make pilgrimages—and its authors are revered as saints or demigods.

Puritanism and Democracy: A Qualification

Associating Puritanism with democracy sounds strange in an age that views Puritans as "insufferable, self-righteous precisionists with narrow minds and blue noses, authoritarian, clericalist, intolerant, and antidemocratic" (Ahlstrom 1965, 95). Historians remind us that Puritan settlements were not motivated by an abstract commitment to religious liberty, which they routinely denied to dissenters in their midst, but rather by the desire to protect their own religious practices. They succeeded magnificently in this objective, imposing on the colonies "a narrower band of religious choices than fellow subjects enjoyed in England" (Murrin 1990, 21). Reflecting "a narrow, sectarian spirit" (Tocqueville 1945, 41), their legal codes mandated church attendance, forbade worship in alien faiths, and "constantly invaded the domain of conscience" by exacting criminal penalties for every imaginable sin. How could such people possibly lay the foundations of a democracy?

Tocqueville supplied one answer when he credited Puritanism with a "spirit of democracy" that sustained freedom and liberty as cultural values (Kessler 1989). This spirit came first from the egalitarian New Testament vision of the church as an association open to all humanity. It was reinforced by the distinctly Protestant view of individuals as capable of discovering religious truth through their own efforts. Both arguments, deployed against the territorial and hierarchical Church of England, mandated that individuals be granted religious choice. Choice was not to be construed, however, as freedom to run riot but rather as a divine gift of "liberty for that only which is just and good" (Tocqueville 1945, 44). Paradoxically, Puritan citizens used freedom to impose on themselves "fantastic and oppressive laws" supposedly in accord with God's plan for humankind. But the potent ideal of liberty, once proclaimed, could not effectively be restricted to the narrow channel approved by Puritan orthodoxy. It eventually challenged the very idea of an "official" religion and undermined any special claims to authority by a religious elite. In the political sphere, the assumption that individuals will discover truth by exercising liberty imparted a sacred character to majority opinion. If the Puritans neither embraced nor practiced democracy as we know it, they nonetheless paved the way for it.

The democratic elements in the Puritan creed were reinforced by institutional interest and the social practices of Protestant Christianity in the New World. The "interest" that first drew Puritans to the New World, a desire to escape the entrenched Church of England, was increasingly threatened by the efforts of the British government to assert greater control over the colonies. Even the transplanted Anglican establishments in the southern colonies had grown accustomed to remarkable autonomy from the mother church in England (Mead 1976, 25–27). In the 1760s, colonists were particularly agitated by plans to appoint Anglican bishops in America. To persons steeped in a tradition of congregational autonomy and religious pluralism, a system in which religious leaders enjoyed minimal civil authority, the prospect of a centralized system of church government seemed to be the opening wedge in a campaign to undo the legacy of their Puritan forebears. As Carl Bridenbaugh (1962) demonstrated in a convincing analysis of the continuing conflict between the Church of England and the colonies, fear of losing religious liberty played a major role in the development of American nationalism and helped to stimulate the drive for independence from Britain.

Viewed as a social force, religion taught the colonists themselves much about the actual practice of democracy. In most of Europe, local churches were held accountable to centralized national hierarchies that prescribed a code of belief, determined acceptable forms of worship, and provided ministers to ensure that local practice conformed to national standards. Membership in the church, determined solely by place of residence, was essentially a matter of passive acceptance rather than active involvement. Colonial religious life, in contrast, developed on the principles of voluntary affiliation and congregational independence. After "planting" a church in the wilderness, the founders could prescribe conditions of membership, formulate their own code of belief and practice, and select a minister who served at the pleasure of the congregants. Membership in a church was an option, rather than an automatic status, and carried with it an obligation to participate actively in the running of the congregation.

The tradition of self-rule that grew up in the churches before and after the Revolution encouraged the corresponding development of a vigorous democratic spirit in the political realm (Hatch 1990). In the judgment of the historian Sydney Ahlstrom (1975, 424), membership in self-governing churches "prepared men to regard the social compact as the proper basis of government." Modern research supports this logic by demonstrating that democratic experience in the home, school, and workplace "spills over" into politics, promoting democratic dispositions (Lipsitz 1964; Renshon 1975). Ahlstrom's conclusion gains further support from the simultaneous development in New England of the congregational principle in church governance and democratic practices in civil life. To a degree unparalleled at that time (though restricted by today's standards), the New England colonies achieved high levels of suffrage, powerful representative institutions, respect for the rule of law, and social policies that encouraged the spread of education, science, culture, and charitable activity (Shipton 1947).

The link between democracy and religion thus turned on all three dimensions of religion. If the creed of Protestant Christianity was ambiguous about democracy as a system of government, the fear of English assaults on the reformed churches and the training in self-government provided by autonomous congregations tipped the scales in favor of the revolutionary cause. For these institutional and social contributions, as much as covenantal theology, the heirs of the Protestant Reformation deserve recognition as precursors of the democratic spirit in America.

"Human Depravity" and Institutional Restraint

Another aspect of Puritanism shaped the new political system that was adopted after the Revolution. The Puritan emphasis on the inherent sinfulness of humankind (a strong theme in Protestant thought) provided principles of governance that the Founders observed in constructing their constitutional alternative to the colonial framework. Though we are apt to think of their creation, the Constitution, as a neutral set of institutional arrangements, the system they fashioned is infused with a moral architecture that still guides the conduct of American political life.

The American governmental system was designed by political architects who assumed that human beings could not be trusted with power. To keep government safely under control, they divided authority among three separate branches, giving each leverage to use against the others, and they added additional safeguards such as powerful territorial governments (the states). As a consequence of that framework, the great challenge to any U.S. political leader is to overcome the inherent division of authority by mobilizing all institutions and levels of government on behalf of a common purpose. Compromise, delay, and deadlock are the characteristics of normal political life, to the frustration of advocates of rapid change.

The ultimate explanation for this aspect of U.S. political life lies in the image of humanity that guided some of the Founders in their deliberations at Philadelphia. Far from adoring "the people," many of the Founders appraised them with a cold eye and found more to say about the defects of popular will than about its virtues. In emphasizing their suspicions about humanity, the Founders repeated a theme found in Reformation theology. For the Puritans, the fate of mortals was symbolized by the story of Adam. In sinning against God, Adam forfeited eternal happiness for a life of toil and sorrow that would end in death. Puritans interpreted this as a statement of the inherent depravity of human beings who, given a choice between good and evil, would often choose the latter. Unlike Catholic doctrine, which taught that the church could offer an escape from damnation, or the religions that held out some hope for mass human regeneration through good behavior, Puritan theology offered little prospect of escape from the curse of Adam. Though a few would enjoy the light of God's grace and become saints on earth, the mass of humankind would know only depravity and sinfulness on earth and eternal torment thereafter.

This perspective led to two important political conclusions. First, because governments were the creations of fallible mortals, no government could be expected to act with rectitude. Quite the contrary, a government that reflected the sinfulness of its human creators would be prone to exceed its rightful authority. Under those circumstances, prudence dictated that the power of government be limited, or, in the words of one Protestant clergyman, that "we should leave nothing to human virtue that can be provided for by law or constitution" (Strout 1974, 61). Second, because God was the only source of redemption, it was not the task of governments to make people good. The highest aspiration for government should be merely to subdue the most blatant excesses of human behavior. Puritan thought acknowledged that these rules could be softened if those who constructed and ran the government happened to be members of God's elect. But even then, it would be wise to put restraints on government lest it fall into the hands of the unregenerate. And even a government of saints, unlikely as that would be, could do no more than promote the conditions under which men and women might have the opportunity to live righteously.

These assumptions weighed heavily in the deliberations of the Constitutional Convention and were offered to justify the document that emerged from that conclave. Although revered as the foundation of a democratic republic, the Constitution was crafted by politicians who made no secret of their faith in the Puritan doctrine of human sinfulness (Wright 1949). In a series of newspaper articles written to encourage ratification by the states and now regarded as the authoritative reflection of the Founders' intentions, Alexander Hamilton, John Jay, and James Madison outdid one another in trumpeting their belief that human beings should not be trusted with unlimited power. The authors of what came to be known as *The Federalist Papers* presented countless historical examples to show that people were inherently prone to choose evil over good, self-interest over the public good, and immediate gratification over prudent delay. Previous attempts at republican government had foundered because organized groups destroyed the institutions of representation in their single-minded pursuit of power and wealth. With its wealth of examples of past failures, *The Federalist Papers* reads like a catalog of human imperfections. This jaundiced (or, to some, realistic) assessment of humankind was accepted as a basic condition, rooted in human nature, revealed in history, and impervious to changing social conditions.

Like the early Puritan settlers, the Founders identified the innate corruption of humankind as the root problem of government and the great challenge to stable democracy. The task of the Constitution they crafted was to permit republican government in spite of human tendencies to destroy liberty. To accomplish this, the Founders broke with traditional political thought by viewing human depravity both as a barrier to liberty and, under the right circumstances, as a republican asset. The problem, they agreed, was to secure a government capable of providing order yet limited enough to maintain a large degree of freedom. In practical terms, this meant that the national or central government must be given greater power than it had been allowed in the aftermath of the Revolution. The question was how to harness and control the power a strong central government would require.

The Founders' principal solution to this problem was to partition the major powers of government by embedding them in distinct and separate institutions. Given an independent base of power, the Founders thought, the three branches of government could be expected to resist encroachments by each other. They would pool their authority to achieve a common goal only when it was clearly in the national interest. By dividing power in this way, John Adams had written earlier, "the efforts in human nature toward tyranny can alone be checked and restrained, and any freedom preserved in the Constitution" (quoted in Wright 1949, 9).

Paradoxically, then, the weaknesses of humankind were called on to fuel the engine of free government. The human shortcomings that other theorists had perceived as the stumbling block to any plan for durable republican government were enlisted by the Founders as the bulwark against tyranny. What would keep the branches independent of one another, the framers predicted, were precisely those less-than-noble qualities that reposed in typical human beings: ambition, envy, greed, lust for power, and so on. Jealous to preserve its own power and status, Congress would never cede to the president the absolute authority of a monarch. Recognizing that their perpetuation depended on preserving the Constitution, the state governments would use the veto power over amendments to retain their role. Judges and executive branch officials would be restrained by the recognition that they could lose their exalted status by impeachment. All in all, as one scholar has written (Diggins 1984, 53), the Founders believed "that the Republic would be preserved by the 'machinery of government,' not the morality of men."

Considering that the Constitution had to be submitted to the people for their evaluation, it may seem remarkable that the Founders were so explicit in denouncing the trustworthiness of human behavior. In one of the most important letters of *The Federalist Papers*, number 51, Madison did little to flatter the citizens whose votes he sought. To control the government, he wrote, it was not enough to rely on the best instincts of the people; it required "auxiliary provisions" such as the various limiting mechanisms of the Constitution. The great hope for the preservation of liberty was to equip each branch of the new government with "the necessary constitutional means and personal motives to resist encroachments of the others." Then, in a phrase that nicely encapsulated the Federalist philosophy of humankind, he reiterated the principal rationale for the various devices that controlled the exercise of governmental authority: "It may be a reflection on human nature that such devices should be necessary to control the abuses of government. But what is government itself but the greatest of all reflections on human nature? If men were angels, no government would be necessary. If angels were to govern men, neither external nor internal controls on government would be necessary" (Rossiter 1961, 322). Precisely because mortals fell short of angelic standards and angels did not deign to rule, prudence demanded that government be restrained from acting on its worst impulses.

That the framers felt free to defend the Constitution in those terms suggests that their image of human depravity was widely shared by the American people. In the fight over ratification, the most effective opposition came from critics who accepted the Puritan diagnosis but doubted that the proposed remedies for it were strong enough to control the weaknesses of human nature (Kenyon 1955). The antifederalists, for example, believed that the framers of the Constitution were naive to imagine that any strong, centralized government could withstand the depradations of greedy and ambitious human beings. Whatever the differences between the proponents and the enemies of the new governmental framework, however, the important point is that the entire debate was conducted within the bounds defined by the Puritan vision of human sinfulness.

Skepticism, rooted in the Puritan view of original sin, also led the Founders to a negative view of government that is still widely shared by American citizens. For all their veneration of the American way of life, Americans are quite cynical about politics and tend to hold its practitioners in low regard. There is a pronounced distrust of the motivations of politicians and an enduring yearning to purify politics by bestowing leadership on persons who have achieved eminence in other fields—

astronauts, business leaders, soldiers, engineers, farmers, and the like. These people, untainted by contact with a corrupting system, must be prevailed upon to relinquish the pleasures of life and to enter the sordid world of political combat. There they are supposed to save the citizenry from "politics" by restoring a measure of sanity and common sense to political life.

The traditional American view of politics as a sordid endeavor derives in part from the Founders. As we have just seen, they perceived government as a necessary evil, an institution that had to exist to preserve order but was not a good thing in itself. By embracing so wholeheartedly the Puritan image of man, emphasizing human bellicosity as the constant threat to liberty, they essentially reduced government to the status of a nightwatchman. Believing that government could just as easily threaten liberty as safeguard it, they called for as little governmental authority as was necessary to prevent society from collapsing into disarray. As for the higher task of cultivating human virtue, that was to be left to private institutions, such as the church, and did not belong in the government's sphere of responsibility (Diamond 1977).

The Founders' concept of government would have astounded the ancient political thinkers, to whom politics, which Aristotle called "the master science," was the highest expression of human capacity (Will 1983). To the ancients, the state was a moral tutor, whose task was to promote certain virtues among its citizens. According to this conception, politics was the realm in which people could overcome narrow self-interest by searching for the best interests of the community. "Citizenship" was not a term denoting a dry legal status, but a title of honor reserved for those who cared deeply about the community and cultivated the public good. A republican form of government could not survive unless it inculcated such virtuous qualities in its inhabitants. According to classical republican thought, the very maintenance of the state depended on its commitment to elevate, to ennoble, to advance the interests of the community by promoting exemplary behavior. To accomplish those ambitious goals, the state had to possess substantial means, even the ability to coerce recalcitrant people to conform to what the community defined as acceptable conduct. Participation in that enterprise was seen as important and honorable.

Nothing could be further from the American conception, which equates good government with limited government. Most Americans operate from the assumption that the inherent rights of individual citizens normally take precedence over the claims of the state or those of any broader social purpose. Because such individual rights can be threatened by an overbearing government, Americans put a premium on protecting individuals from the heavy hand of the state. Following the Founders, Americans have routinely denied government the right or authority to regulate belief or to limit most forms of conduct. Outside a very limited sphere, "personal virtue" is simply not seen as the proper concern of government.

Such a negative interpretation of authority has had a corresponding impact on the image of politicians. Those who are most deeply involved in conducting the business of the state, it has commonly been assumed, do so in pursuit of nothing more than self-interest. The vocation of politics, perceived in the classical tradition as the pursuit of public welfare, appears to the modern age as merely a struggle for power and personal advantage. Under this modern image, the status of the practitioners of politics has been reduced significantly. There is a widespread suspicion that politics attracts people because, as careers go, it is a fairly good way to make a living.

Limitations on government power can certainly be defended by reference to the terrible damages inflicted on other societies by governments that saw themselves as agents of God or history, charged with remaking humanity in a new image. Just as certainly, it presents problems when government tries to persuade the citizenry to undertake actions that contribute in the long run to the public good but run against immediate self-interest. As Robert Horwitz asked, "How can a republic based solely on the principle of individual self-interest continue to defend itself against its external enemies if its citizenry has not an iota of patriotism, public spirit, or any element of that sense of duty that leads men to make sacrifices in defense of their country?" (1977, 333). By teaching that government is a threat to the liberty of free-born citizens, that it is a necessity born of human imperfection, the Founders unwittingly made it difficult for their successors to motivate behavior in the public interest.

One Nation Under God: A Civil Religion

Yet another aspect of American political life, a pronounced tendency to approach political issues in moral terms, owes much to the Puritan inheritance. Commentators have long noted that American political rhetoric is infused with religious symbols and references, and that debates about contending policy choices are frequently couched in terms of competing moral values. According to some scholars, this constant recourse to religious images and symbols in American political culture provides evidence of the existence of what has variously been called a public theology, a political religion, a religion of democracy, a public philosophy or, most commonly today, a civil religion.

At the core of the rich and subtle concept of civil religion is the idea that a nation tries to understand its historical experience and national purpose in religious terms (Bellah 1975; Bellah and Hammond 1980; Richey and Jones 1974). In the same way that religion may endow the life of an individual with a greater meaning than mere existence, so a civil religion reflects an attempt by citizens to give their nation a transcendent value.[3] The nation is recognized as a secular institution, yet one that is somehow touched by the hand of God. British author G. K. Chesterton recognized this tendency in the United States, which he referred to as "a nation with the soul of a church."

The term *civil religion* does not refer to any formal code of beliefs that is fully developed and authoritatively encapsulated by a single written document. Because there is no formal statement of it, the content of a civil religion has to be inferred from the speeches and writings of political leaders. It lacks the status of a state religion, so citizens are not obliged to assent to it. A civil religion is neither the religion of a particular church nor, at the other extreme, a fully articulated religion that competes with existing denominations. Rather, it is a code subscribed to, in varying degree, by all religions in the nation. Accordingly, it closely resembles one anthropologist's definition of a creed: "A constellation of ideas and standards that gives people a sense of belonging together and of being different from those of other nations and cultures" (cited in Mead 1974, 45–46). By imparting a sacred character to the nation, civil religion enables people of diverse faith to harmonize their religious and political beliefs.

In thinking about the transcendent purpose of their nation, Americans traditionally have been drawn to the biblical metaphor of the "chosen people" (Cherry 1972). As noted in the section on covenant theology, the Puritan colonists were prone to interpret their passage to the New World as a reenactment of God's covenant making with the people of Abraham. Like the ancient Jews, the Puritans felt that they had been selected by God for the purpose of bringing redemption to humankind. If they succeeded in establishing Christian communities in the wilderness, creating "God's New Israel," the rest of the world would see how the faithful were rewarded with good fortune. Even though the reality of Puritan settlements strayed far from the Christian models that motivated their founding, the inhabitants were constantly reminded that their success or failure had implications for all of humankind. That the existence of the United States is still viewed as part of a divine plan shows up in the "Pledge of Allegiance" in the phrase, "one nation under God"—which was added only in the 1950s.[4]

Ever since the concept of a civil religion was first suggested, in the late 1960s, its existence has been the subject of a sustained debate among scholars of American society (see Gehrig 1979 for a good summary). Some observers have discounted civil religion as nothing more than a universal tendency among nations to endow themselves with supernatural attributes. Robert Bellah, the sociologist who did more than anyone else to popularize the concept, has argued that the national traumas of the 1960s and 1970s largely eroded American faith in the nation's higher purpose (1975). Against this backdrop, social scientists have tested for the existence of civil religious sentiments with a variety of research tools. Although the findings have not been entirely consistent, most studies have detected in public attitudes something very much like civil religion.[5] A content analysis of the national magazine published by the Masonic fraternal organization identified a large number of statements emphasizing the nation's divine purpose (Joliceur and Knowles 1978). Using questions listed in the box on page 60, Ronald Wimberly and his colleagues have demonstrated a high level of public assent to statements that seem consistent with the civil religion theme (Christenson and Wimberly 1978; Wimberly 1976; Wimberly 1979). Responses to these questions, which have been asked of divergent audiences, do not simply reflect commitment to general religious values or any other background factors. Rather, just as predicted by the scholars who first called attention to an American civil religion, civil religious

Civil Religious Sentiment in the United States

The existence of an American civil religion has been inferred from the responses of American citizens to the following statements:

1. It is a mistake to think that America is God's chosen nation today.
2. I consider holidays like the Fourth of July religious as well as patriotic.
3. We need more laws on morals.
4. We should respect a president's authority since his authority is from God.
5. National leaders should affirm their belief in God.
6. Good patriots are not necessarily religious people.
7. Social justice cannot only be based on laws; it must also come from religion.
8. To me, the flag of the United States is sacred.
9. God can be known through the experience of the American people.
10. If the American government does not support religion, the government cannot uphold morality.

Note: Positive responses to items 2–5 and 7–10 indicate a civil religious orientation, as does disagreement with items 1 and 6.
Source: Ronald C. Wimberly, "Testing the Civil Religion Hypothesis," *Sociological Analysis* 37:341–352.

feelings have been widely diffused among the persons interviewed in the polls. A similar survey among elementary school children in the Midwest yielded comparable support for the civil religion hypothesis (Smidt 1980). On the basis of these studies, it does appear that Americans expect their nation to fill a spiritual purpose.

The presidency appears to play a crucial symbolic role in American civil religion, an observation brought home in an unexpected way by public reaction to the assassination of John F. Kennedy in 1963. Sociological investigators noted a marked increase in prayer, worship, and other forms of religious activity. Despite the formal secularization of the governmental system and President Kennedy's membership in a minority faith (Roman Catholicism), many Americans reacted to the assassination by expressing intense religious commitment. To the political scientist Sidney Verba (1965, 354), the public response revealed that "political commitment in the United States contains a prime component of primordial religious commitment." In mourning the slain president, Americans were honoring a sacred symbol. The discovery that a political leader could take on a religious significance for the public provided further evidence that the nation is viewed in transcendent terms.

Civil religion has also reinforced the "deep-rooted belief in American culture that political and personal virtue should be inseparable" (Sennett 1987, 42). As if to confirm that hypothesis in the 1988 presidential campaign, southern voters told pollsters they believed a candidate's moral behavior in private life foretold success in office.[6] They cited previous drug use, extramarital affairs, and lying as behavior they would weigh against a candidate. Accordingly, one candidate was driven from the race for the nomination by allegations of marital infidelity, another was forced out in response to charges of plagiarism, and two had to endure criticism when they admitted having smoked marijuana in their youth. This was neither the first nor last example of such moral transgressions affecting political standing. Evidence that he had lied about his knowledge of the Watergate burglary drove Richard Nixon from the White House in 1974. By admitting past use of marijuana, a recent nominee for the Supreme Court raised grave questions about his fitness for the post. There is less room for leeway when a public official is also a religious symbol (Fairbanks 1981).

Widespread public affirmation of civil religion has important consequences in political life. In what social scientists call "legitimation," or its "priestly" aspect, civil religion helps to cement loyalty to the nation. God blesses the nation because it serves a sacred purpose. So long as the nation conducts its affairs according to some higher purpose, it warrants allegiance from its citizens on grounds other than mere self-interest. By giving the nation a mission to which citizens are emotionally attached, civil religion may thus counter the tendencies to elevate self-interest into the only basis for loyalty and obedience. The "legitimation" function of civil religion has been confirmed by Corwin Smidt (1982) who found that the children most likely to develop a very positive image of political authority were those who perceived the nation in transcendent terms.

Also, as may be seen in the comments of two very different social critics, Sidney Schanberg and Phyllis Schlafly, civil religion provides standards by which to judge the behavior of a nation. It suggests that there are things higher than the nation and that it is permissible to criticize the nation for its departures from moral codes. As the New Testament taught, a nation "under God" is deemed responsible to God and will be held to a high standard of behavior. Because transgressors suffer severe punishment from a just God, citizens have an incentive to keep the nation firmly on the path of righteousness. This is the ethical or prophetic function of civil religion.

It is true that, by and large, the press in Indochina wrote stories critical of the American policy there. But it was not because reporters were unpatriotic. It was, rather, because reporters saw America slipping toward the habits of totalitarian powers whose activities we deem as less than moral.

What we did was to hold this country to a greater standard. Since our Government says that it stands on higher moral ground than the Communist powers, that it is different, it must behave differently, not just say so. That is the standard by which the press measured its country. (Sidney Schanberg, *New York Times*, Apr. 23, 1985, op-ed)

Q. Who's side *is* God on?

A. Well, I think He's on the side of Right, Justice, and Goodness—all those things. And I think the side anti-ERA is on.

Q. Is God American?

A. No, but He certainly blessed America more than any other country. And with that goes the responsibility to do the right thing and assume that leadership. If America abandons that responsibility, it could face a terrible destruction.

Q. Who is God against? Who's on the other side?

A. The Devil.

Q. Represented by whom?

A. . . . the Devil is a very intelligent creature, who appears in a lot of forms. I do think he's in the Kremlin, among other places. (*Ms.* magazine interview with Phyllis Schlafly, January 1982, p. 92)

Critics of American policy, such as the journalist Sidney Schanberg, quoted here, have usually invoked the prophetic side of civil religion by calling America to honor its own aspirations and standards. When he admonished American Christians to challenge racial segregation, the Reverend Martin Luther King, Jr., imagined what St. Paul would have said to them:

You have a dual citizenry. You live both in time and eternity. Your highest loyalty is to God, and not to the mores or the folkways, the state or the nation, or any man-made institution. If any earthly institution or custom conflicts with God's will, it is your Christian duty to oppose it. You must never allow the transitory, evanescent demands of man-made institutions to take precedence over the eternal demands of the Almighty God. (1963, 128)

The deep hold this concept has had on the American mind is evidenced by the fact that it has recurred with equal intensity among those who have resisted the changes sought by King. In their indictment of American policies, conservative critics like Phyllis Schlafly have stressed that God's blessing on the United States is contingent on the country's adherence to biblical morality. Although they are more prone than King to cite biblical passages that appear to anoint the political system with divine sanction, right-wing leaders such as Schlafly and the Reverend Jerry Falwell also have reserved the right to disobedience when they see human law in conflict with divine law.

No American politician expressed the priestly and prophetic themes of civil religion more eloquently than Abraham Lincoln (Morgenthau and Hein 1983). Although relatively untouched by "church religion," Lincoln saw the United States as a nation with a divine purpose that had been most clearly revealed in the noble principles of the Declaration of Independence. For Lincoln, the commitment to secure free government, which had been sanctified by the sacrifices of the revolutionary generation, was the higher purpose that the United States represented. By adhering to the principles of the Declaration, he told Congress late in 1862, the nation was nothing less than "the last, best hope of earth." Because the Union was the concrete embodiment of that continuing commitment to liberty, Lincoln made its maintenance and eventual restoration his highest priority. At Gettysburg, he interpreted the deaths of Union soldiers in transcendent terms, saying that their sacrifice in the cause of liberty had reaffirmed the sacredness of the American mission. He then asked Americans to respond with "increased devotion" to the cause for which the soldiers have given the "last full measure of devotion" (Lincoln 1959a).

If Lincoln enunciated civil religious themes to sanctify the Union, he was equally willing to call down the wrath of God on the nation when he thought it had strayed from the path of righteousness. Although favoring moderate solutions to slavery, he clearly regarded the maintenance of the institution as a great national sin—perhaps the American equivalent of Adam's fall from God's grace. In his second inaugural address, delivered only a month before his assassination, Lincoln

(1959b) chided Northerners and Southerners alike who claimed God's support for their cause. Quoting from Scripture, he noted that God punished those who committed offenses in the world. Those responsible for the "offense" of American slavery included all Americans, both the Southerners who kept slaves and the Northerners who had acquiesced in its continued existence. He saw the bloodshed and violence of the war as God's retribution: "He gives to both North and South this terrible war as the woe due to those by whom the offense came." Rejecting complacency and self-righteousness, Lincoln called on the nation to accept its punishment and then to rededicate itself to the principles of the Declaration.

Lincoln was far from alone in his invocation of civil religion; in fact, students of political rhetoric have demonstrated its recurrence in the public statements of nearly all American presidents (Hart 1977). In a systematic content analysis of inaugural addresses delivered from George Washington to Ronald Reagan, Cynthia Toolin (1983) found the speeches replete with reference to the nation's divine origin and its corresponding moral obligation to light the way for the remainder of the earth. To judge from the utterances of two recent occupants of the office, the priestly and prophetic strains of civil religion have retained potency. Jimmy Carter's first speech as president encouraged Americans to develop "full faith" in their country—wording that signifies dedication to a transcendent force—and contained numerous references to the country in clearly religious terms (Hahn 1984). Carter also emphasized the prophetic side of civil religion in urging upon the nation the biblical injunction, "to do justly, and to love mercy, and to walk humbly with thy God." In declaring at his inauguration that "I believe God intended for us to be free," Ronald Reagan (1981, 4; also Shannon 1982) made an even more explicit statement of belief in a civil religion. The prophetic side of Reagan's faith can be inferred from his frequent suggestions that the United States has strayed from the intentions of the Founders in asking government to do too much (1981, 3). Though he did not say directly that God had punished Americans by sending an economic recession, that line of reasoning would be consistent with the view that violations of a sacred covenant bring retribution to transgressors.

Civil religion is a double-edged sword. It can ennoble a people by prompting generous instincts and a resolute commitment to the nation's principles. Yet the two streams of civil religion—legitimation and prophecy—can also be vulgarized. Attributing a sacred purpose to the nation can degenerate all too easily into idolatrous worship of the state. The belief that a nation embodies God's will can inhibit the skepticism and self-criticism that is so important to democratic politics (Lipsitz 1968). Similarly, in holding the nation to high standards of conduct, the civil religious tradition may produce a frame of mind that disdains the kind of compromises necessary for an orderly political life. If the standards are rigid and unbending, the system one of moral absolutes, then all deviations are equally reprehensible—a view that does not encourage a sense of proportion.

Although civil religion has been degraded in this manner in domestic politics, the dangers of extremist versions have been most visible in American interactions with the rest of the world (Tiryakian 1982). Barely concealing his irritation, a Canadian described American foreign policy as "a determined ideological and evangelical offensive to redeem the rest of the world from its backward, sinful self" (Rawlyk 1990, 254). Some critics have argued that this sense of mission coupled with a tendency to view international politics as a clash of moral opposites, has undermined the development of an effective foreign policy. An approach to the world built on moral absolutes can distort judgment by blinding policy makers to important subtleties.

Consider for example, the U.S. government's behavior toward international communism in the tense period following World War II. When the wartime alliance between the United States and the Soviet Union broke down in the aftermath of victory, American policy reverted to a position of unrelenting hostility. Whatever the real provocations in Soviet behavior, the U.S. foreign policy leadership was prone to treat the Soviet Union as a moral leper that had to be isolated from the world community (Hoopes 1973). Many thoughtful critics who harbor no illusions about Soviet intentions have wondered if this policy served American interests. They have noted that the moralistic approach to international communism, including denunciations of it in theological terms, may have prevented American policy makers from recognizing and exploiting the split in the late 1950s between the Soviet Union and the People's Republic of China. In this view, an opportunity to assert the national interest by maneuvering between the rival Communist powers was passed over in favor of a crusading approach. If these critics are right—and their views are still debated—the moralistic approach impeded a realistic assessment of American interests.

Such a crusading mentality may also have encouraged the very barbarism it was meant to counteract. As George Kennan (1951) charged, a moralistic streak that stigmatized opponents as the embodiment of evil will be satisfied with nothing less than total victory over the enemy. The result, a "total war" mentality, impedes compromise and thus exacerbates tension. Persons and nations who believed God was on their side have been responsible for some of the most unspeakable horrors of world history (as have people who rejected the notion of God or any higher spiritual realm). Little wonder, then, that civil religion should be regarded as a two-edged sword. Like religion in general, it may call forth the best and worst instincts in human behavior—and there is ample evidence of both in the impact of American civil religion.

It would surely be an exaggeration to state flatly that religion alone *caused* important political attitudes—including the social contract, limited government, and American destiny—to take hold of the American imagination. The link between the ideas of sixteenth-century religious thinkers and eighteenth-century political activists is a tangled and meandering path, not a straight line. Religion, in its various guises, should be recognized as only one of the forces operating in the development of American political culture.

At least two other influences shaped the American political system in its formative period—a new intellectual force and the lure of economic advantage. The foremost intellectual rival to the ideology of the Protestant Reformation was a body of thought developed in seventeenth and eighteenth century Europe under the name of the Enlightenment (May 1976).[7] This movement, characterized above all by a belief in human progress through the systematic application of reason, supplied a heavy dose of optimism to counterbalance the Puritans' stern image of humanity. Without some sense that humans could engage in reasonable conduct under the proper institutional arrangements, the Founders could not have contemplated constructing a democratic political system. Their attempt to create a written constitution alone bespeaks a tremendous confidence in human ability to discover eternal truths by reflection and debate. The influence of the Age of Reason, as the Enlightenment era has been called, was apparent in the thought and behavior of political activists throughout the revolutionary period and during the early history of the nation.

In addition to the sway of intellectual currents from Europe, the colonists were also moved by material forces. Clearly key elements of the political culture served to advance the economic interests of powerful groups in early American society. As generations of schoolchildren have learned, a major incentive to break with Great Britain were economic grievances about taxation and other matters. The Founders' strong commitment to the idea of limited government may have also been the product of economic self-interest, for a government with limited authority was a government incapable of redistributing income from the wealthy to the poor. The Founders generally came from the more affluent stratum of colonial society, and material interests may well have disposed them to want governmental authority tightly reined in. Similarly, the missionary impulse in American political culture permitted the nation to fuel its economic expansion by the constant acquisition of new land, raw materials, sources of labor, and markets.

Given the many factors at work in forming the American political culture, the more appropriate conclusion is that certain patterns of religious thought, habitual ways of reasoning about God and humankind, made it easier for some political ideas to take root in American society. Accustomed to thinking about God and mortals in contractual terms, Americans were receptive to a political theory that treated government in a similar fashion. The widespread belief that humans behave sinfully disposed the colonists to accept the doctrine of limited government. Trained by their religion to see God at work in the daily lives of men and women, Americans could easily imagine a divine hand guiding the destiny of their country. In this view, religion was one of the factors that facilitated the development of a common political outlook.

This qualified judgment, recognizing religion as one among several sources of the founding of America, should also provide a perspective on the debate about the nation's path since the Revolution. Among some contemporary descendants of the Puritan heritage, there is a tendency to treat recent American history in terms of decline and fall. As three evangelical scholars recently conveyed this image, it begins with the assumption that the United States "emerged from the generally Christian actions of generally Christian people [who] . . . bequeathed Christian values, and a Christian heritage, to later American history" (Noll, Hatch, and Marsden 1983). By loosening legal constraints on items as diverse as abortion, school discipline, sexual behavior, drug use, and sex roles, it is charged, the government has betrayed its heritage and abandoned its Christian foundations. But if Christianity certainly played a prominent role in the American founding, the evidence presented herein does not sustain the claim that colonial America was exclusively influenced by Christian values.[8] Whether or not early America was morally superior to present-day society is a question that will continue to be debated; beginning the debate with the image of a golden age, a one-time "Christian America," is a dubious strategy.

When examined from the perspective of political culture, religion has generally been a unifying force in American politics, helping to generate a national consensus on basic political values. Even if the religious inspiration of these core ideas has been forgotten, the political concepts of social contract, limited government, and American destiny remain integral elements of American political culture. As the next several chapters will show, religion can divide as well as unite. Some important features in the body politic originate in differences among religious groups over theology, social standing, and institutional interests. I will first examine how these differences affect mass attitudes on policy issues and behavior in the voting booth.

NOTES

1. As a student once remarked to me, perfectly revealing the cynicism of the age, "People are rich or poor before they are anything else."
2. The development of contract thought among the colonists has traditionally been credited to the "secular" influence of the English philosopher John Locke. But as Winthrop Hudson (1965) argued, Locke drew on the ideas of the Puritans to formulate the doctrine of government by consent of the governed.
3. In a review of the civil religion concept, Richey and Jones (1974, 14–18) identify five overlapping uses of the term. I have adopted the definition of civil religion as a sense of national transcendence because that is the manner in which the "chosen people" metaphor has entered the political culture.
4. The degree to which this type of civil religion is the unique property of American culture or a more universal phenomenon has yet to be fully addressed. Michael Walzer (1985) has found the Exodus metaphor throughout political history. For some suggestive thoughts on civil religion in comparative perspective, see Coleman (1970) and Bellah and Hammond (1980, chaps. 2–4).
5. The exceptions include Thomas and Flippen (1972), who found few references

to any divine plan for the United States in newspaper editorials published during "Honor America" week. In interviews that Benson and Williams (1982) conducted with members of the U.S. Congress, most legislators proved unwilling to endorse statements that interpreted the nation's destiny in transcendent terms.

6. "A Candidate's Morals Matter, and Lying Is the Cardinal Sin," *Atlanta Journal and Constitution,* Jan. 31, 1988.

7. Because the Christianity of the Protestant Reformation was skeptical about the capacity for human regeneration and emphasized revelation as the key to understanding, it may be tempting to portray religion and rationalist thought as incompatible. In practice, the two traditions at times found common ground and at times competed for influence—often within the mind of the same individual.

8. Noll, Hatch, and Marsden (1983) have made a strong case that a "Christian culture" is generally unlikely and that colonial America was a considerable distance away from a scripturally based commonwealth. They also raise doubts that the Christian influence in early America was uniformly positive.

REFERENCES

Ahlstrom, Sydney. 1965. "The Puritan Ethic and the Spirit of American Democracy." In *Calvinism and the Political Order,* edited by George L. Hunt, 88–107. Philadelphia: Westminster.

———. 1975. *A Religious History of the American People.* Vol. 1. New York. Image Books.

Bellah, Robert N. 1975. *The Broken Covenant: American Civil Religion in a Time of Trial.* New York: Seabury.

Bellah, Robert N., and Phillip E. Hammond, eds. 1980. *Varieties of Civil Religion.* New York: Harper and Row.

Benson, Peter L., and Dorothy L. Williams. 1982. *Religion on Capitol Hill: Myths and Realities.* San Francisco: Harper and Row.

Bercovitch, Sacvan. 1975. *The Puritan Origin of the American Self.* New Haven, Conn.: Yale University Press.

Bloch, Ruth H. 1990. "Religion and Ideological Change in the American Revolution." In *Religion and American Politics,* edited by Mark A. Noll, 44–61. New York: Oxford University Press.

Bridenbaugh, Carl. 1962. *Mitre and Sceptre: Transatlantic Faiths, Ideas, Personalities, and Politics, 1689–1775.* New York: Oxford University Press.

Cherry, Conrad, ed. 1972. *God's New Israel: Religious Interpretations of American Destiny.* Englewood Cliffs, N.J.: Prentice-Hall.

Christenson, James, and Ronald C. Wimberly. 1978. "Who Is Civil Religious?" *Sociological Analysis* 39:77–83.

Coleman, John A. 1970. "Civil Religion." *Sociological Analysis* 31:67–77.

Diamond, Martin. 1977. "Ethics and Politics: The American Way." In *The Moral Foundations of the American Republic,* ed. Robert Horwitz, 39–72. Charlottesville: University Press of Virginia.

Diggins, John P. 1984. *The Lost Soul of American Politics: Virtue, Self-Interest, and the Foundations of Liberalism.* New York: Basic Books.

Elazar, Daniel J. 1980. "The Political Theory of Covenant: Biblical Origins and Modern Developments." *Publius* 10:3–30.

Fairbanks, James David. 1981. "The Priestly Function of the Presidency: A Discussion of the Literature on Civil Religion and Its Implications for the Study of Presidential Leadership." *Presidential Studies Quarterly* 11:214–232.

Gehrig, Gail. 1979. *American Civil Religion: An Assessment.* Storrs, Conn.: Society for the Scientific Study of Religion.

Hahn, Dan F. 1984. "The Rhetoric of Jimmy Carter, 1976–1980." *Presidential Studies Quarterly* 14:265–288.

Hart, Roderick. 1977. *The Political Pulpit.* West Lafayette, Ind.: Purdue University Press.

Hatch, Nathan O. 1990. "The Democratization of Christianity and the Character of American Politics." In *Religion and American Politics,* edited by Mark A. Noll, 92–120. New York: Oxford University Press.

Hoopes, Townshend. 1973. *The Devil and John Foster Dulles.* Boston: Atlantic–Little, Brown.

Horwitz, Robert H. 1977. "John Locke and the Preservation of Liberty: A Perennial Problem of Civic Education." In *The Moral Foundations of the American Republic,* edited by Robert Horwitz, 129–156. Charlottesville: University Press of Virginia.

Howe, Daniel Walker. 1990. "Religion and Politics in the Antebellum North." In *Religion and American Politics,* edited by Mark A. Noll, 121–145. New York: Oxford University Press.

Hudson, Winthrop S. 1965. "John Locke: Heir of Puritan Political Theories." In *Calvinism and the Political Order,* edited by George L. Hunt, 108–129. Philadelphia: Westminster.

Jensen, Richard. 1980. "Armies, Admen and Crusaders: Strategies to Win Elections." *Public Opinion* 3:44–53.

Joliceur, Pamela M., and Louis K. Knowles. 1978. "Fraternal Organizations and Civil Religion: Scottish Rite Freemasonry." *Review of Religious Research* 20:3–22.

Kennan, George F. 1951. *American Diplomacy, 1900–1950.* Chicago: University of Chicago Press.

Kenyon, Cecelia. 1955. "Men of Little Faith: The Anti-Federalists on the Nature of Representative Government." *William and Mary Quarterly* 12:3–43.

Kessler, Sanford. 1989. "Tocqueville's Puritans: Christianity and the American Founding." Paper presented at the annual meeting of the American Political Science Association, Atlanta.

King, Martin Luther, Jr. 1963. *Strength to Love.* New York: Harper and Row.

Lincoln, Abraham. 1959a. "The Gettysburg Address." In *The Search for Democracy,* ed. Harry W. Kirwin, 203–205. Garden City, N.Y.: Doubleday Anchor.

———. 1959b. "Second Inaugural Address." In ibid., 102–103.

Lipsitz, Lewis. 1964. "Work Life and Political Attitudes: A Study of Manual Workers." *American Political Science Review* 58:951–962.

———. 1968. "If, as Verba Says, the State Functions as a Religion, What Are We to Do Then to Save Our Souls?" *American Political Science Review* 62:527–535.

Lutz, Donald S. 1984. "The Relative Influence of European Writers Upon Late 18th-Century American Political Thought." *American Political Science Review* 78:189–197.

May, Henry. 1976. *The Enlightenment in America*. New York: Oxford University Press.

Mead, Sidney E. 1976. *The Lively Experiment: The Shaping of Christianity in America*. New York: Harper and Row.

——. 1974. "The 'Nation With the Soul of a Church'." In *American Civil Religion*, edited by Russell Richey and Donald G. Jones, 45–75. New York: Harper and Row.

Miller, Perry. 1956. *Errand into the Wilderness*. Cambridge: Harvard University Press.

——. 1967. *Nature's Nation*. Cambridge: Harvard University Press.

Miller, William Lee. 1961. "American Religion and American Political Attitudes." In *Religious Perspectives in American Culture*, edited by James Ward Smith and A. Leland Jamison, 81–118. Princeton, N.J.: Princeton University Press.

Morgenthau, Hans, and David Hein. 1983. *Essays on Lincoln's Faith and Politics*. Lanham, Md.: University Press of America.

Murrin, John M. 1990. "Religion and Politics in America from the First Settlements to the Civil War." In *Religion and American Politics*, edited by Mark A. Noll, 19–43. New York: Oxford University Press.

Niebuhr, H. Richard. 1959. *The Kingdom of God in America*. New York: Harper Torchbooks.

Noll, Mark A. 1988. *One Nation Under God? Christian Faith and Political Action in America*. San Francisco: Harper and Row.

Noll, Mark A., Nathan O. Hatch, and George M. Marsden. 1983. *The Search for Christian America*. Westchester, Ill.: Crossway.

Rawlyk, George A. 1990. "Politics, Religion, and the Canadian Experience: A Preliminary Probe." In *Religion and American Politics*, edited by Mark A. Noll, 253–277. New York: Oxford University Press.

Reagan, Ronald W. 1981. "Inaugural Address." In *Weekly Compilation of Presidential Documents* 17, January 26, pp. 1–5. Washington, D.C.: Government Printing Office.

Renshon, Stanley Allen. 1975. "The Role of Personality Development in Political Socialization." In *New Directions in Political Socialization*, edited by David C. Schwartz and Sandra Kenyon Schwartz. New York: Free Press.

Richey, Russell E., and Donald G. Jones, eds. 1974. *American Civil Religion*. New York: Harper and Row.

Riemer, Neal. 1980. "Covenant and the Federal Constitution." *Publius* 10:135–148.

Rossiter, Clinton, ed. 1961. *The Federalist Papers*. New York: New American Library.

Rothman, Rozanu. 1980. "The Impact of Covenant and Contract Theories on Conceptions of the U.S. Constitution." *Publius* 10:149–163.

Sandoz, Ellis. 1990. *A Government of Laws: Political Theory, Religion, and the American Founding*. Baton Rouge: Louisiana State University Press.

Schechter, Stephen L. 1980. "The Founding of American Local Communities: A Study of Covenantal and Other Forms of Association." *Publius* 10:165–185.

Sennett, Richard. 1987. "A Republic of Souls: Puritanism and the American Presidency." *Harper's* (July), 41–46.

Shannon, W. Wayne. 1982. "Mr. Reagan Goes to Washington: Teaching Exceptional America." *Public Opinion* 4:13–17, 55.

Shipton, Clifford K. 1947. "Puritanism and Modern Democracy." *New England Historical and Genealogical Register* 101:181–198.

Simpson, Alan. 1955. *Puritanism in Old and New England.* Chicago: University of Chicago Press.

Smidt, Corwin. 1980. "Civil Religious Orientation Among Elementary School Children." *Sociological Analysis* 41:25–40.

———. 1982. "Civil Religious Orientations and Children's Perception of Political Authority." *Political Behavior* 4:147–162.

Strout, Cushing. 1974. *The New Heavens and the New Earth.* New York: Harper and Row.

Swierenga, Robert P. 1990. "Ethnoreligious Political Behavior in the Mid-Nineteenth Century: Voting, Values, Culture." In Mark A. Noll, ed. *Religion and American Politics.* New York: Oxford University Press, 146–171.

Thomas, Michael C., and Charles C. Flippen. 1972. "American Civil Religion: An Empirical Study." *Social Forces* 51:218–225.

Tiryakian, Edward A. 1982. "Puritan America in the Modern World: Mission Impossible." *Sociological Analysis* 43:351–368.

Tocqueville, Alexis de. 1945. *Democracy in America.* Vol. 1. New York: Vintage.

Toolin, Cynthia. 1983. "American Civil Religion from 1789–1981: A Content Analysis of Presidential Inaugural Addresses." *Review of Religious Research* 25:39–48.

Verba, Sidney. 1965. "The Kennedy Assassination and the Nature of Political Commitment." In *The Kennedy Assassination and the American Public,* edited by Bradley S. Greenberg and Edward S. Parker, 348–360. Stanford, Calif.: Stanford University Press.

Walzer, Michael. 1985. *Exodus and Revolution.* New York: Basic Books.

Will, George F. 1983. *Statecraft as Soulcraft.* New York: Simon and Schuster.

Wimberly, Ronald C. 1976. "Testing the Civil Religion Hypothesis." *Sociological Analysis* 37:341–352.

———. 1979. "Continuity in the Measurement of Civil Religion." *Sociological Analysis* 40:59–62.

Wright, Benjamin F. 1949. "The Federalist on the Nature of Political Man." *Ethics* 59:1–31.

4. The Religious Dimension of American Political Behavior

By the side of every religion is to be found a political opinion, which is connected with it by affinity. If the human mind be left to follow its own bent, it will regulate the temporal and spiritual institutions of society in a uniform manner, and man will endeavor . . . to *harmonize* earth with heaven.

—Alexis de Tocqueville, *Democracy in America*

Even in colonial America, a land with a common theological tradition, people did not always see eye to eye on the appropriate political applications of religious ideas. The potential for religiously based political conflict in the United States was further encouraged by the subsequent fragmentation of national religious life. Along with the massive eighteenth- and nineteenth-century migrations from Europe came challenges to Protestant supremacy from perspectives inspired by Catholic and Jewish thought. And just as it began facing competition from immigrant religions, Protestant unity started to give way from within. As new denominations spread rapidly on the expanding southern and western frontiers, the more established branches of Protestantism split into competing denominations over a variety of issues. Owing to these internal fractures, the differences within Protestantism eventually came to rival those between Protestants and non-Protestants. The presence of the new religious groups and the widening fissures within Protestantism undermined the ability of religion to unite Americans in a common body of thought. During much of the nineteenth and early twentieth centuries, religion was a source of continuing social conflict and political dispute.

Despite subsequent convergence on some issues and the decline of much overt religious conflict in politics, differences between religious groups continue to mark political behavior in the United States today. Whatever Americans believe about how religion and politics should interact, their behavior does not always reveal a strict "wall of separation" between religious and political loyalties. Individuals hold opinions and cast votes, but they do so subject to the tug of group tradition and influence. Global studies have revealed that religion, in concert with such factors as social class, race, ethnicity, and region, has continued to exert a major influence on a variety of political orientations (Lijphart 1971; Rose and Urwin 1969). After reviewing numerous studies of voting patterns in different countries, one leading expert on mass political attitudes was forced to conclude that "religious differentiation intrudes on partisan political alignments in [an] unexpectedly powerful degree wherever it conceivably can" (Converse 1974, 734). The use of the word *unexpectedly* reveals that modern observers have been surprised to find political differences tied to "primordial" religious cleavages rather than to thoroughly "modern" inequalities such as social class.

In recognition of the importance of religion in contemporary political loyalties, this chapter describes how religious groups agree or disagree on a variety of political orientations and explains major differences between groups by reference to creedal, institutional, and social/cultural characteristics. Of course, American political attitudes bear the imprint of many factors aside from religious group loyalties. This chapter will not argue either that other group loyalties are absent from the public agenda or that religion intrudes on every political issue of importance. Rather, by charting the contours of denominational differences and evaluating explanations for the link between religious group membership and mass political behavior, it will explore the religious roots of some contemporary political controversies.

Patterns of Religious Affiliation

A valuable perspective on the contemporary relationship between religion and political attitudes in the United States can be gained through a series of public opinion surveys conducted by the National Opinion Research Center at the University of Chicago. Known as the General Social Survey, or GSS, these periodic interviews with representative national samples of the adult population contain a broad range of data about social and political attitudes. Because the surveys also identify the religious preferences of the participants, they make it possible to compare religious groups with one another.[1] In the following analysis, respondents in surveys conducted annually from 1985 through 1989 are combined so as to obtain a data set large enough to permit examination of religious groups that are normally excluded from study because of small representation in any single poll.

For purposes of group analysis, I have subdivided the population into nine religious categories. The initial distinction between *Protestants, Catholics,* and *Jews,* the starting point for any such classification, hardly begins to cover the variety of organized religious expression in the United States (Roof and McKinney 1987). Catholics and Jews form distinctive religious and political communities so their separation from Protestants should come as no surprise. The complexity of the American religious mosaic also mandates separate categories for two other groups outside the Protestant fold: religious *nones* and *Mormons*. In a society that values religion, those who swim against the tide by disclaiming a religious identity might also exhibit unconventional behavior in the political realm. The Church of Jesus Christ of Latter-day Saints, the official label for the Mormon church, has grown larger than many Protestant denominations and adopted an active political role. Taken together, the four groups outside Protestantism compose approximately one-third of the GSS samples.

To those accustomed to thinking of Protestantism as a unified faith with minor denominational differences—"sixty sauces with one flavor" in the sarcastic phrase of a Frenchman—it will be surprising to find the Protestant majority apportioned among five distinct camps. I have carved out separate categories for *black, nontraditional,* and *ambiguous Protestants*. By virtue of its historical situation, social role, and organizational independence, black Protestantism requires separate treatment. So do adherents of Christian Science, Unitarianism, Jehovah's Witnesses, the Society of Friends (Quakers), and other unconventional sects that developed within Protestantism. Because they failed to describe their religious identity beyond such broad phrases as "Protestant" or "Christian," it was necessary to reserve a category for "ambiguous" Protestants.

For the remaining Protestants—almost half the adult population—the principal dividing line runs between the *mainline* and *evangelical* camps. Mainline and evangelical Protestants differ in theology, styles of worship, church governance, and views about the role of religion in society. R. Stephen Warner (1988, chap. 2) argues that this "two-party system" is animated primarily by different understandings of Jesus. Mainline groups regard him predominantly "as a moral teacher who told disciples that they could best honor him by helping those in need," while evangelicals treat Jesus principally "as one who offers [personal] salvation to anyone who confesses his name" (1988, 33–34). This polarization has led to important variations in religious and social practice. Stressing Jesus' role as a prophet of social justice, the mainline tradition sanctifies altruism and regards selfishness as the cardinal sin. In this tradition, which extends membership to all and understands religious duty in terms of sharing abundance, the Bible is treated as a book with deep truths that have to be discerned amidst myth and archaic stories. Consistent with their view of Jesus as personal savior, evangelicals "are obligated above all to share their creed" by bringing others to salvation through a personal embrace of God. The church, a limited community open to those who have attained salvation, sees its principal task as sustaining and extending belief. "Because the Bible is the source of revelation about Jesus," Warner explains (1988, p. 34), evangelicals treasure it and credit even its implausible stories. Unlike mainline Protestants who accept many different sources of religious truth, the evangelicals assign religious authority to the Bible alone.

Applying these subtle and complex outlooks to individuals who participate in attitude surveys is a daunting task. In practice, the evangelical/mainline cleavage often runs through denominations and churches. Other Protestants, particularly in the black denominations, manage to combine the evangelical emphasis on salvation with the mainline commitment to social action. To further confuse the picture, even some Catholics have adopted aspects of the evangelical approach to faith. Nonetheless, there is general consensus among scholars that the evangelical label should be reserved for white Protestants who share core beliefs in the unique authority of the Bible, the divinity of Jesus, and the relevance of his life, death, and resurrection to salvation of the soul (Hunter 1983, 7). Such views are widespread among Protestants variously described as conservative, traditional, fundamentalist, pentecostal, holiness, charismatic, free church, adventist, and reformed. Most evangelicals may be found among Baptists and the southern wings of Methodists and Presbyterians. By contrast, the "mainline" adjective is

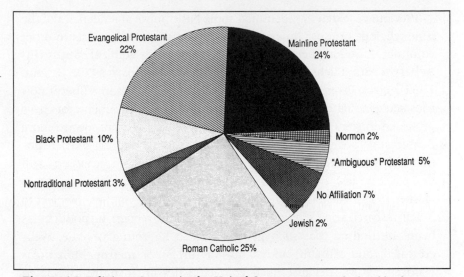

Figure 4.1 Religious Groups in the United States (Source: Calculated by the author from the 1985–1989 General Social Surveys, National Opinion Research Center, Davis and Smith 1990)

sometimes used synonymously with labels such as liberal, moderate, historic, and mainstream. As such, it encompasses most Congregationalists, Methodists, Presbyterians, Episcopalians, and Lutherans. We have followed this denominational strategy in assigning white Protestants to either the evangelical or mainline category.[2]

Figure 4.1 shows the distribution of the almost eight thousand survey participants among the nine basic religious categories. The size of the slices confirms the extent of religious pluralism in the United States. No single religious group comes close to claiming a majority of the population; and were the groups to be subdivided to reflect their internal diversity on issues of theology, worship, and church organization, the sense of religious fragmentation would be reinforced. Roman Catholics constitute the largest single denomination, about one-fourth of the adult population, followed closely by mainline and then evangelical Protestants. The remainder of the adult population is divided among black Protestants (10 percent of the total), persons who claimed no religious preference (7 percent), ambiguous and nontraditional Protestants (5 percent and 3 percent, respectively), Jews (2 percent) and Mormons (2 percent).

Previous research has identified some basic political tendencies of the nine religious groups. American Jews, like their coreligionists in other countries, have long been identified with left-wing political causes (El-Azhary 1980; Fuchs 1956; Guysenir 1958; Liebman 1979; Rischin 1962). Black Protestants have usually supported the same liberal policies and candidates as Jews. Since the 1960s, some commentators have professed to see (and others have hoped for) a movement toward more conservative positions in both groups and the uncoupling of their political alliance. Even with these purported changes, most experts still find black Protestants and Jews on the left side of the political spectrum (Fisher 1979). Although religious nonaffiliates have not been subject to much research, one clue about their general direction in politics has been the finding that such people tend to be young, mobile, well-educated, and affluent, and to live in urban or metropolitan areas (Roozen 1978). Because such characteristics are usually associated with unconventional thinking, it has been thought that the nonaffiliated tend to share the liberal political outlook of Jews and black Protestants.

The white mainline Protestants have been strongly affected by the political and social traumas of recent years. Historically associated with the Republican party and conservative positions on many issues (Berelson, Lazarsfeld, and McPhee 1954; Lazarsfeld, Berelson, and Gaudet 1948; Lenski 1963), the mainline Protestants have been faced with growing liberal sentiment from clergy and denominational leaders (Hadden 1969; Quinley 1974). Conversely, the evangelicals have been encouraged to move in a conservative direction by some of their most vocal pastors. It cannot be assumed that ordinary members of these camps shifted in accordance with their leaders. Many mainline Protestants have strongly resisted the liberalizing tendencies emanating from the pulpit and church officials. And recent reports of evangelical leaders urging their flocks to embrace conservative political causes have diverted public attention from other evangelical voices calling for social justice and world peace through cooperative disarmament (Fowler 1982). The opinion data will reveal how mainline and evangelical white Protestants have responded to these conflicting messages.

Like Jews and black Protestants, Catholics coalesced around the Democratic party in the 1930s; the Catholic commitment to the party was reinforced in 1960 when the Democrats conferred their presidential nomination on a Catholic candidate (Converse 1966; Scoble and Epstein 1964; Greer 1961; Fenton 1960; Baggaley 1962). Some observers have doubted the depth of this commitment, arguing that attachment to the more liberal political party was a transient stage, reflecting the immigrant and working-class background of Catholics. Under conditions of economic parity with Protestants, it has been suggested, Catholics will embrace the political conservatism that appears to be a more natural outgrowth of church doctrine (Phillips 1969, 140–175; Lipset 1964; Crosby 1978; Whyte 1981). Although many Catholics have moved into the economic mainstream and the Republicans have courted them aggressively, using the abortion controversy and other issues, it remains open to debate whether the Catholic masses have moved to the right side of the political spectrum (Hanna 1979; Fee 1976; Greeley 1977). Except on the issue of abortion, members of the Catholic religious elite—priests, bishops, and lay leaders—appear to have moved in just the opposite direction (Hanna 1984).

The remaining Protestant groups inspire mixed expectations. The Mormons have long been regarded as one of the most conservative religious groups. Nontraditional Protestants have appeared on all sides of the political spectrum, and some groups in this category, notably the Jehovah's Witnesses, are famed for their indifference to political life. The ambiguous Protestants are as much a mystery in politics as in religion.

Expectations about religious-group patterns do not always distinguish among different political issues. It is quite possible for a group to stand out as relatively conservative on one policy but to adopt a much more liberal position on another. To take account of this possibility, I have grouped the questions on the General Social Survey into three categories. The first set relates to political identity: preference for a political party, choice of presidential candidates, liberal versus conservative self-image, and general attitude toward government spending. The second taps attitudes toward several political issues of recent import—crime, civil liberties, race relations, and spending for social purposes. The final category is reserved for the "moral" or "social" issues involving behavior that challenges traditional Christian teaching.[3]

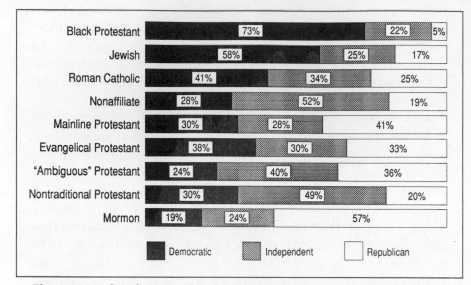

Figure 4.2 Political Partisanship, by Religious Group (Source: Calculated by the author from the 1985–1989 General Social Surveys, National Opinion Research Center, Davis and Smith 1990)

Political Identity

The most basic component of political identity is preference for a major political party. Despite a decline of formal party membership, a rise in the proportion of citizens declaring themselves independent of the parties, and a greater willingness to cross party lines in voting, most Americans still classify themselves, in greater or lesser degree, as supporters of one or the other major political party. The selection of a particular partisan label (including "independent") remains a useful predictor of basic political attitudes, electoral choice, and a wide array of related attitudes and forms of behavior. Though finer distinctions are possible, I have divided the participants in the General Social Survey simply into Democrats (39 percent), Republicans (29 percent) and independents (32 percent). Figure 4.2 shows the partisan breakdown within each of the religious groups.

Pronounced differences among religious groups in patterns of partisan allegiance were apparent. The two most strongly Democratic groups—the only groups giving that party a clear majority—were black Protestants and Jews. At the other extreme, the Mormons were the only religious group with a majority of Republicans, while the mainline Protestants remained true to reputation with a plurality of Republican identifiers. Of the remaining groups, pluralities of Catholics and white evangelical Protestants preferred the Democrats but were less committed to that party than were black Protestants and Jewish respondents. Persons with no religious preference and the two categories of nontraditional and ambiguous Protestants turned out to be predominantly independent in politics as well; of the religiously uncommitted and nontraditional Protestants who did adopt a party label, Democrats outnumbered Republicans. The reverse was true of the ambiguous Protestants.

Another important element of political identity, ideological self-image, can be measured by asking individuals to characterize their political views on a scale from "extremely liberal" to "extremely conservative," with "moderate, middle of the road" as the neutral midpoint. Taken as a whole, the respondents were more comfortable with the neutral designation (39 percent) than with any other classification; after the moderate plurality came persons on the conservative side of the spectrum (34 percent) and then liberals of various degrees (27 percent). With the moderate option so attractive to Americans of all religious preferences, differences among groups can best be gauged by the balance of support between the remaining liberals and conservatives. On that measure, Jewish respondents, black Protestants, nontraditional Protestants, and persons with no religious affiliation were the four most liberal groups, whereas the three remaining types of Protestants and Mormons leaned heavily to the right side of the political spectrum (Figure 4.3). Catholics mirrored the national distribution, with a plurality in the middle and conservatives outnumbering liberals by a clear margin.

The choice between presidential candidates gives citizens an opportunity to act on their more abstract political leanings. Participants in the 1985–1988 surveys were asked about their preferences in the 1984 presidential election; in the 1989 General Social Survey, interviewers canvassed the preferences of participants for the 1988 presidential ballot. In the sample, as in the actual general elections, the Republican candidates were favored over the Democratic nominees. The margin was 62 percent to 38 percent in 1984, when Ronald Reagan trounced Walter Mondale, and a closer 54 percent to 46 percent victory for George Bush

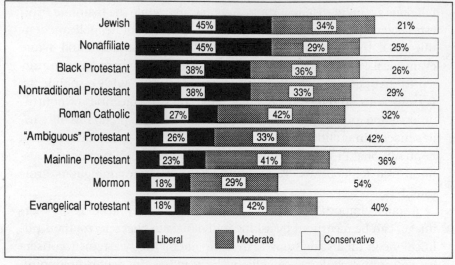

Figure 4.3 Ideology, by Religious Group (Source: Calculated by the author from the 1985–1989 General Social Surveys, National Opinion Research Center, Davis and Smith 1990)

over Michael Dukakis in 1988. How did the religious groups vote in these elections?

Consistent with their party and philosophical leanings, Jews, black Protestants, and persons with no religious preference proved substantially more likely to prefer the Democratic presidential candidate in both the 1984 and the 1988 elections (Figure 4.4). The mainline, evangelical, and ambiguous Protestants, joined again by Mormons, gave correspondingly lopsided proportions of their support to the GOP candidates in 1984 and 1988. That left two groups in the middle. Nontraditional Protestants split equally between the candidates in 1984 but swung decisively behind the Democratic nominee in 1988. Catholics once again came close to the national pattern by giving the Republican candidate about three-fifths of their vote in 1984 and 56 percent in 1988.

The traits of party preference, ideological placement, and voting record can be taken to reflect judgments about how extensively the national government should intervene in daily life—an issue at the root of American politics since at least the 1930s. The General Social Survey does not inquire directly about this principle, but it does ask respondents about their support for spending on a wide range of purposes such as the environment, education, public health, crime control, national defense, and the like. Figure 4.5 represents a summary measure of support in which respondents could receive a maximum of two points for each of eleven areas of government activity that received, in their opinion, too little public money. Perhaps surprisingly in a nation thought to resist active government, the average score on this scale from 0 to 22 was about 15.5.

The differences among groups were relatively small, as only 3.3 points separated the group most supportive of government spending—black Protestants—from those with the lowest level of enthusiasm for government spending—Mormons. Even with these small variations, the general pattern observed in previous tables was repeated. Black Protestants, Jews, the nonreligious, and nontraditional Protestants scored above the national average in support for government spending, while Mormons, mainline Protestants, evangelical Protestants, and ambiguous Protestants averaged below the national standard on the scale. Roman Catholics once again matched the national average.

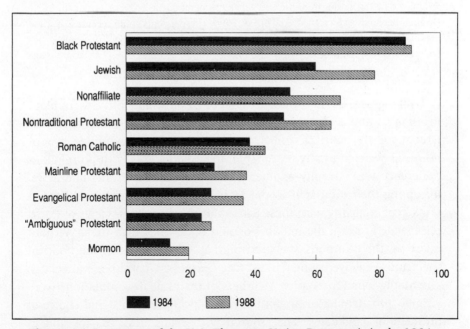

Figure 4.4 Percentage of the U.S. Electorate Voting Democratic in the 1984 and 1988 Presidential Elections, by Religious Group (Source: Calculated by the author from the 1985–1989 General Social Surveys, National Opinion Research Center, Davis and Smith 1990)

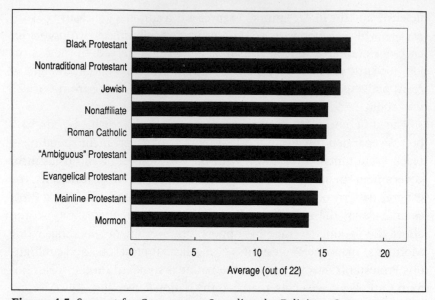

Figure 4.5 Support for Government Spending, by Religious Group (Source: Calculated by the author from the 1985–1989 General Social Surveys, National Opinion Research Center, Davis and Smith 1990). Respondents could receive a maximum of two points for each of eleven areas of government activity that they believed received too little government money.

Looking over the four measures of basic political identity, then, black Protestants and Jews were consistent supporters of the liberal option. Except for the partisan dimension, in which they exhibited a pronounced aversion to any party label, the respondents with no religious preference were usually as liberal as the black Protestants and Jews. Excepting their even split in the 1984 election, nontraditional Protestants kept company with these three liberal groups. The views of Catholics tended toward the middle position on all four measures. Without question, the Mormons anchored the conservative side of the political spectrum. They were joined in varying degrees by mainline, evangelical, and ambiguous Protestants. Members of mainline denominations were strongly pro-Republican in both psychological preference and choice of presidential candidates. They shared with evangelicals an aversion to increased government spending but were somewhat less inclined to see themselves as right of center than members of the most traditional Protestant churches. The evangelicals were most likely of all groups to picture themselves as right-wing and to express a strong desire to hold government spending to its current level. Although conservative in that sense, evangelicals tilted toward a Democratic self-image but were actually slightly more likely than mainliners to favor Republican candidates in recent presidential elections.

Contemporary Political Issues

Do religious group differences in political identity extend to more specific issues and controversies? Analysis of the collective opinions of the religious groups on several issues that have ranked high on the recent American political agenda should shed some light on that question. These issues should not be expected to produce precisely the same patterns of religious group differences as the political identity questions. Since many political issues cannot be defined exactly on the liberal-to-conservative spectrum, and since many Americans react to specific problems without regard to any broad ideological orientation, group opinions on these policies will not necessarily correspond to the distribution of durable political orientations.

As could be expected, inquiries about issues that bear no apparent relationship to religious values revealed nearly identical preferences among the nine religious groups. Overwhelming majorities in all camps believed that courts have been too lenient with criminals and that the government has failed to pay enough attention to average people. Similarly, the religious groups expressed comparable levels of confidence in the branches of national government. On other issues, some differences among religious groups were so peculiar that it was hard to find any meaningful basis for them. Thus, even though the religious groups evinced varying opinions on communism as a form of government and on the advisability of police permits for gun ownership, the group differences conformed to no coherent pattern.

On yet other issues, the dividing line ran between religious groups but reflected racial differences. On the death penalty for murder, to take a clear example, black Protestants were divided almost equally for and against, whereas all other groups favored capital punishment by overwhelming ratios. Black Protestants also stood out from all other denominations by a greater sympathy for governmental action to reduce income differences through progressive taxation and other devices.

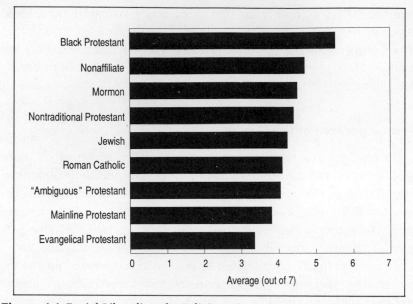

Figure 4.6 Racial Liberalism, by Religious Group (Source: Calculated by the author from the 1985–1989 General Social Surveys, National Opinion Research Center, Davis and Smith 1990). Respondents were asked seven questions to measure racial liberalism; the answers were rated on a scale from 0 to 7.

What best accounts for this type of pattern, I would venture, is not that black religion has some unique message about these themes, but rather that blacks are represented disproportionately among the poor and among those who receive death sentences.

Thus, religion was not—nor should it have been expected to be— relevant to all controversies nor as relevant as it was for political identity. Yet the basic patterns observed on questions about fundamental political identity recurred on civil rights, perhaps the most important issue in American politics over the past thirty years. The racial liberalism scale in Figure 4.6 was created from seven separate questions on the General Social Survey. One series of questions asked respondents if they were willing to send their children to schools with a plurality or majority of black students or if they would try to change the rules of a social club that prohibited black members. In the other four questions, respondents could attribute racial differences in income and housing to discrimination and education barriers or to factors like ability and motivation. On a scale that ranged from 0 to 7, the sample averaged about 4.0.

As can be seen in Figure 4.6, the religious groups followed a by-now familiar pattern of responses: black Protestants, Jews, nontraditional Protestants, and respondents with no affiliations were most receptive to racial liberalism, the mainline and evangelical camps were least receptive and Catholics, as usual, fell midway between the clusters. The only departure from the patterns observed earlier was the very strong racial liberalism scores earned by Mormons. Otherwise, alignments on the racial issue followed the trends established on partisanship, ideology, vote choice, and support for government spending.

The "Social Issue"

In the late 1960s, a new type of political issue appeared on the national political agenda. What was labeled the "social issue" was actually a packet of controversies revolving around drug usage, new patterns of sexual behavior, equal rights for women, and similar matters. At base, these issues all raised questions about the place of traditional social and moral values in public policy. Even though they do not touch upon the formal role of the churches in American society, the social issues have frequently been debated with reference to religious values. For many observers, the phrase "religion and politics" has come to encompass matters such as abortion, pornography, drug use, and nontraditional sexual practices. Any comprehensive discussion of religious-group differences in American politics must consider this newer type of conflict, in addition to the long-standing debates examined above.

Differences about social values often arise in the context of debates over civil liberties—as when Republicans and Democrats split over a 1989 Supreme Court decision that extended the first amendment guarantee of freedom of expression to physical desecration of the flag. That item did not appear on the GSS, but the surveys included a series of questions about the rights that should be extended to five unpopular groups—atheists, racists, Communists, militarists, and homosexuals. Survey participants were asked whether members of these groups should be allowed to speak in their community and whether the public library should remove books advocating their point of view. An individual who supported the rights for all groups would receive the

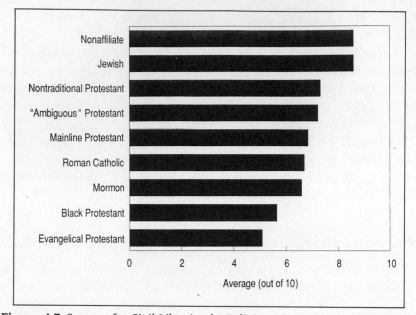

Figure 4.7 Support for Civil Liberties, by Religious Group (Source: Calculated by the author from the 1985–1989 General Social Surveys, National Opinion Research Center, Davis and Smith 1990). Respondents were asked a series of questions about the rights of five unpopular groups; the answers were rated on a scale from 0 to 10.

maximum scale score of 10. The population averaged about 6.5, as illustrated in Figure 4.7.

The group answers show how thoroughly social regulatory issues crosscut traditional alignments based on political identity. On the one hand, consistent with earlier patterns, we find Jews, nontraditional Protestants, and the nonreligious to be the most liberal, and evangelical Protestants the most conservative on civil liberties. Yet on the other hand, black Protestants deserted the liberal coalition to join the conservative bloc, while three normally conservative groups—mainline Protestants, Mormons, and ambiguous Protestants—scored above the average for blacks. The Catholics were close to the national pattern on attitudes regarding civil liberties.

Many debates about traditional values turn on the role of women in society. The General Social Survey contained four such questions that were combined in a feminism scale. Three of these items asserted the superiority of the mother who stayed at home over the mother employed outside the home while the fourth contended that the latter could have just as close relationships with their children as mothers who stayed at home. Respondents who disagreed with the three statements favoring mothers who work at home and thought mothers employed outside the home could have equally close relationships with their children were assigned the maximum value of four. The American public was closely divided as indicated by an average score of 2.3 on a scale that ranged between extremes of 0 and 4.

The pattern on this scale in Figure 4.8 produced some interesting variations. To summarize the major differences from the basic patterns observed on other questions, mainline Protestants were among the four groups most supportive of a nontraditional role for women. Nontraditional Protestants, normally among the most liberal religious groups, joined with Mormons and evangelicals in adhering to a more traditionalist role regarding women's rights.

The group tendencies were further scrambled on a scale measuring

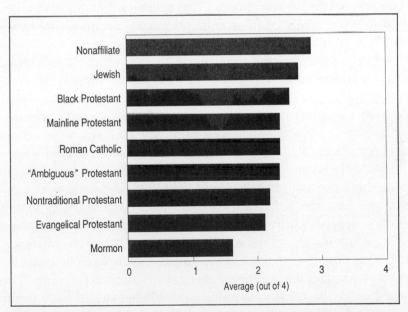

Figure 4.8 Support for Feminism, by Religious Group (Source: Calculated by the author from the 1985–1989 General Social Surveys, National Opinion Research Center, Davis and Smith 1990). On a scale from 0 to 4, respondents were questioned about mothers who work and mothers who stay at home.

support for a permissive policy toward pornography (not shown). The highest level of tolerance for the availability of sexually explicit material was shown by Jews and the nonreligious, while Mormons and evangelical Protestants favored the most restrictive policy. On this social policy question, blacks were allied with the liberal groups. The other four religious groups were tightly clustered between the two extremes.

The disease caused by the HIV virus, Acquired Immune Deficiency Syndrome (AIDS), has joined the list of policy questions under the "social issue" heading. Questions about the disease did not enter the General Social Survey questionnaire until 1988, so it is necessary to consult other sources to establish the attitude of religious groups. A 1986 ballot referendum in California, which would have declared AIDS a contagious disease and subjected infected persons to the state's quarantine and isolation laws, provides such an opportunity (Le Poire et al., 1990). Although views about the appropriate treatment of AIDS might be rooted in medical judgment, the issue has often been approached as a referendum on the "life-style" of homosexuals. Even though Californians rejected the harsh proposals in the ballot referendum, about one-third of voters contacted in an exit poll voiced support for what was known as Proposition 64. In a finding consistent with the patterns revealed in this chapter, researchers found that Jews and those with no religious preference were substantially less likely to support the proposition, while "born-again" Christians, a classification roughly equivalent to white evangelical Protestants, were the strongest proponents of the quarantine. Blacks, other Protestants and Catholics were neither more nor less likely to support the proposition than the typical voter.

Then there is abortion. Since the Supreme Court's historic ruling of 1973, this contentious issue has been the subject of intense debate and even more intense action. Experts have found that attitudes toward abortion depend heavily on the circumstances of the case (Granberg 1978; McIntosh, Alston, and Alston 1979). The different circumstances that might prompt a woman to terminate a pregnancy can be evaluated on two separate scales. The first scale measures support for abortion on *social* grounds that the woman is single, poor, or has already had a family and wanted no more children. "Social" abortion has proved to divide the American public almost equally between those who reject abortion under any of these circumstances and those who endorse the availability of abortion under one or more of the conditions. If we assign one point

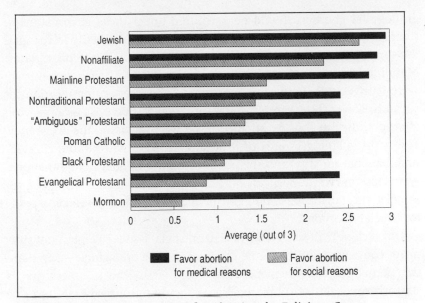

Figure 4.9 Conditional Support for Abortion, by Religious Group
(Source: Calculated by the author from the 1985–1989 General Social Surveys, National Opinion Research Center, Davis and Smith 1990). Respondents' answers were measured on a scale from 0 to 3.

for supporting abortion under any of the three social conditions, the national average is just 1.3. Public support for legalized abortion is much higher when there is a likelihood of birth defects, health threats to the mother, or pregnancy as a result of rape. The *medical* scale that includes these three situations drew wholehearted support from three-quarters of the persons surveyed in the General Social Survey. The mean score was 2.5 out of a maximum of three.

The placement of the religious groups on the two scales is shown in Figure 4.9. Even though the level of support for abortion differed significantly according to the justification offered, the religious groups placed in almost the same order on both scales. A majority of Roman Catholics, white evangelicals, black Protestants, and Mormons rejected all social reasons for abortion—poverty, the mother's marital status, or the desire to limit family size. The same four groups were relatively the least supportive of abortion even in circumstances of birth defects, threats to the mother's health, or rape. Although majorities of the three groups said abortion should be permitted under these circumstances, their support for abortion on health grounds was markedly lower than the support registered by Jews, mainline Protestants, and nonaffiliates. Mainline Protestants were not indiscriminately prochoice; rather, they were fairly equally between opposition to and support for abortion for social reasons. They were virtually unanimous, however, in approving abortion if health considerations or rape were factors in the pregnancy. The two remaining groups of Protestants, those with ambiguous denominational identity and members of nontraditional denominations, were close to the evangelicals on the "medical-abortion" scale but resembled their mainline coreligionists in above-average levels of support for "social abortion."

Does religion affect public opinion on social issues? Yes, but not simply or consistently. While some groups are quite predictable—Jews and the nonreligious in their permissiveness, evangelical Protestants as staunch advocates of traditional values—other groups differ from one issue to the next. When the issue is abortion or feminism, then Mormons are overwhelmingly conservative. But they part company with the conservative camp on civil liberties, scoring above the national average, and appear to be strong racial liberals. Black Protestants, normally synonymous with liberal political outlooks, are markedly more restrictive than most religious groups on abortion and questions about civil liberties. Nontraditional Protestants are strongly civil libertarian but centrist on abortion and strongly inclined to defend the traditional role of women in society. The mainline Protestants, a conservative mainstay on questions of political identity, prove to be closer on many social issues to Catholics than to Protestants with an evangelical outlook. And the ambiguous Protestants look like evangelicals on one abortion scale but like members of mainline denominations on the other.

Religious Differences and Social Standing

To understand why religion may influence mass political opinions and behavior, it is necessary to consider several factors that could account for the group patterns delineated in previous sections. This task would be much easier if social scientists had thought more systematically about the role of religion in the political outlooks of individuals and religious communities. Because relatively little such work has been done, however, knowledge about the sources of linkage between religious and political loyalties must take the form of hypotheses, offered tentatively and with caution.

One common reaction to revelations of some of the more dramatic political differences among religious groups, such as the pronounced disagreement over public spending or the equally significant variations in partisan identification, is denial that these patterns "really" have anything to do with religion per se. Skeptics tend to view the ties between religious and political views as spurious; members of a religious group, they argue, think alike about politics not because of their religion but because they share other characteristics that directly influence political attitudes.

The most commonly cited sources of unity linked to religion have been historical experience and economic or social standing. Jews tend toward liberalism, it is argued, because of their experience as an oppressed people whose emancipation was part of the liberal agenda and frequently resisted by conservative movements. Jews are said to have inherited from this tradition a sympathy for liberal values and a suspicion of conservatism. Similarly, proponents of an economic explanation would attribute the conservatism of mainline Protestants to their high social status and economic privileges, not to religious convictions. In this view, differences in political orientations between religious groups generally can be reduced to social characteristics that happen to be associated with membership in the various denominational families (Allinsmith and Allinsmith 1948; Ebersole 1960).[4]

Attempts to trace denominational political distinctiveness back to social standing are based on the discovery of major variations in the profiles of American religious groups. The denominational groups have been shown to exhibit striking differences in ethnic and racial composition, geographical distribution and concentration, and, most important, social and economic achievement (Roof and McKinney 1987). In Figure 4.10, the nine religious groups are compared in terms of educational achievement, a major influence on social status and political outlooks in the United States. Consistent with many other studies, the figure shows Jewish respondents with the highest levels of formal education in the population, followed at some distance by the participants who did not report any religious affiliation. These two groups are followed by another three groups with very similar educational profiles,

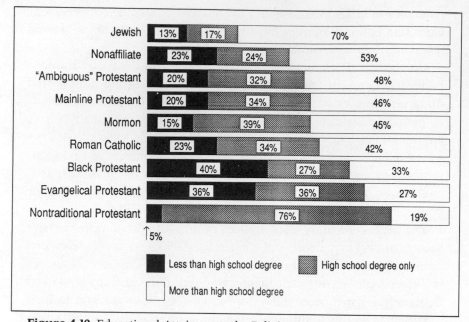

Figure 4.10 Educational Attainments, by Religious Group (Source: Calculated by the author from the 1985–1989 General Social Surveys, National Opinion Research Center, Davis and Smith 1990).

the ambiguous Protestants, mainline Protestants and Mormons. Roman Catholics follow. Then, clustered at the lowest level of educational achievement, come white evangelicals and black Protestants. Nontraditional Protestants are difficult to classify because so few of them are found at the extremes. If we use the proportion with at least some college education as the critical measure, they actually rank last among the nine groups. Analyses of religious group differences on related indicators of social standing such as income and occupational attainment have disclosed very similar patterns.

The claim that political differences among religious groups reflect only the social composition of denominations can be tested by a comparison of religious group attitudes with social standing held constant. Using party identification as an example of a political difference, one would try to discover if, for example, Jews of high education reported the same level of attachment to the Democratic party as did persons with similar educational levels but different religious preferences. If religious group differences were shown to narrow at each level of education, then education apparently could contribute to political variations. But if the political differences were shown to persist—if, sticking with the same example, college-educated Jews were to be still more strongly attached to the Democratic party than were college-educated Catholics, evangelical Protestants, or other groups—then religious differences in politics could not be attributed wholly to a factor such as education.

The test results for the nine denominational groups appear in Figure 4.11. Members in each group were subdivided by education into three categories: no high school degree, a high school degree only, and a high school degree with some additional schooling. For each group, we calculated the percentage of participants who identified with the Democratic party.

The figure shows social status (in the form of education) to be an important but not altogether complete explanation for denominational differences in partisanship. For five groups—Catholics, Mormons, and Protestants from the mainline, evangelical and ambiguous categories—

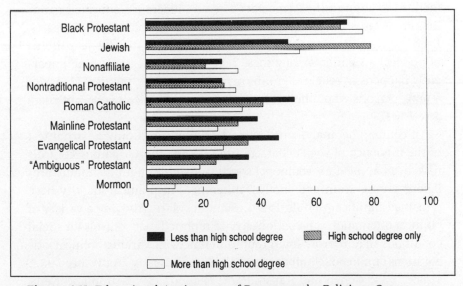

Figure 4.11 Educational Attainments of Democrats, by Religious Group (Source: Calculated by the author from the 1985–1989 General Social Surveys, National Opinion Research Center, Davis and Smith 1990).

gains in education were clearly associated with movement toward the Republican party. Put another way, the level of Democratic identification declined steadily as members of these groups moved from the least to the most educated categories. However, the other four groups contradicted this tendency. There were no significant differences among educational categories for black Protestants. For Jews, the nonreligious, and nontraditional Protestants, the Democratic affiliation among the best educated actually exceeded the Democratic percentage registered by those with less than a high school degree.

Even if social status clearly influences party loyalties for the largest denominations, as demonstrated in Figure 4.11, it does not eliminate the full measure of religious-group differences. If education were all that mattered, partisanship would be identical among persons from different religious groups but with the same level of formal education. In fact, the general level of partisanship differed considerably among denominations even with educational level held constant. Catholics remained more Democratic than white Protestants of comparable education from all four categories. Jews with advanced education were more Democratic than the least educated from all groups save black Protestants. Conversely, poorly educated Mormons were almost as disinclined to support the Democrats as even moderately educated mainline Protestants, normally regarded as a pillar of the Republican party. Even taking education into account, there remain distinctive patterns of political affiliation among these religious groups. Something apparently happens in religious groups to foster distinctive political identities among persons who otherwise differ on many politically relevant characteristics.

Of course, the analysis in Figure 4.11 represents only a partial test of the influence of social characteristics. When more rigorous controls have been applied for additional social traits that might distinguish religious groups from one another, differences in political identity have remained significant (Wald 1989). Many scholars, studying a variety of political orientations and outlooks, have reported that controls for social conditions may narrow intergroup differences in various political orientations but do not eliminate them altogether (Beatty and Walter 1982, 1983, 1984; Cohen and Kapsis 1977; Glantz 1959; Grupp and Newman 1973; Laumann and Segal 1971; Maddox 1979; Miller 1974). That conclusion has stood whether the social status indicator has been education, income, urbanization, ethnicity, or occupational status. Thus the religious-group variations in attitudes to AIDS reported earlier are net differences after controlling for the impact of socioeconomic factors, gender, and age.

Even if denominational political differences are affected to some degree by social forces—the strongest conclusion warranted by current research—that still does not mean that religion is irrelevant to political attitudes and orientations. If religion confers an economic disadvantage or advantage on members of a group, it contributes in a major way to the shaping of political outlooks. From both the world and the American experience, it is not hard to identify religious groups that have suffered from economic discrimination because their creed differed from that of the majority of the community. The informal restrictions that once confined most Catholics to the working class probably go a long way toward explaining why Catholics were so receptive to Democratic party efforts to build social programs such as unemployment insurance, workers' compensation, federal aid to education, and the like (Buenker 1973). Membership in a high-status church may provide individuals with social ties, business connections, and opportunities to gain considerable position in society. With such a strong stake in the existing order, members of prestigious denominations may develop a conservative outlook on social change.

To make the argument more strongly: religious values may be the critical element in determining the social status of the denomination and, thus, a powerful if indirect influence on political orientations. In *The Protestant Ethic and the Spirit of Capitalism,* one of the classic (and most controversial) works of modern sociology (first published in 1920), the German scholar Max Weber advanced a theory linking certain religious values to success in the economic realm. Trying to explain why Protestants had surpassed Catholics in economic achievement since the advent of capitalism in Europe, Weber suggested that the cause lay partly in the different social values inspired by the two traditions. The Protestant emphasis on discipline and self-control, born of the Puritan desire to illustrate God's blessing, was nicely suited to the demands of work life in a capitalist economy. By comparison, Weber argued, Catholic values encouraged behavior that was not conducive to economic achievement. In particular, the tendency to regard life on earth as mere preparation for the next world and to equate material poverty with spiritual grace handicapped Catholics in competitive economic struggle. If this "Protestant ethic" thesis is correct—and there is enormous controversy about it—then the economic standing of religious groups is even more strongly connected with denominational values. Thus, although it is possible to apportion some of the credit for denominational differences in politics to economic factors, the pattern of economic status itself may ultimately have much to do with religion.

In addition to relatively "hard" differences shown on objective measurement scales of education, income, and so forth, religious groups may also differ from each other in subjective social standing. High income does not necessarily confer social acceptability, and advanced education does not invariably correlate with prestige. Too, such subjective assessments may influence the perspectives of group members and thus help to account for unique political traditions. Subjective social standing is frequently invoked to explain the persistence of Jewish liberalism. Why should Jews, by objective standards one of the highest-status groups in the United States, maintain such a firm commitment to liberal political values—a commitment that seems, contrary to all common sense, to *increase* with economic achievement (Maller 1977; Fuchs 1955)? As measured by social attitudes, Jewish standing in society has not matched the level of Jewish economic and educational attainment. Because of a strong collective memory of persecution, it has been claimed, Jews tend to think of themselves not as part of the established elite, but rather as a group on the margin of society, defensive and vulnerable to attack by the majority. The social insecurity of American Jews has been said to make Jews especially wary of any political movements that appear to encourage intolerance and bigotry (Cohn 1957; C. Liebman 1973; Petrusak and Steinart 1976; Rothman and Lichter 1982). Hence, Jews make common cause with other subordinate groups in clear defiance of their immediate economic interests.

The concept of subjective status can be extended to explain the political activism of the black Protestant churches. Denied the most elementary forms of family life, access to education, and any opportunity to develop an independent community life, black slaves were allowed only the church as a focus of collective loyalty. Not surprisingly under such conditions, the church developed into the social, cultural, and intellectual center of black life. To a degree unmatched in white society, the black church provided its members some protection from a hostile

outside world, a durable source of collective identity, training in organizational skills, and the opportunity to nurture native leadership
(Colombo 1984, 23). When blacks began to challenge the system of
segregation that remained in place a century after the passing of slavery,
the church became the crucible of action, and it continues today as the
principal agent in black political action. Even though race defined the
ghetto, the black political response was heavily conditioned by the intense religious commitment that developed in social isolation.

This same line of argument has been advanced to account for the
political mobilization of evangelical Protestants in the late 1970s and
1980s. Although this subject will be examined more thoroughly in
Chapter 7, there is some evidence that evangelical Protestants have been
driven to undertake political action in response to perceived attacks on
their way of life and social standing. In a study of Protestant churchgoers in one southern community, support for the political goals of the
so-called New Christian Right was strongly related to a sense that
groups representing "traditional" values were given less respect by society than they warranted (Wald, Owen, and Hill 1989). For a variety
of religious groups, subjective social standing may be as important in
the forging of political views as factors that can be measured in dollars
or years of schooling.

Religion and Political Values

Some observers have not been reluctant to attribute religious-group
differences in politics to the values, teachings, and ideas of the various
traditions. The application of religious creeds to politics is most visible
when the leaders of a faith assert that their religion demands a particular
political stance. In the United States, where official political announcements by churches have traditionally been comparatively rare, the overt
linking of religious ideas with political positions has recently become
much more common among almost all denominations.

The Catholic hierarchy, for example, has insisted that church teachings about the nature of life impose on Catholics the obligation to reject
both artificial methods of birth control and abortion. As these are medical procedures governed by public policy, Catholic doctrine has drawn
some members of the faith into political action. Catholic public officials
who disagree with official teaching on abortion have been denied var-

ious religious rites and threatened with eternal damnation for their actions. The Catholic hierarchy has not been alone in translating faith into political principles. Members of the clergy who participated in the drive for civil rights insisted that segregation was incompatible with Judeo-Christian values. In the 1960s and 1970s, some leaders of mainline white Protestantism urged on biblical grounds that members of the churches oppose the Vietnam War and work for a broad-ranging program of social reform and welfare services. Most recently, some leaders of the evangelical wing of Protestantism have asserted biblical support for programs on the conservative agenda. Each basic plank in the program put forward by the Moral Majority, an organization supporting conservative social policy on moral grounds, was accompanied by a reference to a specific passage in Scripture. In excommunicating a supporter of the Equal Rights Amendment for disobedience, the elders of the Church of Jesus Christ of Latter-day Saints (the Mormons) surpassed other groups in enforcing compliance with political doctrine as a condition for church membership. Nonetheless, it would be hard to think of a religious group whose leaders have not defended some political position on theological grounds.

The connection between doctrine and politics may also draw upon theological tradition in more subtle ways. Rather than speak directly to political issues, it has been suggested, certain common ways of thinking about religion spill over into politics (Laitin 1978). According to most observers, the differences in style and approach between a "conservative" and a "liberal" orientation in religion may well correspond to the political orientations of the same name.[5] Michael Parenti has suggested four key dimensions on which conservative and liberal religions differ:

(a) The extent to which divine teaching is considered fixed, final, and unchallengeable, as opposed to being susceptible to rational investigation and modification; and consequently, the extent to which intellectualism and many of the values associated with it are opposed or welcomed.

(b) The extent to which the drama of redemption and atonement is defined as a personal battle waged for one's soul for the sake of eternal salvation, rather than as a moral commitment to a worldly social betterment of mankind.

(c) The extent to which sin and evil are defined as inherent in human nature (e.g., original sin) and inevitable in human behavior (e.g., concupiscence), rather than as social effects of widespread environmental causes.

(d) The extent to which human well-being and natural pleasures are manifestations of a "lower," corrupting realm of nature, something to be repressed as the contamination of the spiritual, rather than responsibly cultivated as the fulfillment of God's beneficence. (1967, 268)

Recent research has suggested another major difference between conservative and liberal religions—their images of God. According to Andrew Greeley (1982), the concept of God evokes for some people a "warm" image of friendship, nurturance, caring, and love, but for others a "cold" image of discipline, order, and punishment. Additional research on the same theme has revealed that religions may convey different messages about God's presence in the world and responsibility for the flow of human events (Piazza and Glock 1979; O'Grady 1982).

How might these dimensions of religious belief take on political significance? Because of their emphasis on faith in fixed authority over the free play of intellect, persons of a conservative orientation are more likely than religious liberals to stress the need for obedience than to encourage skepticism or dissent (Rokeach 1969). If redemption is interpreted to mean bringing the Kingdom of God to realization on earth, as liberal religions seem to argue, movements for political change are infused with a transcendent purpose. But if, as in conservative religion, life is seen as a mere preparation for the next world or the imminent return of God to earth, then little can be done except to live as righteously as possible and to guard the integrity of one's soul from temptation and corruption (Kleppner 1970). An emphasis on sinfulness as the essential condition of humankind seems quite compatible with a skeptical orientation toward the prospect of improving conditions through political action (Rosenberg 1956). Similarly, if human pleasures are judged inferior to spiritual rewards, there is little urgency about improving material conditions. The liberal belief in "social" sin and the dignity of earthly existence, which contrasts sharply with conservative religious assumptions, spurs efforts to eradicate structural barriers to justice and to improve the material conditions of life. Belief in a warm, caring God who is part of the world tends to enhance commitment to social welfare, whereas the image of a cold and authoritative deity lends support to government's role in securing order and property.

These contrasting modes of thought are illustrated by the way in which Jews and Lutherans apply their differing religious styles to the political realm. A classic example of a liberal faith, Judaism venerates learning and charity as major virtues and is relatively silent about the origin of sin and the prospect of life after death. That combination of values encourages optimism about the human condition and a sense of urgency about the application of reason to human problems. As described by some experts, the Jewish outlook seems almost to demand social and political involvement on behalf of liberal causes:

Implicit in this style is the view that man and his environment are malleable, that he is much more the creator of history than its creature. Implicit, too, is the notion that man's environment and his polity are made for him. Implicit is a dynamic view of law, that it is changing and made for man. . . . And especially implicit in such a style is the belief that what happens in this life on this earth is very important, what happens here and now matters very much. (Fuchs 1984, 70)

Subject to the influence of this body of assumptions, little wonder that Jewish voters have been strongly attracted to political leaders and movements that promote social change—drawn so strongly, in fact, that they have occasionally preferred activist liberals from Christian denominations to more conservative Jewish candidates (Leventman and Leventman 1976). For a people normally given to such high levels of solidarity, crossing denominational lines is strong evidence for the political impact of a liberal religious style.

The Jewish stress on human capacity to remake the world through political action finds barely an echo in Lutheran doctrine. Martin Luther taught that salvation would come only to the person who submitted thoroughly and wholeheartedly to the will of an omniscient God. In sharply contrasting the evil of mortals to the perfection of God, Lutheran thought treats humans as creatures of passion and sin who should not interfere with the divine plan for the world. Based on an extensive survey of Lutheran laypersons in the Detroit metropolitan area, Lawrence K. Kersten found that Luther's spiritual descendants accepted his counsel to take the world as it is: "Lutheran social philosophy suggests that true happiness for man and total release from the bondage of sin are not possible until after death. If earthly conditions are undesirable, man should patiently endure them, for they may actually be a test of his faith. Man must trust that God will change the social structure or social conditions when He sees fit" (1970, 31). Such religious beliefs may help to account for the pronounced economic, social, racial, and political conservatism exhibited by Lutherans (M. C. Weber 1983).

At this point, it should be emphasized that links between attitudes and religious orientations have been more often asserted than proved.

Attempts to assess the connection between religious belief and political outlook have yielded mixed results. The most consistent relationships between theological beliefs and political outlooks have been found with samples of the clergy, a group that should have the firmest grasp of the political implications of religious thought. In almost every study of the clergy I have located, commitment to a conservative religious style correlated with conservative outlooks on politics and social issues (Beatty and Walter 1989; Balswick 1970; Guth 1989; Hadden 1969; Hero 1973; Driedger 1974; Eckberg and Blocker 1989; Jeffries and Tygart 1974; Johnson 1966, 1967; Schindeler and Hoffman 1968; Zehner 1967). As for surveys of more typical people, some empirical studies have reported a relationship between commitment to the tenets of conservative religion and (1) conservative beliefs about race and ethnic relations, (2) membership in the Republican party, (3) resistance to liberal initiatives on environmental and social welfare policy, (4) support for traditional beliefs about sexual roles and behavior, and (5) a low level of toleration for "deviant" political ideas (Johnson 1962, 1964; Rokeach 1969; Orum 1970; Glock and Stark 1966; Hendricks 1977; Stellway 1973; Hand and Van Liere 1984; Steiber 1980). Similarly, the "image of God" studies have for the most part linked the image of a stern and vengeful deity with various manifestations of political conservatism (Greeley 1988; Hoffman 1982, 1985; Welch and Leege 1988—but see Jelen 1985).

Nevertheless, this type of relationship between theological and political outlooks has not always been sustained by empirical research. On the basis of an exhaustive review of previous research, Robert Wuthnow (1973) pointed out that well-designed studies were just as likely to report no relationship between religious beliefs and political attitudes as they were to find a positive association. Even in studies of the clergy, as Beatty and Walter (1989) discovered, the relationship was far from complete. Baptist ministers with liberal theological outlooks were still more conservative in politics than Episcopalians, Methodists, and Congregationalists of comparable religious views. Focusing exclusively on studies about racial beliefs, Gorsuch and Aleshire (1974) discovered that persons committed to religion for its intrinsic value were the least likely to hold prejudiced views of blacks. Responding to the emergence of organized political activity by leaders of the evangelical Protestant churches, several studies have found that in general, church members tie religious and political attitudes together only in the domain of sexual and social roles (Wald and Lupfer 1983). The idea that Jewish political values derive from the content of the religion has been challenged by the discovery that the most religiously observant Jews, who should have the greatest exposure to the implicit liberal messages of Judaism, in fact constitute the most politically conservative element of the community (Cohen 1983, 143–153; Liebman 1973, 139–144). An inverse relationship between attachment to traditional religion and racial militance has been reported in studies of black Protestants (Marx 1967, chap. 4; Madron, Nelsen, and Yokeley, 1974; Nelsen, Madron, and Yokeley, 1975). Even when survey findings have appeared to support connections between denominational belief and political outlook, the conclusions have been challenged on grounds that they really represented social background influences of the kind examined in the previous section (D. Anderson 1966; Henriot 1966; Jay 1981; Rojek 1973; Roof 1974; Summers et al. 1970).

Those who would insist on drawing too strong a connection between religious orientations and particular forms of political belief should remember the many exceptions to the rule. Left-wing movements for social reform have frequently been inspired by Christian doctrine (Murchland 1982; Littell 1970). William Jennings Bryan, the defender of religious conservatism par excellence, had no difficulty combining a deep commitment to fundamentalist theology with passionate conviction in international arbitration, the rights of urban workers, women's suffrage, public ownership of utilities, and, in general, support for an extensive government effort to secure social and economic justice. The same Bryan who condemned evolution, in large part for its pernicious social implications, saw his commitments to social reform as the logical outgrowth of Christian morality (Levine 1975). Like Bryan, many black Protestants, white evangelicals, and Roman Catholics find no contradiction between theological conservatism and political liberalism. Even the Pentecostal movement, normally regarded as the politically most regressive wing of Protestantism, has found biblical sanction for racial integration (Elinson 1965, 414–415). The confluence of liberal theology with conservative politics can also be found in American political life. Despite a traditional commitment to liberalism, some Jews have enlisted on behalf of conservative programs and policies. Milton Friedman, the dean of laissez-faire economists, is Jewish; so is Howard

Phillips, leader of the Conservative Caucus and a long-time activist in right-wing political movements. Much to the dismay of many liberals in the Jewish community (see Shorris 1982), the principal leadership of the American neoconservative movement comprises Jewish intellectuals disillusioned by events in the 1960s and 1970s.

These exceptions suggest that there are limits to simple theological explanations of political attitudes. On the one hand, the lack of an authoritative source of interpretation for most American religions leaves believers free to develop their own understanding of sacred texts and teachings. And even where the religious tradition seems clearly to point to a logically related political position, church members may keep the religious values segregated in their minds, limiting the application to politics. Perhaps that is why Lupfer and Wald (1985) found in their Memphis study that evangelicals did not judge humanity in the harsh manner that most lay persons assume would follow from the doctrine of original sin. On the other hand, most religious traditions are elastic enough to support very different political applications. Drawing on a common sacred text, for example, Jerry Falwell and Martin Luther King, Jr., ended up in remarkably different places. Elasticity also shows up when denominations or individuals change political behavior despite an unchanging religious outlook (Balswick, Ward, and Armstrong 1975). Where influential leaders of evangelical protestantism once read the Bible as a blueprint for the Social Gospel, in the 1920s the predominant interpretation shifted to emphasize biblical passages that promoted political withdrawal. Before then, evangelicals provided many of the leaders of progressive causes such as the antislavery movement and populism and supported other policies, such as Prohibition, that can now be understood as sincere attempts to improve social conditions (Clark 1976; T. L. Smith 1965; Hammond 1974).

If we still suspect a link between political and religious values, even after recognizing the potential obstacles to a relationship, what is to be done? The first step is recognizing that the deeper content of religious values is only imperfectly captured by denominational affiliation, rates of church attendance, and other simple measures of religiosity frequently employed in studies of political behavior. Demonstrating how to go beyond those traditional measures, Benson and Williams (1982) explored the "mental maps" of religion held by members of Congress. Recognizing religious belief as a complex and multifaceted phenomenon, they questioned each representative about four different aspects of his or her personal religious philosophy. These aspects or dimensions represented different ways of understanding religious truth. The agentic-communal dimension indicated whether religion focused more on personal or social problems. The second dimension concerned religious messages—were they restrictive, setting limits and regulating conduct, or did they offer release through forgiveness? In the third dimension, religion might be perceived as vertical, with the lines of communication flowing down from God, or horizontal, from person to person. In the final dimension, the primary task of religion was either to offer comfort to individuals or, alternatively, to challenge them to rebuild society. When used to compare voting records, the authors found that advocates of communal, horizontal, challenging, and release-oriented religions were much more likely to support liberal political causes than their religious opposites. These findings are important given the prevailing tendency to dismiss religious influences on the behavior of elected officials.

The value of this approach has also been suggested in several studies based on interviews with more than two thousand Catholics. The directors of the Notre Dame Study of Catholic Parish Life approximated the agentic-communal dimension by asking their respondents to identify the basic human problem addressed by religion, the path to salvation, and the results of salvation (Leege 1989). The agentic, or individualist, mode was illustrated by those who selected fear of the unknown as the primary problem, accepting God's will as the path to salvation, and eternal life as the consequence of salvation. By contrast, the communal label was assigned to individuals who identified the human problem as lack of community and fellowship, regarded working for social justice as the route to salvation, and expected their efforts to produce peace and harmony on earth. Trying to assess the vertical/horizontal dimension, the researchers also measured individuals' feeling— was the presence of God felt most intensely in situations that linked them to other people or was God experienced primarily in formal rituals that stressed authority.

As expected, the individualist/communal dimension proved to be a strong predictor of political ideology and a significant influence on attitudes toward social regulatory policies; in both cases, the communal approach to religion was associated with more liberal outlooks (Leege and Welch 1989). Even more powerfully, those who felt close to God when working for justice and peace were disposed to political liberalism in general and to liberal preferences on issues like abortion, defense spending, and school busing (Welch and Leege 1988). However, these innovative measures of religion did not influence a number of other important political orientations and frequently had less impact than other religious beliefs (ibid.). Even with such mixed findings, it seems likely that more sensitive measures of religion have a great potential to uncover the full impact of religious belief on political outlooks.

The larger point is to treat with caution the apparent compatibility of religious with political thought. Even when religious orientations are found to be consistently in league with corresponding political outlooks, the links should be treated as dispositions that allow some room for exceptions. If one should not claim too little for religion, in the manner of those who always see social standing as the "real" cause for denominational political differences, neither should one claim too much. Tocqueville and Weber were correct in using the term *affinity* instead of *cause* to examine how different religions related the Kingdom of God and humanity.

Religion and Group Interests

Institutional interest provides the last major line of explanation for denominational differences in political attitudes and behavior. At first glance, churches may not appear to fit in with other organized institutions that make claims on government. The principal concern of churches, after all, is to minister to the spiritual needs of the membership. Yet because their wide scope of activity inevitably brings them into contact with government, churches, like secular groups, develop interests that may require defense in the political realm. Of concern in this regard is how the assertion of institutional interests may affect the basic attitudes and loyalties of the church and its supporters.

In the United States, as in other countries, the issue of education has frequently drawn churches into the political realm. Partly in an effort to maintain themselves (although for other reasons as well), American churches have supported extensive systems of elementary, secondary, and postsecondary education. These schools provide both instruction in basic skills and training in religious traditions and practice. The Catholic parochial schools provide the best-known example of religious education, but many denominations have built their own facilities in locations where their members are concentrated. As of the early 1980s, approximately 11 percent of school-age children attended church-related elementary and secondary institutions, and churches supported almost eight hundred institutions of higher learning in the United States (Vance and Snyder 1983, 46, 105).

The maintenance of these institutions is an enormous drain on the financial resources of the churches, and so several efforts have been undertaken to relieve the burden. In each case, the relief efforts have impinged on the public sector. One persistent line of attack has been to seek some sort of state support, either through direct payments to church schools for the nonreligious part of their efforts (salary supplements, supply of textbooks for secular subjects) or through requirements that public schools share resources with their nonpublic counterparts. The interests of the private schools also touched the public systems when taxation levels have been set to support the latter. Most recently, supporters of religious education have tried to persuade Congress to grant tax relief for tuition payments.

In each of these cases, the affected churches and their members have a straightforward financial incentive to support policies that favor the religious schools. With state support, churches can maintain an institution that helps ensure continuity of belief across generations. Under these circumstances, it is hardly surprising that polls have shown very strong support for various forms of state aid among denominations that maintain schools and much more resistance in churches in which the bulk of children attend public institutions (Menendez 1977, chap. 11; Rothenberg and Newport 1984, 58–61). Conversely, studies of voting on urban bond issues dedicated to financing public education have revealed a high level of opposition from Catholics—who have a financial interest in minimizing the cost of a school system many do not utilize (Cataldo and Holm 1983).

Interests do not have to be restricted to the financial sphere nor to single issues. In the late 1920s and 1930s, a convergence of interests brought first- and second-generation Catholics and Jews, previously inactive or pro-Republican, into the New Deal Democratic coalition fashioned by Franklin D. Roosevelt. Part of Roosevelt's appeal to these groups lay in his commitment to economic policies that addressed their economic needs; at the same time, however, Roosevelt was also seen as a defender of the religious minorities from attack by the Protestant culture. As immigrants became more numerous in cities from the late nineteenth century onward, Protestants more and more looked askance at the challenge to their norms and beliefs posed by the influx of Catholics and Jews. The period from approximately 1880 to the 1920s was marked by Protestant efforts to preserve their image of the Christian America by invoking the force of law to support "pious behavior" in matters of personal conduct (Handy 1984). For their part, the immigrants grew increasingly to resent Protestant crusades for immigration restriction, the prohibition of liquor, and the imposition of Sunday closing laws. The implementation of these policies represented a victory for Protestant ideas of morality, which were far more restrictive on such issues than were Jewish or Catholic thought.

As the minority party in the United States, the Democrats had a strong incentive to court the as-yet unattached potential voters. The party's urban organizations proved highly receptive to the interests and concerns of the immigrant workers, and this receptivity was finally matched at the national level in the 1928 presidential nominating convention. There, the party formally repudiated the Ku Klux Klan, then principally an extremist Protestant group attacking Catholics and Jews, and conferred the presidential nomination on New York governor Alfred E. Smith, a Catholic who embodied "the revolt of the underdog, urban immigrant against the top dog of 'old American' stock" (Lubell 1965, 53). Although he lost badly to Herbert Hoover in the 1928 presidential election, Smith brought over to the Democratic side the votes of Catholics in urban America (Lichtman 1979; Burner 1967). Four years later, Roosevelt would capitalize on that cultural conflict and on the nation's economic disarray to claim the presidency for the Democrats.

Roosevelt's policies in 1932 and thereafter cemented the alliance of Jews and Catholics with the Democratic party (Flynn 1968). Catholics were favorably disposed toward a presidential candidate who had denounced religious bigotry in the heated 1928 campaign and who quoted a papal encyclical in support of his plans for economic recovery. Roosevelt further recognized the church by appointing two Catholics to cabinet positions (half the number who had held such posts in all previous U.S. administrations combined), naming Catholics to other important positions in government, and, in an important symbolic gesture, opening up direct contacts between the church and the White House. Roosevelt cultivated Jewish support with similar actions but earned the highest degree of loyalty for his leadership of the war against Hitler. Jews thereupon embraced the Democratic party with a tenacity matched by few groups—a commitment that was redoubled when Roosevelt's successor made the United States one of the first countries to recognize and endorse the formation of a Jewish state in Israel.

By means of such actions, political leaders attempt to convey to members of religious groups their understanding of the group's situation and sympathy for its goals. Eventually, if the conditions are ripe and the romance is conducted with sufficient skill, political elites can forge strong ties between a party and the members of denominations. Unlike some political parties in other countries, the major American parties have never appealed for support solely as the representatives of a specific religious interest. But they have signaled their willingness to make room for members of religious groups in the party coalition. Through the process known as "political socialization," group members may even come to regard affiliation with a particular party as one element of their religious identity (Irvine 1974). Support for the party becomes, in essence, a natural reflex for members of the religious group. Studies of group-based political loyalties have underscored the durability of the associations between religious commitment and political loyalties. Despite the obsolescence of many of the issues that prompted Jewish and Catholic support for the Democratic party under Franklin Roosevelt, the connection has persisted. Political commitments by denominations based initially on common interests thus may broaden into durable loyalties that outlive their original causes (Leege, Lieske, and Wald 1989).

The Role of Social Integration

Very little has been said thus far about how members of groups acquire the outlooks characteristic of their religion. By what process do adherents of a denomination learn about its theology, institutional interests, and subjective social standing—the principal routes by which political traits are forged? In order to answer the question, it is important to think of "religion" as an activity pursued (usually) in groups. The same principles that govern the organization and maintenance of other groups apply equally well to groups defined by a religious purpose:

Members of religious groups have a common identity, interact with one another regularly, and expect each other to think and act in certain ways. These expectations, which are commonly called group norms, are enforced by sanctions, i.e., rewards and punishments which group members administer to each other. The norms of a religious group constitute its special culture, a culture that is usually distinct in some ways from the culture of other groups in its environment. (Johnson and White 1967, 31)

In that description, Johnson and White call attention to the means by which religious groups create a common consciousness that may extend to political ideas.

By participating in a religious group, the individual learns what is expected of him or her and what behavior patterns are required for maintaining membership. When attending church, the affiliate enters a world with a communication network that reinforces the sense of group awareness. Both inside and outside the church, the member may come to have more and more social contact with like-minded persons from the religious community. In the case of the young, the church creates special educational institutions for the express purpose of transmitting group norms. These formal networks are supplemented by informal messages from various agents, especially parents, about what constitutes appropriate behavior for members of the denomination. The minister is an additional source of cues about norms. In most churches the clergy is recognized as the source of spiritual leadership and is expected, as an integral part of worship, to provide guidance about church doctrines. When these elements are put together, they provide the church with impressive potential to influence the outlooks of the membership (Cornwall 1987).

Through each of these routes—restricted communication, social interaction, formal training, informal education, ministerial guidance—the church impresses on the individual member a commitment to its norms. In American churches, these norms may include informal commitment to a party or political outlook, or at least agreement on some of the elements that can influence political perspectives: theological assumptions, a sense of social status, and a belief that group members share certain interests. Through these avenues of influence, churches may provide cues that reinforce political differences between denominations (Converse and Campbell 1969; Kaplan 1969). Most Americans, while frowning on explicit political direction from the clergy, are less resistant to the relatively subtle means of political education that may emanate from the church.

The tie between religion and politics, which produces the denominational differences depicted earlier in the chapter, also operates powerfully at the level of the individual congregation or parish. Roozen, McKinney, and Carroll (1984) found that congregations in Hartford, Connecticut, adopted very different stances toward the role of the church in society, "missions" that powerfully influenced the form and amount of outreach actually practiced by the congregation. In a study of Protestant congregations in one community, my colleagues and I discovered that the acceptance of conservative or liberal politics depended less on an individual's religious outlook than on the religious values held by a majority of fellow congregants (Wald, Owen, and Hill 1988). We interpreted this finding as evidence that subtle messages from the clergy and fellow congregants provide guidance about the appropriate political conclusions that should be drawn from religious principles. The relative power of congregational influence as opposed to residential forces or other personal traits has been the focus of important research by Huckfeldt, Plutzer, and Sprague (1990). Recall from earlier in the chapter that mainline Protestants tend toward both Republican partisanship and liberal views on abortion. Using a unique set of interviews that assessed the views of individuals, their fellow parishioners, and neighbors, Huckfeldt and his colleagues found that the opinions of fellow congregants enhanced the underlying attitudes of the denomination. That is, both the level of republicanism and prochoice sentiment among individual Protestants increased when other church members were predominantly Republican and liberal on abortion. These findings held even allowing for education, income level, and residential context. Further analysis of attitudes toward abortion in Protestant congregations suggests "that members learn more from one another than they do from abstract church pronouncements." Whatever the mechanism of influence, churches—by which I mean individual congregations— are an important crucible where the connections between religion and politics are forged.

Because individuals are not equally involved in churches, they are not equally receptive to the political messages flowing from them. The extremes of involvement run from the person with no religious background or connection to any denomination to the cult member whose immersion in the religious community cuts off all outside sources of political information. Not surprisingly, the nonaffiliate is likely to develop political ideas independent of traditional church doctrine, whereas the cult member is likely to follow the church's political guidance with complete loyalty. Between these poles lay a wide range of religious commitments and, presumably, of responsiveness to the political cues given out directly or indirectly by the religious group. This factor accounts for the consistent finding that commitment to the denomination strengthens conformity to the political norm of the religious group and accentuates attitude differences between persons from different groups. Hence the discovery, to cite only one of many available from the literature, that religious group differences in party identification and presidential voting are greatest among persons with the strongest involvement in their respective religious families (C. Anderson 1973; Knoke 1974). What is true for individuals also holds for congregations. The more a church dominates and circumscribes the life of its members, the greater the political cohesion among congregants (Wald, Owen, and Hill 1990).

Strength of commitment to the religious group has been measured in different ways—frequency of attendance at worship, involvement in the organizational life of the church, level of social interaction with church members, length and intensity of exposure to church doctrine, and even the individual's subjective assessment of the importance of religious identity relative to other group loyalties. Whatever the measure of commitment, research both in the United States and elsewhere has suggested, political loyalty to a denominational pattern builds as the individual's life becomes more nearly encapsulated by the religious group (Wald 1989).

Levels of religious participation may also minimize the impact of nonreligious factors on the political loyalties of church members. The church is an arena that frequently brings together people from different social backgrounds. Although the point should not be overstated, a strong sense of collective religious identity, with its associated political messages, may override the other sources of political cues available to the church members. Instead of picking up political orientations from the newspaper, neighbors, coworkers, or other secondary organizations, the individual may imbibe loyalties from the church members and leaders who are the principal partners in social interaction. The muted level of class differences in politics found between members of the same religious denomination appears to confirm the operation of this process

(Bochel and Denver 1970). To the extent that they actually forge a common political approach among persons of diverse social standing, churches may account for the persistence of political differences independent of social forces such as income, occupation, and education.

Religion is relevant to some types of political conflict but not to all others. When they do appear, political differences among denominations cannot be reduced to a single source, be it theology, social standing, or institutional interest. All these factors may play a role in forging the patterns of belief observed at the beginning of the chapter. Whatever the source of political identity, the transmission of group-based political ideas appears to depend on the individual's level of involvement in the religious community. For individuals whose lives are the most deeply merged with the church, politically distinctive behavior appears to be the rule.

Most of the political differences examined in this chapter do touch directly on religion. American history is rife, however, with conflicts about the place of the church in public life. In the next chapter, we turn to these traditional church and state issues.

NOTES

1. In the General Social Survey (Davis and Smith 1989), the participant is asked to identify his or her "religious preference" from a list of "Protestant, Catholic, Jewish, some other religion, or no religion." Those who pick "Protestant" are asked a follow-up question about their specific denomination. It is important to recognize that such denominational labels, and the categories based on them, fall far short of perfection. However, the difficulty of developing meaningful schemes for classifying religious preferences is no greater than the obstacles facing researchers who seek to categorize people by social class, ethnicity, regional background, or political loyalty. All measurement schemes are approximations of the concept they are meant to represent. Provided that the purpose of the exercise is kept in mind—to identify religious group tendencies in the political realm—the religious-preference questions on the General Social Survey are adequate to the purpose. For an extended discussion of techniques for assessing the religious orientation of individuals, see the excellent essays by Roof (1979) and Wilson (1978, app.). A systematic comparison of different techniques is available from T. W. Smith (1990).

2. Without implicating him in this particular analytical scheme, I must thank Lyman Kellstedt of Wheaton College for his counsel and advice. My distinction between evangelical and mainline Protestants follows as closely as possible the techniques we utilized in revising the religious coding rules for the 1989 Pilot Survey of the National Election Study (Leege, Kellstedt, and Wald 1990). Readers of the first

edition will note that Figure 4.1 reports a significantly smaller proportion of evangelical Protestants in the total sample. That is attributable both to greater specificity in the GSS religious codes since 1984 and to revised rules of classification.

3. The questions about political identity were asked in each annual GSS survey. For the other two categories, questions were asked on a rotating basis. Each of the attitude scales referenced in the text meets acceptable levels of internal consistency.

4. The low level of support for capital punishment by black Protestants can also be used to illustrate the concept of spurious association. Their standing as the minority group most likely to suffer capital punishment, not their religious values, better explains why blacks expressed the greatest resistance to the death penalty.

5. Even though the differences are frequently used to characterize entire religious traditions as conservative or liberal, they constitute tendencies that may divide people of a common heritage.

REFERENCES

Allinsmith, Wesley, and Beverly Allinsmith. 1948. "Religious Affiliation and Politico-Economic Attitudes: A Study of Eight Major U.S. Religious Groups." *Public Opinion Quarterly* 12:377–389.

Anderson, Charles H. 1973. "Religious Communality and Party Preference." In *Research in Religious Behavior,* edited by Benjamin Beit-Hallahmi, 336–352. Monterey, Calif.: Brooks Cole.

Anderson, Donald. 1966. "Ascetic Protestantism and Political Preference." *Review of Religious Research* 7:167–171.

Baggaley, Andrew. 1962. "Religious Influence on Wisconsin Voting." *American Political Science Review* 56:66–70.

Balswick, Jack O. 1970. "Theology and Political Attitudes Among Clergymen." *Sociological Quarterly* 11:394–404.

Balswick, Jack, Dawn M. Ward, and David E. Armstrong. 1975. "Theological and Socio-Political Belief Change Among Religiously Conservative Students." *Review of Religious Research* 17:61–67.

Beatty, Kathleen Murphy, and Oliver Walter. 1982. "Religious Belief and Practice: New Forces in American Politics?" Paper presented at the annual meeting of the American Political Science Association, Denver.

———. 1983. "The Religious Right and Electoral Change." Paper delivered at the annual meeting of the Midwest Political Science Association, Chicago.

———. 1984. "Religious Preference and Practice: Reevaluating Their Impact on Political Tolerance." *Public Opinion Quarterly* 48:318–329.

———. 1989. "A Group Theory of Religion and Politics: The Clergy as Group Leaders." *Western Political Quarterly* 42:129–146.

Benson, Peter L., and Dorothy L. Williams. 1982. *Religion on Capitol Hill: Myths and Realities.* San Francisco: Harper and Row.

Berelson, Bernard, Paul Lazarsfeld, and William N. McPhee. 1954. *Voting: A Study of Opinion Formation in a Presidential Campaign.* Chicago: University of Chicago Press.

Bochel, J. M., and D. T. Denver. 1970. "Religion and Voting: A Critical Review and a New Analysis." *Political Studies* 18:205–219.

Buenker, John D. 1973. *Urban Liberalism and Progressive Reform.* New York: Scribner's.

Burner, David. 1967. *The Politics of Provincialism: The Democratic Party in Transition, 1918–1932.* New York: Norton.

Cataldo, Everett F., and John D. Holm. 1983. "Voting on School Finances: A Test of Competing Theories." *Western Political Quarterly* 36:619–631.

Clark, Norman H. 1976. *Deliver Us From Evil: An Interpretation of American Prohibition.* New York: Norton.

Cohen, Steven M. 1983. *American Modernity and Jewish Identity.* New York: Tavistock.

Cohen, Steven M., and Robert E. Kapsis. 1977. "Religion, Ethnicity, and Party Affiliation in the United States: Evidence from Pooled Election Surveys, 1968–1972." *Social Forces* 56:637–653.

Cohn, Werner. 1957. "The Politics of American Jews." In *The Jews,* edited by Marshall Sklare, 614–626. New York: Free Press.

Colombo, Furio. 1984. *God in America: Religion and Politics in the United States.* New York: Columbia University Press.

Converse, Philip E. 1966. "Religion and Politics: The 1960 Election." In *Elections and the Political Order,* edited by Angus Campbell, Philip E. Converse, Warren E. Miller and Donald Stokes, 96–124. New York: Wiley.

———. 1974. "Some Priority Variables in Comparative Electoral Research." In *Electoral Behavior,* edited by Richard Rose, 727–745. New York: Free Press.

Converse, Philip E., and Angus Campbell. 1969. "Political Standards in Secondary Groups." In *Readings in Reference Group Theory and Research,* edited by Herbert H. Hyman and Eleanor Singer, 473–489. New York: Free Press.

Cornwall, Marie. 1987. "The Social Bases of Religion: A Study of Factors Influencing Religious Belief and Commitment." *Review of Religious Research* 29:44–56.

Crosby, Donald F. 1978. *God, Church and Flag: Senator Joseph R. McCarthy and the Catholic Church, 1950–1957.* Chapel Hill: University of North Carolina Press.

Davis, James A., and Tom W. Smith. 1989. *General Social Surveys, 1972–1989: Cumulative Codebook.* Chicago: National Opinion Research Center.

Driedger, Leo. 1974. "Doctrinal Belief: A Major Factor in the Differential Perception of Social Issues." *Sociological Quarterly* 15:66–80.

Ebersole, Luke. 1960. "Religion and Politics." *Annals of the American Academy of Political and Social Sciences* 332:101–111.

Eckberg, Douglas Lee, and T. Jean Blocker. 1989. "Varieties of Religious Involvement and Environmental Concern: Testing the Lynn White Thesis." *Journal for the Scientific Study of Religion* 28:509–517.

El-Azhary, M. S. 1980. *Political Cohesion of American Jews: A Reappraisal of Their Role in Presidential Elections.* Washington, D.C.: University Press of America.

Elinson, Howard. 1965. "The Implications of Pentecostal Religion for Intellectualism, Politics, and Race Relations." *American Journal of Sociology* 70:403–415.

Fee, Joan L. 1976. "Party Identification Among American Catholics, 1972, 1973." *Ethnicity* 3:53–69.

Fenton, John H. 1960. *The Catholic Vote.* New Orleans: Hauser.

Fisher, Alan. 1979. "Realignment of the Jewish Vote." *Political Science Quarterly* 94:97–116.

Flynn, George Q. 1968. *American Catholics and the Roosevelt Presidency, 1932–1936.* Lexington: University of Kentucky Press.

Fowler, Robert Booth. 1982. *A New Engagement: Evangelical Political Thought, 1966–1976*. Grand Rapids, Mich.: Eerdmans.

Fuchs, Lawrence H. 1956. *The Political Behavior of American Jews*. Glencoe, Ill.: Free Press.

———. 1955. "American Jews and the Presidential Vote." *American Political Science Review* 49:385–401.

———. 1984. "The Political Behavior of American Jews." In *American Political Theology*, edited by Charles W. Dunn, 70–78. New York: Praeger.

Glantz, Oscar. 1959. "Protestant and Catholic Voting Behavior in a Metropolitan Area." *Public Opinion Quarterly* 23:73–82.

Glock, Charles Y., and Rodney Stark. 1966. *Christian Beliefs and Anti-Semitism*. New York: Harper and Row.

Gorsuch, Richard L., and Daniel Aleshire. 1974. "Christian Faith and Ethnic Prejudice: A Review and Interpretation of Research." *Journal for the Scientific Study of Religion* 13:281–307.

Granberg, Donald. 1978. "Pro-Life or Reflection of Conservative Ideology? An Analysis of Opposition to Legalized Abortion." *Sociology and Social Research* 62:414–429.

Greeley, Andrew M. 1982. *Religion: A Secular Theory*. New York: Free Press.

———. 1988. "Evidence That a Maternal Image of God Correlates With Liberal Politics." *Sociology and Social Research* 72:150–154.

———. 1977. "How Conservative Are American Catholics?" *Political Science Quarterly* 92:199–218.

Greer, Scott. 1961. "Catholic Voters and the Democratic Party." *Public Opinion Quarterly* 25:611–625.

Grupp, Frederick W., and William M. Newman. 1973. "Political Ideology and Religious Preference: The John Birch Society and the Americans for Democratic Action." *Journal for the Scientific Study of Religion* 12:401–413.

Guth, James L. 1989. "Southern Baptists and the New Right." In *Religion in American Politics*, edited by Charles W. Dunn, 177–190. Washington, D.C.: CQ Press.

Guysenir, Maurice G. 1958. "Jewish Vote in Chicago." *Jewish Social Studies* 20:195–214.

Hadden, Jeffrey. 1969. *Gathering Storm in the Churches*. Garden City, N.Y.: Doubleday Anchor.

Hammond, John M. 1974. "Revival Religion and Anti-Slavery Politics." *American Sociological Review* 39:175–186.

Hand, Carl M., and Kent D. Van Liere. 1984. "Religion, Mastery-Over-Nature, and Environmental Concern." *Social Forces* 63:555–570.

Handy, Robert T. 1984. *A Christian America?* 2d edition. New York: Oxford University Press.

Hanna, Mary T. 1979. *Catholics and American Politics*. Cambridge: Harvard University Press.

———. 1984. "From Civil Religion to Prophetic Church: The Bishops and the Bomb." In *American Political Theology*, edited by Charles W. Dunn, 144–153. New York: Praeger.

Hendricks, John S. 1977. "Religious and Political Fundamentalism: The Links Between Alienation and Ideology," Ph.D. diss., University of Michigan.

118   Religion and Politics in the United States

Henriot, Peter. 1966. "The Coincidence of Political and Religious Attitudes." *Review of Religious Research* 8:50–58.

Hero, Alfred O., Jr. 1973. *American Religious Groups View Foreign Policy: Trends in Rank-and-File Opinion, 1937–1969.* Durham, N.C.: Duke University Press.

Hoffman, Thomas J. 1982. "Religion and Politics: An Empirical Inquiry." Ph.D. diss., University of Arizona.

————. 1985. "Religion and Political Change: The Impacts of Institutional Connectedness and Religious Imagery." Paper delivered at the annual meeting of the American Political Science Association, New Orleans.

Huckfeldt, Robert, Eric Plutzer, and John Sprague. 1990. "Alternative Contexts of Political Behavior." Political Science Paper #136. St. Louis, Mo.: Washington University.

Hunter, James Davison. 1983. *American Evangelicalism: Conservative Religion and the Quandary of Modernity.* New Brunswick, N.J.: Rutgers University Press.

Irvine, William P. 1974. "Explaining the Religious Basis of the Canadian Partisan Identity: Success on the Third Try." *Canadian Journal of Political Science* 7:560–563.

Jay, Evelyn D. 1981. "Religious Commitment: Its Origins and Its Consequences for Social Conservatism," Ph.D. diss., University of California, Berkeley.

Jeffries, Vincent, and Clarence Tygart. 1974. "The Influence of Theological Denomination and Values upon the Positions of Clergy on Social Issues." *Journal for the Scientific Study of Religion* 13:309–313.

Jelen, Ted G. 1985. "Images of God as Predictors of Attitudes on Social Issues Among Fundamentalists and Non-Fundamentalists." Paper delivered at the annual meeting of the Society for the Scientific Study of Religion, Savannah, Georgia.

Johnson, Benton. 1962. "Ascetic Protestantism and Political Preference." *Public Opinion Quarterly* 26:35–46.

————. 1964. "Ascetic Protestantism and Political Preference in the Deep South." *American Journal of Sociology* 69:359–366.

————. 1966. "Theology and Party Preference Among Protestant Clergymen." *American Sociological Review* 31:200–208.

————. 1967. "Theology and the Position of Pastors on Public Issues." *American Sociological Review* 32:433–442.

Johnson, Benton, and Richard H. White. 1967. "Protestantism, Political Preference, and the Nature of Religious Influence: Comment on Anderson's Paper." *Review of Religious Research* 9:28–35.

Kaplan, Norman. 1969. "Reference Groups and Interest Group Theories of Voting." In *Readings in Reference Group Theory and Research,* edited by Herbert H. Hyman and Eleanor Singer, 461–472. New York: Free Press.

Kersten, Lawrence K. 1970. *The Lutheran Ethic.* Detroit: Wayne State University Press.

Kleppner, Paul. 1970. *The Cross of Culture.* New York: Free Press.

Knoke, David. 1974. "Religious Involvement and Political Behavior: A Log-Linear Analysis of White Americans, 1952–1968." *Sociological Quarterly* 15:51–65.

Laitin, David D. 1978. "Religion, Political Culture, and the Weberian Tradition." *World Politics* 30:563–592.

Laumann, Edward O., and David R. Segal. 1971. "Status Inconsistency and Ethnoreligious Group Membership as Determinants of Social Participation and Political Attitudes." *American Journal of Sociology* 77:36–61.

Lazarsfeld, Paul F., Bernard Berelson, and Hazel Gaudet. 1948. *The People's Choice: How the Voter Makes up His Mind in a Presidential Campaign.* New York: Columbia University Press.

Leege, David C. 1989. "Toward a Mental Measure of Religiosity in Research on Religion and Politics." In *Religion and Political Behavior in the United States*, edited by Ted G. Jelen, 45–64. New York: Praeger.

Leege, David C., Lyman A. Kellstedt, and Kenneth D. Wald. 1990. "Religion and Politics: A Report on Measures of Religiosity in the 1989 NES Pilot Study." Paper presented at the annual meeting of the Midwest Political Science Association, Chicago.

Leege, David C., Joel A. Lieske, and Kenneth D. Wald. 1989. "Toward Cultural Theories of American Political Behavior: Religion, Ethnicity, and Class Outlook." Paper delivered at the annual meeting of the Midwest Political Science Association, Chicago.

Leege, David C., and Michael R. Welch. 1989. "Religious Roots of Political Orientations: Variations Among American Catholic Parishioners." *Journal of Politics* 50:137–162.

Lenski, Gerhard. 1963. *The Religious Factor.* Garden City, N.Y.: Doubleday Anchor.

Le Poire, Beth A., Carol K. Sigelman, Lee Sigelman, and Henry C. Kenski. 1990. "Who Wants to Quarantine Persons with AIDS?" *Social Science Quarterly* 71:239–249.

Leventman, Paula Goldman, and Seymour Leventman. 1976. "Congressman Drinan, S.J., and His Jewish Constituents." *American Jewish Historical Quarterly* 66:215–248.

Levine, Lawrence W. 1975. *Defender of the Faith: William Jennings Bryan—The Last Decade, 1915–1925.* New York: Oxford University Press.

Lichtman, Allan J. 1979. *Prejudice and the Old Politics: The Presidential Election of 1928.* Chapel Hill: University of North Carolina Press.

Liebman, Arthur. 1979. *Jews and the Left.* New York: Wiley Interscience.

Liebman, Charles. 1973. *The Ambivalent American Jew.* Philadelphia: Jewish Publication Society.

Lijphart, Arend. 1971. "Class Voting and Religious Voting in the European Democracies." Glasgow, Scotland: Survey Research Centre, University of Strathclyde.

Lipset, Seymour Martin. 1964. "Three Decades of the Radical Right: Coughlinites, McCarthyites, and Birchers." In *The Radical Right*, edited by Daniel Bell, 373–446. Garden City, N.Y.: Doubleday Anchor.

Littell, Franklin H. 1970. "The Radical Reformation and Revolution." In *Marxism and Radical Religion*, edited by John C. Raines and Thomas Dean, 81–100. Philadelphia: Temple University Press.

Lubell, Samuel. 1965. *The Future of American Politics.* Third edition. New York: Harper and Row.

Lupfer, Michael, and Kenneth D. Wald. 1985. "An Exploration of Adults' Religious Orientations and Their Philosophies of Human Nature." *Journal for the Scientific Study of Religion* 24:293–304.

McIntosh, William A., Letitia T. Alston, and John P. Alston. 1979. "The Differential Impact of Religious Preference and Church Attendance on Attitudes Toward Abortion." *Review of Religious Research* 20:195–213.

Maddox, William S. 1979. "Changing Electoral Coalitions from 1952–1976." *Social Science Quarterly* 60:309–313.

Madron, Thomas W., Hart M. Nelsen, and Raytha L. Yokeley. 1974. "Religion as a Determinant of Militancy and Political Participation Among Black Americans." *American Behavioral Scientist* 17:783–796.

Maller, Allen S. 1977. "Class Factors in the Jewish Vote." *Jewish Social Studies* 39:159–162.

Marx, Gary T. 1967. *Protest and Prejudice: A Study of Belief in the Black Community.* New York: Harper and Row.

Menendez, Albert J. 1977. *Religion at the Polls.* Philadelphia: Westminster.

Miller, Abraham. 1974. "Ethnicity and Party Identification: Continuation of a Theoretical Dialogue." *Western Political Quarterly* 27:470–490.

Murchland, Bernard. 1982. *The Dream of Christian Socialism: An Essay on Its European Origins.* Washington, D.C.: American Enterprise Institute.

Nelsen, Hart M., Thomas W. Madron, and Raytha L. Yokeley. 1975. "Black Religion's Promethean Motif: Orthodoxy and Militancy." *American Journal of Sociology* 81:139–146.

O'Grady, John F. 1982. *Models of Jesus.* New York: Image.

Orum, Anthony M. 1970. "Religion and the Rise of the Radical White: The Case of Southern Wallace Support in 1968." *Social Science Quarterly* 51:674–688.

Parenti, Michael. 1967. "Political Values and Religious Cultures: Jews, Catholics, and Protestants." *Journal for the Scientific Study of Religion* 6:259–269.

Petrusak, Frank, and Steven Steinart. 1976. "The Jews of Charleston: Some Old Wine in New Bottles." *Jewish Social Studies* 38:337–346.

Phillips, Kevin P. 1969. *The Emerging Republican Majority.* Garden City, N.Y.: Doubleday Anchor.

Piazza, Thomas, and Charles Y. Glock. 1979. "Images of God and Their Social Meanings." In *The Religious Dimension: New Directions in Quantitative Research,* edited by Robert Wuthnow, 69–91. New York: Academic.

Quinley, Harold E. 1974. "The Dilemma of an Activist Church: Protestant Religion in the Sixties and Seventies." *Journal for the Scientific Study of Religion* 13:1–22.

Rischin, Moses. 1962. *The Promised City: New York's Jews, 1870–1914.* New York: Harper and Row.

Rojek, Dean. 1973. "The Protestant Ethic and Political Preferences." *Social Forces* 52:168–177.

Rokeach, Milton. 1969. "Religious Values and Social Compassion." *Review of Religious Research* 11:24–39.

Roof, Wade Clark. 1974. "Religious Orthodoxy and Minority Prejudice: Causal Relationship or Reflection of Localistic World View." *American Journal of Sociology* 80:643–664.

———. 1979. "Concepts and Indicators of Religious Commitment: A Critical Review." In *The Religious Dimension: New Directions in Quantitative Research,* edited by Robert Wuthnow, 17–45. New York: Academic.

Roof, Wade Clark, and William McKinney. 1987. *American Mainline Religion: Its Changing Shape and Future.* New Brunswick, N.J.: Rutgers University Press.

Roozen, David A. 1978. *The Churched and the Unchurched in America: A Comparative Profile.* Washington, D.C.: Glenmary Research Center.

Roozen, David A., William McKinney, and Jackson W. Carroll. 1984. *Varieties of Religious Presence: Mission in Public Life*. New York: Pilgrim.

Rose, Richard, and Derek Urwin. 1969. "Social Cohesion, Political Parties, and Strains in Regimes." *Comparative Political Studies* 2:7–67.

Rosenberg, Morris. 1956. "Misanthropy and Political Ideology." *American Sociological Review* 21:690–695.

Rothenberg, Stuart, and Frank Newport. 1984. *The Evangelical Voter.* Washington, D.C.: Free Congress Research and Education Foundation.

Rothman, Stanley, and S. Robert Lichter. 1982. *Roots of Radicalism: Jews, Christians, and the New Left*. New York: Oxford University Press.

Schindeler, Fred, and David Hoffman. 1968. "Theological and Political Conservatism: Variations in Attitudes Among Clergymen of One Denomination." *Canadian Journal of Political Science* 1:429–441.

Scoble, Harry M., and Leon D. Epstein. 1964. "Religion and Wisconsin Voting in 1960." *Journal of Politics* 26:381–396.

Shorris, Earl. 1982. *Jews Without Mercy: A Lament*. Garden City, N.Y.: Doubleday Anchor.

Smith, Timothy L. 1965. *Revivalism and Social Reform: American Protestantism on the Eve of the Civil War.* New York: Harper and Row.

Smith, Tom W. 1990. "Classifying Protestant Denominations." *Review of Religious Research* 31:225–245.

Stark, Rodney, and William Sims Bainbridge. 1985. *The Future of Religion*. Berkeley and Los Angeles: University of California Press.

Steiber, Steven R. 1980. "The Influence of the Religious Factor on Civil and Sacred Tolerance." *Social Forces* 58:811–832.

Stellway, Richard J. 1973. "The Correspondence Between Religious Orientation and Socio-Political Liberalism and Conservatism." *Sociological Quarterly* 14:430–439.

Summers, Gene F., Richard L. Hough, Doyle P. Johnson, and Kathryn A. Veatch. 1970. "Ascetic Protestantism and Political Preference: A Reexamination." *Review of Religious Research* 12:17–25.

Tocqueville, Alexis de. 1945. *Democracy in America*. Volume 1. Edited by Phillips Bradley. New York: Vintage Books, 310.

Vance, Grant W., and Thomas D. Snyder. 1983. *Digest of Education Statistics, 1983–84*. Washington, D.C.: National Center for Educational Statistics.

Wald, Kenneth D. 1989. "Assessing the Religious Factor in Electoral Behavior." In *Religion in American Politics*, edited by Charles W. Dunn, 105–122. Washington, D.C.: CQ Press.

Wald, Kenneth D., and Michael B. Lupfer. 1983. "Religion and Political Attitudes in the Urban South." In *Religion and Politics in the South: Mass and Elite Perspectives*, edited by Tod A. Baker, Robert B. Steed, and Laurence W. Moreland, 84–100. New York: Praeger.

Wald, Kenneth D., Dennis E. Owen, and Samuel S. Hill, Jr. 1988. "Churches as Political Communities." *American Political Science Review* 82:531–548.

———. 1989. "Evangelical Politics and Status Issues." *Journal for the Scientific Study of Religion* 28:1–16.

———. 1990. "Political Cohesion in Churches." *Journal of Politics* 52:197–215.

Warner, R. Stephen. 1988. *New Wine in Old Wineskins: Evangelicals and Liberals in a Small-Town Church*. Berkeley and Los Angeles: University of California Press.

Weber, Mary Cahill. 1983. "Religion and Conservative Social Attitudes." In *Views from the Pews: Christian Beliefs and Attitudes*, edited by Roger A. Johnson, 103–122. Philadelphia: Fortress.

Weber, Max. 1958. *The Protestant Ethic and the Spirit of Capitalism*. New York: Scribner's.

Welch, Michael R., and David C. Leege. 1988. "Religious Predictors of Catholic Parishioners' Sociopolitical Attitudes: Devotional Style, Closeness to God, Imagery, and Agentic/Communal Religious Identity." *Journal for the Scientific Study of Religion* 27:536–552.

Whyte, John H. 1981. *Catholics in Western Democracies: A Study in Political Behavior*. New York: St. Martin's.

Wilson, John. 1978. *Religion in American Society: The Effective Presence*. Englewood Cliffs, N.J.: Prentice-Hall.

Wuthnow, Robert. 1973. "Religious Commitment and Conservatism: In Search of an Elusive Relationship." In *Religion in Sociological Perspective*, edited by Charles Y. Glock, 117–132. Belmont, Calif.: Wadsworth.

Zehner, Paul. 1967. "Beliefs and Political Behaviors of Chicago Clergymen from Nine Denominations." Ph.D. diss., Northwestern University.

5. Religion and the State

When Caesar, having exacted what is Caesar's, demands still more insistently that we render unto him what is God's—that is a sacrifice we dare not make.
—Alexander Solzhenitsyn

It may not be easy, in every possible case, to trace the line of separation between the rights of religion and the Civil authority with such distinctiveness as to avoid collisions and doubts on unessential points.
—James Madison, *In God We Trust*

Because Americans frequently fail to recognize the subtle religious influences on political life, I have devoted two chapters in this book to examining the contributions of religion to important themes in American political culture and to political differences among the major religious groups. It is now time to move on to an analysis of those open conflicts between government and religion that often come to mind with the phrase "church and state."

Popular discussions of this topic often reveal deep disagreements over the meaning of provisions of the Constitution relating to religion and how the Constitution has been interpreted by the Supreme Court and other government agencies.[1] This confusion frequently extends to basic claims about the role of religion in American political history. In the perennial debate over the religious motivations of the Founders, the framers are frequently described as deists and freethinkers who were highly skeptical about traditional forms of religion and who wrote a Constitution intending to subdue political activism by churches. That interpretation clashes sharply with other writers who portray the Founders as deeply religious men, Christian statesmen who believed as a matter of course that the state should support the institutions of religion. If it is hard to gain agreement on the question of what a particular group of men thought about the relation of religion to the government, it is doubly difficult to interpret the motives and consequences of subsequent decisions about church-state relations.

This chapter supplies some perspective on these issues by discussing the reasons for church-state tension and how the solution worked out by the Founders has been modified by the Supreme Court to fit the changing circumstances of the country. Government policy on the subject is not fixed in stone. The United States may now be entering a new phase in church-state relations under the leadership of a more conservative Supreme Court. The chapter concludes with an examination of the new approach taken by the Court and how it might affect the shape of church-state relations in coming years.

The Genesis of Church-State Conflict

The relationship between church and state presents two sets of problems for all governments. On the most fundamental level, governments must decide what legal status to grant to churches, the institutional expression of religion. Should government take account of religious sentiments, treat churches as just another type of interest group, or try to restrict the public role of the churches? The problem is particularly severe when, as in the United States, many types of churches compete for the loyalty of the citizens. In such a situation "taking account" of the public's religious sentiment may inflame members of religious minorities and persons who are not religious. Yet by ignoring religion or limiting its public role in the interest of preserving harmony, the government runs the risk of alienating citizens for whom religion is an important source of personal identity.

The second type of church-state problem stems from possible conflicts between religious motivation and behavior in secular realms. Religions provide guidance about how people should live their lives. In some cases, religious beliefs may counsel individuals to undertake actions that violate the duly established laws of the state. Government may demand behavior that a church forbids or may prohibit actions that the church requires. In either case, the citizen is forced to choose between loyalty to the public law and loyalty to religious faith. What should be done when church and state provide conflicting guidance about appropriate or permissible behavior?

Because it involves the rights and privileges of two different institutions, the question of the legal status granted to churches is known as the boundary problem or, from the phrase first used by Thomas Jefferson, that of the "wall of separation" between church and state.[2] The second type of church-state problem, collision between the teachings of church and state, is usually described as the free-exercise controversy— a label that recognizes the possibility that the free exercise of religious belief may run afoul of limits established by secular law. Both types of problem have repeatedly found their way onto the American political agenda. From any number of possible examples, two recent incidents will be used to illustrate each type of church-state problem.

Two court cases raised in the starkest possible way the religious basis of disobedience to secular law (Zlatos 1984).[3] On February 16, 1984, an Indiana infant named Joel David Hall died of pneumonia. Less than four months later, in a neighboring town, nine-month-old Allyson Bergmann died of bacterial meningitis. The parents of both children had refused to seek medical care because of religious convictions. The Hall and Bergmann families belonged to Faith Assembly Church, a large congregation in northern Indiana that preaches faith in God as an alternative to medical care. Believing that God will conquer disease and pain if souls are pure, church members regard illness as a sign of defective spiritual commitment by individuals and their families. They also believe that any resort to professional medical care will only hasten death because God will interpret it as evidence of diminished faith. Consistent with their understanding of life as a divine gift dependent on intense spiritual devotion, the church members avoid hospitals, reject medical devices such as eyeglasses and hearing aids, refuse immunizations, and do not maintain life insurance or use seatbelts. For failing to seek timely medical care, the parents of the two infants were charged under Indiana laws with reckless homicide and child neglect, convicted in jury trials, and sentenced to prison terms. Similar charges are frequently filed against Christian Scientists who may refuse on religious grounds to obtain conventional medical treatment for children.

These cases represent, in extreme form, the free-exercise basis of church-state conflict. Government and religion came into conflict because each claimed the authority to set standards for human behavior. The right of government to limit what citizens may do is widely accepted by most modern societies. The authority of government is recognized in codes of law that state the types of behavior that are unacceptable and define the penalties for disobedience. Religions also take positions on what behavior is permissible, and they embody their beliefs in sacred documents and religious codes. Recognizing the authority of government in most spheres, churches frequently urge the state to make religion the basis for deciding what types of behavior are to be encouraged or forbidden. But when the laws do not agree with the doctrines of a church, the religious may claim for themselves a right to follow what they see as God's "higher law." That was the premise of Martin Luther King, Jr., when he openly defied laws on racial segregation as incompatible with Christianity; that was also the premise of the parents of Allyson Bergmann and Joel David Hall for not seeking medical care.[4]

In the Faith Assembly cases, government demanded one standard of behavior and the church another. Based on the widespread belief that government should protect children, who usually cannot defend themselves, the state of Indiana invoked laws calling for heavy fines and jail terms for parents who do not seek timely medical care for sick children. In moving against the parents of the Bergmann and Hall infants, the state was particularly alarmed by evidence that infant mortality rates among Faith Assembly members were three times the state average, even though church members could have afforded professional treatment. According to the prosecutor, the substitution of prayer for effective medical care constituted "negligence and criminally reckless conduct" under secular law. On their part, the Halls and Bergmanns claimed that faith healing was a legitimate exercise of their religion and that the state of Indiana had no legal basis on which to force them to act against their beliefs by calling in a physician. The bedrock of their defense, however, was the claim of moral superiority for church doctrine over the state laws. Asked by the judge if she would ever seek medical treatment for her children, the mother of Joel David Hall declared, "On the basis of my convictions, and of my fear of God almighty, I could not provide medical care." What the state required as evidence of reasonable behavior by a parent, the church denounced as a form of blasphemy. In such a case, the parents asserted the right to follow their conscience.

The so-called boundary problem does not usually appear in so dramatic a form, but it probably arises more frequently. A typical illustration of the boundary problem was the controversy that arose in the central Florida town of Sanford over the recognition of religious holidays in public schools.[5] During the week before Christmas in 1983, Olivia Myers bought cards for her second-grade classmates at Pine Crest Elementary School and put a Jesus sticker on each of the cards. Concerned that such a religious symbol might violate school regulations about religious practices, Olivia's teacher consulted with the school's assistant principal and was told not to allow distribution of the cards during class. Like many public school systems, that of Seminole County had a policy forbidding celebrations on religious themes. Under this policy, religious holidays could be studied as cultural events, but calling attention to the theological basis of holidays was prohibited as constituting an endorsement of a particular religion. Hence, although cultural symbols such as Christmas trees or Santa Claus were acceptable under the guidelines, a religious symbol, such as a picture of Jesus, appeared to touch on matters of personal faith that public schools were supposed to avoid. The decision to prohibit distribution of Olivia's cards and similar attempts to minimize religious themes drew criticism from some churches in the county.

In focusing on these two major types of church-state conflict, I do not mean to suggest that the two institutions are permanently locked into a battle for supremacy. Though conflicts occur, not all church-state interaction is marked by hostility. On some occasions, churches have actually called in government agencies to resolve situations beyond their power to remedy. Thus, church members and the diocesan hierarchy of the Lutheran Church in America asked the police and the court system to remove a Pennsylvania minister who refused to accept dismissal from his pulpit.[6] As corporate institutions, churches are entitled to the protection of government in such matters of property. Government may also be asked to help individuals secure religious liberty from threats posed by other, non-governmental, institutions. For example, the federal courts have been petitioned to require businesses to recognize the conscience of employees whose faith does not permit them to work on certain days of the week or to perform certain responsibilities. But in most cases, and particularly in those that draw headlines, controversies arise over where to draw the proper line between the institutions (boundary) and the moral authority (free exercise) of church and state. This source of the controversy may be as seemingly trivial as an eight-year-old's wish to distribute Christmas cards to her classmates in public school or as significant as a parent's decision to withhold medical care from a critically ill child.

Principles of Church-State Relations

The American approach to the boundary and free-exercise problems is governed by the famous phrase from the Constitution's first amendment: "Congress shall make no law respecting an establishment of religion, or prohibiting the free exercise thereof." That statement and a prohibition on "religious tests" for holding public office in Article VI are the only formal reference to religion in the Constitution. This brevity in the discussion of religion has inspired continuing debate over what kinds of government action toward religion are permitted and how far individuals may go in claiming religion as justification for violating secular law. The constitutional language on religion, like that on so many other subjects, has been interpreted differently from one generation to the next. The debate over the precise meaning of the words in different circumstances, a source of passionate controversy and fierce argument, is examined in later sections. Despite its intensity, however, that debate should not disguise what has been a strong American consensus on the role of religion in the state.[7]

For the more than two hundred years it has existed as an independent nation, the United States has pursued what might best be described as a "partial" separation of church and state. There has been virtually unanimous agreement that the establishment clause ("Congress shall make no law respecting an establishment of religion") forbids the government to grant preference to any particular religion. Together with the corresponding free-exercise clause (". . . or prohibiting the free exercise thereof"), it also seems clearly to rule out the possibility of the government imposing one religion as the official faith or prosecuting members of another because their beliefs are repugnant. But if "separation of church and state" is interpreted to mean that government should make no allowances for religion or belief, then the United States is a long way from complete separationism. In numerous ways, the government has recognized the strong religious beliefs held by many citizens of the nation and made it clear that separation does not require state hostility to religious influence (Kirby 1977).

The currency, national seal, "Pledge of Allegiance," national anthem, legislative prayers, and oaths sworn in federal courts all make explicit reference to belief in God. Most of these practices have been upheld in court challenges. In such political events as a presidential inauguration, the religious motif is readily apparent through the Bible on which the oath is sworn and the prominent participation of clergy in the ceremony. In addition, the churches on occasion have been asked to participate in the formation of public policy. Until the Supreme Court broadened the grounds for "conscientious objection" to military participation, it was customary for members of the clergy to sit in judgment on the moral sincerity of persons who applied for exemption from military service. Even today, the clergy may be sought out to review public policies that raise moral issues. Pursuing a middle ground between the extreme alternatives, the United States has on one hand avoided the option of submerging the state to the church, as in a theocratic system of government, and on the other refused to restrict the church to a nonpolitical role.

Choosing neither theocracy nor subordination of religion to government, Americans must still resolve what Madison described as "collisions and doubts" vis-à-vis church and state issues. In so doing, they choose among three competing interpretations of the Constitution's religious language. Favoring Jefferson's "high wall," advocates of *separation* believe that "government and religion will better achieve their ends if they remain independent of each other" (Adams 1986, 69). This doctrine takes a dim view of any government aid or support for religion but is generally sympathetic when individuals seek exemption from laws on religious grounds. The separationist viewpoint was most forcefully expressed by Justice Hugo Black in a 1947 Supreme Court decision:

The "establishment of religion" clause of the first amendment means at least this: Neither a state nor the Federal Government can set up a church. Neither can pass laws which aid one religion, aid all religions, or prefer one religion over another. Neither can force nor influence a person to go to or to remain away from church against his will or force him to profess a belief or disbelief in any religion. No person can be punished for entertaining or professing religious beliefs or disbeliefs, for church attendance or non-attendance. No tax in any amount, large or small, can be levied to support any religious activities or institutions, whatever they may be called, or whatever form they may adopt to teach or practice religion. Neither a state nor the Federal Government can, openly or secretly, participate in the affairs of any religious organizations or groups and vice versa. (*U.S. Reports*, 330 U.S. 15 [1947])[8]

In sharp distinction, the doctrine of *accommodation*, sometimes known as "benevolent neutrality," or nonpreferentialism, urges government to protect the nation's Judeo-Christian heritage. Accommodationists believe that government may extend benefits to religion in a nondiscriminatory manner. The clarion call for accommodation was sounded by Justice William O. Douglas in 1952:

We are a religious people whose institutions presuppose a Supreme Being. We guarantee the freedom to worship as one chooses. We make room for as wide a variety of beliefs and creeds as the spiritual needs of man deem necessary. We sponsor an attitude on the part of government that shows no partiality to any one group and that lets each flourish according to the zeal of its adherents and the appeal of its dogma. When the state encourages religious instruction and cooperates with religious authorities by adjusting the schedule of public events to sectarian needs, it follows the best of our traditions. For it then respects the religious nature of our people and accommodates the public service to their spiritual needs. (*U.S. Reports*, 343 U.S. 310 [1952])

The doctrines of accommodation and separation pit "those who think that government should accommodate and encourage the sort of religion that they see as a foundation of our culture" against "those who think that the government should not extend aid or support to religion in any way" (Wilson and Drakeman 1987, xviii). Offering a third alternative, the doctrine of *strict neutrality* holds that government should neither confer benefits nor disabilities on individuals based on religion (Weber 1989). In terms of the establishment clause, strict neutrality insists that religious groups be treated no differently from other organizations—neither given exclusive rights nor subjected to any particular limitations. In the same way, individuals would have difficulty claiming exemption from secular laws because of religious beliefs but could challenge laws that imposed burdens on them primarily because of their religious standing.

The American public partakes to some degree of all three doctrines (Figure 5.1). When asked whether government should provide no support to any religion or should support all religions equally, a narrow majority opts for the accommodationist perspective by selecting the latter option. But when the issue is phrased another way, the majority shifts

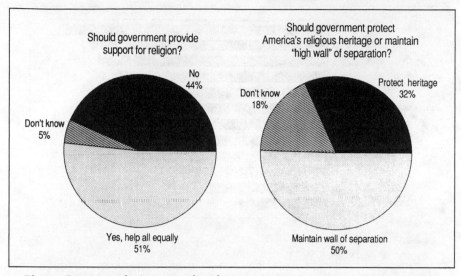

Should government provide
support for religion?

No
44%

Don't know
5%

Yes, help all equally
51%

Should government protect
America's religious heritage or maintain
"high wall" of separation?

Don't know
18%

Protect heritage
32%

Maintain wall of separation
50%

Figure 5.1 General Views on Church-State Separation (Source: Williamsburg Charter Foundation, 1988, Washington, D.C.)

to something closer to the separationist perspective. In the second question, individuals were asked whether government should take special steps to protect the Judeo-Christian heritage of the United States or, rather, if there should be a "high wall" of separation between church and state. The majority supports Jefferson's wall.

Figure 5.2 shows public reaction to specific church-state relationships. Accommodationists could point to majority support for several types of government recognition of religion—practices such as military chaplains, religious displays on public property, voluntary student religious groups in high schools, and prayers at the beginning of high school sporting events. Yet, to prove that public opinion demands a high wall between church and state, separationists could seize on the emphatic rejection of aid to religious schools and the requirement that public schools emphasize Judeo-Christian values. On some questions, such as "moment of silence" laws allowing private prayers in school, the public appears to take a strong stand in favor of "free-exercise" rights. Yet to judge by the large proportions of individuals favoring legal restrictions on religious cults and minority faiths, the public does not want to extend such rights in a nondiscriminatory manner.

Each doctrine of church-state relations claims that history is on its

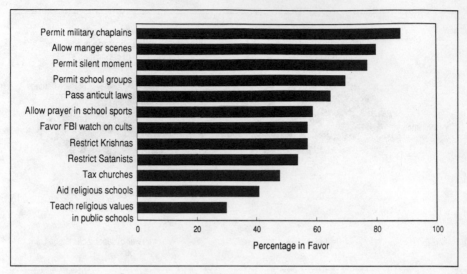

Figure 5.2 Specific Views on Church-State Separation (Source: Williamsburg Charter Foundation, 1988, Washington, D.C.)

side. That makes it important to examine what the American Founders said and did about the role of religion in government. As we shall see, the scheme of partial church-state separation in the First Amendment reflected a compromise between persons who disagreed about the political value of religion. Rather than fit neatly into the categories of religious supporters or opponents, most of the Founders recognized religion as a force with the potential both to enhance and to undermine political stability. Hence the particular arrangement of church-state relations in the United States constitutes neither a wholehearted endorsement of religious influence on government nor unremitting hostility to it. To appreciate the American solution to the boundary and free-exercise problems, it is essential to examine the circumstances under which it evolved.

The Founders and Religion

When the Founders prohibited "religious tests" for holding federal office, they were reacting against both their understanding of British history and common practices in the colonies. From the Reformation, which had inspired the settlement of America, they acquired the belief that alliances between a powerful church and an absolute state would corrupt both institutions. More immediately, they observed how some of the North American colonies appeared to court that same danger by providing religion with the sanction of government in the form of religious requirements for public office, the establishment of an official faith, and denial of religious freedom to members of minority religions.

Many colonies demanded that public office be filled only by persons who could pass some test of acceptable faith. Even where a relatively wide range of religions was recognized, as a rule, Christianity was the basis for these religious tests. Pennsylvania reserved public office for persons who would swear, "I do acknowledge the Scriptures of the old and New testament [sic] to be given by divine inspiration" (Schappes 1971, 68). Belief in God was not sufficient in Maryland; although one of the most tolerant colonies, it further demanded that officeholders accept the concept of the Holy Trinity (Kirwin 1959, 24–29). North Carolina also went one step further than Pennsylvania, excluding not only Jews but also Catholics from holding executive or judicial office (Schappes 1971, 598). In addition to such religious tests, most of the colonies formally endowed certain religions with official status. Under this system, citizens could be obliged to attend services at a church of the favored denomination and were taxed to provide revenue for the dominant religion. Besides enjoying material support from the government, the clergy of the established church were often granted legal privileges such as exemption from certain types of civil laws. Competing faiths were put at a further disadvantage by laws making worship the privilege of the established church. As an example, the charter for New York colony limited the right of public worship to all "who profess faith in God by Jesus Christ" (cited in ibid., 18–19).

The degree to which legal support of one church hampered the free exercise of other faiths was apparent in several restrictive features of colonial law. In some colonies, conformity to the official faith was a condition of residence and dissent the grounds for expulsion or worse. The "worse" in Massachusetts was death. According to that colony's charter of 1641 (cited in Dunn 1984, 22), "If any man after legal conviction shall have or worship any other god, but the lord god, he shall be put to death." What it meant to "have any other god" was spelled out by another law that warranted the death penalty for anyone who cursed or blasphemed "the name of God, the father, Son or Holy ghost."

This law was invoked in 1660 to hang a Quaker woman who had refused repeated orders to stay out of Massachusetts (Marty 1984, 86–87). For denying the divinity of Jesus, the doctrine of the Resurrection, and the occurrence of miracles, a Jewish resident of Maryland faced the possibility of death and the loss of property (Schappes 1971, 13–15). Under these conditions, the free exercise of religion applied only to the established religion of the colony.

Although differing over how far the government might go in recognizing religion, the men who most influenced the Constitution and operated the new system of government in its first years were virtually unanimous in rejecting state support for a national faith. Such support was deemed bad for the state because it promoted false values, undermined respect for the law, and introduced an unhealthy fanaticism to public affairs. As men of strong if unorthodox faith, the Founders also shared a belief that establishment of a national religion or government support for religions would do religion more harm than good. Because each of these objections is relevant to current debate over church-state relationships in the United States, the Founders' logic demands careful review.

For some of the founding generation, notably Thomas Jefferson and John Adams, organized religion deserved no government support because, among other reasons, it was thought to pervert the true meaning of religion. Their extended correspondence shows that the architects of the Declaration of Independence and Washington's successors to the presidency both agreed that true religion consisted of benevolent conduct toward one's fellow human beings. They outdid one another in denouncing the "irrelevance" and "superstition" of the dogma that priests and clergy had encrusted over the simplicity and beauty of religion's moral content (Cousins 1958, 85, 139, 283; see also the comments of Ben Franklin, 25–26). All that was important in Christianity and the other religions, Adams wrote (ibid., 81, 281), could be found in the Sermon on the Mount and the Ten Commandments. Jefferson agreed heartily: years before, he had tried to rewrite the Scriptures by pruning away all the doctrines that he saw as unnecessary—including the divinity of Jesus, the Holy Trinity, and the structure of the church (ibid., 173–216). Precisely because formal religion appeared to give more attention to such mystical concepts than to emphasize the essential truths of the Golden Rule, it evoked little enthusiasm from Adams and Jefferson. Hence, they believed that organized religion would not contribute to the public good if it enjoyed the patronage of government.

Establishment was also considered unwise by some of the Founders because it seemed likely to bring the law into low esteem. As deeply held matters of personal belief, religious views could move people to take extreme actions in defense of conscience. History seemed to demonstrate that attempts to impose a uniform faith by government action would inevitably unleash passion and violence. With so many different religious groups in the colonies, each offering its own distinct version of the truth, any national establishment would be certain to offend the many citizens who subscribed to different faiths. Under these circumstances, a law commanding support for an established church could not realistically be enforced. According to Madison, the consequence of an unenforceable law would be a striking demonstration of government's impotence and a reproach to its authority (ibid., 108). In the absence of consensus, he thought, it would be better to pass no law at all than one certain to elicit widespread disobedience.

The final political problem connected with establishment was the Founders' firm belief in the inevitable degeneration of a state church into a system of religious tyranny. The experience of the colonies suggested to them, that although establishment might begin as a mild and benign preference for one church, the privileges of governmental support would almost certainly encourage attempts to suppress alternate views. John Adams, whose skepticism of the churches earned him an unwarranted reputation for irreligion, asked rhetorically, "When or where had existed a Protestant or dissenting sect who would tolerate a free inquiry?" Answering his own question, he noted that the clergy would accept all manner of brutality and ignorance in the name of preserving the one true faith. "But," he wrote from personal experience, "touch a solemn truth in collision with a dogma of a sect, though capable of the clearest proof, and you will soon find you have disturbed a nest, and the hornets will swarm about your legs and hands and fly into your face and eyes." Having experienced similar condemnation for his attempt to reduce all religions to a common core of moral commands, Jefferson echoed Adams's appraisal of the tendency of churches to persecute those who did not fully accept their doctrines. To give such an institution access to the full powers of the state, they agreed, would create a powerful engine of oppression.

The harmful political consequences of a national religion were not the only reasons the Founders rejected establishment. They also argued that political support would make for bad religion. As Jefferson observed, a government that compelled religious exercises could dictate other terms to a church, reducing it to a servant of power (Cousins 1958, 137). More fundamentally, the Founders concurred that religion was meaningful only when it was a sincere expression from the heart and mind of a free people. Second to none in his admiration of religion as a spur to upright conduct, George Washington repeatedly emphasized the need to keep religion a matter of personal conscience, free of government intervention. To do otherwise, Washington argued, was to put human beings in God's role as the judge of other people's conscience (ibid., 49). Jefferson advised his nephew to "question with boldness" even the existence of God because, if a Supreme Being existed "he must more approve of the homage of reason than that of blindfolded fear" (ibid., 128–129). Although the government could force people to swear loyalty to a public faith, it could not make their hearts pure or their behavior any better. From this evidence, it seems clear that resistance to establishment did not grow out of hostility to faith. Even Tom Paine, the Founder most widely regarded as an enemy of Christianity, believed that the practice of true religion would improve if churches were separated from the state.

All these supposed defects of establishment would be turned into benefits if government refrained from endorsing a religion or from trying in any way to regulate acceptable belief. Freed from state support, political leaders in the early Republic predicted, the false churches would collapse as humanity returned to the essentials of religion (ibid., 320). Instead of undermining respect for the law by insulting the conscience of dissenters, a government that respected religious freedom would enjoy widespread popular support and obedience in the legitimate exercise of its power. In fact, citizens watchful of their religious freedom would be equally sensitive to safeguard their other fundamental and natural liberties. Finally, in the absence of attempts to enforce a single faith, the Founders expected an even greater number and diversity of churches. In religion, as in politics, they thought that diversity would make tyranny less likely, and so they welcomed the prospect of the growth in the number of denominations. On top of these political benefits, of course, rested a firm belief that religion would be purified as its practice was freed from compulsion and hypocrisy.

So long as it was "universal, noninstitutional, and uncoerced" (Diggins 1984, 80), religion could contribute to good government by teaching men restraint and instilling in them a commitment to good works (see Tocqueville 1945, 1: chap. 17; 2: book 1, chap. 5). It was that kind of faith that was endorsed when, for example, Washington in his farewell address referred to the importance of religion to morality. In that sense, the Founders treated religion as a factor with the potential to stabilize republican government. Yet they remained aware that religion in a particular, institutional, and coerced form could do as much damage to the stability and reputation of republican government as any other source of social conflict (Cousins 1958, 67). That is why they attached so much importance to denying any religion a favored status.

At a minimum, the Founders did not want the national government to prefer any one religion or faith over another. Accommodationists have suggested that that is *all* they wanted or meant. In particular, it has been argued recently, the First Amendment to the Constitution was written only to prohibit the establishment of a *national* faith and governmental preference for one particular denomination (Malbin 1978; Curry 1986). In this view, nothing in the Constitution prohibits states from endorsing a particular faith or the national government from providing nondiscriminatory support for religion in general. In terms of the specific intentions operating at the time of the First Amendment, this narrow interpretation has much to commend it. Many states maintained a religious establishment and other forms of official recognition of religion at the time the Constitution was passed. Because these establishments were not challenged on legal grounds, it has been contended, the First Amendment must not have been intended to limit the states. Moreover, the Founders accepted a level of official recognition for religion far beyond what is tolerated today.

None of the Founders appeared to believe that government must ignore religious feeling in its official actions. Thinking that God's blessings would be important in the outcome of the revolutionary war, Washington ordered officers and soldiers in the Continental Army to maintain "punctual attendance" at worship services (Cousins 1958, 50). Samuel Adams, the least reluctant of the founding generation to limit religious expression, used his position as governor of Massachusetts to issue religious proclamations (ibid., 355–356); Washington did the same when he called for the first day of "thanksgiving" by the new nation (ibid., 71–72). Even Jefferson, who provided the famous (or infamous) interpretation of the First Amendment as building "a wall of separation" between church and state, had no objection to the use of municipal buildings for worship by the different congregations in his village (ibid., 163). Though he steadfastly recommended against paying for religious instruction at the state university he founded in Charlottesville, Jefferson advised the Virginia legislature to encourage the denominations to fund professorships of their own (ibid., 164). By accommodating the claims of different churches in this manner, he thought the university could counter the false impression that it stood "against all religion." James Madison, usually portrayed as the strictest separationist among the founding generation, also appears to have conceded religion an important public role (Weber 1982).

If one looks beyond the immediate circumstances of the adoption of the First Amendment, however, it becomes more difficult to sustain the very narrow interpretation of motives that some ascribe to the Founders. In a frontal assault upon the accommodationist interpretation, Leonard Levy (1986) contends that the Founders meant the First Amendment expressly to prohibit any form of government assistance to any and all churches. He points out that the colonial establishments deviated from the European pattern of a single official religious faith. When the First Amendment was framed, "all state establishments that existed in America were general or multiple establishments of all the churches of each state, something unknown in the Europe familiar to Americans" (ibid., 9). If "establishment" meant that all churches were eligible to be supported by tax revenue, as Levy argues, then the First Amendment's prohibition against establishment must be read as a separationist mandate against any government support for religion—even if that support is neutral vis-à-vis competing denominations.

Beyond the letter of the law, there is evidence for this position in the actions of several Founders. Although they conceded the continuation of establishment at the state level, Jefferson and Madison had made clear their opposition to official religion by waging a continuing battle for disestablishment of the Episcopal church in their native Virginia. Other members of the founding generation were involved in similar struggles throughout the states. It appears that Madison accepted limiting the disestablishment clause to the national government only as a way of strengthening support for the Constitution as a whole.

Just as important, some of the Founders appeared to have doubts about the very idea of governmental aid to religion, even if it were to be allocated on a nondiscriminatory basis by state governments. Washington objected on principle to a bill introduced in the Virginia legislature to pay religious teachers from tax revenue. Rather than rankle the consciences of dissenters and so "convulse the State" with religious conflict, he much preferred a scheme like Jefferson's compromise on religious instruction at the state university. In a letter to a political friend, Washington expressed himself as favoring the obligation of all religions—Christianity no less than Islam or Judaism—to pay for their own religious instruction (Cousins 1958, 64–65). "I wish an assessment had never been agitated," he wrote, "and . . . that the Bill could die an early death." Madison, the most relentless critic of public aid to religion, responded with vehemence the same year to a proposal in Congress that would set aside a section of the Northwest Territories to support the church favored by a majority of the inhabitants. He denounced the proposal as "unjust" and "hurtful," a bill "smelling so strongly of an antiquated Bigotry" that it would reduce international respect for the country" (ibid., 306–307). Although neither Washington nor Madison might have considered such proposals as unconstitutional under the terms of the First Amendment, they did declare them to be unwise.

The strongest evidence that the Founders did not favor even nondiscriminatory aid or noncoercive state recognition lay in their expressed sensitivity to the feelings of religious minorities. Their apparent awareness of how state recognition might injure the feelings of religious minorities can be interpreted to support preference for governmental aloofness to any religious expression, however bland and noncontroversial. A deeply religious man who served several terms as president of the American Bible Society, John Jay of New York objected to opening the sessions of the Continental Congress with a prayer. Citing the diversity of belief and custom among the delegates, he doubted that a prayer could be found that would not offend some member of the assembly. To the commander of a military expedition in Canada, General Washington stressed the need "to avoid all disrespect to or contempt of the religion of the country" (ibid., 49). More than just a tactic to neutralize the French-Canadian Catholics, Washington's statement reflected his belief that one nation seeking freedom of conscience should not infringe the same right of another. As president, Washington showed the same sympathy to the religious groups that suffered the brunt of exclusion under state laws of establishment. He told a general meeting of Quakers that he believed that "the conscientious scruples of all men should be treated with great delicacy and tenderness" and wrote to the Jewish community in Newport, Rhode Island, of his belief that religious freedom was a "natural right," not a mere "indulgence" of toleration to minority faiths that the majority could grant or withdraw at will (ibid., 60–61). Jefferson provided the clearest display of sensitivity to the implications of state recognition of religion when, as president, he was asked to proclaim a religious holiday (ibid., 136–137). Reluctant to assume an authority that was, if it existed at all, reserved for state governments, he refused to issue a watered-down proclamation encouraging national prayer with nothing more than the force of public opinion behind it. Challenging the proponent of such a plan, he asked: "Does the change in the nature of the penalty make the recommendation less a *law* of conduct for those to whom it is directed?" Jefferson doubted the Constitution gave the president "the authority to direct the religious exercises of his constituents" even if such "direction" was nothing more than bland verbal encouragement.

Given their sense that taking note of any denomination or even recognizing something as broad as Christianity might offend the sentiments of good citizens, it seems unlikely that the Founders would have approved what the Constitution may have permitted. Their approval of religious freedom extended to almost any form of faith that did no harm to the public good (ibid., 61). As political scientist Michael Malbin (1978) has emphasized, the leaders of the new government thought that the state should judge religions not by their beliefs but by the behavior those beliefs produced.[9] In his *Notes on the State of Virginia*, Jefferson made the point very clearly:

The legitimate powers of government extend to such acts only as are injurious to others. But it does me no injury for my neighbor to say there are twenty Gods, or no God. It neither picks my pocket nor breaks my leg. If it be said his testimony in a court of law cannot be relied on, reject it then, and be the stigma on him. Constraint may make him worse by making him a hypocrite, but it will never make him a truer man. It may fix him obstinately in his errors, but will not cure them. (Cousins 1958, 123)

The state had a just interest in religion, Madison concurred, only when faith impelled a believer to "disturb the peace, the happiness, or safety of Society" (ibid., 301). Even then, it was the actions, not beliefs, that constituted an offense. On this reading, the Founders appear to have been as eager to keep the state from limiting religious expression as they were to keep the government from promoting it.

The prevailing attitudes about church and state in the early Republic were reflected in the thoughts and actions of political leaders other than the major participants in the Constitutional Convention. A more complete sense of how early American political leaders understood the Constitution's religious policy can be gained through examination of an instructive controversy that began in the early years of the nineteenth century (Blakeley 1970). Since the founding of the nation, the government had always permitted the mail to be transported between communities on Sunday, the Christian Sabbath. In 1810, Congress enacted a law requiring post offices that received Sunday mail to stay open on that day and directing postmasters to make deliveries the same day they received shipments. Despite numerous protests from Christian organizations over defamation of the Lord's Day, Congress not only repeatedly refused requests to repeal the law but also extended it on several occasions. Early reports from the House committee with jurisdiction over the Post Office stressed that suspension of Sunday mail would impede the efficient performance of a major and legitimate government function. But as the protests mounted, the committee increasingly cited religious considerations as the basis for refusal to end Sunday delivery of posts.[10]

The language of a report issued in 1830 made the case for continued Sunday delivery in terms that would probably have pleased the founding generation. By acceding to requests to end mail delivery on Sunday, it was argued, Congress would effectively be granting official recognition to the Christian Sabbath. Withholding the mail on Sunday would force non-Christians to respect a holiday that they did not recognize in their hearts. In strong language, the House committee reminded the petitioners that the Constitution gave religious equality to all people by denying privileges to any—even if the faith in question was shared by the vast majority of the population. Echoing the fear of the Founders that even slight concessions to one faith might open up a wedge for greater government regulation in the future, they wrote that:

the conclusion is inevitable, that the line cannot be too strongly drawn between Church and State. If a solemn act of legislation shall, in *one* point, define the law of God, or point out to the citizen one religious duty, it may, with equal propriety, proceed to define *every* part of divine revelation; and enforce *every* religious obligation, even to the forms and ceremonies of worship; the endowment of the church, and the support of the clergy. (Committee on Post Offices and Post Roads 1830, 1)

Rather than coerce individuals by using the authority of government, the committee recommended that petitioners try to "instruct the public mind" on the evils of the practice that they condemned. If all men and women truly came to believe in the evil of Sunday mail, the practice would wither instantly; so long as people did not unanimously share the views enunciated by critics of Sunday mail, governmental intervention could only inflame religious passions.

Whatever their merits or demerits, the committee reports reveal a view of church-state relations that appears to have prevailed in the minds of early legislators. As the 1830 report emphasized, any governmental recognition of religion appeared to be forbidden under the First Amendment. Although this view was not unanimously accepted, as indicated by dissents from the 1830 report and by language in earlier committee documents, the ideas of the Founders were interpreted as supporting the "wall of separation" that Thomas Jefferson sought between the institutions of government and the churches.

The Wall of Separation Grows Higher

Despite the constant potential for controversy, neither the boundary problem nor the free-exercise concept excited much national attention in the first 150 years under the Constitution. Over that span, the controversy over Sunday delivery of mail was one of the few church-state items to engage Congress. At the state level, fierce battles were fought over proposals to drop establishment and to soften other forms of official support for religion. Although denominational competition and conflict remained important elements of political controversy, the constitutional status of religious institutions and belief was simply not a pressing item on the national agenda.

Church-state relations became a major topic of political discussion only in the 1940s, when the United States Supreme Court began to reinterpret the First Amendment's language on religion. During a period of reappraisal that stretched from the mid-1940s to approximately the mid-1970s, the Court provided a new legal framework that, although under serious challenge today, has since governed American practice about church-state relations.

During this era of judicial ferment, the Supreme Court departed from previous church-state doctrine in three important respects. First, it abandoned the traditional distinction between national and state action toward churches. Whatever the First Amendment forbade or required the national government to do about religion, it was now held by the Court, also applied to the state and local levels of government. Second, the Court attempted to fortify the boundary between church and state by broadening the list of government actions that constituted an impermissible establishment of religion. Formerly understood to forbid only actions that treated religious groups unequally, establishment was now seen to encompass many activities that appeared to favor religion in general. Last, the Court became much more sensitive to claims that government rules and regulations unconstitutionally interfered with the free exercise of religion. Before this period, the justices had tended to strike down only those practices that seemed to force individuals to endorse religious beliefs that might be contrary to their own. Now, however, they began to identify a wide range of actions that produced the same effect and either prohibited their enforcement or required government to exempt persons from certain practices on grounds of conscience.

As noted above, the First Amendment says only that *Congress* is forbidden to make laws about religious establishment or otherwise restrict religious exercise. In practice, the courts had interpreted that language as binding all agencies of the national government, those of the judicial and executive branches included, but leaving states free to support religion through their own constitutions. Many did, maintaining customs and practices that gave religion a favored legal standing. The different treatment of religion by nation and state was first rejected in principle by a 1940 Supreme Court decision; eight years later, a policy developed by an Illinois school board became the first state or local regulation actually struck down by the Supreme Court as being in conflict with the establishment clause in the Constitution. The Court has since applied its doctrine of church-state separation uniformly to all levels of government. In so doing, it did nothing to the religion clauses of the

First Amendment that it had not previously done to the rest of the Bill of Rights. By restricting states in the same way as the federal government, the Court treated religion as part and parcel of a national list of rights that all governmental institutions must respect.

The extension of the First Amendment to the states became so important because the Court widened its definition of what the Constitution had meant by "establishment." Most of the important cases in which this concern arose had to do with actions affecting public elementary and secondary schools. Because children are thought to be especially open to influence, Americans have been most sensitive to government's treatment of religion insofar as it affects the youngest members of society. That concern has been magnified because children are required by law to attend school, and most of them do so in educational institutions paid for by tax revenue. In such politically delicate circumstances, any apparent favoritism toward a creed can appear to constitute government endorsement of religion. Because attendance at institutions of higher learning represents a voluntary choice by more mature individuals who often bear a substantial part of the costs of schooling, the courts in general have allowed much greater latitude for proposals to assist religiously affiliated colleges and universities.

The progress of the Supreme Court's ideas was uneven, and the new doctrine about establishment did not unfold clearly from one case to the next. A pattern of fits and starts is common when the Court changes direction; it was especially marked in the "boundary" cases because the Court itself underwent changes in composition and because the problems of interpretation in the area were so very difficult.

In 1947 the Court decided a case that was to herald a flood of litigation about the modern meaning of First Amendment prohibitions "respecting an establishment of religion." In *Everson v. Board of Education*, the justices ruled that New Jersey could constitutionally compensate the parents of all children, including those attending religious schools, for the expenses of bus transportation to and from school. Defraying the cost the parents incurred for sending their children to religious schools, the Court held, did not involve an excessive degree of state support for religion. Even though this ruling appeared on the surface as a victory for advocates of government aid to religious education, the language of the majority opinion made it clear that breaches of the wall of separation would be tolerated only under the narrowest of circumstances. Consistent with that warning, in *McCollum v. Board of Education* (1948), the Court said that the school board in Champaign, Illinois, could not allow students in public schools to receive religious instruction on the premises even though attendance at such classes was voluntary and paid for privately. Opening up the school building to religious training while other classes were in session struck the Court as virtual endorsement of religion by the local government, an action that fell within the meaning of the establishment clause. But suppose that instead of inviting religious teachers to offer voluntary instruction in the school building, the state simply allowed students to travel off-campus for that purpose during the school day? In a 1952 decision, *Zorach v. Clausen*, the justices ruled that a New York City law releasing students from normal classes to attend religious classes somewhere else did not offend the establishment clause. This pattern of ruling first to permit some action, then to deny others, has persisted to the present day.

Rulings about how far the state could go in helping students receive religious training did not settle the issue of what the public schools could do about religious ideas. The two decisions that spoke clearly to that issue rank among the most unpopular rulings in the history of the Supreme Court. The 1962 case of *Engel v. Vitale* raised a challenge to the prayer that New York State required teachers to read at the beginning of the day. Because a government agency composed the prayer and insisted it be read as part of the daily routine, six justices declared that the New York practice illustrated precisely the type of action that the First Amendment forbids as an establishment of religion. A year later in *Abington Township School District v. Schempp*, the Court extended the ban on state-mandated religious ceremonies to cover a Pennsylvania law requiring the reading of Bible verses and recitation of the Lord's Prayer at the beginning of the school day. By these two decisions, the Court seemed to say that "establishment" included any celebration of religion conducted by an agency of the government.[11] Such actions have since been routinely struck down by courts across the land.

Once that precedent had been established, the focus of debate over the church-state boundary in education shifted back to government action vis-à-vis religious schools. In a 1968 case, *Board of Education v. Allen*, the Court decided that New York State could lend parochial school students the same textbooks provided free of charge to students in the public schools without violating the First Amendment. The *Allen* decision, which appeared to open the door to several different types of state support for church-related schools, inspired legislatures throughout the country to funnel various forms of aid to parochial schools. As these laws were challenged and the cases eventually made their way through the appeals process to the Supreme Court, it became clear that the justices viewed the provision of textbooks, like reimbursement for bus transportation, as one of very few ways that government could legitimately assist schools that taught religious faith. In a string of cases decided during the 1970s, the Court ruled that the boundary was violated if states contributed to the salary of parochial school teachers to cover their "nonreligious" responsibilities (*Lemon v. Kurtzman*, 1971), allowed church schools to finance the upkeep of their buildings with tax money (*Committee for Public Education v. Nyquist*, 1973), reimbursed parents for the costs of private school tuition (same case), paid religious schools for the cost of educational testing required by state law (*Levitt v. Committee for Public Education*, 1973), or lent instructional materials other than textbooks to schools supported by religious institutions (*Meek v. Pittenger*, 1975). The justices appeared to relent a bit when, in *Wolman v. Walter* (1977), they held that the state of Ohio was allowed to defray parochial schools' expenses incurred in conducting diagnostic and therapeutic services and in purchasing textbooks and some standardized test material. But the Court invalidated those parts of the law authorizing the state to help pay church-related schools for field trips, some instructional materials, and equipment. Continuing the restrictive trend in two 1985 decisions (*Grand Rapids v. Ball*; *Aguilar v. Fenton*), the Court forbade public funding of even part-time or remedial teaching in religious schools.

For a judicial system that puts a high value on clarity, consistency, and tradition, the record in the establishment cases does not reveal many of those qualities. Part of the difficulty in this regard stemmed from the division of the Court into factions with different interpretations of the meaning of the First Amendment's language (Pritchett 1984, 158). Because these groupings were fluid and relatively evenly balanced, changes in circumstances from one case to another could swing enough votes to produce apparent contradictions between decisions. Over time, however, the Court moved closer to a common set of standards for determining if certain activities undermined the Constitution by establishing religion. Stated most fully by Chief Justice Warren

Burger in the 1971 *Lemon* decision (cited in Pfeffer 1977, 30), the Court's standard required that a law must pass three tests before it could be deemed compatible with the antiestablishment language of the First Amendment: a primarily secular purpose, primarily secular consequences, and no excessive entanglement of church and state.

To pass the first test, a law's major purpose must be to further some secular mission of government. Though it may touch on religion in so doing, that cannot be its principal intention. Thus, compensation for bus transportation was valid because New Jersey wanted *primarily* to get all children safely to and from school—a perfectly reasonable state policy not connected to religion. Because of this legitimate secular purpose, the law was acceptable even though it indirectly helped religious schools by marginally reducing the transportation costs that would otherwise have been borne by the parents. In contrast, an Arkansas law that prohibited the teaching of evolution in public schools had no discernible purpose except to give legal support to a tenet of the religious faith predominant in the state and hence was voided by the Court (*Epperson v. Arkansas*, 1968). On similar grounds, the Court in 1987 rejected a Louisiana law that mandated the religiously inspired theory of divine origin alongside evolution (*Edwards v. Aguillard*).

The second test set up by the Court applies the same standard of secularity to primary *effects*. Because lending textbooks to all students, in private and public schools alike, would principally expand knowledge in secular subjects, New York was authorized to keep its law on distribution. As long as the undeniable benefit to religion was not the principal outcome of the legislation, the law fell within the Supreme Court's view of legitimate public policy. But the New York law that permitted parents to receive tax credits for private school tuition had the primary effect of supporting instruction for religious purposes. Children would certainly benefit from attending schools with greater resources, but that was not deemed to be the primary consequence of the state law. Hence the tuition tax credit was rejected for breaching the boundary.

Even if a law is deemed principally nonreligious in purpose and result, it must still satisfy the requirement that it does not "excessively entangle" the church and government. That means a law should neither bring the government too deeply into the affairs of religion nor encourage religious groups to enter the political process as religious groups. The first type of entanglement was cited when the Court ruled that paying parochial school teachers for secular instruction imposed on government a responsibility to see that the teachers did not let their religious values intrude on that portion of their work supported by tax revenue. To enforce such a provision, the justices decided, the government would have to monitor teaching in church schools and so involve itself deeply in matters best left free from state action. The other entanglement the Court wanted to avoid was the encouragement of continuous political activism by churches as corporate bodies. If local school boards had the discretion to give certain types of assistance to private religious schools, the justices thought, school board elections would inevitably become transformed into conflicts between churches and candidates would be judged primarily by their religious affiliations.[12] Acknowledging that church members could and should get involved in politics as individuals, the Court sought to discourage the evolution of churches into political parties.

What kind of state action could survive scrutiny on this entanglement rule? The Court pointed with approval to a New York law that exempted churches and church-related institutions from property tax. In *Walz v. Tax Commission of New York* (1971), it upheld the state's decision to keep religious property and the holdings of other nonprofit institutions off the tax rolls. Reasoning that taxation of churches would require local governments to assign a monetary value to church property and might even lead the state to put liens on the property or foreclose if taxes were not paid, the Court preferred exemption as much the lesser evil. Once certified as a nonprofit institution, exempt from the taxing authority of government, the church would be relatively free from the excessive entanglement that threatened the wall of separation. For that reason, among others, the Court's majority sustained tax exemption for property held by religious bodies. So, "entanglement" prohibited programs that might enable the church to draw on the resources of the government, as in the case of salary supplements for parochial school teachers, or policies of taxation that gave government potential power to interfere with the mission of religious bodies. Whatever the effect, too much intermingling of church and state made government action unconstitutional.

The *Lemon* test did not shield churches from any sort of contact with the state. Early in 1990, the Supreme Court upheld California's right to tax sales of religious material by a televised ministry. In *Swaggart Min-*

istries v. Board of Equalization, the Court concluded that the general sales tax had an undeniable secular purpose—raising revenues—and no significant effect on religion. Even though the tax satisfied the first two prongs of the *Lemon* standard, the ministry argued that it "excessively entangled" church with state because of the administrative burden of complying with the law and possibility of a state audit of its records. The Court rejected the entanglement claim principally because the California tax did "not require the State to inquire into the religious content of the items sold or the religious motivation for selling or purchasing the items." This suggests that governments have the right to tax or to exempt religion so long as churches are treated the same way as other organizations.

Under the Court's three-part rule, statutes involving religion were presumed to violate the establishment clause unless they could be shown to meet all three requirements. Challengers had to demonstrate only one failing for the law to be declared invalid. With such a demanding set of conditions, it is hardly surprising that the advocates of a high wall of separation won most of the critical Supreme Court cases and generally succeeded in church-state litigation when cases were decided by lower courts (see Sorauf 1976). If the Court nonetheless appeared indecisive in accepting some actions and rejecting others, that probably reflected the inherent difficulty of applying these rules to specific cases.

Nowhere was the tyranny of circumstances more evident than in several cases involving government sponsorship of religious symbols. In the 1984 case of *Lynch v. Donnelly,* a divided Court ruled that the city of Pawtucket, Rhode Island, could constitutionally erect a Christmas nativity display without violating the establishment clause. Acknowledging the Christian origin of the crèche, the Court nonetheless found that it was a "passive" endorsement of religion. Placed among holiday symbols such as Christmas trees, carolers, candy-striped poles, and a Santa Claus sleigh pulled by reindeer, the crèche was adjudged to be primarily a cultural and historical symbol, part of a legitimate government effort to engender "a friendly community spirit of good will in keeping with the season" (Miller and Flowers 1987, 363). Five years later, in *Allegheny v. ACLU,* the Court followed this somewhat tortuous logic by upholding the constitutionality of a large Chanukah menorah placed outside one government building in Pittsburgh while simultaneously ruling against a Christmas crèche displayed on a staircase in a nearby courthouse. The menorah was acceptable, despite its religious significance in Judaism, because it was deemed to include cultural and historical references and because it was placed among other holiday symbols. By standing alone as an unadorned symbol of Christianity, a seeming endorsement of a particular faith, the crèche ran afoul of the establishment clause. Unsure about how many other holiday symbols would be necessary to denude the crèche of its religious symbolism, Pittsburgh officials decided to leave it in storage during the next holiday season rather than risk the censure of what one legal scholar cuttingly described as "those interior decorators" on the Supreme Court.[13]

Critics have argued that the Court could have avoided the problem altogether by either leaving alone the tradition that granted states substantial freedom in promoting religion or, failing that, accepting the judgment of democratically elected legislatures about what "establishment" means to modern public opinion. To supporters of the courts' understanding of the "wall of separation," however, the states had brought the problems on themselves by failing to heed clear signals to restrict their support for religion.

Extending Free-Exercise Claims

Even as it was broadening the meaning of "establishment" and thus restricting the scope of state action to encourage religion, the Supreme Court was growing markedly more receptive to individuals who challenged governmental actions as barriers to the practice of their faith. The same justices who demonstrated a concern to protect individuals from unwanted religious influences emanating from the government also showed a willingness to defend worship and other forms of religious activity from interference on the part of public authorities. The Court's concern was particularly likely to surface in cases where the faith was unconventional and the restrictive government regulation may have reflected hostility to the minority religion by better-established religious groups.

The Court's initial concern in this regard was to ensure that religious groups enjoyed full freedom to practice their faith and to undertake activities related to it. For religions outside the mainstream, such as the Jehovah's Witnesses and Seventh-Day Adventists, the practice of religion involved public activities that might run afoul of local and state ordinances regulating access to public facilities or limiting door-to-door soliciting. Given its propensity to support speech and other forms of public expression about political ideas, the Court had little difficulty offering the same support to religious ideas.

As Pritchett has noted (1984, 133–134), many of the critical decisions in this area asserted that religious minorities should enjoy the same basic freedoms extended to unpopular political movements and causes. As early as 1938, the Court cited freedom of the press in allowing Jehovah's Witnesses to sell literature door-to-door without first having to obtain a municipal permit. The same rationale was cited in a 1943 ruling that exempted Jehovah's Witnesses from a Pennsylvania municipal license fee required of all door-to-door commercial solicitors. The free-speech clause of the First Amendment provided the basis for a 1948 decision upholding the right of a preacher from the same sect to broadcast his sermons in a public park. In a Maryland case decided in 1951, the justices overturned the conviction of some Witnesses who had preached in a public park in defiance of municipal ordinances prohibiting such activity. Noting that the ordinance was enforced against the Witnesses but had not been used when mainstream religious groups held prayer services in the same location, the Court decided that the law was enforced unequally—a violation of the Fourteenth Amendment's requirement that all must enjoy the equal protection of the laws.

The Supreme Court also moved to defend religious freedom by explicit reference to the free-exercise clause. The majority opinion in *Cantwell v. Connecticut* (1940) was the first to enshrine the principle of free exercise on its own terms and became a powerful precedent. The case arose when three ministers from Jehovah's Witnesses were convicted of several offenses against municipal ordinances in New Haven, Connecticut. The key conviction of soliciting without a license was overturned on the grounds that the law unconstitutionally allowed the state government to determine if the ministers' actions were motivated by genuinely religious convictions. For the government to screen religions in this manner, Justice Robert Jackson wrote, would "lay a forbidden burden upon the exercise of [religious] liberty protected by the Constitution" (cited in Pfeffer 1977, 137). In subsequent cases, the Court struck down a number of laws, regulations, ordinances and administrative practices for interfering with religious exercise or preaching.

Even when respect for free-exercise rights might prove burdensome in some way, the Supreme Court generally insisted they take precedence. For example, prison authorities have been required to extend a number of privileges to inmates who practice Muslim, Buddhist, and Native American religions.

Worship and preaching clearly fall under the scope of free exercise. But what happens when the exercise of religion appears to be inconsistent with an obligation that government imposes on citizens? In dealing with this type of free-exercise question, the Court has distinguished between government-mandated expressions of political sentiment, which have usually been invalidated, and government-mandated action, which generally have been judged acceptable under the Constitution.

At first, the Court sided with the state in compelling certain expressions of political sentiment even when they violated religious belief. In *Minersville School District v. Gobitis* (1940), a controversial decision that unleashed violence in several states, the Supreme Court backed a Pennsylvania school board that had expelled two young members of the Jehovah's Witnesses for refusing to salute the flag in a public school ceremony (Manwaring 1962). In its opinion, the Supreme Court recognized that the children were sincere in their belief that saluting the flag was akin to worshipping a "graven image," a practice apparently forbidden by a literal reading of some passages in the Book of Exodus (20:4–5). Yet, the majority argued, government had an overriding interest in promoting patriotism and national unity, for liberty was not possible without a strong sense of national community. As the flag symbolized the nation, government could legitimately insist that it be honored by schoolchildren.

Just three years later, in what must be close to a record turnaround, the Supreme Court overturned the *Gobitis* decision. Inspired by the ruling on behalf of Pennsylvania and by the wartime atmosphere of intense patriotic sentiment, West Virginia's Board of Education had demanded that public school students salute the American flag or face punishment for insubordination. Members of the Jehovah's Witnesses had sued on the grounds that salutes conflicted with the biblical injunction. In terms of issues and combatants, therefore, the case of *West Virginia State Board of Education v. Barnette* was identical to *Gobitis*. This time, however, the Supreme Court sided with the Witnesses against the state, arguing that the regulation unconstitutionally enforced belief rather than conduct.

The flag was a symbol of state, comparable to the banner of a fraternal organization or the cross of a church, and the salute meant nothing more than a gesture of respect. As such, it was an expression of opinion that could not be forced on a person who was unwilling, for any reason, to endorse the sentiment. As the majority opinion stated, the constitutional provision that "guards the individual's right to speak his own mind" did not give government the authority "to compel him to utter what is not in his mind" (cited in Pfeffer 1977, 130). Ever since that landmark decision, the courts have generally supported religious minorities seeking the protection of the First Amendment against different types of required patriotic expression, such as reciting the "Pledge of Allegiance" or standing during the national anthem. In 1977, to take one of the most recent cases of this type, the Court supported New Hampshire residents who had taped over the "Live Free or Die" slogan on their license plates as inconsistent with their faith.

The Court has been slower to free religious groups from laws alleged to impose behavior repugnant to religious scruples. Even though the Court has not sided consistently with such claims, it has moved away from the traditional presumption that the needs or purposes of government must take precedence over conscience. Under that presumption, for example, the Supreme Court ruled in the 1934 case of *Hamilton v. Regents of the University of California* that a state was entitled to require military training for able-bodied male students enrolled at state universities. In that case, the paramount need for military preparedness was seen as taking precedence over religiously grounded objections to participation in military activity. In time, the presumption was relaxed, if not discarded, as the Court insisted that government must have a very strong reason to force people to act against religious conscience. Unless the government could show that exemption would do severe damage to some important national or state function, the Court insisted that "free exercise" of conscience had priority. In the words of a 1972 opinion, assigning a "preferred position" to the First Amendment rights meant that "only those interests of the highest order not otherwise served can overbalance legitimate claims to the free exercise of religion" (Pfeffer 1977, 35).

In decisions handed down in several cases involving national security and loyalty, the Court explicitly recognized motives as a basis for principled dissent and limited forms of disobedience. In 1943 a Seventh-

Day Adventist from Canada was refused American citizenship because he said religious beliefs would prevent him from taking up arms to defend the United States. Like other members of his faith who had served as noncombatants in the military and contributed in nonviolent ways to the war effort, the applicant was willing to support the nation by other means. Hence, Justice William O. Douglas argued for the majority in *Girouard v. United States* (1946), any attempt to demand the willingness to fight as a condition for citizenship contravened religious scruples for no good purpose. The right to seek noncombatant status, which Congress had granted to persons with religious scruples, was upheld when the Court ordered a draft board to grant conscientious-objector status to a member of Jehovah's Witnesses (*Sicurella v. U.S.*, 1955). The types of religious scruples protected under the free-exercise clause were enlarged by the Court's 1965 decision in *United States v. Seeger.* In this and related cases, it ordered local draft boards to treat applications for conscientious-objector status with the same respect whether the individual cited nontraditional forms of belief in a Supreme Being or orthodox ideas of God as the basis for exemption.

Considering that the Court recognized the primacy of faith in so sensitive an area as national security, it is not surprising that rules conflicting with faith were challenged successfully in several other areas. In *Wisconsin v. Yoder* (1972), the Court upheld the right of Amish parents to keep their children out of public school after the age of fourteen. As the state could not convince the justices that an additional year or two of schooling was critical for any social purpose, the Court was more impressed by Amish fears that exposure to additional secular instruction might undermine the children's commitment to their community's values. Similar rulings upheld religious belief as a warrant for refusing jury duty and prohibited state governments from denying unemployment benefits to persons whose religious beliefs against work on Saturday kept them out of a job. As recently as 1989, the Court demanded that Illinois pay unemployment compensation to a man who, though belonging to no church, nonetheless refused on "Christian" grounds to take a job that required him to work on Sunday. By decisions such as these, free exercise has been extended to support mandatory exemption from a variety of obligations imposed on American citizens.

As noted above, the Court defined "free exercise" for individuals both as religious activity and as conscientious objection to selected government policies. But the Court also moved more aggressively to extend to churches as collective institutions "a right to be left alone by government so that they may freely exercise religion" (Laycock 1986, 37). The doctrine emerged slowly from a variety of specific decisions. As much as possible, the Court took itself out of the business of resolving internal church disputes over property, recommending that the judiciary generally defer to the decision of the supreme authority in the church. The Court has also upheld the right of churches to impose religious requirements on employees of its "nonreligious" enterprises. The churches have been shielded from lawsuits alleging malpractice by members of the clergy and given protection against outside attempts to monitor church political activity. Although advocates of this third type of free exercise worry about government "intrusion" in several realms, the trend since the 1940s has been toward greater autonomy.

Despite this general trend toward expanding the list of state actions that unconstitutionally interfere with the free exercise of religion, the Court from time to time has permitted some limitations. Recognizing the state's interest in protecting public health and safety, the Court has approved compulsory vaccination and other medical procedures, especially those involving children, and permitted government to ban religious practices that might endanger the participants. (Such precedents suggest that the Faith Assembly members in the Indiana cases mentioned earlier would not find the Court very receptive to their pleas.) The Supreme Court has also upheld the constitutionality of the so-called blue laws, state statutes that compel businesses to close on Sunday. Originally passed as part of the Protestant campaign to give legal support to the Sabbath—clearly a religious purpose—they were upheld by the Court because they had become a species of welfare legislation, serving the interests of public safety and employee health by stopping business activity on one day of the week. Over the protests of some Orthodox Jewish merchants, for whom the law meant another day of shutdown after the Jewish Sabbath, the Court adjudged the laws reasonable and saw no alternative to achieve a valid public purpose. Similarly, the Court has declared that employers need only make a reasonable effort to accommodate the religious beliefs of their workers; there is no legal obligation to incur financial hardship.

Over time, the Supreme Court has developed a two-part test to evaluate free-exercise claims that resembles the standard it has used in judging cases involving the establishment clause (Miller and Flowers 1987, 59). When confronted with charges that a secular law or custom unconstitutionally limits the right of free exercise, the Supreme Court asks if the policy places a burden on the exercise of religion by individuals or groups. If so, the government, first, must demonstrate that it has a compelling interest in the law or policy and, second, that its goal cannot be achieved without hindering religious observance. The spirit of this standard was illustrated in a recent lower court ruling in a free-exercise case. On safety grounds, a local school board prohibited an Orthodox Jewish student from wearing a *yarmulke* (skull cap) while playing basketball for his school. The Court accepted the student's argument that forcing him to remove the yarmulke during games constituted interference with the right of free exercise. Yet it also acknowledged the school board claim that the skull cap might be dislodged during play, potentially causing another player to slip and fall. Rather than side with the government, however, the Court asked if player safety could not be achieved by allowing the student to affix the skull cap firmly to his head with an elastic band that would fasten under the chin. The presumption of this test normally places a burden of proof on the government, which must demonstrate that it cannot find an acceptable alternative that leaves persons free to exercise their faith.

The Court's tendency to support religious objections to secular law has inspired a substantial growth in the filing of such cases and a dramatic increase in the success of such suits. A recent study by Way and Burt (1983) illustrated the magnitude of the trend away from the presumption favoring government. During the first decade covered by their study, 1946–1956, the state and federal courts decided thirty-four cases in which minority religions—groups outside the Protestant, Catholic, and Jewish families—claimed free-exercise rights. Although the courts sustained the claims in only 20 percent of the cases, the significance of the decisions apparently stimulated more litigation. Between 1970 and 1980, the number of such cases more than quadrupled to 145. Over that period "marginal" religious groups won slightly more than half of the cases they brought; in contrast, victories resulted in only about one-third of the lawsuits involving mainstream religions. The minority religious groups were more likely to succeed in legal challenges to laws or practices that limited efforts to spread the faith and in suits brought to extend rights of practice to prisoners. They broke even in cases related to employment and taxation and lost more attempts to gain exemptions from secular laws governing schools or to refuse medical care for minors.

Thanks to almost forty years of intense judicial activity, both the free-exercise and establishment clause of the First Amendment have taken on new and broader meanings. In the process, the actions of the courts raised new issues and fueled compelling debates about the place of religion in American society.

The Politics of Church-State Relations

In the majesty of their surroundings and the dignity of their procedures, the courts often appear isolated from the normal processes of political conflict. Despite the exalted image of the judiciary, its behavior is permeated by the same types of political influences that affect other arenas of government. Any discussion of church-state relationships must, therefore, take account of the larger political context in which the judicial decisions are made. An investigation of the politics of church-state interaction is necessary to understand why the issue became so important when it did, how the religious community reacted to the crucial court decisions, and whether or not a restoration of the pre–World War II legal framework is likely.

The Supreme Court's radical transformation of church-state doctrine from the 1940s through the 1970s did not occur in isolation. As noted above, one source of revision was the general tendency of the justices to extend the First Amendment to cover the actions of state and local governments. In that sense, the new limitations on government action toward religion were a by-product of a broader tendency to "nationalize" the Bill of Rights. But beyond this general shift in the constitutional interpretation, another factor was involved in the Court's specific rulings about religion. As is often the case in political and legal change, the consciousness of the Court was shaped by intensive grass-roots political activity that raised the church-state issue to a high place on the national agenda (Morgan 1968; Sorauf 1976). Throughout the era of judicial activism on the church-state question, the churches, allied groups of laypeople and interfaith organizations functioned much like classic interest groups—designing legislation, raising public support in well-orchestrated campaigns for public opinion, lobbying legislatures and courts, bringing and defending lawsuits. This description fits both the coalition that supported state aid to religious schools and those who sought to defend Jefferson's "wall of separation" from state aid to church-affiliated education.

Many of the state aid laws evaluated by the Supreme Court in the decades after World War II were inspired by religious groups as a means of supporting church-affiliated schools, whose financial health had been seriously impaired by a combination of social changes. As most of these schools were Roman Catholic, the principal groups defending aid to parochial schools were Catholic organizations, such as the Education Division of the United States Catholic Conference, the National Catholic Educational Association, the Catholic League for Religious and Civil Rights, and the Knights of Columbus. They were joined by several organizations representing non-Catholic private schools: Citizens for Educational Freedom, the National Association for Hebrew Day Schools, the National Jewish Commission on Law and Public Affairs, and others. Ranged on the other side were liberal Protestant groups in the National Council of Churches, those conservative Christian denominations that feared state aid as the opening wedge in a government drive to take over the schools (e.g., the Baptist Joint Committee on Public Affairs), secular groups such as the American Civil Liberties Union and the American Association of Humanists, and the major umbrella organizations for the American Jewish community. As should be evident from the diversity of these coalitions, the conflicts involved cannot be reduced simply to proreligion versus antireligion or to a simple Christian versus anti-Christian dimension. Although some of the opponents of state aid were motivated by hostility to Catholicism in particular or to religion in general, the debate also split many religious communities internally.

Even though most of the constitutional battles were won by groups that opposed state aid, the Court's decisions limiting government support and restricting religious observance in the schools inspired much discontent. Public opinion polls have consistently revealed that a clear majority of Americans—possibly as many as two-thirds of the population—favors some sort of organized prayer in public schools. The apparent public support for restoration of school prayer has made it politically appealing to challenge the *Engel* and *Schempp* rulings. When Court rulings strike an exposed nerve, those most affected will sometimes attempt to get around them by interpreting the decision narrowly, by evading them, or, those options having failed, by trying to override the Court by changing the Constitution. In the case of the school prayer decisions, critics of the Court rulings tried each of these strategies.

As an example of the first strategy, the courts were besieged with new state laws attempting to alter this or that feature of a school prayer policy that had previously been struck down. The hope—which had been rewarded in some other types of cases—was that the courts might relent, allowing some variant of state-supported prayer to stand as law. However, the Court consistently ruled against the constitutionality of governmental efforts to celebrate religion in public schools. Undaunted, supporters of religious observance then tried to undermine the prayer decisions with "silent meditation" laws. Passed by more than half the states, these statutes typically provided for a moment of silence or meditation during the school day. Challenges to these procedures as attempts to sneak in organized prayer by the back door were sustained by some lower courts but dismissed by others. The Supreme Court subsequently ended most doubts about the constitutionality of this newest form of school prayer law when it struck down Alabama's silent meditation statute in *Wallace v. Jaffree* (1985).

Rather than petition the courts for an allowable practice short of organized prayer, some authorities attempted to evade the rulings. Because control over school religious practices effectively rests with thousands of local school districts and tens of thousands of classroom teachers, the prayer and Bible-reading decisions offered greater-than-normal opportunities for noncompliance. In a study of Tennessee reactions to the Court's prohibition of Bible reading, Robert Birkby (1966) discovered that all but one school district had allowed the forbidden practice to continue. At the advice of the state superintendent of education, most districts simply revised their policies to leave the question of religious ceremonies in the classroom to the discretion of the teacher. Even though the Court had ruled that voluntary religious activity was no more constitutional than coerced worship, local school boards adopted it unless they were faced with legal challenges. Similar patterns of widespread local evasion were apparent following the *Schempp* decision on Bible reading, as well as earlier Supreme Court decisions restricting religion in the public schools (Patric 1957; Katz 1965; Sorauf 1959).

The widespread adoption of the teacher discretion policy throughout the United States did not prevent a substantial decline in formal religious observance in the classroom. A nationwide survey of public school teachers during the 1964–1965 school year found that the incidence of morning prayers declined from 60 percent before the *Engel* decision to 28 percent after, and that Bible reading, a regular practice in the classrooms of 48 percent of the teachers before *Schempp*, survived in only 22 percent after the case was decided (Way 1968, 191; see also Dierenfeld 1967). Reported compliance was lowest in the southern states, where nearly three-fifths of the teachers continued reading the Bible and just under two-thirds maintained the practice of morning prayers. Twenty years later, noncompliance was still widespread in those parts of the country where evangelical Protestantism is strongest.[14] Studies of compliance patterns in local communities by Muir (1967), Johnson (1967), and Dolbeare and Hammond (1977) have suggested that the degree of conformity to the Court's will depended on a variety of factors—the religious composition of the area, the prestige of the Supreme Court, the willingness of individuals to demand implementation, and the position taken by political elites. Depending on the mix of circumstances in the local environment, the Court decisions were either implemented in full, accepted in a half-hearted manner, or treated as a dead letter.

Other critics have mounted a frontal attack on the Court's rulings, without much success. The favorite instrument, a constitutional amendment to overturn *Engel* and *Schempp*, has failed repeatedly to obtain the required two-thirds majority in the House and Senate. (Unless they receive that extraordinary majority in both houses of Congress, amendments cannot be submitted to the states for approval.) In 1984, President Ronald Reagan supported an amendment to permit vocal prayer by individuals or groups in public institutions, schools included.[15] Although the amendment was supported by fifty-six senators, it still fell eleven votes short of the required sixty-seven needed for further action. The diversity of both the support for and the opposition against the proposal underlines how such church-state issues split normal coalitions in American politics. Supporters of the proposed amendment included liberals and conservatives (e.g., Sen. William Proxmire of Wisconsin and Sen. Jesse Helms of North Carolina), Jews and Mormons (Sen. Edward Zorinsky of Nebraska and Orrin Hatch of Utah), and representatives of both the mainline and evangelical wings of Protestantism. The forty-four Senate opponents of organized school prayer included some of the most conservative members of that body (Barry Goldwater of Arizona), its only clergyman (John Danforth of Missouri, an ordained Episcopal priest), and one of its most prominent evangelical spokesmen (Mark Hatfield of Oregon). With the subsequent replacement of several supporters of the prayer amendment by opponents of the measure, the prospects for amending the Constitution to overturn the prayer decisions now seem remote.[16]

The failure to capitalize on such a strong public mood favoring the return of school prayer has been ascribed to several factors. Although the polls indicated support for overturning the Court decisions, the level of support may not have been intense enough to prompt legislative action. Unless legislators judge that public sentiment is very deeply engaged over an issue, they may not respond even when polls show majority approval. The advocates of school prayer have been put at a further disadvantage by the fact that citizens who support such legislation have tended to be less educated and less affluent than supporters of the current policy (Elifson and Hadaway 1985). Accordingly, those seeking to overturn the restrictive policy on religious observance in the schools must rely on a constituency that has relatively few political resources. Moreover, the church organizations that might be expected to lead the effort have divided over the wisdom of challenging school prayer restrictions.

Although efforts to bring organized prayer back into the classroom have not gained much ground, Congress did give tangible support to religious observance by passing in 1984 an "equal access" law. Under its provisions, high schools that allow noncurricular student groups to meet on campus before or after classes must extend the same privileges to students who want to form religious associations. This apparent concession to the advocates of school prayer, passed shortly after the Reagan prayer amendment was defeated, was qualified in several respects. For one thing, it applies only to high school students, whereas many prayer advocates regard elementary school students as especially in need of moral guidance. Also, in recognition of the Court's insistence on governmental neutrality, the law stipulates that no teachers or other school personnel may participate actively or supervise worship. Even more significantly, the equal access law appears to give administrators several openings for evasion. By prohibiting the government from denying or withholding education funds from noncomplying school districts, Congress reduced the incentive for compliance. Furthermore, the requirement that religious groups enjoy the same access to facilities as other noncurricular groups may have undermined the law's intent by giving school boards a basis to refuse facilities to all groups. Largely on free-speech grounds, the Supreme Court upheld the constitutionality of the equal access law in 1990.

A Constitutional Counterrevolution?

Advocates of accommodation—the doctrine that smiles on general government support for religion—never approved the Supreme Court's post–World War II movement toward separationism. To these critics, the Court disregarded both the intentions of the Founders and the predominant body of constitutional interpretation by interfering with state actions and broadening the meaning of "establishment" (Cord 1982; Howe 1965; Morgan 1984). Court decisions—especially those limiting state aid to parochial schools—have also been denounced for their allegedly adverse policy consequences. Isolating the churches behind a wall of separation, it is charged, prevents the state from cooperating with institutions that could advance the quality of national education (Berger and Neuhaus 1977). By issuing decisions that fly in the face of public support for religion, it has also been claimed, the Court diminishes the public esteem for the rule of law and reduces the likelihood of compliance with its rulings. (Note that these are precisely the consequences that Madison cited to argue against establishment.) These arguments received strong support from key members of the Reagan administration.

Defenders of the Supreme Court's postwar church-state rulings have offered several responses, ranging from an insistence that the Court has correctly read the Constitution to the argument that the interpretation of ambiguous phrases such as "establishment" and "free exercise" must be allowed to evolve with changing social conditions and religious diversity (Fey 1963; Gordon 1963; Pfeffer 1967). The Court's defenders have also made use of public opinion polls to dispute the claim that religious rulings have undercut public support for the judiciary. Although the public appears to disagree with a number of Court rulings (see Figure 5.2), studies have suggested only a modest spillover onto the general image of the Court (Kessel 1966; Dolbeare 1967; Caldeira and Gibson 1989). The most useful information was uncovered in a 1966 poll of voting-age American citizens (Murphy, Tanenhaus, and Kastner 1973). Of nearly 1,300 persons surveyed in the study, only about 500 made any responses when asked if there was something they liked or disliked about the recent work of the Supreme Court. If less than 40 percent of the sample felt the need to volunteer any praise or condemnation of the Court just four years after the first decision on school observance, the salience of the issue for the general public must be questioned. It is not clear what to make of the further finding that the school prayer and Bible-reading decisions were the source of 30 percent of the actions that displeased respondents. On the one hand, the fact that no other set of decisions accounted for more criticism suggests that the issue was relatively important. On the other, 70 percent of the critical remarks were directed to different issues. It should also be kept in mind that unhappiness with the Court's religious rulings may have been part and parcel of more general displeasure with the Court's liberal orientation on questions of civil rights, prisoner rights, reapportionment, and other policy areas. To the extent public opinion polls can gauge such matters, the broadening of the establishment clause was not the object of widespread enthusiasm, particularly insofar as it prohibited religious observance as an official part of the school day; but the hostility it engendered should not be overstated, either.

Ever since Richard Nixon assumed the presidency in 1969, inaugurating a long period of Republican dominance, Court watchers have waited for a return to traditional understandings of the religion clauses. More than twenty years later, they are still waiting. Without doubt, recent Supreme Court decisions have substantially qualified some of the pioneering doctrines first advanced in the 1940s and 1950s. The Court now seems disposed to permit more state action on behalf of religion—as when it upheld Pawtucket, Rhode Island's Christmas crèche in *Lynch v. Donnelly*—and to give less support to individuals who cite conscience as the basis for exemption from secular law. That trend was exhibited in 1990 when the Court upheld Oregon's right to deny unemployment compensation to members of the Native American church who were fired for using an illegal drug in religious ceremonies.

Yet for every decision said to herald a return to accommodation, it is possible to identify other recent cases which reaffirmed separationism.

On establishment grounds, the Court struck down state practices of posting the Ten Commandments on classroom walls (*Stone v. Graham,* 1980), printing a "motorists' prayer" on state maps (*Bradshaw v. Hall,* 1981), and extending veto power over liquor licenses to churches close to the site of the application (*Larkin v. Grendel's Den,* 1982). On the issue of religious observance in the public schools, the Court sustained lower court decisions prohibiting voluntary organized prayer (*Treen v. Karen B.,* 1982) or prayers before high school sporting events (*Jager v. Douglas County Board of Education,* 1989), and struck down Alabama's attempt to achieve the same purpose through a "moment of silence" law (*Wallace v. Jaffree,* 1985). The justices have also refused to grant religious organizations blanket exemptions from minimum wage and tax laws. And if the Court has slackened in its support for marginal religions, recall a series of other rulings that mandated unemployment insurance for workers who refused jobs or assignments out of religious convictions. The same Court that refused a claim by Native Americans that social security numbers robbed them of their spirits agreed to let the Amish in Minnesota forgo the use of reflectorized triangles on their vehicles because the safety devices expressed greater confidence in the devices of humans than God.

Separationists, accommodationists, and strict neutralists can each find recent decisions that appear to sustain their favored doctrines. That suggests a Court with no fixed principles on establishment and free exercise, responding to cases depending on local circumstances or its own judgments about what is the most reasonable course of action (Shapiro 1990).

As this litany of Supreme Court cases has demonstrated, conflict between church and state may arise under a variety of circumstances. My clipping file bulges with news reports of incidents that will probably never make it to a high appellate court: debates about the legal status of information disclosed to clergy during counseling sessions, a church's request for exemption from a proposed historic preservation district, the conviction of two fundamentalist Christian families for educating their children at home, cases involving the rights of preachers on public property, and the dismissal of an elementary school principal for illegally teaching religion in a public school. As argued above, conflict and interaction of this kind are inevitable, because the two institutions involved, church and state, each claim authority to regulate human behavior.

When faced with such competing claims, some political systems have given supreme authority to the church and others have subordinated the religious institutions to the state. Characteristically, the playing out of this issue in the United States has taken place in the middle ground. As commonly understood today, the Constitution prevents the government from granting its authority to any particular church or from routinely using that authority to restrict religious liberty. As the detailed examination of Supreme Court decisions demonstrated, deciding just how to implement these principles can be a daunting and confusing task. In an effort to maintain neutrality toward religion, the government may act in ways that appear to imperil the free-exercise rights of majority religions. Thus, the Court decisions prohibiting organized prayer sessions in the classroom on establishment grounds have been attacked by some religious people as interference with their First Amendment rights. Yet by accommodating religious sentiment, as when the Court permitted Amish children to leave school at age fourteen, the government may be granting favors to a religion in direct violation of the "no establishment" requirement. Even people committed to reason and goodwill may find it difficult to strike the proper balance.

Despite the emphasis in this chapter on church-state conflict and tension, it is worth remarking that the American compromise seems to have worked quite well. As a rule, the churches have remained relatively independent of government and the latter appears to have recognized the rights of persons of diverse faith. The current balance of power does not make everyone happy, but it appears to have helped to prevent the widespread religious and political violence that has plagued other societies.

The relative independence of religion from the government has left the churches and religious people free to pursue political ends. In some cases, as this chapter outlined, this power has been used to secure the immediate interests of the religious group. But churches and religious coalitions have also been involved in a wide range of public controversies that raised questions of belief and morality outside the narrow bounds of issues like public prayer or state aid to religious schools. The next chapter examines the role of religion in the formation and execution of public policy.

NOTES

1. A "Dear Abby" column illustrates how much the facts can be scrambled in discussion of this subject. The columnist answered a letter from a woman who was unhappy about her daughter's decision to raise her child outside the family faith. According to the columnist, the constitutional guarantee of freedom of religion meant that the letter writer had no right to criticize her daughter's choice in religion. Although the free-exercise clause of the Constitution does prohibit interference with an adult's choice of faith, it does not compel tolerance.

2. The "wall of separation" phrase is from Jefferson's letter to some Connecticut Baptists. Contrary to the impression of some students, neither this phrase nor "church and state" appears in the Constitution. If the language does not appear, it is arguable nonetheless that the sentiment does.

3. "Faith Healers Convicted of Homicide and Child Neglect in Daughter's Death," *Gainesville Sun,* Sept. 12, 1984, 4A; "Faith-Healing Couple Sentenced to Five Years in Death of Infant," *Gainesville Sun,* Dec. 21, 1984, 6B.

4. The major difference was that King did not seek to escape punishment for his behavior; indeed, he hoped that the conscience of the nation would be so moved by the example of unjust suffering that the law in question would subsequently lose credibility and be repealed. From the newspaper accounts of the Indiana trial, it seems that the accused parents denied that their behavior constituted a breach of the law.

5. "Girl's Mom Belittles School Decision to Forbid Cards," *Gainesville Sun,* Dec. 21, 1984, 4A.

6. "Synod-Splitting Rift Causes Lutherans 'Enormous Pain'." *Gainesville Sun,* Jan. 5, 1985, 1B.

7. In attempting to reconcile the claims of church and state, other societies have experimented with a variety of policies. Some, such as contemporary Iran, have melded the two institutions so closely that they constitute what is known as theocracy. Motivated by pronounced hostility to religious influences, the government of Mexico has strictly separated religion from the protection of the state and severely limited its permissible activities. Similarly hostile to a force that it identifies with counterrevolutionary activity, the Soviet Union has attempted to reduce the church to the status of a government department that can be carefully regulated to prevent excessive authority. For information about these policies, see Bellah and Hammond (1980); Kramer (1980); Fireside (1971); and Sawatsky (1977).

8. The full text of the Supreme Court decisions referred to in this chapter can be found in either the *United States Reports* or the privately published *Digest of U.S. Supreme Court Reports.* Useful compilations of the most important decisions include Pfeffer (1977), Miller and Flowers (1987), Wilson and Drakeman (1987), and Alley (1988). The quarterly *Journal of Church and State* publishes a valuable preview of court cases as well as the full decisions in important cases.

9. Malbin has argued that when behavior collides with secular law, there is no justification for exempting people who claim religious motivation. He therefore applied his interpretation to limit free-exercise claims rather than to uphold a strong separationist position. As indicated in the paragraph above, I find the distinction

between belief and behavior supports a strong interpretation of the establishment clause.

10. The reports of the committee also stressed uncertainty that Congress had the right under the First Amendment to legislate on a religious matter. Despite this uncertainty, the reports denounced the proposals as unwise even if Congress could rule in their favor.

11. The critical issue appeared to be the role of governmental authorities—specifically, teachers and other school personnel—in leading religious ceremonies. When officials take the initiative in leading prayers or reading from the Bible, the state appears to be endorsing a particular doctrine. Inflamed rhetoric about "banning God from the schools" notwithstanding, the rulings do not prohibit prayer by individual students. The circumstances of individual prayer may be regulated so that it does not disrupt educational activities, but voluntary prayer is permissible if the student can find an opportunity for it.

12. That appears to have been precisely the case in Great Britain during the period 1870–1902, when that nation experimented with elective school boards (see Cruickshank 1963).

13. Originally a defendant, the city of Pittsburgh became a plaintiff late in 1989 when it sued to have the large menorah removed from the steps of the same City-County building that had previously housed the unconstitutional crèche!

14. "Prayer in Many Schoolrooms Continues Despite '62 Ruling," *New York Times*, Mar. 11, 1984.

15. "Amendment Drive on School Prayer Loses Senate Vote," *New York Times*, Mar. 21, 1984.

16. In 1985 the Senate overwhelmingly rejected a bill that would have withdrawn the issue of school prayer from the jurisdiction of the federal courts. This approach to restoring the pre-1960s situation was defeated so handily (by a 62–36 vote) both because of its dubious constitutionality and because of a reluctance to give states such wide latitude to restore prayer to the classroom.

REFERENCES

Adams, Arlin. 1986. "Is the Supreme Court Making a Significant Shift in Church-State Jurisprudence?" In *Government Intervention in Religious Affairs II*, edited by Dean M. Kelley, 69–78. New York: Pilgrim.

Alley, Robert S., ed. 1988. *The Supreme Court on Church and State*. New York: Oxford University Press.

Bellah, Robert N., and Phillip E. Hammond, eds. 1980. *Varieties of Civil Religion*. New York: Harper and Row.

Berger, Peter L., and Richard John Neuhaus. 1977. *To Empower People: The Role of Mediating Structures in Public Policy*. Washington, D.C.: American Enterprise Institute.

Birkby, Robert H. 1966. "The Supreme Court and the Bible Belt: Tennessee Reactions to the 'Schempp' Decision." *Midwest Journal of Political Science* 10:304–319.

Blakeley, William Addison, comp. 1970. *American State Papers Bearing on Sunday Religion*. Revised and enlarged edition. New York: Da Capo.

Caldeira, Gregory A., and James L. Gibson. 1989. "The Etiology of Public Support for the Supreme Court." Paper delivered at the annual meeting of the Midwest Political Science Association, Chicago.

Committee on Post Offices and Post Roads. 1830. *Report No. 271.* Twenty-first Congress, 1st sess. Washington, D.C.: U.S. House of Representatives.

Cord, Robert L. 1982. *Separation of Church and State: Historical Fact and Current Fiction.* New York: Lambeth.

Cousins, Norman, ed. 1958. *In God We Trust: The Religious Beliefs and Ideas of the American Founders.* New York: Harper and Row.

Cruickshank, Marjorie. 1963. *Church and State in English Education.* New York: St. Martin's.

Curry, Thomas J. 1986. *The First Freedoms: Church and State in America to the Passage of the First Amendment.* New York: Oxford University Press.

Dierenfeld, R. B. 1967. "The Impact of the Supreme Court Decisions on Religion in the Public Schools." *Religious Education* 62:445–451.

Diggins, John P. 1984. *The Lost Soul of American Politics: Virtue, Self-Interest, and the Foundations of Liberalism.* New York: Basic Books.

Dolbeare, Kenneth. 1967. "The Public Views the Supreme Court." In *Law, Politics, and the Federal Courts,* edited by Herbert Jacob, 194–212. Boston: Little, Brown.

Dolbeare, Kenneth, and Phillip Hammond. 1977. *The School Prayer Decisions: From Court Policy to Local Practices.* Chicago: University of Chicago Press.

Dunn, Charles W., ed. 1984. *American Political Theology.* New York: Praeger.

Elifson, Kirk W., and C. Kirk Hadaway. 1985. "Prayer in Public Schools: When Church and State Collide." *Public Opinion Quarterly* 49:317–329.

Fey, Harold E. 1963. "A Protestant View: An Argument for Separation." In *The Wall Between Church and State,* edited by Dallin H. Oaks, 26–40. Chicago: University of Chicago Press.

Fireside, Harvey. 1971. *Icon and Swastika: The Russian Orthodox Church Under Nazi and Soviet Control.* Cambridge: Harvard University Press.

Gordon, Murray A. 1963. "The Unconstitutionality of Public Aid to Parochial Schools." In *The Wall Between Church and State,* edited by Dallin H. Oaks, 73–94. Chicago: University of Chicago Press.

Howe, Mark DeWolfe. 1965. *The Garden and the Wilderness: Religion and Government in American Constitutional History.* Chicago: University of Chicago Press.

Johnson, Richard M. 1967. *The Dynamics of Compliance: Supreme Court Decision-Making from a New Perspective.* Evanston, Ill.: Northwestern University Press.

Katz, Ellis. 1965. "Patterns of Compliance with the Schempp Decision." *Journal of Public Law* 14:396–408.

Kessel, John H. 1966. "Public Perceptions of the Supreme Court." *Midwest Journal of Political Science* 10:167–191.

Kirby, James C. 1977. "*Everson* to *Meek* and *Roemer*: From Separation to Detente in Church-State Relations." *North Carolina Law Review* 55:563–575.

Kirwin, Harry W., ed. 1959. *The Search for Democracy.* Garden City, N.Y.: Doubleday Christendom.

Kramer, Martin S. 1980. *Political Islam.* Washington Papers, no. 73. Beverly Hills, Calif.: Sage.

Laycock, Douglas. 1986. "The Right to Church Autonomy as Part of Free Exercise of Religion." In *Government Intervention in Religious Affairs II*, edited by Dean M. Kelley, 28–39. New York: Pilgrim.

Levy, Leonard W. 1986. *The Establishment Clause: Religion and the First Amendment*. New York: Macmillan.

Malbin, Michael J. 1978. *Religion and Politics: The Intentions of the Authors of the First Amendment*. Washington, D.C.: American Enterprise Institute.

Manwaring, David R. 1962. *Render Unto Caesar: The Flag Salute Controversy*. Chicago: University of Chicago Press.

Marty, Martin E. 1984. *Pilgrims in Their Own Land*. Boston: Little, Brown.

Miller, Robert T., and Ronald B. Flowers, eds. 1987. *Toward Benevolent Neutrality: Church, State, and the Supreme Court*. 3d ed. Waco, Tex.: Baylor University Press.

Morgan, Richard E. 1968. *The Politics of Religious Conflict*. New York: Pegasus.

———. 1984. *Disabling America*. New York: Basic Books.

Muir, William K., Jr. 1967. *Prayer in the Public Schools: Law and Attitude Change*. Chicago: University of Chicago Press.

Murphy, Walter F., Joseph Tanenhaus, and Daniel L. Kastner. 1973. *Public Evaluations of Constitutional Courts: Alternative Explanations*. Beverly Hills, Calif.: Sage.

Patric, Gordon. 1957. "The Impact of a Court Decision: Aftermath of the McCollum Case." *Journal of Public Law* 6:455–464.

Pfeffer, Leo. 1967. *Church, State, and Freedom*. Revised edition. Boston: Beacon.

———, ed. 1977. *Religious Freedom*. Skokie: National Textbook.

Pritchett, C. Herman. 1984. *Constitutional Civil Liberties*. Englewood Cliffs, N.J.: Prentice-Hall.

Sawatsky, Walter. 1977. "Religious Administration and Modernization." In *Religion and Modernization in the Soviet Union*, edited by Dennis J. Dunn, 60–104. Boulder: Westview.

Schappes, Morriss U., ed. 1971. *A Documentary History of the Jews in the United States*. 3d edition. New York: Schocken.

Shapiro, Martin. 1990. "The Supreme Court from Early Burger to Early Rehnquist." In *The New American Political System*, edited by Anthony King, 47–86. New version. Washington, D.C.: American Enterprise Institute.

Sorauf, Frank J. 1976. *The Wall of Separation: The Constitutional Politics of Church and State*. Princeton, N.J.: Princeton University Press.

———. 1959. "*Zorach v. Clausen*: The Impact of a Supreme Court Decision." *American Political Science Review* 53:777–791.

Tocqueville, Alexis de. 1945. *Democracy in America*. 2 volumes. New York: Vintage.

Way, Frank, and Barbara J. Burt. 1983. "Religious Marginality and the Free Exercise Clause." *American Political Science Review* 77:652–665.

Way, H. Frank, Jr. 1968. "Survey Research on Judicial Decisions: The Prayer and Bible-Reading Cases." *Western Political Quarterly* 21:189–205.

Weber, Paul J. 1982. "James Madison and Religious Equality: The Perfect Separation." *Review of Politics* 44:163–186.

———. 1989. "Strict Neutrality: The Next Step in First Amendment Development?" In *Religion in American Politics*, edited by Charles W. Dunn, 25–35. Washington, D.C.: CQ Press.

Williamsburg Charter Foundation. 1988. *The Williamsburg Charter Survey on Religion and Public Life.* Washington, D.C.: Williamsburg Charter Foundation.

Wilson, John F., and Donald L. Drakeman, eds. 1987. *Church and State in American History.* 2d edition. Boston: Beacon.

Zlatos, Bill. 1984. "When Faith Lets Children Die." *Washington Post Weekly Edition,* October 15, pp. 31–32.

6. Religion and American Public Policy

The American public is divided on the merits of political involvement by religious groups. When asked if the clergy should speak out on public issues in their places of worship, churchgoers split almost evenly between support and opposition for such involvement (Welch et al. 1990). Even while accepting the constitutional right of churches to take positions on public issues, the public is also quick to note the potentially divisive consequences of such political involvement (Williamsburg Charter Foundation 1988). As suggested in Chapter 1, Americans tend to look to their religion for solace and comfort, not political direction.

Despite these concerns, American religious institutions have been repeatedly drawn into the thick of the political process. On some occasions, as the previous chapter recounted, churches have entered the public realm because they felt that their spiritual mission was endangered by some action of government or of another secular institution. Yet the churches have also become important participants in public decision making about issues that do not appear to touch on their immediate interests. Religious institutions have taken public stands on issues as narrow as the zoning decisions of local planning boards and as broad as the state of the national economy. The focus of recent political activity by American religious bodies has ranged from government policy on the morality of personal conduct to global problems of hunger and war.

Of course, religious groups do not always take the initiative in these battles. At times, they are drawn into controversies at the urging of secular political forces. In the debate over revisions of the federal tax code, for example, political leaders structured their proposals so as to bring certain religious groups into the conflict. To enlist conservative evangelical Protestants on behalf of President Reagan's plan, the administration put a great deal of rhetorical emphasis on the proposed doubling of the personal exemption. The proposal was offered to "profamily" groups on the grounds that it would relieve large families of extra financial burdens; presumably, that would reduce incentives for women to enter the labor force and, by making another child less expensive, discourage elective abortion for economic reasons. The proponents of the plan hoped that these features would appeal to the socially conservative values of the evangelical lobby, bringing in additional congressional support for a plan that covered many sections of the federal tax code.[1]

Whatever the basis for political involvement—be it a policy affecting the ability of churches to perform religious activities, an issue that addresses the social concerns of church members, or a government action that is seen to challenge church doctrine—religion is a potentially significant factor in the policy-making process. Because we have examined religion's contribution to some other dimensions of political life, it is time to turn to the role of religion informing public policy. In the first part of this chapter, "religion" appears as a political actor in the guise of churches and church-related interest groups. In exploring the day-to-day political activity of religious groups, the chapter describes the methods by which they attempt to influence government decision making, along with other avenues through which religious and moral considerations may bear on public issues. The remainder of the chapter is devoted to the task of estimating the impact of religious forces in resolving certain policy disputes. Is religious influence most apparent on well-focused issues about personal behavior, a domain in which churches have traditionally taken strong stands? And on larger issues involving many participants, are religious institutions equipped with sufficient resources to compete effectively for influence with major secular actors and institutions? The answers to such questions will help to illuminate the significance of the churches relative to other agencies that participate in public decision making.

Interest Group Activities

The techniques used by religious groups in attempts to shape public policy are conditioned by the U.S. political process. Like other participants in the policy-making process, religious groups confront a system of extraordinary complexity. Political decision making takes place in three different spheres of authority—the legislative, judicial, and executive branches of government. Overlaying this division of power among the relatively equal branches is a further division of political authority among local, state, and national levels of government. To further complicate matters, many areas of public life are left altogether outside the scope of government action, reserved instead for private associations such as business corporations. The diverse political strategies of "religion"—a term that encompasses individuals, congregations, denominations, church-affiliated groups, and interchurch organizations—are dictated by this fragmentation of political influence in the American system.

For any group that wants to influence public life, the complexity of political structure creates a multitude of opportunities and access points. Churches may try to pursue political goals through statutes, administrative procedures, and/or court cases. Along with a choice of arenas, they can decide to concentrate on influencing local, state, or national authorities or to apply pressure on nongovernmental organizations. The options for involvement also extend to the various stages of the policy process: churches and religious groups can specialize in raising awareness of problems, shaping policy alternatives, trying to influence the content of policies, or monitoring the implementation of government action. Like all interest groups, religious groups can employ strategies that fall into four major categories: direct public action, lobbying the government, campaign-related activities, and what I choose to call "infiltration." Although the strategies differ in levels of risk and likelihood of success, each has at one time or another been adopted by groups and individuals motivated by religious concern.

Direct Action

The strategy of direct action may entail activities as diverse as peaceful demonstrations, public relations campaigns, civil disobedience, and in extreme cases, violence. These techniques, utilized extensively by persons on both sides of the civil rights and Vietnam controversies, have been widely adopted by various religious groups.

Peaceful demonstrations have been particularly attractive to groups motivated by intense and deeply felt commitments but lacking in other resources such as money, political experience, and organization. By holding prayer services in public, religiously motivated demonstrators have tried to add moral weight to the force of their argument. In my community, open-air services have been conducted both outside the walls of the state prison, to protest capital punishment, and on the sidewalk outside a medical clinic, to protest abortions performed there. Rather than concentrate on sporadic demonstrations, other religious groups have organized boycotts against institutions that offended their religious principles. Over the past twenty years or so, many clergy have participated in nationwide boycotts of certain agricultural products as a way to force growers to bargain collectively with their workers. The boycott was the weapon favored by an interfaith coalition that successfully persuaded international corporations to change their practice of marketing potentially dangerous infant feeding products in poor countries (Ermann and Clements 1984). The American Family Association, led by the Mississippi minister described in Chapter 2, has used boycotts against companies for advertising on "immoral" television programs or selling what he regards as "pornographic" reading material (see Swatos 1988).

In an attempt to gain public sympathy for their efforts, religious groups may reach out to a larger audience by using sophisticated public relations techniques. The Church of Scientology has advertised regularly in the pages of the *Washington Post*, seeking public support as it contests several indictments by the federal government. Subscribers to national newspapers and magazines should be familiar with other religiously sponsored advertisements, addressing issues such as abortion, school prayer, and foreign policy. Borrowing a page from family-planning groups, the Roman Catholic bishops recently committed several million dollars to a major public relations offensive against abortion.[2] The church will use the services of two major marketing research companies to conduct public opinion studies and to develop public education campaigns. For groups without the resources to mount such expensive public relations exercises, free publicity can be obtained by letters to the editor, press releases, and guest appearances on local talk shows or news broadcasts. In this way, religious groups can attempt to create a favorable climate of opinion for their causes.

Peaceful demonstrations, boycotts, and public relations campaigns are types of public actions that normally fall within the letter of the law. Sometimes, though, frustrated by the failure of more conventional efforts to influence policy, religiously oriented persons have purposely taken actions that violated the law. Religion has inspired many campaigns of civil disobedience, in which protesters have intentionally challenged laws in the name of higher religious values. One such recent effort, the Sanctuary movement, attempted to provide asylum in the United States for refugees from civil strife in Central America (Murphy 1984). Defying a national policy limiting immigration from Central America, Sanctuary workers went to prison for smuggling refugees into the United States and harboring them in churches, religious houses, and private homes. Despite the alleged illegality of the actions, the program was endorsed by national organizations affiliated with a wide range of churches: the American Friends (Quakers), the Conservative wing of Judaism, United Presbyterians, United Methodists, and the American Baptist Association. More than 150 local congregations, including Roman Catholics, Unitarians, ecumenical groups, as well as the denominations mentioned above, supported the movement financially and were willing to offer a place of refuge. Considering that much of the leadership of the movement consists of clergy and other devout believers, it is not surprising that the illegal actions taken have been defended in the name of moral and ethical premises derived from religious teaching. Under the same claim of conscience, groups morally opposed to nuclear armaments have committed symbolic acts of sabotage and withheld income tax payments.

The most extreme form of public action, calculated acts of violence, has occasionally been undertaken by people who claimed to hear God's command. No modern moral issue can match abortion as a focus of religiously connected violent protest. The Supreme Court justice who wrote the majority opinion in *Roe v. Wade* (1973), in which the Court removed many restrictions on the availability of the controversial medical procedure, apparently was the target of an assassination attempt. And in 1983 and 1984 alone, the U.S. Justice Department recorded nearly two hundred attacks, incidents ranging from minor vandalism to arson and lethal bombings, on medical clinics that performed abortions.[3] Although violence has been denounced by virtually all leaders of the antiabortion movement, some of the persons convicted of major assaults have cited religious convictions in their defense. (They also claim that attacks on abortion facilities represent a measured response to the much greater violence used against the aborted fetus.) The ambivalent

attitude of some religious leaders toward antiabortion violence was symbolized by the Baptist minister who hailed as "heroes" the four young
people accused of bombing two facilities in a Florida city.[4] There is nothing particularly new about the use of violence to further moral causes.
The antislavery movement of the nineteenth century, thoroughly infused by religious passion, decried the "martyrdom" of John Brown,
who had killed unarmed civilians in assaults on proslavery settlements
and government facilities. Like some of today's antiabortion zealots,
Brown portrayed himself as the instrument of God's will, wreaking ven-
geance in the name of higher law. Those who have associated the "holy
war" mentality only with fanatical sects in the Middle East should be
reminded that intense religious commitment has occasionally prompted
the systematic use of violence in this nation, too.

Lobbying

Religious groups have also turned to lobbying, a term signifying efforts to influence public officials. With its unsavory connotations of using pressure, bribery, and corruption to advance self-interest, lobbying
might seem like a strange activity for groups committed to high moral
standards. The very use of the term clearly makes religious interest
groups nervous (Zwier 1988). Yet most lobby work is ordinary and morally unobjectionable—monitoring government actions, assembling facts
and figures, making public presentations, visiting offices, negotiating
the details of legislation and government regulations. These "insider"
tactics, available to groups with personal access to government elites,
require the resources to support professionals for whom lobbying is a
primary responsibility.

By Allen Hertzke's estimate (1988, 5), more than eighty religious
groups—churches, religious organizations, moral reform campaigns—
now maintain permanent offices for advocacy purposes in Washington,
D.C.[5] This represents a significant increase over the past (Adams 1970;
Dexter 1938; Ebersole 1951). Staff members employed by these groups
spend their time much like lobbyists for secular organizations, "draft-
ing bill language, offering amendments, forging coalitions behind the
scenes, negotiating with opponents over compromise provisions, and
providing useful facts and arguments to members during legislative debates" (Hertzke 1988, 70). Even though direct communication with
members of the Supreme Court is not deemed appropriate in the Amer-

ican political system, the religious groups lobby justices by submitting "friend of the court" briefs, written arguments about cases under Supreme Court review. In the important case in which the Court first evaluated the constitutionality of affirmative action for disadvantaged minority groups, the flood of briefs sent to the justices included submissions from the National Council of Churches, the Young Women's Christian Association, and the Anti-Defamation League of B'nai B'rith. Issues that touch directly on religious interests bring out appeals from an even broader range of religious groups.

Lobbying may be undertaken to advance the theological, institutional, or communal interests of a religious group. Consider the report of the official lobbyist for the Florida Catholic Conference for one week in 1985, which highlighted three bills under consideration by the state legislature.[6] The church opposed on theological grounds one bill that permitted withdrawal of intravenous food and fluids from terminally ill patients. Because food and water are necessities of life rather than forms of medical treatment, the official testified, their withdrawal would constitute a type of euthanasia, which church doctrine condemned. A concern for the institutional strength of the church was evident in the lobbyist's support for a bill to grant privileged status to communication between clergy and church members in cases involving child and adult abuse. Without the protection of the law, it was argued, the church's counseling programs might be threatened. Finally, the lobbyist expressed grave concern about a bill on the state senate floor to repeal all state and local tax exemptions, including those for the religious, educational, and charitable activities sponsored by churches. Even though the repeal was merely a device designed to permit the legislature to consider each category of tax exemption on the books, the church opposed the bill because it threatened "the freedom of religion, the separation of church and state, and the orderly planning for . . . institutions which provide basic necessary services." It should be pointed out that the Catholic church was not the only participant in lobbying on these bills, and that its lobbying was not successful in two of the three cases. Even more important, although each bill touched a particular facet of the Catholic religion, it would be foolish to claim that one particular motivation was paramount in any one issue. The churches, like other interested actors, may intervene for a variety of religious and secular reasons.

The use of professional advocates is only one prong of the effort to lobby public officials. To a much greater extent than secular interest groups, religious lobbies attempt to reinforce their influence by such classic "outsider" strategies as demonstrations, public relations campaigns, and other efforts at grass-roots mobilization (Hofrenning 1989, 23). Through these tactics, religious groups try to convey the impression that their constituencies stand ready to support officials who go along and to penalize legislators who do not. Because more Americans belong to religious organizations than to any other voluntary association, public officials are disposed to listen.

The views of churchgoers are made known to public officials in several ways. The American tradition of letter-writing campaigns to public officials has been followed by many religious organizations engaged in matters of public controversy. When, for example, President Gerald Ford proposed to sell several sophisticated intelligence-gathering airplanes to Saudi Arabia, several Jewish groups fought the proposal as a threat to Israeli security. In a coordinated campaign to defeat the sale, members of the Jewish community in some cities were sent preprinted postcards addressed to congressional representatives. By flooding Capitol Hill mailbags with messages opposing the sale, the Jewish groups hoped (unsuccessfully) that Congress would overturn the president's decision. Because of the importance of the president in the process of policy making, the same strategy is often aimed at the White House. By spearheading the sending of telegrams, letters, postcards, petitions, and telephone calls, a religiously affiliated organization may attempt to enlist the executive branch on one side or another of a policy controversy.

Often portrayed as spontaneous outbursts by enraged congregants, mass mobilization usually results from campaigns that are meticulously planned by the Washington office of the religious group. Media-based ministries have effectively used mass mailings, phone banks, computerized telephone messages, and broadcast programs to generate letters, telegrams, personal visits, and telephone calls by their supporters (Hertzke 1988, 50). Less common on the religious left, similar techniques have been used effectively by the peace movement to mount grass-roots campaigns against such initiatives as the MX missile or U.S. assistance to the Nicaraguan *contras*. In those campaigns, the appeals were targeted to the small churches with pacifist traditions, such as Mennonites, as well as to mainline Protestants who were sympathetic

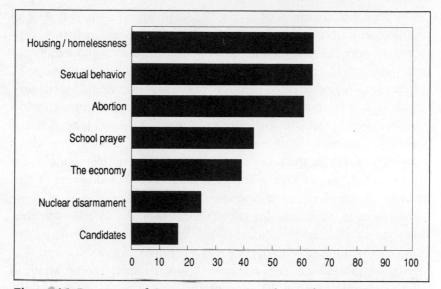

Figure 6.1 Percentage of Congregants Hearing Clergy Discuss Political Issues (Source: Calculated by Welch et al. [1990] from the 1989 pilot study, American National Election Study)

to calls for disarmament. The ground for appeals to congregants is planted in the tradition of church guidance on public issues. Church-goers hear from their leaders on a broad range of public issues (Figure 6.1). Clear majorities indicate that religious leaders have spoken out on homelessness, sexual behavior, and abortion. Sizable minorities also report similar efforts on school prayer, the economy, and nuclear disarmament. These issue appeals are far more common than communication about candidates for public office.

Political Campaigning

Lobbying is likely to be especially powerful if the person on the receiving end thinks the lobbyist can affect his or her chances for retaining public office. Hence, some religious groups have become involved in various phases of political campaigning at all levels of the government. For some religiously affiliated groups, campaign involvement may take the form of merely questioning candidates about issues in which the church takes an interest. That familiar mixture of theological, institutional, and social concern was very much in evidence in the questions sent to the

1984 presidential nominees by the St. Augustine (Florida) diocese of the Roman Catholic church.[7] The candidates were asked if they supported or opposed a constitutional ban on abortion, elimination of capital punishment, cutbacks in the deployment of nuclear weapons, income tax credits for private school tuition, and major new federal programs to combat hunger and increase housing opportunities. In addition to indicating their orientations on human life issues (abortion and capital punishment), state legislative candidates were asked their views on welfare funding, the provision of services to nonpublic schools, ratification of the Equal Rights Amendment, and the broadcasting of "indecent" material on cable television. Having defined each of these concerns as moral issues, the church encouraged its members to consider the candidates' response before casting their ballots. Forbidden from endorsing candidates or parties as a condition for maintaining tax-exempt status, the churches can nonetheless use such interrogations to let the members know that one of the candidates is closest to the church's preferred position on the issue.

The prohibition on formal endorsement by churches as churches does not prevent the clergy from attempting to influence the votes of church members or from participating as private citizens in political campaigns. By extolling the moral virtues of one candidate and pointedly refraining from comment about the competition, a minister can clearly indicate a preference without actually recommending a vote from the pulpit. Even that fine line can be breached when ministers make explicit endorsements of candidates from a platform outside the church. Does ministerial support pay off at the polls? When asked where they turn for political advice and guidance, Americans do not frequently mention the church. That finding may indicate only that Americans feel it is improper for churches to take sides in elections—not that they are unaffected by clergy influence. In the black community, where the clergy have long been recognized as an important source of political authority, voters certainly seem to respond to cues from the pulpit (Vedlitz, Alston, and Pinkele 1980).

In an age of weak political parties and generally low rates of political participation, the support of religious groups is usually seen as a valuable asset in a political campaign. Through several mechanisms, religiously involved people can supply resources to help favored candidates or, conversely, to defeat candidates they find unacceptable. Simply providing the candidate a forum from which to address the membership gives free publicity and the opportunity to spread a message among attentive audiences. As organizations possessing membership lists and other resources, the churches may even be pressed into action as the core of a candidate's campaign effort. In bidding for presidential nomination in 1988, both Jesse Jackson and Pat Robertson, ordained ministers, relied heavily on sympathetic churches for leadership, funding, platforms, and various types of support services (Wald forthcoming). Though major political parties in the United States attempt to draw support from different religious groups, several minor parties have been built almost exclusively on specific religious constituencies. That was true of the antislavery and prohibitionist parties in an earlier age. Since 1978, antiabortion activists in New York have supported the Right-to-Life party, which as of 1984 had more than 17,000 enrolled members. Though not formally tied to any church, the leaders and members of the party appear to have been recruited mainly from denominations that favor conservative theology and positions on public issues (Spitzer 1987).

Infiltration

Finally, there is the method called *infiltration*. Reasoning that the most reliable kind of official is the one who shares the group's values, a religious organization may seek to place one of its members in office. If the office is filled by public election, members of a religious group may organize to win the seat for a fellow member. Although the Constitution forbids the government to impose "religious tests" for holding office, it does not restrict citizens from supporting candidates out of religious loyalty.

Judging by their determined efforts to publicize religious affiliation and church membership, candidates seem to have recognized the electoral power of religious affiliation. In 1982 a candidate with the decidedly non-Jewish name of Larry Smith wanted to indicate his Jewish identity to voters in a Florida congressional district. Concerned that his name would be a handicap in a race against other Jewish candidates in a district with a predominantly Jewish electorate, Smith had his wife introduced to district residents by her maiden name, Sheila Cohen, and distributed campaign literature with pictures of his son's Bar Mitzvah ceremony (Ehrenhalt 1983, 333). Also, in a packet of material sent out to influential leaders and community groups, the candidate called attention to his active membership in a local synagogue and reminded readers that he had helped to found a chapter of B'nai B'rith and been named "Man of the Year" by the local chapter of the Jewish National Fund. Consistent with the tactics that eventually brought victory in the election, Smith's 1984 campaign biography called attention to his membership in the congressional Caucus for Soviet Jewry and an award received for zeal in promoting the sale of Israeli bonds. Quite the opposite problem faced Marc Holtzmann, a Jewish candidate for a Pennsylvania congressional seat with a majority of Roman Catholic voters (Taylor 1985). To offset the potential disadvantage of a Jewish-sounding name, Holtzmann asked the American ambassador to the Vatican to arrange a meeting with Pope John Paul II. Despite blanketing the district with pictures of his meeting with the spiritual leader of the Catholic church, Holtzmann lost.

Do voters actually respond positively to such appeals to vote for "their own kind" of people? Although complex motivations cannot be attributed to any single factor, a candidate's religious affiliation clearly can play a role in voter decision making. The most persuasive evidence leading to this conclusion has been obtained in experiments simulating the electoral process. In a classic study by the psychologist Leon Festinger (1947), a group of female college students was asked to listen to speeches by candidates for the presidency of a college club. On contrived grounds, the first vote (in which the name and religious identities of the candidates were not revealed) was voided. After a suitable interval, during which the participants learned the candidates' religious affiliation, a second ballot was conducted. Festinger interpreted the changes in preference between ballots as evidence that knowledge of a candidate's religious identity inflated support among members of the candidate's religious family. That conclusion has been sustained by studies in which voters have been asked to choose between hypothetical candidates for public office. In these studies the ethnic identity of the candidate, a quality frequently associated with religious affiliation, apparently brought in additional support from members of the same ethnic group (Kamin 1958; Lorinskas, Hawkins, and Edwards 1969—see Pomper 1966 for actual election data). Studies of Catholic voting patterns in 1956 and 1960 showed that Catholic candidates running for national offices against candidates from other faiths earned substantially more support from their coreligionists than party ties could have explained (Campbell et al. 1960, 319–321; Converse 1966).

All other things being equal—and they rarely are in electoral politics—voters usually favor a candidate of their own religion.[8] Religious affiliation is only one element in the voters' image of the candidate, which is, in turn, only one of the three factors that strongly sway electoral choice. The other two factors—partisanship and the issues—may limit or offset the impact of religious affiliation. In two studies that examined the impact of candidates' ethnic and religious traits under partisan conditions, the effect was clearest when the normal party cues were absent (Kamin 1958; Pomper 1966). When a voter has to cross party lines to support a candidate with the same ethnic or religious identity, the religious factor has a much smaller impact. The candidate's stands on the issues may also deter members of his or her religious community from giving additional support. As has been shown by studies of predominantly Jewish districts, Jewish candidates whose political views differed from those of most of their coreligionists have lost badly to non-Jewish candidates whose policies are more closely attuned to public opinion (Leventman and Leventman 1976). These studies have suggested that voters do not attribute quite as much significance to a candidate's personal religious affiliation as candidates seem to imagine.

The religious factor has also played a role in the politics of appointments. When President Ronald Reagan filled an important position in the U.S. Department of Education with an official from the conservative religious group Moral Majority and named a leader of the antiabortion movement to the post of surgeon general, he reenacted the familiar American ritual of awarding patronage to a group that had supported his election (Schuster 1981). Moral Majority undoubtedly welcomed the appointment providing a way to safeguard its growing private school movement and to interject its moral concerns into the decision-making process on education policy. If that case illustrates how religious groups may take the initiative to receive appointments, it is worth remembering that public officials may seek out religious leaders for positions on public bodies. As respected community leaders with considerable prestige, members of the clergy may seem to be perfectly positioned to lend credibility to policies that would otherwise inspire political controversy.

Given the central role of judges in the policy process, it should not be surprising that judicial appointments have also been the subject of intense religious-group activity. When Catholics and Jews were still struggling for political recognition, it was customary to reserve a seat on the U.S. Supreme Court for each group. In the modern period, more interest is focused on the specific views of nominees for judgeships. At congressional hearings on the appointment of federal judges, representatives of church groups have testified in favor of or against nominees because of preferences on policy issues. Antiabortion groups persuaded the Republican conventions of 1980 and 1984 to pledge support for restricting federal judicial nominations to persons who "respected the sanctity of human life." What might sound like routine political rhetoric struck many observers as a commitment to make opposition to abortion a requirement for judicial appointment. Studies of the judicial appointment process in the Reagan administration suggest that the platform pledge was carried out (Kurtz 1985b). In 1984 the Reagan administration withdrew support from its own nominee for a seat on the District of Columbia Court of Appeals, in part because of conservative complaints that he belonged to the National Abortion Rights Action League and Planned Parenthood. In a questionnaire sent by three Republican senators, a nominee for a federal judgeship in New Jersey was asked seven questions about the legalization of abortion and about such religiously based issues as school prayer, the death penalty, the Equal Rights Amendment, and public financing for private schools. And when the administration was considering the appointment of an outspoken evangelical Protestant to chair the Justice Department committee on judicial selection, fears of religious tests for the judiciary inspired fierce, and ultimately successful opposition (Kurtz 1985a). Supreme Court nominations were also made very much with an eye toward the likely impact on decisions involving religious claims.

Churches resemble secular interest groups in their ability to use several or all of the methods of political action. Few religious groups have used as many different techniques as the Unification church, a religious and political movement founded by the Reverend Sun Myung Moon, a South Korean businessman (Horowitz 1978; Isikoff 1984; Boyer and Alem 1985a, 1985b). A fervent if unorthodox Christian, Moon has propagated a worldview in which international communism is seen as a representative of the anti-Christ and the church exists as "the instrument to be used by God" in his unceasing battle against Marxism (Isikoff 1984, 8). Financed by several profitable international business ventures (as well as the smaller-scale soliciting so familiar to airport travelers), the Unification church deployed a vast array of devices in its anti-Communist crusade. To influence American public opinion directly, the church publishes daily newspapers in Washington and New York, as well as a nationally distributed Spanish-language daily. Aiming to win over opinion leaders and, through them, the mass public, the church has also established a "think tank" in Washington and underwritten seminars and conferences throughout the nation. In addition, it has transported journalists, scholars, congressional staff members, black ministers, and other influential citizens to national and international meetings. The Unification church also has been involved in direct lobbying in Washington, D.C. It has contributed to an alliance of conservative groups that lobby Congress on behalf of anti-Communist measures and has paid for Central American trips by some congressional staff assistants. Church officials were linked to the effort by the Korean government to influence congressional and executive branch officials in the 1970s (Horowitz 1978, chaps. 8, 10, 11; Isikoff 1984, 7). Church leaders were strong supporters of President Richard Nixon, and their Spanish-language newspaper endorsed Ronald Reagan in his 1980 campaign for the Republican nomination. One church leader apparently met with President Reagan, and several key officials in the administration, the president included, and granted exclusive interviews to the *Washington Times*, the newspaper financed by the Unification church. A congressional committee investigated charges that the church funneled aid to the *contras* at the behest of the Reagan administration.[9] These political connections did not prevent the prosecution and imprisonment of the Reverend Sun Myung Moon on charges of fraud and misrepresentation.

Organizing for Political Action

Like American religion itself, the efforts of religious groups in politics are remarkably diverse. In surveying seventy-five groups that maintained offices in the nation's capital in 1981, Paul Weber (1982) was particularly struck by the diversity of the groups on a number of dimensions. In terms of denominational orientation, there were groups representing the views of Catholics, Jews, mainline and evangelical Protestants, black Christians, and secularists with a strong interest in church-state relations. Some groups represented single denominations, others broad coalitions with common interests. As organizations, some relied on dues-paying individual members, whereas others were subsidized departments of national church organizations whose very existence might not be known by the church members who supported them financially. The social issues pursued by the groups were in some cases identified by an elaborate system of consultation reaching down to member churches and in others left to the discretion of centrally based leaders of the church organization. Politically, the groups ranged from narrowly conceived single-issue movements that worked alone to organizations with a broad range of concerns that were willing to coalesce with secular groups if that would advance their preferred policies. These differences extended to groups representing the same religious denomination. Thomas O'Hara (1989b) found important policy and strategy differences among Washington lobby groups established by the Catholic church, independent groups representing different orders of the Catholic clergy, and lobbies founded by Catholic laity.

This diversity was strikingly evident in the five-year battle over a key piece of civil rights legislation (O'Hara 1989a). The issue arose from a 1984 U.S. Supreme Court decision that exempted institutions or their programs from penalties for discrimination levied against a subdivision. Under the ruling, federal grants to a university could no longer be cut off if a program within it, such as the athletic department, had discriminated against women. Fearing that this narrow interpretation crippled enforcement efforts against race, sex, and age discrimination, civil rights groups determined to make the entire institution liable for discrimination by any of its programs or divisions. They turned for support to the same religious communities that had promoted the civil rights legislation affected by the Court decision.

But unlike the 1960s and 1970s, when virtually every religious lobby had enlisted on their behalf, deep divisions among religious groups prevented passage of the bill for five years and limited the scope of the law finally approved in 1989. The struggle for the Civil Rights Restoration Act was supported enthusiastically by most mainline Protestant and Jewish groups, important allies since the 1960s, but encountered serious resistance from other religious interest groups. The remedial legislation was opposed outright by groups that had not been active during the heyday of civil rights—Christian schools associations, various conservative social movements like Moral Majority and Christian Voice, and several major televised ministries. Never known for moderate rhetoric, the Reverend Jerry Falwell expressed his opposition in extreme form when he claimed the proposed act would define sin as a disease or handicap, thereby forcing church-related institutions to accept "active homosexuals, transvestites, alcoholics and drug addicts, among others" (quoted in O'Hara 1989b, 18). The United States Catholic Conference, once an integral part of the civil rights coalition, also opposed the bill. Their representatives expressed fears that the prohibition against sex discrimination might force them to offer abortion coverage in benefit programs for university students and staff and, equally troublesome, render every Catholic institution in a diocese liable for the actions of a single offender.

In the five years it took to resolve these concerns, the religious groups also embraced a variety of strategies. The Catholic Conference worked closely with the congressional committees to revise the language of the bill and to round up support for an amended version. Most of the conservative Protestant opponents never accepted the legislation, first trying to load it down with amendments that would kill the bill, then persuading President Reagan to veto it. When Congress threatened to pass it over the veto, these groups mounted a massive campaign of public mobilization.

Diversity also characterizes the manner in which religious groups formulate their public agenda. In particular, aspects of a denomination's religious tradition, and particularly its preferred form of organization, may shape the process by which it develops a position on a public issue and attempts to persuade policymakers to adopt it. For purposes of comparison, the Catholic and Jewish communities provide an excellent contrast (Fisher and Polish 1980). Catholicism is organized on a hierarchical basis with centralized decision making; Judaism, in this respect resembling many of the Protestant denominations in the United States, accords individual congregations a very high degree of autonomy.

The American Jewish community is divided into four major theological camps that support a wide range of organizations for both religious and secular purposes. Many organizations function at the local level to secure the immediate interests of the Jewish community. In addition to these local organizations, there are a number of national groups and federations of congregations. Furthermore, the spiritual leaders of Judaism, the rabbis, have traditionally enjoyed wide latitude in making social pronouncements as individuals or as members of rabbinic associations. Each of these groups may take public positions on issues of national and international concern, leading to a chorus of voices singing in different keys.

To date, as Peter Medding (1989, 28) notes, "American Jews remain fiercely united around the principle that no single body speaks for the entire community." Attempts at coordination can be made through the National Jewish Community Relations Advisory Council (NJCRAC), described as "an umbrella body consisting of all national Jewish organizations and 106 local Jewish Community Relations Councils drawn from almost every community in the country containing an organized Jewish community" (Brickner 1980, 9). However, the NJCRAC is merely an advisory body that lacks the authority to issue binding pronouncements on questions of public policy. The awkwardly named Conference of Presidents of Major Jewish Organizations has also attempted to speak in the name of the entire Jewish community, but it too enjoys only limited legitimacy. When an authoritative Jewish voice is sought out by the media—as it was, for instance, when President Bush proposed major arms sales to Arab nations following Iraq's invasion of Kuwait—there is no single obvious place to go.

In the Catholic church, in which the lines of authority are much more clearly drawn, political decision making seems to follow a hierarchical pattern.[10] As the apex of the authority pyramid, the pope may issue binding statements about Catholic policy on social issues. These statements of church policy may not persuade all Catholics, but the pope wields enough disciplinary power to enforce some compliance. Thus, Pope John Paul II had ordered priests and nuns to avoid public office, forcing the resignation of a U.S. congressman, and has threatened expulsion from religious orders for clergy who publicly challenge the papal policy on abortion. Within the United States, the Catholic church addresses public issues through the Catholic Conference, an organization of bishops from the dioceses who meet periodically and issue various types of statements on questions of public policy. The head of the conference, elected by the bishops, is widely recognized as the authoritative spokesman for the church and may even become a major public figure.

The Jewish and Catholic policy-making procedures clearly reflect differing ideas about organization and authority, but they do not necessarily differ in effectiveness. Depending on the circumstances, both approaches can yield political cohesiveness or contribute to disarray. Thus, despite its organizational fragmentation, the American Jewish community rallied with extraordinary unity to the defense of Israel when it was attacked by Egypt during the fall of 1973 (Elazar 1976, app. A). Under the threat of an external enemy, the local and national Jewish organizations cooperated in a fund-raising drive aimed at the collection of almost $1 billion in emergency aid. The organizations also exhibit efficiency in coordinating volunteers for service in Israel and in local fund drives. In terms of direct political action, the heads of major Jewish organizations lobbied the administration and Congress to provide assistance to Israel and worked to enlist American public opinion on behalf of that country. By all accounts, these efforts at mobilization contributed to subsequent Israeli success.

These examples of successful group mobilization can be countered by stories illustrating the limits of organized political activity by religious groups. The American Jewish community, united behind Israel under the impetus of the Egyptian invasion, split into competing camps once the immediate threat abated. Even as American Jews have strongly supported Israel, they have differed over some Israeli policies. Likewise, American Catholics have not been of one mind about how to implement their church's formal condemnation of abortion. Proponents of restrictive policies have argued over the best mechanism to achieve their goal, and opponents have insisted that Catholics have no obligation to follow church doctrine. In a telling comment on the limits of church authority, scholars have reported that the contraceptive practices and abortion attitudes of American Catholics do not differ significantly from those followed by persons from other churches (Greeley 1977, 141–151, 245–247; Westoff and Bumpass 1973; Westoff and Ryder 1970; Jaffe, Lindheim, and Lee 1981, 106; Henshaw and Silverman 1988). In that sense, the bishops' resort to the public relations campaign described above may be an admission that preaching has been ineffective. Religious groups, like other politically organized interests, cannot simply command their members to toe the line.

The Question of Representation

The political intervention of churches and religious groups has been condemned as divisive, politically motivated, naive, unconstitutional, and theologically wrong (Atkins and McConnell 1986). Although some of these complaints probably represent dissatisfaction with the positions taken rather than with the act of advocacy itself, many critics have argued that churches and religious groups are prone to misrepresent the views of their members (Reichley 1985; Hallum 1989). In formulating church statements on public policy, it is charged, religious elites take advantage of their power to foist their own views on denominations, speaking in the name of the church when its members may be divided or ranged predominantly on the other side of the issue. This charge, long made against the liberal Washington representatives of the mainline Protestant churches, has recently been lodged against the Roman Catholic bishops for their public opposition to support for the Nicaraguan *contras,* abortion, nuclear weapons, and "supply-side" economic policy. Despite a constituency that is deeply troubled by human rights abuses, some Jewish organizations have seemingly given uncritical support to Israeli actions against Palestinians on the West Bank. The most recent entrants on the scene, the conservatives who claim to speak for the white evangelical Protestants, have also been charged with misrepresenting the more moderate views of their members on several issues.

The charge of misrepresentation is doubly serious. First, it impugns the religious organizations by suggesting they are out of touch with their members. The "correct" stance on public policy may be chosen at the expense of alienating congregants and weakening the church. Second, the charge of misrepresentation undermines the effectiveness of church representatives. An advocate who confronts a public official without the support of the membership has little credibility with the official. In response to such criticisms and as a defense for staking out church positions on controversial issues, religious elites often claim a prophetic role for the church. In this view, churches are not democracies that determine policy on the basis of majority votes. Rather, the church must follow the dictates of religious values and educate the membership to understand its obligations. If the price of prophecy is dissension in the ranks, they reply, so be it. This response does not deny that official positions may differ from the preferences of the laity; it justifies such deviation in terms of moral imperatives.

American religious elites certainly appear to differ from the citizenry. Leaders of Catholic and mainline Protestantism are much more likely than their parishioners to identify with liberalism, support Democratic candidates for president, and hold liberal views across a range of political and social issues (Lerner, Rothman and Lichter 1989). But do the advocacy groups that profess to speak for denominations accurately represent the policy views of congregants when they engage in lobbying? Allen Hertzke's answer (1989, 134; see also 1988, chap. 5), based on comparing lobbying positions with poll data, is mostly yes. Although mainline Protestant lobbies diverged from member preferences on social issues, their opposition to aiding the Nicaraguan *contras* and to support for both food stamps and environmental protection matched both the substance and priorities of the active members of their churches. Almost a mirror image of mainline lobbying, evangelical lobbying reflected member concerns about social policy while taking a more conservative line than the laity on several domestic and foreign policy issues. Both Catholic and Jewish representatives in Washington were close to member opinion on most issues. Like Hertzke, Daniel Hofrenning (1989) observed that lobby positions were closest to the views of parishioners on the most salient issues, less so on issues that did not arouse the interest of congregants. These studies suggest that religious elites blend a concern for rank-and-file opinion with a prophetic orientation. If not perfectly representative of mass opinion, neither are they consistently out of step.

Paths of Influence

Up to now, religious groups have been viewed as supplicants for power, outsiders trying to influence the decisions of insiders. This is consistent with the image of the policy process as a struggle for influence in which the government simply bends to the will of outside pressure. But in fact, religion may also influence policy more directly, through its impact on the views and preferences of policymakers. Religion can become the foundation for public policies in several ways. When laws are decided through public referenda, religious groups may simply vote their preferences into law. That has been the case for evangelical Protestants in voting against referenda proposals relaxing limits on alcohol and gambling (Morgan and Meier 1980; Wasserman 1989). Voting patterns have followed religious lines in other policy areas. Howard Hamilton (1970) noted a peculiar pattern in the relationship between religion and support for "open housing" laws in three referenda conducted during the early 1960s. In two of the contests, persons with no religious preference gave greater support to the proposals than did members of Christian churches—a finding consistent with survey data (cited in Chapter 4) on the greater racial liberalism of the "no preference" respondents. But in a similar referendum in Toledo, Ohio, all groups of churchgoers were more likely than nonmembers to endorse antidiscrimination housing legislation. Hamilton explained this deviation by noting that the Toledo churches had taken a strong and active role on behalf of the fair housing ordinance (ibid., 719), apparently exposing churchgoers to positive information and mobilizing them to vote in favor of the proposal. Religious values are most likely to influence voting on questions of public policy when the church provides unambiguous clues for its membership (see Richardson 1984).

Most laws are enacted, not by a public vote, but by the concerted action of elected officials. Religion can play a role in this process by influencing the values of officeholders. Particularly when they are chosen by public election, government officials are likely to share the dominant religious values of their community. Even if the officials come from another religious tradition, a dependence on public approval for reelection should motivate them to express the preferences of their constituents. In either case, government officials could play a crucial role in translating religious sentiment into public law.

It is important to recognize the limits of the hypothesis, that the behavior of political elites can be shaped by their personal religious orientations. Political scientists continue to debate the relative weight to assign the many factors that influence the behavior of public officials. In deciding how to cast a roll call vote, for example, members of Congress are subject to the pull of party loyalty, regional culture, judgments about constituency preferences, the influence of the president, the flow of national public opinion, staff recommendations, the lobbying efforts of myriad groups, and other personality characteristics. Although the sources of influence might be different, officials in the executive and judicial spheres are similarly buffeted by forces that could override any single personal characteristic. Religion is just one of the factors that might account for an official's decision to favor or oppose a particular course of action on a public problem.

Considering the clear importance of religion in mass voting, it is remarkable to discover how little attention has been devoted to the study of the religious factor in congressional behavior. Most systematic research has simply attempted to establish if members of Congress vote as religious blocs on issues decided by roll call votes. Even with a limited focus on basic denominational differences, the studies have not reached consensus. John Fenton (1960) compared the behavior of Catholic and Protestant members of the House and Senate during the 1959–1960 session of Congress. Fenton found that for the most part, when compared with members from the same party and region, Catholics and Protestants did not differ much in their support for civil rights legislation, foreign aid, or bills affecting organized labor. In contrast, Leroy Rieselbach (1966) showed consistent differences between Catholic and Protestant representatives on foreign aid votes in five Congresses from 1934 to 1964. In most cases, Catholics were more supportive of foreign aid appropriations than their fellow partisans, whether Democratic or Republican, or representatives from urban districts. This difference did not extend, however, to the realm of foreign trade issues, the other dimension of Rieselbach's study. Using roll call votes on those social welfare issues that had elicited policy statements from mainstream Protestant denominations, John Warner, Jr. (1968), also observed significant differences among Catholic, Protestant, and Jewish members of the Eighty-ninth Congress. Like other observers Warner found Protestants to be the most conservative and Jews to be the most liberal, but he also found no significant policy differences between mainstream and evangelical Protestant legislators once party affiliation had been taken into account.

Denominational affiliation might prove to exert a significant impact on legislative voting only when the issue under consideration has been the subject of intense religious controversy. The abortion issue, which has long engaged the attention of many churches, would seem to offer a good test case for this proposition. Two studies of voting on abortion laws in the American West have indeed revealed clear differences in legislative behavior by different religious groups.[11] In a study of legislators from an unnamed state, Richardson and Wightman Fox (1972, 1975) sought evidence for the impact of religious affiliation in votes on bills to liberalize abortion policy. Taking into account the urbanization levels of the districts and the legislators' age and party—factors likely to influence votes on moral issues—they found support for more liberal access to abortion among the Protestant and Jewish members of the lower house, and opposition to the proposals from the Catholic representatives. The Mormon legislators switched to the opposition side after their church issued clear statements about the incompatibility of liberalized abortion with Mormon doctrine. Observing a similar battle in another western state, O'Neil (1970) found essentially the same pattern of conflict in the Senate committee that killed a proposal for liberalized abortion. The ill-fated bill was supported by all liberal Protestants and Jewish members of the committee and opposed by every Roman Catholic and conservative Protestant.

The principal weakness of these studies was their failure to sort out systematically the impact of personal religion from either district composition or the other sources of influence on congressional voting. That problem has been addressed in three published studies. In the first, which examined roll call voting records for approximately one-fourth of House members in the Ninety-fifth Congress (Page et al. 1984), the legislators were ranked according to their attitudes toward social welfare spending, race relations, women's rights, law and order, and, finally, abortion. Using a powerful statistical technique, the researchers then attempted to assess the influence on this ranking the demographic characteristics of the district, its collective opinions on public issues, the representative's party affiliation, and his or her personal traits (including religious affiliation). On most issues, the investigators found little significance for personal traits. Abortion was an exception. Even taking into account the impact of district characteristics, the religious affiliation of the representatives exerted a significant impact by prompting Catholic members to support restrictive procedures on abortion. The same conclusion emerged from a study of three votes on abortion taken by the House of Representatives in 1976 (Vinovkis 1979). Through a complex statistical analysis, this study found legislators' personal religious affiliation to be one of the most powerful predictors of a vote on a motion to prohibit the use of federal funds for abortions. Even after the application of controls for personal traits, partisanship, liberalism, and several district characteristics, Catholics gave disproportionate support to the amendment, Protestants gave a low level of support, and Jewish representatives were strongly opposed to it. Finally, when the Senate voted in 1983 to reject a constitutional amendment that would have overturned the *Roe v. Wade* decision, Catholic and evangelical Protestant legislators were more likely to support the amendment than non-Catholics (Gohmann and Ohsfeldt 1990; Granberg 1985b). The impact of religious affiliation in this case withstood controls for a host of state-level influences.

As valuable as they are, these statistical investigations of denominational differences in legislative behavior only scratch the surface of possible religious effects on political elites. Much additional light has been shed by a pair of studies that transcended simple denominational classification by interviewing legislators to learn their religious values. Based on her interviews with twenty-five Catholics serving in the United States Congress in the period 1973–1974, Mary Hanna (1979) concluded that Catholics did not form a separate bloc and, with a few exceptions on issues such as abortion, were not strongly influenced by their Catholic constituents or the lobbying efforts of the church. Rather, Hanna found, the principal contribution of faith to Catholic legislators' political identity was its influence on their basic political attitudes. Two different streams of Catholicism guided their values: "A religious formation that emphasized strict codes of conduct, rules and guidelines, a rather rigid, puritanical devotion to duty and order; and one which stressed Christian love, compassion, and concern for one's fellowman, especially the poor, the helpless, and the unfortunate" (Hanna 1979, 99). Not surprisingly, adherents of the first tradition were conservative Republicans and legislators who drew on the social reform stream were liberal Democrats.

As discussed in Chapter 4, a similar distinction between different types of religion was noted by Peter L. Benson and Dorothy L. Williams (1982), who interviewed eighty members of the House of Representatives from a wide range of denominations. Politically conservative and liberal representatives were found in each major American denomination, but members of the two camps tended to stress different aspects of belief. The conservatives conceived of religion as something for the individual, a force that gave them comfort in times of distress, strength of conviction, self-discipline, and the promise of eternal reward. In contrast, political liberals put a great deal of emphasis on the communal aspect of religion. Where conservatives saw religion as a one-to-one relationship between individuals and God, the theology of liberalism stressed the oneness of humanity, and the need for social transformation on earth if God's will is to be recognized adequately. These differences in ultimate value showed up in voting on specific types of legislation. "Individualism-preserving" religion was correlated with support for free enterprise, private ownership, and military expenditures and with opposition to government spending on social programs. Its opposite, what Benson and Williams labeled "community-building" religion, encouraged support for programs of foreign aid, hunger relief, civil liberties, and liberalized abortion. These differences in religious style appeared much stronger than the group differences normally observed when legislators are divided into broad families, such as Protestant, Catholic, and Jew, or classified according to denominations. For elites just as the masses, studies using denominational affiliation may underestimate the connection between religious values and legislative behavior.

The Judiciary and the Bureaucracy

If legislators may be influenced by religious backgrounds, the same force could in principle affect the decisions of judges. Some scholars have argued that in the American political system, which gives judges broad discretion to interpret the laws, a complete understanding of judicial decisions requires the use of information about personal and social background. Although this point has by no means been universally accepted by judicial scholars, it has inspired several careful studies that have traced patterns of judicial behavior to the traits of individual judges. The need to be cautious in ascribing religious motives to public acts must once again be recognized. A judge's decision is likely to reflect certain norms of the legal profession—a respect for precedent, the quality of advocacy, views about the proper scope for judicial discretion, and, of course, the facts surrounding any particular case. If religion fits into the equation, it does so merely as one factor among many.

Systematic analysis of religion has been as scarce in research on judicial behavior as in studies of legislative behavior. Probably the best evidence for a religious effect can be found in Sorauf's (1976, chap. 9) analysis of denominational differences in voting on church-state issues by judges on high appellate courts. In analyzing nonunanimous decisions during the 1950s and 1960s, he found that more than 80 percent of Jewish judges favored a strict "separationist" policy that limited government's ability to recognize religion, whereas Roman Catholic judges, by an equally lopsided margin, voted to endorse policies and practices that accommodated religious interests. Protestants, who made up by far the bulk of the judges hearing the church-state issues, split roughly in half between the separationist and accommodationist camps. The historic tension between Protestants and Catholics in the United States was apparent in the tendency of Protestant judges to become more accommodationist when Catholics were not a party to a lawsuit and for Catholics to become decidedly more separationist when non-Catholic groups were involved in the case (ibid., 225). As Sorauf realized, this set of cases was particularly conducive to the operation of a denominational effect because "the religious affiliation of the judge relates in the judicial decision to the direct and immediate interests of his religious group as well as to the social values derived from the religious tradition and its belief system" (ibid., 222). When the interests of specific denominations are not so self-evident, religious affiliation should play a lesser role.

The existing research supports the foregoing conclusion. Analyzing the decisions issued by state and federal supreme court justices in 1955, Stuart Nagel (1962) found statistically significant differences between Protestants and Catholics in four out of fifteen categories of cases. In three of the types that fit into a conservative-liberal spectrum, the Catholic judges were more liberal: they were more likely than their Protestant colleagues to rule on behalf of convicted criminals appealing a verdict, government agencies engaged in regulating business practices, and employees seeking compensation for injuries. In divorce cases, however, the Catholic judges exhibited a much higher tendency to rule in favor of the wife—perhaps a reflection of the tradition of Catholic conservatism in family matters. Most of the difference between Catholics and Protestants was associated with partisanship rather than religion, however (Nagel 1961). Skepticism about a religious effect on judicial decisions was supported by Goldman's (1966, 1975) studies of decisions issued by the federal courts of appeal during the 1960s. In only two of the ten areas examined by Goldman did significant Protestant/non-Protestant differences surface, and most of the apparently greater conservatism of Protestant judges could be explained by the high proportion of Southerners in the Protestant category. S. Sidney Ulmer (1973) extended this type of social background analysis to the U.S. Supreme Court in examining voting patterns on criminal cases from 1947 to 1956. He concluded that Protestants were more likely than non-Protestants to support the government side against appeals by convicted criminals.

Rather than investigate a range of issues, some scholars have concentrated on one particular area of judicial activity—race relations. The courts were the catalyst for racial change in the southern states, and some observers have thought that religious values could have accounted for the willingness of federal judges to challenge the deeply entrenched system of segregation in the South. The guiding hypothesis has been that those judges who were least immersed in the southern culture of segregation, including those who were not affiliated with the numerically dominant evangelical Protestant churches, would be most inclined to rule on behalf of another out-group. Kenneth Vines (1964), the first to check out this expectation with social scientific methods, examined judicial rulings in nearly three hundred civil rights cases decided in southern circuits from 1954 through 1962. On the basis of decisional patterns, thirty-seven federal district judges were classified as segregationist, moderate, or integrationist. As one might expect, there was a demonstrable difference in ruling associated with religious affiliation. The "orthodox Protestants," a term Vines used for denominations defined here as evangelical, were principally found in either the segregationist (45 percent) or moderate (36 percent) camps, leaving less than 20 percent for the integrationist. At the other extreme, the two Catholic judges were classified as integrationists. That left the middle position for judges who were presumed to be mainline Protestants. They were less likely to be integrationist than Catholics (45 percent) but also less likely to issue rulings in favor of segregation (21 percent).

Despite its conformity to prediction, the Vines study suffered from weaknesses of technique. By using religion without any controls for possibly related factors, he exposed himself to a charge of spurious correlation. Furthermore, because the cases differed from circuit to circuit, he may have, in effect, compared apples with oranges. To remedy those defects and to update the findings, Giles and Walker (1975) examined the problem anew. Rather than use dissimilar cases, they used the same measure in each circuit—racial imbalance in public schools. Because all schools were under court order to implement antisegregation policies, Giles and Walker contended, the measure of racial imbalance remaining in 1970 indicated "the district judge's policy decision in implementing the [desegregation] mandate at the local level" (ibid., 924). Trying to capture the religious factor, the analysis compared judges from what the authors labeled as "fundamentalist Protestantism" with members of all other religious affiliations. Religion, included as a social background factor in an equation that also contained a measure of the racial climate, the judge's connection to the community, and several characteristics of the school district, was not found to exert a substantial influence on the racial imbalance permitted in the district. Whether these conflicting findings can be laid to different techniques or to a real change cannot be determined; on balance, however, the systematic studies examined in this section do not strongly support the notion of a religious effect in judicial decisions.

If analysis of religion in Congress were similarly dependent solely on statistical studies, negative conclusions about religious effects in that branch might also have been reached. A fuller understanding of the legislative arena was possible because members of Congress were available for interviews that could elicit religious beliefs beyond mere denominational affiliation. Because judges rarely submit to such interviews, it has been difficult to find out if more sensitive measures of religious values might account for behavioral differences. Some judicial biographies have speculated about possible religious influences on particular decisions or even judicial style. Late in 1981, when the Equal Rights Amendment (ERA) to the U.S. Constitution was in the waning days of its unsuccessful ratification period, a federal judge from Idaho issued an adverse ruling that further reduced the amendment's slim chances for passage. Because the judge held a position of authority in the Mormon church, which vehemently opposed the ERA, several critics charged that his ruling improperly reflected his religious values. Then, too, in a psychologically oriented analysis of the great Supreme Court justice Felix Frankfurter, H. N. Hirsch (1981) argued that religion influenced the judge's high combative and aggressive style. Though the point is too complex to summarize easily, Hirsch argued that Frankfurter, the child of Jewish immigrants from Austria, was caught between the attractiveness of the Protestant establishment that dominated the legal profession and his standing as a conspicuous outsider who was reminded powerfully that he did not fit in. Consequently, he developed a personality and style highly conducive to the role of the outsider. That kind of linkage cannot as yet be subjected to systematic testing, but at least it suggests how religion may contribute to judicial behavior by an indirect path.

Because laws are not self-executing, the administrative agencies of government play an important part in public policy making. Yet, as little as is known about religion in the legislative and judicial branches, even less seems clear about the executive wing. For the political appointees and career civil servants who staff the executive branch and its agencies, only fragmentary evidence about religious values is available. From time to time, for example, we hear about zealous federal prosecutors whose crusades against pornography are reported to be a function of their intense religiosity.

As the official head of the executive branch and the principal focus of American government, the president has a unique opportunity to affect both the substance and tone of public policy. In this area, as in the others examined in the chapter, scholars have disagreed about the importance of social background factors relative to the many competing influences brought to bear on presidential decision making. The specific influence of religion has been even harder to assess, because almost all recent presidents have come from the mainline Protestant tradition. Nonetheless, there is at least suggestive evidence that religious background may affect a president's approach to politics, if not the specific policies of a chief executive. This can best be demonstrated by comparing two recent occupants of the White House.

To a degree that had not been common in the twentieth century, Jimmy Carter brought questions of religious values and character to the center of his political campaigns. A devout Southern Baptist, churchgoer and "born-again" Christian who was familiar with the work of modern theologians and experienced in missionary work, Carter was a novel factor in the 1976 presidential campaign (Kucharsky 1976; Miller 1978; Pipert 1978). His candidacy appeared to hearten evangelical Protestants and worry many mainline Protestants, Catholics, Jews, and the nonaffiliated. Partly because of unfamiliarity with the Southern Baptist tradition and partly because of the presumed association of evangelical

Christianity with social conservatism and intolerance, many worried that a deeply religious president would try to enforce his "narrow" moral preferences on the nation or, fortified by a belief in a personal relationship with God, would reject compromise and negotiation with those who did not see the world in the same way. Throughout the campaign, Carter attempted to assure voters that he did not see God's hand in every policy proposed in his platform and that he would not use the law to enforce narrow standards of moral rectitude. Rather than prompting an unshakable faith in the rightness of his own preferences, he argued, his religious values had taught him the need to recognize his own fallibility. And to those who expressed concern about the Baptist social agenda, Carter emphasized the Social Gospel tradition of religion as a force for economic and political reform.

In practice, few observers were able to link Carter's major political tendencies to his personal religiosity. On church-state issues, for example, he adhered to the traditional Baptist insistence on a sharp wall of separation, even refusing to hold worship services in the White House (Flowers 1983). His religious background showed up, however, in several ways that might not have been apparent to most observers. According to one analysis, Carter's personal style—marked by enormous self-discipline, a commitment to hard work, orderliness, and fiscal conservatism—bore the unmistakable traces of Puritanism from which his faith had descended (Mazlish and Diamond 1979, 253). In his insistence that other nations be held to high standards of behavior, as in the crusade for international human rights, Carter might have been exhibiting a "typical" evangelical's missionary tendency. Another scholar attributed Carter's discomfort with power politics to the Baptist disapproval of conflict (Speer 1988). A fellow Southern Baptist (Baker 1977) suggested another carryover of Carter's religion into his politics. One of Carter's first and most controversial acts as president was to issue a pardon to draft evaders—not an amnesty, which declares that a person did no wrong, but a pardon, which forgives a wrongdoer. In that distinction, Baker argued, lay evidence of the biblical spirit of grace that offers love and forgiveness to the sinner. Carter's major triumph, bringing the leaders of Egypt and Israel together on a framework for peace in the Middle East, has also been attributed to a religious trait. Only a person of sublime self-confidence, a faith in himself born of religious certainty, and one who was more than usually committed to bringing peace to the Holy Land would have the audacity to undertake such a challenging mission or the stamina to succeed in it.

Unfortunately, the validity of this analysis is anything but certain. The only other Southern Baptist to hold the presidency, Harry Truman, exhibited few traits in common with his coreligionist. And some presidents from different religious traditions acted in ways similar to Carter. John Kennedy spoke in missionary terms about the nation's world role. Gerald Ford issued an even more controversial pardon (of former president Richard Nixon). Few presidents in history could match Lyndon Johnson's skill as a negotiator and persuasive advocate. Because each of these men was far removed from Carter's religious background, it is clearly dangerous to draw too firm a conclusion about the impact of theology on politics.

Carter's successor, Ronald Reagan, also described himself as a born-again Christian and argued strongly for the relevance of religion to public policy. But unlike Carter, whose theology treated politics as a calling to establish social justice, Reagan viewed government intervention as more likely to create problems than solve them. In one sense, Reagan's political theology was close to that of the Puritans, with whom he shared a dismal assessment of humanity's natural impulses. Like them, Reagan tended to regard human beings as creatures of impulse who needed the hand of government "to restrain the darker impulses of human nature" (Reagan 1981). In this light, the only legitimate role of government is negative: to maintain order so that humanity's goodness and creativity can flourish in the social and economic realms. This view of government recalls the emphasis of the Founders on politics as a barrier to the worst excesses of sinful people and nothing more. Such a perspective may explain why Reagan foresaw dramatic improvements in the quality of life with a reduction in the level of government activity (Thomas 1984).

By his penchant for quoting Bible verses to support certain policies (Reagan 1985, 130) and his references to the Soviet Union as the "focus of evil" in the modern world, Reagan certainly encouraged observers to analyze his political preferences in terms of explicit theological values. During the 1984 campaign, critics expressed concern about the influence of what has been called "Armageddon theology" on Reagan's attitude toward the use of force in world politics.[12] The phrase refers to an interpretation of the Bible that foresees a time of worldwide turbulence, including the possibility of a nuclear war in the Middle East, on the eve of the Second Coming of Jesus. A president who subscribed to that apocalyptic view of the world, it has been argued by some theologians, would have less incentive to strive for peace or nuclear arms control and might be tempted to ignore the long-run costs of social policies. (That theological issue cropped up in the confirmation hearings for James Watt, Reagan's first secretary of the interior, who was reported to have expressed the view that Jesus' imminent return meant that preservationist environmental policies could be relaxed.) To counter this interpretation, Reagan declared during a televised debate that his interest in prophecies would not inhibit his efforts to secure peace.

The impact of religion on presidential behavior might take several different forms (Monsma 1977). In one such model, closest to the Reagan style, the president serves as the "high priest of American civil religion," calling the nation to righteousness through order and obedience. Alternatively, the personal morality model, expressed to some degree by President Carter, expects the president to express religiosity by living up to Christian moral standards in personal conduct. Yet a third option is for the president to pursue policies "molded by basic Christian principles and insights such as justice, healing, man's purpose as an image-bearer of God, and the sinfulness of human nature." This is not a call to theocracy but an insistence that presidents recognize moral imperatives when they act.

Religious Values and Government Activities

Whatever types of influence religious groups may attempt to wield, is the political system responsive to religious values and appeals? Although it is very difficult to sort out the relative importance of all the factors that influence government decisions in any policy area, there is much evidence linking general patterns of public policy to religious factors.

Because American churches have traditionally given major priority to questions of personal conduct, it should not be at all surprising to find a strong link between religious affiliation and government "morality" policies. This has been demonstrated in a series of studies tracing policy differences between the states to variations in religious composition. David Fairbanks (1977) discovered a strong correlation between the proportion of the population belonging to Protestant churches and the restrictiveness of state statutes affecting gambling and liquor. Because the evangelical churches have usually regarded these activities as inconsistent with Christian orthodoxy, it seems reasonable to conclude that state laws have reflected community values. Similarly, the clearly expressed resistance of the Catholic church to artificial birth control and divorce probably explains why in the various states, the strictness of contraception and marriage laws has varied directly with the proportion of Catholics in the population (ibid., 1979). Because these relationships have survived the application of several environmental factors that might be supposed to underlay them, it appears that the moral values of a state's dominant religious group are somehow conveyed to lawmakers.

In abortion, a policy area heavily laden with moral issues, religious groups also appear to have played a decisive role in determining how the Supreme Court's decision was implemented. John R. Bond and Charles A. Johnson (1982) surveyed a national random sample of hospitals in 1979, six years after the Supreme Court struck down legal restrictions on a woman's right to terminate a pregnancy. They found that despite a national policy of permitting abortions without restrictions during the first six months of pregnancy, only about one-fifth of the hospitals surveyed provided abortion services to the full limit allowed by the *Roe v. Wade* decision. A substantial percentage allowed abortion only during the first three months (39 percent) or under specified conditions (13 percent). Of those that did not allow abortions to be performed, the policy ranged from facilitating abortion by providing referrals to other facilities to discouraging it by counseling on the medical and moral issues of abortion. In trying to explain differences among hospitals, the authors hypothesized that community preference would be a critical influence; accordingly, they tested the permissiveness of the policy against hospital administrators' perceptions of community and elite-group opinion about abortion, the level of interest-group activity on the issue, and a measure of the level of church membership in the community. Two of the three measures of community preference (interest-group activity was the exception) were found to exert a significant influence on hospital abortion policy. The more supportive the personal attitudes of the community and elites and the lower the level of church membership, the more permissive the abortion policy. In that public opinion on the issue has been shown to be strongly related to religious affiliation and activity, it seems appropriate to credit the religious characteristics of a community with substantial influence on the availability of facilities for abortion.

That conclusion was supported by Susan B. Hansen's (1980) study of state-level differences in 1976 abortion rates. If all states were operating under the same Supreme Court ruling, why did New York and California report approximately 40 abortions per 1,000 women of childbearing age whereas the comparable rate was only about 3 per 1,000 in Mississippi and West Virginia? Like Bond and Johnson, Hansen observed that the major direct influence on the performance rate was the availability of hospitals willing to offer abortion services. The restrictiveness of hospital policy, in turn, depended on a number of factors including the state's religious composition. The percentage of Mormons in the population had a negative impact on community tolerance for abortion and a direct depressive effect on the rate of abortion.[13] Similarly, the greater the Catholic share of the state population, the lower the community support for abortion and the more restricted the availability of facilities offering abortion.[14]

Given that churches have often spoken out forcefully on matters of personal conduct, it should not be surprising to discover a correlation between legal restrictions on unorthodox activities and religious geography. But studies of the American states have supplied much evidence that religious composition is related to policy patterns that do not have such an obvious link to theological values. Most such studies have built on the hypothesis that religion contributes in a major degree to the assumptions, values, and habits that may define policy preferences over a wide range of public issues.

In the area of race relations, for example, Fenton and Vines (1967) argued that the level of voter registration of Louisiana blacks depended largely on the religious values of the politically dominant whites in the community. More than a decade after the Supreme Court struck down state laws excluding blacks from voting in public elections, local communities had found ways to keep more than two-thirds of black adults off the electoral registers. As a rule, the level of black registration in Louisiana was much higher in the predominantly Catholic parishes (counties) of the southern area of the state than in the northern area, where Protestant groups predominated. Finding that this difference held up in the face of checks for the influence of various nonreligious social, political, and cultural factors, the investigators pointed to differences in social attitudes between Catholics and Protestants:

Permissive attitudes toward Negro registration in French-Catholic parishes seem expressive of the basic value that the Negro is spiritually equal in a Catholic society. Such a view of man's relation to man, a scheme of elementary justice implicit in a Catholic society, some Catholics maintain, is sustained by traditional Catholic theology and actively promoted by the Church in Louisiana. There is little evidence in the Protestant parishes of cultural values assigning the Negro a spiritually equal place in the community or of activity by the church itself toward these values. (ibid., 176)

In addition to a doctrinal basis for racial tolerance, the Catholic church also had institutional and social reasons to discourage ill treatment of blacks. As a universal church that crosses racial and ethnic boundaries, Catholicism would be threatened if all the faithful were not treated on equal terms. Moreover, because the Catholic church was one of the few integrated institutions in the South, its members were given the opportunity to dispel their prejudices and stereotypes. In contrast, the segregated white Protestant churches of northern Louisiana catered to the segregationist values of their members and did little to promote the contact between races that might have fostered mutual tolerance.

Religion may affect an even broader range of policies through its influence on attitudes toward the role of government in society. In Chapter 3, I noted that one way religion might shape American political behavior is by its general effect on the national political culture. Along the same lines, a leading authority on American federalism has suggested that the religious and ethnic groups that settled the various American states were the carriers of particular cultural values that have left a mark on contemporary state politics and policy. According to Daniel Elazar (1970, 476), migrating groups subscribed to different views about the nature and purpose of government, the role of politics in society, and other politically relevant beliefs. For example, he noted the emphasis in Puritan thought on using the power of the state to create a holy commonwealth on earth. In the parts of the country settled by Puritans, their successors, and immigrants with similar religious traditions, this conception of politics as a calling has survived in a highly moralistic approach to politics:

Politics, to the moralistic political culture, is considered one of the great activities of humanity in its search for the good society—a struggle for power, it is true, but also an effort to exercise power for the betterment of the commonwealth. Consequently, in the moralistic political culture both the general public and politicians conceive of politics as a public activity centered on some notion of the public good and properly devoted to the advancement of the public interest. Good government, then, is measured by the degree to which it promotes the public good and in terms of the honesty, selflessness, and commitment to the public welfare of those who govern. (Elazar 1984, 117)

This approach, like those of the individualistic and traditionalistic cultures elsewhere, dictates a particular configuration of values that should affect the scope, nature, and style of political practice. Noting that religious groups with such distinctive political conceptions clustered in different parts of the country, Elazar predicted a correlation between state policy orientations and ethnoreligious settlement patterns.

Although it was developed principally to account for contemporary policy differences, Elazar's theory has been strikingly confirmed by studies of political conflict in the nineteenth-century United States (Hammond 1979; Kleppner 1979). Movements for abolition of slavery, Prohibition, and a host of other social reforms were fired by the enthusiasm and crusading mentality that characterizes a moralistic culture and resisted in terms of values that sound remarkably like Elazar's description of the traditionalist culture. What is more, according to the influential "ethnocultural" school of American history, the basic groupings of voters were defined largely by the type of religious values that Elazar identified as the core of differing political cultures. Whatever its historical value, Elazar's assertion about the policy impact of religiously based value systems has inspired several research projects on contemporary state-level variations in public policy. Although the specific predictions have not always been confirmed (Schiltz and Rainey 1978), several scholars have detected affinities between the concentration of certain religious groups and particular sets of policies enacted by the states.

Based on statistics of church membership, Hutcheson and Taylor (1973) classified American states in terms of the proportion of the population affiliated with fundamentalist denominations—defined in the study as religious groups who believe the Bible is the literal word of God. The groups in Hutcheson and Taylor's "fundamentalist" category—essentially the same denominations classified as evangelical Protestants in Chapter 4—have been identified by Elazar (1984, 130–131) as carriers of the "traditionalistic" political culture. Precisely as would be expected from a culture that wants government to play a "conservative and custodial" role (ibid., 119), the fundamentalist share of the population was associated with a high teacher-pupil ratio in public schools and a low level of state taxation. Using a similar technique, Johnson (1976) reported that the concentration of religious groups with a moralistic orientation correlated strongly with high levels of spending for social welfare programs but that the proportion of traditionalistic denominations depressed governmental efforts in that area. Klingman and Lammers (1984) confirmed that conclusion with a different approach. The states were ranked on a scale of "general policy liberalism" in which high scores identified a willingness to utilize government power on behalf of disadvantaged groups. The scale included such diverse components as state efforts to combat racial discrimination, spending for child welfare and social services, ratification of the Equal Rights Amendment, and the level of consumer protection efforts. Although no direct measure of religious concentration was included in the long list of factors tested as possible influences on policy liberalism, the analysis did rank each state by the moralism of its political culture. As it happens, the measure of state political culture turned out to be one of the two strongest predictors of a state's ranking vis-à-vis policy liberalism. The states with the most moralistic political cultures were the most likely to adopt innovative policies designed to improve the status of disadvantaged groups.

In one of the most imaginative studies of its kind, Michael Johnston (1983) managed to demonstrate a connection between religious geography and what Elazar described as the "moralistic approach" to politics. As an expert on political corruption, he wanted to test an explanation for what appears to be very different levels of toleration for illegal acts by public officials. In some communities, official misconduct is accepted as a fact of life, something as inevitable and irresistible as bad weather; other communities react to governmental malfeasance with shock and horror, deploying the full resources of the law to combat it. On the assumption that communities with high concentrations of moralistic denominations would be especially averse to such misconduct, he included religious affiliation in a model to explain the rate of conviction for public officials. As it did in the other studies conducted in Elazar's framework, the variable that tapped the moralism of political culture exerted a strong influence in the predicted manner. The higher the concentration of denominations that Elazar identified as carriers of a moralistic outlook on politics, the greater the number of successful prosecutions for official lawbreaking.

On the basis of this evidence, it appears that political culture—which Elazar traced specifically to the beliefs and historical experience of religious denominations—affects not only the content of state policy but its style as well. This conclusion could be subjected to the same criticism about spurious relationships that was raised in the discussion of religion as mass political behavior. Surely, a state's level of spending, its social programs, and its record of prosecution for corruption and other actions depend, for the most part, on its governmental capacity and level of economic development. In each of the studies cited above, that possibility was taken into account by the inclusion of variables to represent the social and economic status of the areas under comparison. Although the precise measures differed somewhat, the application of controls for economic development did not eliminate the linkage between religious groups and policy patterns. Religion, which according to the previous chapters has left its mark on American political values, mass political behavior, and the law, apparently has also contributed to the different configurations of public policy pursued by the states.

Limitations on Religious Influence

The influence of a particular religious group in a particular policy area represents only one force in the struggle to shape government action. Because of the complexity of public policy making in the United States, it is important to appreciate how religion and moral influences compete with other factors for an impact on decisions. The need for a balanced appraisal can best be conveyed through a case study of American policy in the Middle East. Though frequently cited to illustrate the potential impact of religious considerations, this case also points to conditions that limit religious influence on public policy.

Since the state of Israel was founded in 1948, the United States has consistently supported it with vigorous diplomatic action, military aid, and significant amounts of economic assistance. That support has frequently been attributed to a pair of "religious" factors—namely the actions of the "Jewish lobby" in the United States and the moralistic strain in American foreign policy. American Jews have used their considerable political resources—voting strength, organizational ties, campaign contributions, access to decision makers, media influence—to mount an energetic campaign on behalf of Israeli interests. The campaign has succeeded because a pro-Israel position fits in well with the moralistic style of American foreign policy. Formed in the shadow of the Holocaust, besieged by hostile neighbors, and holding steadfastly to the same democratic political values as the United States, Israel had drawn on a powerful current of goodwill in American opinion. As Lyndon Johnson is said to have told the Soviet leader who asked why America was pledged to Israel, "We think it's right" (Glick 1982, 106). Taken together, the political strength of American Jews and the moralistic tendency of American foreign policy seem to explain American policy in the Middle East and to illustrate the importance of religious influence.

Yet before too much influence is conceded to religion, it is crucial to put U.S. policy toward Israel into a broader context. According to scholars who have studied foreign policy making, the critical element in American support for Israel has been a perception of national self-interest rather than Jewish lobbying or attachments of sentiment. After a careful reconstruction of the events that led President Truman to make the initial commitment to Israel, Ganin (1979) concluded that the chief motivations were fear of disorder and bloodshed in Palestine, competition with the Soviet Union for Middle East influence, and Truman's desire to assert his primacy over the U.S. State Department. The American commitment to Israel was maintained and expanded by successive administrations because it served their overriding foreign policy objectives (Spiegel 1985). The Carter administration, preoccupied with maintaining American access to Middle East oil supplies, valued Israel because of its location near the crucial transportation lanes for petroleum exports. Concerned above all else to counter alleged Soviet expansionism, the Reagan administration saw great benefits in cooperating with a nation that had the military might to deter Soviet action in the Middle East. With the end of the Cold War, the Bush administration has seemingly attached lower priority to the American-Israeli alliance. To counter Iraq's invasion of Kuwait in 1990, Bush assembled a multinational military coalition that included many Arab states but pointedly excluded Israel from an active role. Hence, although religious factors help to explain the pro-Israel thrust of U.S. Middle East policy, most authorities have given precedence to the overriding strategic objectives and perceptions of American foreign policy decision makers.

To the extent that religion has facilitated a pro-Israel policy, that issue illustrates how many factors must fall into place before religion assumes an important role. There are several unique aspects to the origins of U.S. policy toward Israel. To begin with, the religious group in question, the American Jewish community, was overwhelmingly united behind a common goal that it considered extraordinarily important. Jewish support for Israel arises from the combination of institutional self-interest, social concerns, and theology. Israel represents a chance for the survival of Judaism as a religion and the Jewish people as a distinct community—and no institutional interest could be more basic than self-preservation (Medding 1989). The fate of Israel also touches the social aspirations of Jews who have been a minority, and often a despised one, throughout their history. Israel's success thus serves to provide "psychological, ethnic, and religious pride" for American Jews (Glick 1982, 126). An additional basis for American Jewish support of Israel can be found in the theological call for a return to Zion and the opportunity it provides for realizing Jewish social values. The combination of these factors raised Israel to the forefront of political consciousness of many American Jews, and they provided ample resources to promote Israeli interests in Washington. It certainly helped the Israeli cause that no opposing religious groups have been able to match the American Jewish community in political sophistication and strength of purpose. Unlike many religious lobbies, which are poorly staffed, broadly focused, inexperienced, and unschooled in the art of compromise (Hertzke 1988, 70–79), the Israeli lobby in Washington has learned to concentrate its efforts with considerable sophistication.[15]

As to the issue itself, Israel's moral claim for support was compatible both with the U.S. government's secular interest and with religious values almost universally shared by Americans. As few other political causes have done, Zionism appealed to a broad spectrum of American Christianity. Israel earned sympathy from the politically liberal segments of American religion because of its social and ethical values. At the other extreme, the most politically conservative wing of Protestantism could find support for the restoration of a Jewish state in Bible prophecy.[16] In such a supportive environment, the moral justification for Israel's existence was not challenged.

These conditions, which are highly conducive to religious impact, have not been common in other areas of policy making. To begin with, few political issues are as salient and unifying to members of a religious group as the cause of Israel was for American Jews. The abortion issue, which has become the basis of political mobilization for some Catholics, has actually divided church members and reduced political unity. As a political issue becomes further removed from the religious group's self-interest or traditional level of concern, cohesion becomes even harder to maintain. Without a common front, a religious group has a lesser chance of influencing public policy. Furthermore, because of differing institutional interests, social status, and theological traditions, religious groups usually have not made common cause on most issues of public policy. Whether the issue has been something as basic to religious interests as prayer in public schools or as global as the policy to freeze production of nuclear weapons, denominations have rarely spoken with a single voice. Divisions within the religious community have further retarded the impact of moral concern on public policy.

Religious groups often lack the means of influence available to secular interests. In carrying out their lobbying, for example, religious interest groups are typically at a severe disadvantage because of minimal budgets, small staffs, and limited government experience—the latter a particularly important quality that bestows both credibility and access (Zwier 1988). Resources alone do not guarantee success, but they probably correlate with scope of influence. However, the religious interest groups can compensate somewhat for this comparative disadvantage by intelligent use of their limited resources (Weber and Stanley 1984). This means, among other things, focusing on a limited set of issues, attempting to influence the early stages of legislation through contacts with key officials, and developing expertise and effective communication skills. With their highly positive images and substantial social prestige, the religious lobbies have enjoyed some success, particularly in securing religious liberty or other concerns where they supported very specific goals.

The Middle East policy-making process, unusual in several respects, also contributed to the apparent influence of religious factors. Religious pressure could be brought to bear effectively because the decision-making process was relatively centralized, involving only a handful of officials. The authority to extend diplomatic recognition and to cooperate militarily belonged to the president alone. When military and economic assistance was proposed, Congress entered the process. Neither the courts nor state and local government agencies played a role. With the decision makers reduced to a select few, each possessing clear authority, lobbying efforts could be concentrated for maximum effectiveness and opposing forces had fewer avenues for delay and appeal. In addition to the elite nature of the decision, the Israeli case was unusual because the fundamental issues were presented in fairly straightforward terms and embodied in a series of concrete decisions: Should the United States extend diplomatic recognition to Israel? How much U.S. economic and military aid should Israel receive? Should the United States provide Israel with military intelligence and emergency supplies in armed conflict with the Arab states? Because these questions were often posed in what amounted to life-or-death situations, there was an opportunity for decisive action with relatively clear understanding of the implications of each potential course of action.

In most policy areas, religious influence is inhibited from bearing heavily on decision making. In the typical policy debate, power and authority are widely diffused among many actors, making it unclear who, if anyone, has the decisive role. With fragmented authority, a victory at any level has less long-term significance. Even more fundamentally, the typical government policy is rarely so clear-cut as it was with Israel. As many authorities have concluded, policy making is a process rather than an event. When issues enter the process, they are often subdivided into components and acted on by different authorities rather than treated as a single problem. A decision reached in one sector is not binding on another; a victory in one arena can be reversed in another. In any case, the consequences for a particular course of action are likely to be uncertain. This is all the more relevant when religious lobbies forgo involvement with legislative detail to concentrate instead on "witnessing" for such broad goals as social justice and world peace.

For these reasons, policymakers usually stress the difficulty of applying moral insights to items on the public agenda. According to Senator Paul Simon of Illinois (1984, 131), "Practical dilemmas that real-life politicians face do not fit into easily wrapped packages to which moral labels can be attached." As an example, Simon cites a 1977 congressional debate on a bill to renew a federal program that sent American agricultural products to countries facing food shortages (ibid., 22–23). When a representative introduced an amendment to prohibit the purchase of tobacco for export under the program, Simon faced a moral dilemma. Because tobacco was a significant crop in nearly a hundred House districts, the amendment might endanger support for the program, resulting possibly in the "clearly immoral" denial of food to starving people. Yet without the amendment, the government would spend money that could buy food for 900,000 hungry people on a product with lethal consequences for public health. As Simon asked rhetorically, "What could be a clearer moral issue?" The testimony of other legislators and administrators amplified Simon's conclusion that policymakers normally confront choices between conflicting moral norms, rather than simply between good and evil (Anderson 1970; Haughey 1979).

From the evidence presented in this chapter, it seems clear that religious influence can be brought to bear on political decision making, particularly when issues are narrow in scope, but that it is rarely the decisive factor in the outcome of a complex policy. Aside from competing interests, the major limits on religious impact are divisions of opinion within and among religious groups and the inherent confusion of the policy-making process.

The decision to enter the political arena, whether taken by a religious group of its own volition or virtually imposed on it by external authorities, may impose a significant cost. Political conflict is characterized by disagreement, strife, and competition. In associating itself with such a process—or being seen as part of it—the church may lose its reputation as a place of refuge from the sordid reality of life. Yet, paradoxically, abstention from politics may also diminish the church's stature. If members of the community perceive religious values as relevant to a political issue or under threat from some external actor, they may lose faith in a church that stands idly by. Because religious values are so all-encompassing, and couched in a universal language, it is difficult to defend indifference as a political strategy.

Throughout the chapter, it has largely been taken for granted that religious groups declare positions on public issues in order to focus on how such positions are advocated in the public realm. Left open was the vital issue of what different religious groups actually stand for and how they have come to favor certain political options. Because shifting patterns of religious group politics have undermined many comfortable images inherited from the past, such as the stereotypes of conservative Catholicism or apolitical evangelicalism, the next topic of inquiry is the emerging pattern of political identity among the major denominational families in the United States.

NOTES

1. "Substance, Tactics of Tax Revision Cause Conflict Among Administration Hard-Liners, Pragmatists," *Wall Street Journal,* Oct. 8, 1985, 64.

2. "Catholic Bishops Hire Firm to Market Abortion Attack," *New York Times,* Apr. 6, 1990, 10A.

3. "Abortion Issue Takes Violent Turn," *New York Times,* Nov. 25, 1984, 2E.

4. "Defense Fund Set Up for Bombing Suspects," *Gainesville Sun,* Mar. 19, 1985, 11A.

5. Under federal law, a nonprofit organization can maintain tax-exempt status so long as less than 20 percent of its budget is used to influence the decisions of public authorities.

6. "Lawmakers Debate Three Critical Issues," *Gainesville Sun,* April 21, 1985.

7. "Candidates' Poll, General Election, 1984," *Gainesville Sun,* Oct. 28, 1984.

8. Before jumping to the conclusion that voters are bigoted and irrational in favoring a candidate of the same religion just because of the common tie of church membership, consider another possibility. Because religion is an important element in influencing the social system, persons from the same religious community may share similar experiences and develop similar views about the issues of the day. These features, not the mere fact of common religious affiliation, can make a candidate attractive to a voter. It is worth keeping in mind that the studies cited on this subject (except for Pomper) used hypothetical candidates in fictitious races; hence, there were few cues other than ethnicity or religion to guide electoral choice. As Donald Granberg (1985a) demonstrated with both survey and experimental data, voters who lack information about a candidate's position on an issue—particularly an issue with religious implications—may infer a position by using religious affiliation as a cue.

9. "Did Moon Give Aid to the Contras?" *Miami Herald,* Jan. 30, 1985.

10. Using the issue of the Equal Rights Amendment, White (1984) has shown how the Mormon system for reaching judgments on public issues also follows a very centralized pattern.

11. On such a sensitive issue as abortion, participants in legislative struggles may be unwilling to confide in academic researchers. To alleviate fears that their comments may become public knowledge, researchers have sometimes had to disguise the state in which the study was conducted.

12. "Armageddon View Prompts a Debate," *New York Times,* Oct. 24, 1984, 1, 13; "Religious Debate Fueled by Politics," *New York Times,* Oct. 28, 1984, 31; and

"Reagan Looks Down on 'Blessed Are the Peacemakers'," *Gainesville Sun*, April 23, 1984, 11A.

13. Lacking any direct measure of community support for abortion, she used a surrogate measure indicating the proportion of a state's congressional delegation supporting federal abortion funding in several 1977 votes.

14. The finding that a concentration of antiabortion religious groups diminishes the availability of abortion facilities may well explain why Borders and Cutright (1979) failed to find a significant Catholic effect on abortion rates in metropolitan areas. Once the level of services enters the analysis, it masks the impact of religious composition—suggesting the need for a two-step analysis such as that performed by Hansen.

15. "Political Contributions from Pro-Israel PACs Suggest Coordination," *Wall Street Journal*, June 24, 1987, pp. 1, 21.

16. For those Christians who were not moved by either appeal, it might not have escaped notice that the probable alternative to a Jewish state was further migration of Jewish refugees to the United States.

REFERENCES

Adams, James L. 1970. *The Growing Church Lobby in Washington*. Grand Rapids, Mich.: Eerdmans.

Anderson, John B., ed. 1970. *Congress and Conscience*. Philadelphia: Lippincott.

Atkins, Stanley, and Theodore McConnell, eds. 1986. *Churches on the Wrong Road*. Chicago: Regnery Gateway.

Baker, James T. 1977. *A Southern Baptist in the White House*. Philadelphia: Westminster.

Benson, Peter L., and Dorothy L. Williams. 1982. *Religion on Capitol Hill: Myths and Realities*. San Francisco: Harper and Row.

Bond, John R., and Charles A. Johnson. 1982. "Implementing a Permissive Policy: Hospital Abortion Services After *Roe v. Wade*." *American Journal of Political Science* 26:1–24.

Borders, Jeff A., and Phillips Cutright. 1979. "Community Determinants of U.S. Legal Abortion Rates." *Family Planning Perspectives* 11:227–233.

Boyer, Jean-François, and Alegandro Alem. 1985a. "Moon in Latin America: Building the Bases of a World Organization." *Manchester Guardian Weekly*, Mar. 3, pp. 12–14.

———. 1985b. "The Moonies: A Power in the Service of Anticommunism." *Manchester Guardian Weekly*, Feb. 24, pp. 12–13.

Brickner, Balfour. 1980. "Social Policy-Making Structures of the Jewish Community." In *The Formation of Social Policy in the Catholic and Jewish Traditions*, edited by Eugene J. Fisher and Daniel F. Polish, 5–14. Notre Dame, Ind.: University of Notre Dame Press.

Campbell, Angus, Philip E. Converse, Warren E. Miller, and Donald Stokes. 1960. *The American Voter*. New York: Wiley.

Converse, Philip E. 1966. "Religion and Politics: The 1960 Election." In *Elections and the Political Order,* edited by Angus Campbell, Philip E. Converse, Warren E. Miller and Donald Stokes, 96–124. New York: Wiley.

Dexter, Lewis Anthony. 1938. "Administration of the Social Gospel." *Public Opinion Quarterly* 2:294–299.

Ebersole, Luke E. 1951. *Church Lobbying in the Nation's Capital.* New York: Macmillan.

Ehrenhalt, Alan, ed. 1983. *Politics in America: Members of Congress in Washington and at Home.* Washington, D.C.: CQ Press.

Elazar, Daniel J. 1970. *Cities of the Prairie.* New York: Basic Books.

———. 1976. *Community and Polity: The Organizational Dynamics of American Jewry.* Philadelphia: Jewish Publication Society of America.

———. 1984. *American Federalism: A View from the States.* Third edition. New York: Harper and Row.

Ermann, M. David, and William H. Clements II. 1984. "The Interfaith Center on Corporate Responsibility and Its Campaign Against Marketing Infant Formula in the Third World." *Social Problems* 32:185–196.

Fairbanks, David. 1977. "Religious Forces and 'Morality' Policies in the American States." *Western Political Quarterly* 30:411–417.

———. 1979. "Politics, Economics, and the Public Morality: Why Some States Are More 'Moral' Than Others." *Policy Studies Journal* 7:714–720.

Fenton, John H. 1960. *The Catholic Vote.* New Orleans: Hauser.

Fenton, John H., and Kenneth N. Vines. 1967. "Negro Registration in Louisiana." In *Negro Politics in America,* edited by Harry A. Bailey, 166–177. Columbus, Ohio: Charles E. Merrill.

Festinger, Leon. 1947. "The Role of Group Belongingness in a Voting Situation." *Human Relations* 1:154–180.

Fisher, Eugene J., and Daniel F. Polish, eds. 1980. *The Formation of Social Policy in the Catholic and Jewish Traditions.* Notre Dame, Ind.: University of Notre Dame Press.

Flowers, Ronald B. 1983. "President Jimmy Carter, Evangelicalism, Church-State Relations, and Civil Religion." *Journal of Church and State* 25:113–132.

Ganin, Zvi. 1979. *Truman, American Jewry, and Israel, 1945–1948.* New York: Holmes and Meier.

Giles, Michael, and Thomas G. Walker. 1975. "Judicial Policy-Making and Southern School Desegregation." *Journal of Politics* 37:917–936.

Glick, Edward Bernard. 1982. *The Triangular Connection: America, Israel, and American Jews.* London: George Allen and Unwin.

Gohmann, Stephan F., and Robert L. Ohsfeldt. 1990. "U.S. Senate Voting on Abortion Legislation: A More Direct Test for Ideological Shirking." Working Paper Series #90-14, Dept. of Health Care Organization and Policy, School of Public Health. Birmingham: University of Alabama.

Goldman, Sheldon. 1966. "Voting Behavior on the U.S. Court of Appeals, 1961–64." *American Political Science Review* 60:374–383.

———. 1975. "Voting Behavior on the U.S. Court of Appeals Revisited." *American Political Science Review* 79:491–506.

Granberg, Donald. 1985a. "An Anomaly in Political Perception." *Public Opinion Quarterly* 49:504–516.

————. 1985b. "The United States Senate Votes to Uphold *Roe v. Wade.*" *Population Research and Policy Review* 42:115–131.

Greeley, Andrew. 1977. *The American Catholic: A Social Portrait.* New York: Basic Books.

Hallum, Anne Motley. 1989. "Presbyterians as Political Amateurs." In *Religion in American Politics,* edited by Charles W. Dunn, 63–74. Washington, D.C.: CQ Press.

Hamilton, Howard D. 1970. "Voting in Open Housing Referenda." *Social Science Quarterly* 51:715–729.

Hammond, John L. 1979. *The Politics of Benevolence: Revival Religion and American Voting Behavior.* Norwood, N.J.: Ablex.

Hanna, Mary T. 1979. *Catholics and American Politics.* Cambridge: Harvard University Press.

Hansen, Susan B. 1980. "State Implementation of Supreme Court Decisions: Abortion Rates Since *Roe v. Wade.*" *Journal of Politics* 72:372–395.

Haughey, John C., ed. 1979. *Personal Values in Public Policy.* New York: Paulist.

Henshaw, Stanley K., and Jane Silverman. 1988. "The Characteristics and Previous Contraceptive Use of U.S. Abortion Patients." *Family Planning Perspectives* 20:158–168.

Hertzke, Allen D. 1988. *Representing God in Washington.* Knoxville: University of Tennessee Press.

————. 1989. "The Role of Religious Lobbies." In *Religion in American Politics,* edited by Charles W. Dunn, 123–136. Washington, D.C.: CQ Press.

Hirsch, H. N. 1981. *The Enigma of Felix Frankfurter.* New York: Basic Books.

Hofrenning, Daniel J. 1989. "Beyond Oligarchy: The Internal Politics of Mainline Protestant Denominations." Paper presented at the annual meeting of the Midwest Political Science Association, Chicago.

Horowitz, Irving L., ed. 1978. *Science, Sin, and Scholarship: The Politics of Reverend Moon and the Unification Church.* Cambridge: MIT Press.

Hutcheson, John D., and George A. Taylor. 1973. "Religious Variables, Political System Characteristics, and Policy Outputs in the American States." *American Journal of Political Science* 17:414–421.

Isikoff, Michael. 1984. "What the Moon Church Wants for Its Millions." *Washington Post Weekly Edition,* December 10, pp. 7–8.

Jaffe, Frederick S., Barbara Lindheim, and Philip R. Lee, eds. 1981. *Abortion Politics: Private Morality and Public Policy.* New York: McGraw-Hill.

Johnson, Charles A. 1976. "Political Culture in American States: Elazar's Formulation Examined." *American Journal of Political Science* 20:491–509.

Johnston, Michael. 1983. "Corruption and Political Culture in America: An Empirical Perspective." *Publius* 13:19–39.

Kamin, Leon J. 1958. "Ethnic and Party Affiliations of Candidates as Determinants of Voting." *Canadian Journal of Psychology* 12:205–212.

Kleppner, Paul. 1979. *The Third Electoral System.* Chapel Hill: University of North Carolina Press.

Klingman, David, and William W. Lammers. 1984. "The 'General Policy Liberalism' Factor in American State Politics." *American Journal of Political Science* 28:598–610.

Kucharsky, David. 1976. *The Man from Plains.* New York: Harper and Row.

Kurtz, Howard. 1985a. "The Ideology of Federal Judgeships." *Washington Post Weekly Edition*, April 15, pp. 9–10.

———. 1985b. "Opposition to Reagan's Choice for Legal Policy Job Is Mounting." Ibid., August 5, p. 34.

Lerner, Robert, Stanley Rothman, and S. Robert Lichter. 1989. "Christian Religious Elites." *Public Opinion* (March/April), 54–58.

Leventman, Paula Goldman, and Seymour Leventman. 1976. "Congressman Drinan, S.J., and His Jewish Constituents." *American Jewish Historical Quarterly* 66:215–248.

Lorinskas, Robert A., Brett W. Hawkins, and Stephen D. Edwards. 1969. "The Persistence of Ethnic Voting in Urban and Rural Areas: Results from the Controlled Elections Method." *Social Science Quarterly* 49:891–899.

Mazlish, Bruce, and Edward Diamond. 1979. *Jimmy Carter: A Character Portrait.* New York: Simon and Schuster.

Medding, Peter Y. 1989. *The Transformation of American Jewish Politics.* New York: American Jewish Committee.

Miller, William Lee. 1978. *Yankee from Georgia: The Emergence of Jimmy Carter.* New York: Times Books.

Monsma, Stephen V. 1977. "The Oval Office: Three Models for a Christian." *Christianity Today,* January 21, pp. 28–29.

Morgan, David R., and Kenneth J. Meier. 1980. "Politics and Morality: The Effect of Religion on Referenda Voting." *Social Science Quarterly* 61:144–148.

Murphy, Caryle. 1984. "Sanctuary: How Churches Defy Immigration Law." *Washington Post Weekly Edition,* September 17, pp. 8–9.

Nagel, Stuart. 1961. "Political Party Affiliation and Judge's Decisions." *American Political Science Review* 55:843–850.

———. 1962. "Ethnic Affiliations and Judicial Propensities." *Journal of Politics* 24:92–110.

O'Hara, Thomas J. 1989a. "The Civil Rights Restoration Act: The Role of the Religious Lobbies." Paper delivered at the annual meeting of the American Political Science Association, Atlanta.

———. 1989b. "The Multifaceted Catholic Lobby." In *Religion in American Politics,* edited by Charles W. Dunn, 137–144. Washington, D.C.: CQ Press.

O'Neil, Daniel J. 1970. *Church Lobbying in a Western State: A Case Study in Abortion Legislation.* Tucson: University of Arizona Press.

Page, Benjamin I., Robert Y. Shapiro, Paul W. Gronke, and Robert M. Rosenberg. 1984. "Constituency, Party, and Representation in Congress." *Public Opinion Quarterly* 48:741–756.

Pipert, Wesley G., comp. 1978. *The Spiritual Journey of Jimmy Carter.* New York: Macmillan.

Pomper, Gerald A. 1966. "Ethnic and Group Voting in Non-Partisan Municipal Elections." *Public Opinion Quarterly* 30:79–99.

Reagan, Ronald. 1981. "Remarks at the Annual Meeting of the International Association of Chiefs of Police." *Weekly Compilation of Presidential Documents* 17, September 28, pp. 1039–1046.

———. 1985. "Remarks at the Annual Convention of the National Religious Broadcasters Association." *Weekly Compilation of Presidential Documents* 21, February 4, pp. 129–131.

Reichley, A. James. 1985. *Religion in American Public Life.* Washington, D.C.: Brookings.

Richardson, James T. 1984. "The 'Old Right' in Action: Mormon and Catholic Involvement in an Equal Rights Amendment Referendum." In *New Christian Politics,* edited by David G. Bromley and Anson Shupe, 213–234. Macon, Ga.: Mercer University Press.

Richardson, James T., and Sandie Wightman Fox. 1972. "Religious Affiliation as a Predictor of Voting Behavior on Abortion Reform Legislation." *Journal for the Scientific Study of Religion* 11:347–359.

———. 1975. "Religion and Voting on Abortion Reform: A Follow-Up Study." *Journal for the Scientific Study of Religion* 14:159–164.

Rieselbach, Leroy N. 1966. *The Roots of Isolationism: Congressional Voting and Presidential Leadership in Foreign Policy.* Indianapolis, Ind.: Bobbs-Merrill.

Schiltz, Timothy D., and R. Lee Rainey. 1978. "The Geographic Distribution of Elazar's Political Subcultures Among the Mass Population: A Research Note." *Western Political Quarterly* 31:410–415.

Schuster, William G. 1981. "Appointments." *Christianity Today,* March 13, p. 58.

Simon, Paul. 1984. *The Glass House.* New York: Continuum.

Sorauf, Frank J. 1976. *The Wall of Separation: The Constitutional Politics of Church and State.* Princeton, N.J.: Princeton University Press.

Speer, James Allen. 1988. "An Examination of the Influence of Baptist Belief on the Governing Style of President Jimmy Carter, 1977–1980." Ph.D. diss., University of Georgia.

Spiegel, Stephen. 1985. *The Other Arab-Israeli Conflict.* Chicago: University of Chicago Press.

Spitzer, Robert J. 1987. *The Right to Life Movement and Third Party Politics.* New York: Greenwood.

Swatos, William H., Jr. 1988. "Picketing Satan Enfleshed at 7-Eleven: A Research Note." *Review of Religious Research* 30:73–82.

Taylor, Paul. 1985. "He Went Out for Pizza and Came Back the Definitive Campaigner." *Washington Post Weekly Edition,* September 30, p. 12.

Thomas, J. Mark. 1984. "Reagan in the State of Nature." *Christianity and Crisis* (September 17), pp. 321–325.

Ulmer, S. Sidney. 1973. "Social Background as an Indicator to the Votes of Supreme Court Justices in Criminal Cases: 1947–1956 Terms." *American Journal of Political Science* 17:622–630.

Vedlitz, Arnold, Jon P. Alston, and Carl Pinkele. 1980. "Politics and the Black Church in a Southern Community." *Journal of Black Studies* 10:367–375.

Vines, Kenneth. 1964. "Federal District Judges and Race Relations Cases in the South." *Journal of Politics* 26:337–357.

Vinovkis, Maris A. 1979. "The Politics of Abortion in the House of Representatives in 1976." *Michigan Law Review* 77:1790–1827.

Wald, Kenneth D. Forthcoming. "Ministering to the Nation: The Campaigns of Jesse Jackson and Pat Robertson." In *Nominating the President 1988,* edited by Emmet Buell and Lee Sigelman. Knoxville: University of Tennessee Press.

Warner, John B., Jr. 1968. "Religious Affiliation as a Factor in the Voting Records of Members of the 89th Congress." Ph.D. diss., Boston University.

Wasserman, Ira M. 1989. "Prohibition and Ethnocultural Conflict: The Missouri Prohibition Referendum of 1918." *Social Science Quarterly* 70:886–901.

Weber, Paul J. 1982. "Examining the Religious Lobbies." *This World* 1:97–107.

Weber, Paul J., and T. L. Stanley. 1984. "The Power and Performance of Religious Interest Groups." *Quarterly Review* 4:28–43.

Welch, Michael R., Lyman A. Kellstedt, David C. Leege, and Kenneth D. Wald. 1990. "Are the Sheep Hearing the Shepherds? Pastoral Cues, Congregational Responses and Political Communication Processes." Unpublished paper, University of Notre Dame.

Westoff, Charles F., and Larry Bumpass. 1973. "Revolution in Birth Control Practices of United States Roman Catholics." *Science* 179:41–44.

Westoff, Charles F., and Norman R. Ryder. 1970. "Contraception Control Among American Catholics." In *Catholics/USA*, edited by William T. Liu and Nathaniel J. Pallone, 257–268. New York: Wiley.

White, O. Kendall, Jr. 1984. "Overt and Covert Politics: The Mormon Church's Anti-ERA Campaign in Virginia." *Virginia Social Science Journal* 19:11–16.

Williamsburg Charter Foundation. 1988. *The Williamsburg Charter Survey on Religion and Public Life.* Washington, D.C.: Williamsburg Charter Foundation.

Zwier, Robert. 1988. "The World and Worldview of Religious Lobbyists." Paper presented at the annual meeting of the Midwest Political Science Association, Chicago.

7. The Political Mobilization of Evangelical Protestants

Get 'em saved; get 'em baptized; get 'em registered.

—Slogan at an evangelical workshop on political action, Mark Silk, *Spiritual Politics: Religion and America Since World War II*

It has been said that the political tone of the 1980s took root in 1976, labeled the "Year of the Evangelical" by *Time* magazine, matured with the 1978 electoral defeat of several Democratic incumbents over abortion and other social issues, and reached fruition in 1980, when the enthusiastic support of evangelical voters helped Republicans seize the White House, the Senate, and the national agenda. Struck by the new political assertiveness of conservative evangelicals, journalists suggested that the self-centeredness dominating the "Me" decade of the 1970s had given way to the piety of the "Thee" decade. Political scientists also took note of the increasing tendency among voters to insist on the political relevance of their religious and cultural values. But by the end of the 1980s, with scandals and financial collapse afflicting several media-based ministries, the collapse of the Pat Robertson presidential campaign, and the decision to disband conservative organizations like Moral Majority, some began to write an epitaph for the evangelical political movement (D'Antonio 1989).

Just as some observers overreacted to the new militancy of conservative Protestants, exaggerating its political impact, so others now seem likely to make the opposite mistake of writing off the evangelical offensive. With the benefit of hindsight, this chapter examines the upsurge in political activity by theologically conservative Christians. What do evangelical Protestants think about contemporary political issues? What caused their apparent increase in political action? Has the attempt to mobilize them altered the pattern of American political life? Will the activism persist and in what form? These questions will guide the anal-

ysis of a new political force that some observers denounced as dangerous to the political system and others heralded as a movement to revitalize American politics.

The Political Background

Of all the shifts and surprises in contemporary political life, perhaps
none was so wholly unexpected as the political resurgence of evangelical
Protestantism in the 1970s. As noted earlier, modernization theory had
led many observers to treat traditional religion as a spent force in the
United States and to discount its influence in the realm of national
politics.[1] Like other predictions rooted in secularization theory, this assessment was rudely challenged by evidence that evangelical Christianity had achieved new strength and was ready to assert that power in
political activity. The nomination of Jimmy Carter in 1976, the rise to
national notice of organizations such as Moral Majority, the restoration
of spirited public debate about certain "moral" issues—all these signs
of evangelical political awakening marked the return to national prominence of a force that knowledgeable observers had long ago written off.

Until the 1920s, evangelical Protestantism was an animating force in
American political life. It had contributed greatly to the growth of antislavery sentiment in the Northern states during the period leading up
to the Civil War and, paradoxically, reinforced the commitment of
Southerners to the maintenance of the slave economy. In the decades
following that great conflict, evangelicals generally sided with a variety
of movements designed to purify American politics of various corrupting
influences. In the twenty years before World War I, when it was embodied in the national arena by William Jennings Bryan, the evangelical
impulse was a driving force behind such disparate movements as currency reform, women's suffrage, regulation of corporate abuses, arbitration of international conflicts, and adoption of "direct democracy"
through the initiative, referendum, and recall election (Levine 1975).
These reforms of the Progressive era were advanced as means to defend
the economic interests and social values of traditional Protestantism.
Their widespread adoption before World War I attested to the central
place of evangelicalism in American culture.

In the period following World War I, evangelical Protestantism was
displaced from its perch as a major cultural force by a series of major

social developments that culminated in a virtual social revolution. It is important to recognize the shattering impact of these trends.

The disintegration of traditional American values—so sharply recorded by novelists and artists—was reflected in a change in manners and morals that shook American society to its depths. The growing secularization of the country greatly weakened religious sanctions. People lost their fear of Hell and at the same time had less interest in Heaven; they made more demands for material fulfillment on Earth. . . . Most important, the authority of the family, gradually eroded over several centuries, had been sharply lessened by the rise of the city. "Never in recent generations," wrote Freda Kirchwey, "have human beings so floundered about outside the ropes of social and religious sanctions." (Leuchtenburg 1958, 158)

Under the impact of rapid urbanization, the spread of science and technology, and skyrocketing birth rates in the predominantly non-Protestant immigrant communities, the conditions that had once favored traditional Protestant religion began to lose hold. The weakening of the social values associated with evangelicalism was apparent in such disparate trends as the growth in women's employment, the loosening of restraints on sexuality, the rising prestige of science, and a general tendency to exalt hedonism and materialist values. Even many Protestants, later recognized as founders of the "mainline" approach, began to doubt the literal authority of the Bible and its superiority relative to science.

Whether these developments were ever as widespread as imagined is really beside the point. Accurately or not, evangelicals thought they were confronted with threats to orthodox Christianity, and they reacted with furious defensive activity. Attempting to resist the encroachments of secularism in the political realm, they concentrated in the 1920s on a pair of causes—the campaigns to restrict the sale of intoxicating liquor and to prohibit the teaching of evolution in the public schools. Both movements attained temporary success, but in the end, neither could withstand the shift of power to the burgeoning cities, where evangelicalism was weak and a new set of issues commanded public interest.

The fate of evangelicalism was tied to "a receding and beleaguered small-town culture" (Burner 1967, 4). As many predominantly northern denominations embraced modernity and expressed a willingness to apply scientific insight to religious belief, the center of gravity in evangelicalism shifted to the rural South. There were significant political implications in the increasing southern orientation of traditional Protestantism. Unlike northern evangelicals, who had argued that salvation depended on both faith and works, the southern variety of Protestant Christianity stopped short of demanding social transformation as a condition for salvation. To most southern theological conservatives,

salvation was an act, a transaction between God and the individual that was separable from the life that followed. Those who had been born again were expected to practice Christian morality, to behave rightly in their own lives, and to work and pray for the conversion of others. Yet these expectations were never connected with any imperative to transform their culture in the name of Christ. They did not deprecate the world about them; they simply saw religious life as something to be carried on in a separate compartment. (Kleppner 1979, 187)

From its new southern base, evangelicalism thus chose to remain outside the political arena—a withdrawal broken only by participation in sporadic rearguard actions through fringe movements and extremist crusades. Whether scholars studied the Ku Klux Klan, segregationists, book censors, or virulent anti-Communists, they found evangelical Protestants overrepresented (Clabaugh 1974; Craig 1987; Grupp and Newman 1973; Orum and McCrane 1970; Ribuffo 1983). These links between evangelicalism and regressive political movements fixed traditional religion with a public image as narrow-minded, bigoted, and backward looking—an image that obscured earlier associations between the same religious community and progressive political causes (Warner 1979).

Observers relied on social and theological factors to explain the political style of traditional Protestantism after World War I. The social and economic deprivation that typified evangelicals denied them the time, energy, or skill to carry on sustained political participation and isolated them from experiences that would have promoted tolerance, compromise, and other democratic values. Lesser educational opportunities were said to afflict evangelicals with cognitive rigidity, an inflexibility of mind that kept them at a disadvantage in genuinely democratic political competition (Lipset 1960, 100). Furthermore, the otherworldly orientation of southern religion, the divorce between religion and social conditions, discouraged participation in the earthly process of political action. Many observers who associated evangelicalism with reactionary and violent movements, such as the Ku Klux Klan, shared an unspoken assumption that political abstinence by evangelicals contributed to the stability of the political system.

To the extent that evangelicals participated in national political life after Bryan's eclipse, their sympathies remained with the Democratic party.[2] The alliance between theological conservatives and the more liberal of the national parties can be explained largely in regional and class terms. The force of tradition kept white Southern Baptists, the largest evangelical denomination, firmly attached to the party that had reestablished white political dominance in the late nineteenth century. To placate the white South, the Democratic party usually selected its vice-presidential nominee from the region. The linkage was further cemented in the 1930s by the popularity of the New Deal social welfare programs that attacked poverty and agricultural distress in the region. The first academic studies of public opinion and party allegiance, published in the 1940s and 1950s, confirmed what southern election returns had suggested—that white Southern Baptists were disproportionately attached to the Democratic party and much more prone than other groups to support government programs of economic security (Allinsmith and Allinsmith 1948; Pope 1953). Though the "states' rights" revolt at the 1948 Democratic National Convention had demonstrated the capacity of the civil rights issue to draw southern whites away from a Democratic allegiance, the partisan impact of the controversy was checked by the similarity of the Democratic and Republican positions until the 1960s.

The first stirrings of change in the pattern of evangelical politics were visible in presidential elections of the 1960s. When the Democratic party nominated a Catholic for president in 1960, large numbers of white, churchgoing southern Protestants defected to the Republican candidate (Converse 1966; Pool, Abelson, and Popkin, 1965, 115–122; Dawidowicz and Goldstein 1974, 41–48). Four years later, the same parts of the country that had given William Jennings Bryan his greatest margins of support responded favorably to the candidacy of Barry Goldwater, a Republican who had cultivated their favor by emphasizing conservative social values (Burnham 1968). Goldwater's candidacy appeared to galvanize many evangelicals who had previously stayed outside the political arena. In 1968, George Wallace's independent presidential candidacy showed extraordinary strength among southern whites belonging to theologically conservative denominations (Crespi 1971; Orum and McCrane 1970; Oldendick and Bennett 1978). By the end of the decade, the level of psychological attachment to the Democratic party and voting support for its presidential candidates had eroded considerably among white Southerners (Knoke 1976, 23; Ladd and Hadley 1975, 229).

These trends did not wholly prepare observers for the subsequent attempts to turn evangelical Protestants to the political right. The changing voting patterns in the South were not interpreted principally in terms of a revolt by theological conservatives but rather in racial and economic terms.[3] The Republican surge in 1960 was attributed directly to anti-Catholic sentiment, but most observers perceived it in the context of a steady postwar erosion of Democratic support in the region, occasioned by the increasing liberalism of the national Democratic party on race and social welfare issues and the corresponding move to the right by the Republican leadership. Unaware that the partisan reaction was especially pronounced among persons deeply committed to orthodox Protestantism, most influential commentators on southern politics did not dwell on the role of religious values in stimulating voter transitions.

The rise of Jimmy Carter to national power both focused public attention on the growing political significance of evangelical Protestantism and further undermined the stereotype of rabid extremism. A well-educated and scientifically trained person, comfortable with contemporary culture and familiar with modern theology, Carter advocated moderate to liberal policies without the excited appeals to emotion that had been the hallmark of evangelical politics. In the face of publicly expressed doubts by Catholic, Jewish, and black leaders who associated southern evangelicals with religious and racial bigotry, Carter's moderation seemed to promise a welcome break with that unpleasant historical tradition. In the election of 1976, he carried Catholic and Jewish voters by the same or greater margins as had most other postwar Democratic presidential candidates and, like Lyndon Johnson and Hubert Humphrey, received virtually unanimous support from blacks (Miller, Miller, and Schneider 1980, 332). That Carter could appeal so strongly to liberal social groups and carry most of the southern states suggested the end of evangelical political distinctiveness. That impression might not have been so widely accepted if more people had realized that a majority of white Southerners voted for Carter's Republican opponent (*Public Opinion* 1985).

The "New Christian Right"

The return of evangelicals to organized political action, manifested in what has been labeled the New Christian Right (NCR), or the New Religious Right, was facilitated by a number of local movements that developed during the social ferment and upheaval of the 1970s. Alan Crawford (1980), a conservative journalist who looks with disfavor on the evangelical influence in politics, has argued that the ground for national organizations such as Moral Majority was prepared by three grass-roots campaigns that unexpectedly caught fire: a textbook controversy in West Virginia, a gay-rights referendum in Dade County (Miami), Florida, and a spirited campaign to defeat the proposed Equal Rights Amendment to the Constitution. In each case, evangelicals rallied strongly to the defense of traditional cultural and social values.

In the mid-1970s, protesters in a mining valley of West Virginia challenged some of the English textbooks that the Kanawha County Board of Education had approved for use in public schools. Led by the wife of a fundamentalist minister, who denounced most of the books as "disrespectful of authority and religion, destructive of social and cultural values, obscene, pornographic, unpatriotic, or in violation of individual and familial rights of privacy" (Jenkinson 1979, 18), the campaign ignited a massive boycott of the schools by the parents of most students, sympathetic wildcat strikes by coal miners, mass picketing all across the county, a teachers' strike, temporary closure of the schools, and several violent assaults on people and property. Although all of the books were eventually approved for classroom use, the controversy led to the resignation of the school superintendent and a new textbook adoption procedure that made it easier for parents to screen out "offensive" books. The apparent success of the parent groups in the Kanawha County "Battle of the Books" inspired similar challenges around the country (Goff 1977; Richburg 1986).

The seeds of the New Christian Right were also planted by the 1977 Dade County, Florida, referendum on a gay-rights ordinance. As part of a nationwide campaign to gain legal protection, homosexuals had persuaded the Dade County Commission to pass an ordinance prohibiting discrimination on the basis of sexual preference in housing, employment, and public accommodations. The ordinance prompted formation of a new organization, called Save Our Children, which claimed that the law would require private and religious schools to employ homosexuals as teachers (Bryant 1977). After a petition drive led by the singer Anita Bryant and many religious leaders, the ordinance was submitted to a popular referendum and voted down by more than a 2–1 margin. Similar ordinances were subsequently repealed elsewhere around the country.

The potential clout of religious conservatism was also on display in the remarkable campaign that defeated the proposed Equal Rights Amendment to the Constitution (Boles 1979). Approved by Congress early in 1972, the amendment prohibiting sexual discrimination by the states and the federal government quickly sailed through ratification votes in twenty-two state legislatures, leaving it only sixteen states short of formal adoption. The seemingly inevitable path to constitutional status was interrupted by the formation of "Stop-ERA" under the leadership of Phyllis Schlafly, a longtime activist in conservative political causes. In the face of determined lobbying by Schlafly's organization and allied groups, the rate of ratification dropped sharply and the amendment ultimately died three states short of the thirty-eight needed. To underline the religious dimension to the conflict, most of the states that failed to ratify had substantial concentrations of Mormons (Utah, Nevada, Arizona) or evangelical Protestants (all the southern states except Texas and Tennessee), and conservative churches supplied the recruitment base for most of the antiratification leaders and activists (Arrington and Kyle 1978; Brady and Tedin 1976; Conover and Gray 1983; Mueller and Dimieri 1982; Jones 1983; Tedin 1978; Tedin et al. 1977; Wohlenberg 1980). Among ordinary citizens, both membership in fundamentalist churches and high rates of church attendance were associated with opposition to the amendment (Burris 1983).

Although motivated by different issues, these three campaigns were tied together by common dissatisfaction with what the participants saw as a godless society that had replaced firm moral standards with a system of relativism (Phillips 1982, chap. 14). The campaigns against "obscene" schoolbooks, gay-rights ordinances, and the ERA attracted a variety of supporters but appealed most strongly to evangelical Protestants, who saw each movement as a crusade in defense of traditional Christian values and institutions. The particular value presumed under attack ranged from respect for social conventions in West Virginia to heterosexual marriage in Miami to the maintenance of traditional social roles for women in the struggle over the ERA. Underlying the challenges to orthodox Christian values, it was argued by some leaders of the movement, was a doctrine called "secular humanism." Although definitions of that concept varied from one critic to another, social conservatives generally agreed that at its core lay a belief in the supremacy of humanity rather than of God. According to the advocates of traditional social values, the doctrine of secular humanism had become entrenched in the government, schools, media, and other institutions that molded public perceptions. Through state and local campaigns against particular outcroppings of what they saw as a pernicious idea, conservative religious activists began to forge organizational links and a common view about the source of major social problems. Eventually they moved to counter the evils of secular humanism with a positive program of "profamily" issues.

These movements represented a sea change in the thinking of evangelical Protestants, a "coming out" almost as dramatic as the political awakenings of feminists and homosexuals that had triggered it. Once ridiculed as being "so heavenly minded they were of no earthly good," evangelicals had been theologically unequipped for regular participation in society. Their ministers had long warned them to steer clear of "secular" politics and focus their energies on "getting saved." But now, in response to the menacing social trends unleashed in the 1960s, they were counseled to

reject the division of human affairs into the "secular" and "sacred" and insist, instead, that there is no arena of human activity, including law and politics, which is outside of God's lordship. The task is not to avoid this world, but to declare God's Kingdom in it. (Buzzard 1989)

Animated by this ideal, evangelicals began to apply to politics the same missionary zeal they had traditionally shown in converting individuals.

The political successes of grass-roots evangelicalism did not go unnoticed by "secular" conservative activists. Casting about for a strategy to restore a Republican party dispirited by consecutive electoral defeats in 1974 and 1976, they attempted to capitalize on the political energy displayed by evangelicals and to transfer it from the local to the national arena. The effort to build bridges between secular and religious conservatives was spearheaded by four activists who had no background in the evangelical community: Howard Phillips of the Conservative Caucus; John "Terry" Dolan of the National Conservative Political Action

Committee; Paul Weyrich of the National Committee for the Survival of a Free Congress; and Richard Viguerie, a major fundraiser for conservative causes.

Spurred on by the availability of a large pool of potential allies, Phillips and his colleagues offered assistance to the emerging leaders of the Christian conservative movement and urged the most vocal leaders of the evangelical community to make common cause with other single-issue groups. The basis for coalition would be a frontal attack on "big government" as a threat to traditional religious and economic values. With that theme, they hoped to harness evangelicals to a comprehensive conservative program, including opposition to liberal policies on gun control, the treaty relinquishing American control over the Panama Canal, nonrestrictive abortion laws, compulsory unionization, and defense cutbacks. Using their contacts and ample political resources—in particular, the ability to raise money through direct-mail appeals to sympathizers—the secular conservatives helped build up several national organizations designed to appeal to evangelical Protestants and other theological conservatives.

The most prominent of the new organizations, Moral Majority, became synonymous with the entire religious right. Properly speaking, Moral Majority was a lobbying organization founded in 1979 by television evangelist Jerry Falwell, the minister of the nation's largest independent Baptist church, in Lynchburg, Virginia. Falwell, who had assisted Anita Bryant in the Dade County repeal campaign, used the mailing list for his "Old Time Gospel Hour" television program to recruit supporters and solicit financial contributions. Concentrated mostly in the southeastern states, Moral Majority drew most of its membership from independent Baptist churches and virtually all of its leadership from pastors of that confession. Organized in state chapters, it concentrated on encouraging church members to register as voters and to support staunch conservatives.

To reach into the Southern Baptist Convention, the largest association of evangelical Protestants, as well as other conservative denominations, a retired Memphis sales executive named Ed McAteer founded the Religious Roundtable. Unlike Moral Majority, which aimed at building a mass movement of evangelicals, the Roundtable (which dropped the "Religious" from its name) was intended primarily to provide a common meeting ground where theologically conservative pastors could learn the fine art of political mobilization on behalf of various conservative causes. This was accomplished by periodic mass meetings, or "public affairs briefings," featuring conservative speakers and workshops on various aspects of political action.

Christian Voice, the oldest national organization in the New Christian Right, grew out of an unsuccessful attempt by California evangelicals to pass a state law prohibiting the employment of either homosexuals or advocates of homosexuality in publicly supported teaching positions. Similar in many respects to Moral Majority, it has a western and southwestern base and a particular appeal to members of the Assemblies of God. More so than the other two organizations, Christian Voice concentrated its efforts on electioneering—compiling information on candidates, offering lists of favored and opposed candidates, and raising funds to support independent campaigns for favored candidates. It also had an active lobbying presence in Washington, D.C.

Initially formed to defend the interests of the burgeoning Christian schools movement in 1977, the National Christian Action Coalition (NCAC) was a multipurpose organization (Moen 1989, 71–73). It lobbied on Capitol Hill, raised funds for candidates, compiled the first "family issues" scorecard for congressional representatives, and supported both a research foundation and a publishing firm. The organization, which remained committed above all else to defending Christian schools from governmental intrusion, was rewarded when its founder was named by President Reagan to a post in the U.S. Department of Education.

There were other smaller groups that focused on a narrower range of issues yet drew in one way or another on the same concerns that motivated the larger organizations. Although the existence of so many different organizations reflected some of the diversity in the evangelical community and a degree of rivalry among the prominent television ministers, the different groups shared members, staff, support services, funding sources, and office space (Hill and Owen 1982, 56). The principal leaders formed something of an interlocking directorate, holding seats on the boards of one another's organizations and leadership positions in the secular conservative groups with whom they were allied. All the organizations established at the end of the 1970s also drew on the experience and expertise of earlier movements designed to spur evangelicals into political action, including some that had ties to the unsuccessful attempt by Ronald Reagan to win the 1976 Republican nomination for president (Pierard 1983b; Blumenthal 1984).

Most important, Moral Majority, Christian Voice, the Roundtable, and NCAC capitalized on essentially the same set of issues to rally evangelicals to political action (Shriver 1981). Described by the Christian Right as the "profamily" program, the same specific proposals showed up in the literature of all four organizations. Reverend Falwell's "Christian Bill of Rights" stressed opposition to abortion, support for voluntary prayer and Bible reading in public schools, the responsibility of government to encourage the "traditional family unit," maintenance of tax exemption for churches, and noninterference by the authorities with Christian schools. The Moral Majority's ten "amendments" are given below:

Christian Bill of Rights

Amendment I. We believe that, from the time of conception within the womb, every human being has a scriptural right to life upon this earth. (Ex. 20:13; Ps. 139:13–16)

Amendment II. We believe that every person has the right to pursue any and all scriptural goals that he or she feels are God-directed during that life upon this earth. (Prov. 3:5–6)

Amendment III. We believe that, apart from justified capital punishment, no medical or judicial process should be introduced that would allow the termination of life before its natural or accidental completion. (Ps. 31:15)

Amendment IV. We believe that no traitorous verbal or written attack upon the beloved nation advocating overthrow by force be permitted by any citizen or alien living within this country. (Rom. 13:1–7)

Amendment V. We believe that all students enrolled in public schools should have the right to voluntary prayer and Bible reading. (Josh. 24:15)

Amendment VI. We believe in the right and responsibility to establish and administer private Christian schools without harassment from local, state, or federal government. (Deut. 11:18–21)

Amendment VII. We believe in the right to influence secular professions, including the fields of politics, business, legal, medical, in establishing and maintaining moral principles of Scripture. (Prov. 14:34)

Amendment VIII. We believe in the right to expect our national leaders to keep this country morally and militarily strong so that the religious freedom and Gospel preaching might continue unhindered. (I Pet. 2:13–17)

Amendment IX. We believe in the right to receive moral support from all local, state, and federal agencies concerning the traditional family unit, a concept that enjoys both scriptural and historical precedence. (Gen. 2:18–25)

Amendment X. We believe in the right of legally-approved religious organizations to maintain their tax-exempt status, this right being based upon the historical and scriptural concept of church and state separation. (Matt. 22: 17–21)

In an effort to explain the need for mobilizing evangelicals, Christian Voice expanded the list of social evils to include the teaching of evolution, pornography, the celebration of "immoral" behavior on television, and liquor and drug abuse. The same topics were stressed in Roundtable briefings and embodied in the Family Protection Act, a composite piece of legislation introduced by Senator Paul Laxalt of Nevada. True to its roots in the Christian school movement, NCAC pressed relentlessly for income tax credits to offset private school tuition.

Although assigning preeminence to family issues, the leaders of these movements did not ignore the issues that concerned "secular" conservatives, including increased defense spending, support of anti-Communist movements around the globe, anti-inflationary policies, efforts against street crime, and calls for a balanced budget. In each case, conservative positions on these issues were advocated with a religious rationale. Thus, increased defense spending was justified as a way of keeping the nation free for the continued preaching of the Gospel and support for the governments of Taiwan and South Africa was defended as necessary to protect Christian allies from the "Godless forces of anti-Christ Communism." Similarly, Jerry Falwell asserted a scriptural basis for low inflation, flat-rate taxation, and a balanced federal budget. In practice, however, family issues consumed most of the energy the New Christian Right directed toward politics.

Evangelical Political Action in the 1980s

The New Christian Right, as it was styled by media and academic observers, first gained widespread national attention during the presidential campaign of 1980, when its leaders coalesced, formally or informally, around the candidacy of Ronald Reagan. Divorced, an intermittent churchgoer from a mainline denomination, the father of children who have pursued unconventional lives and a veteran of show business, Reagan seemed a most unlikely object of support for the devout—doubly so in a race with two other evangelical Protestants, Jimmy Carter and John Anderson. But as Reagan alone endorsed the political efforts of the conservative evangelical leaders and pledged to work for enactment of the "profamily" agenda, he increasingly drew the New Christian Right into his camp. Christian Voice was the first and most enthusiastic supporter, creating a political action committee called Christians for Reagan to raise funds and propagandize on behalf of the Reagan campaign. The Roundtable brought Reagan to speak at its major public affairs briefing in Dallas during the summer of 1980, an event that gave him direct access to more than 15,000 clergymen and brought national attention to the movement. Moral Majority refrained from formal endorsement but conveyed its enthusiasm in every possible way short of outright recommendation. All the groups encouraged pastors to sign up evangelicals on the voter rolls and to impress upon churchgoers the necessity of expressing their religious convictions in the polling booth. These efforts led to a substantial evangelical presence in political party activities during the 1980 campaign (see chaps. 5–7 in Baker, Steed, and Moreland 1983). Only twenty years earlier, John Kennedy had traveled to Houston in a well-publicized effort to reassure Protestant clergy that he would not attempt to impose Catholic doctrine on the nation. As recently as 1976, Jimmy Carter had felt it necessary to emphasize his intention to respect the separation between personal religious values and public policy. By 1980, the circle had come full turn, the joining of the religious and political wings of conservatism was epitomized by a bumper sticker bearing the word "vote" with the *t* in the shape of a cross.

Despite criticism of the administration's failure to push hard enough on the profamily agenda, the leaders of the New Christian Right lined up even more enthusiastically behind the Reagan reelection effort in 1984. In states such as Minnesota, where Republicanism had been a weak force, members of the religious right virtually took over the party apparatus (Pressman 1984, 2317–2318). In July 1984, three hundred conservative Christian ministers, including most of the prominent television evangelists, met at the White House with the president, the vice-president, and two cabinet members.[4] Shortly before the Republican national convention began in August, the campaign chairman solicited the support of Christian leaders in a letter sent to 45,000 ministers. Plans to include a copy of the New Testament in the welcoming kit prepared for delegates to the Dallas convention were dropped only at the last moment (Bergstrom and Saperstein 1984).

The 1984 Republican convention opened with a prayer by the Reverend James Robison, a Texas evangelist who had been vice-president of the Roundtable, and closed with a benediction from Moral Majority president Jerry Falwell, who referred to the Republican presidential and vice-presidential nominees as "God's instruments in rebuilding America."[5] The platform committee, liberally staffed with legislators who had been strong supporters of the New Christian Right in Congress, produced a document that called for a constitutional amendment to restrict abortion, legalization of prayer and religious meetings in public schools, a ban on abortion, and no pledge of support for the Equal Rights Amendment. In language that spoke directly to the concerns that had prompted formation of the evangelical political movement, the platform accused the Democrats of "assaulting our basic values," stating: "They attacked the integrity of the family and parental rights. They ignored traditional morality. And they still do."[6] To hammer home the point about the differing stands taken by the two major parties, speakers referred constantly to their opponents as "the San Francisco Democrats," linking the freewheeling city where the Democrats had met for their convention with the policies pursued by the party. And on the morning of his renomination, President Reagan brought religion even more firmly into the campaign by giving a speech at a prayer breakfast that had been organized by the convention host committee (Reagan 1984).

The same techniques that had been used in 1980 were tried again in 1984. As in 1980, Moral Majority and Christian Voice appealed to their members on a profamily basis. (The Roundtable and NCAC were less in evidence.) Under the leadership of the American Coalition for Traditional Values (ACTV—pronounced "active"), an umbrella group whose board included Falwell and Robison but whose director and key staff members came from Christian Voice, $1.5 million was budgeted to mount voter-registration drives in evangelical churches. The organization was structured as a pyramid, with the ACTV national field director supervising the work of 350 field directors, who, in turn, oversaw the work of "church captains" in individual congregations. In order to maintain its tax-deductible status, ACTV could not endorse any candidate. However, its literature made it clear to the new voters that the organization's preferred moral stands were fully represented in the Republican platform, and it distributed a leadership manual for which President Reagan had written an introduction (Spring 1984).

Without the unifying presence of Ronald Reagan at the head of the ticket, evangelical leaders split during the 1988 Republican primary campaign. Jerry Falwell endorsed George Bush, while Jack Kemp and Robert Dole drew support from other New Christian Right activists. With the decline of the four major groups active in 1980, the significance of these endorsements was dubious. Moreover, the major focus of evangelical activism in 1988 was the campaign for the Republican nomination by Pat Robertson, an ordained Southern Baptist minister who had built the Christian Broadcasting Network into the nation's largest religious broadcasting empire. Though he stood aloof from the earliest efforts to mobilize conservative Christians, Robertson apparently began planning for a presidential candidacy early in the 1980s.[7] Relying on a network of supporters recruited primarily from viewers of his popular television talk show, the "700 Club," Robertson announced his interest in running for president during a 1986 campaign rally broadcast over closed-circuit television to an audience of 200,000 supporters gathered in evangelical churches (Diamond 1989, 73). The campaign, formally announced one year later, was buoyed by the extraordinary financial resources available to the candidate, several strong showings in early party gatherings, and the stunning second-place finish ahead of George Bush in the Iowa caucus. But Robertson's hopes of riding to the nomination on the basis of a strong showing in the "Super Tuesday" southern primaries in March were dashed by his poor showing throughout the region. He eventually withdrew. Robertson's failure was attributable to the strength of the competition, his own verbal gaffes and limited experience, and strong divisions within the evangelical camp (Wald forthcoming).

Though less in evidence in the 1988 convention and subsequent campaign, most of the organized Christian Right closed ranks behind the Bush campaign. The scandals engulfing several television ministries made Bush somewhat wary of too public an embrace by the Christian Right. Nonetheless, the Republican campaign stressed the conservative cultural themes associated with the Religious Right. The latter reciprocated by mobilizing for the Republican ticket.

Theories of Evangelical Mobilization

Describing the origins and development of the New Christian Right is much easier than explaining it. The emergence of the movement contradicted social science research about the secularization of political conflict and the social and doctrinal basis for evangelical political apathy. Initially caught off guard by the upsurge in evangelical political action, scholars soon began to analyze the new coalition according to theories and concepts that have been applied to similar social movements of the past. Because no single factor is sufficient to explain such an unexpected social development, the responsibility for the New Religious Right must be apportioned among the three facets of religion previously shown to have political relevance: social group, institution, and values (see Wald 1990).

Social Influences

As a social group, the evangelicals have achieved dramatic gains in socioeconomic status since the end of World War II (compare Roof and McKinney 1987 with Pope 1953; Lazerwitz 1961; Bogue 1959, 697–709). From the late 1940s and through the mid-1950s, white Southern Baptists averaged just under eight years of formal education, and roughly two-thirds did not complete high school. By the 1970s, the average years of school completed by the same group had risen to almost eleven, and the proportion with less than a high school degree declined to substantially less than half. These gains in education signaled the growing presence of evangelicals in urban areas, higher income brackets, and white-collar occupations. Though evangelicals continued to lag behind the rest of the white population on most measures of socioeconomic achievement, the younger members of the community came to resemble mainstream American groups. The development of an evangelical middle class was symbolized by the replacement of modest, ramshackle churches with lavish and well-appointed centers of worship.

This objective gain in economic standing contributed in several ways to undercutting evangelical traditions of political apathy and Democratic partisanship. As evangelicals moved into the middle class, they gained resources that encouraged political participation, such valuable assets as increased free time and energy, organizational skills, access to social and communication networks, contacts with government officials, and greater exposure to information. As it often does for other groups, social change also produced an evangelical leadership class of clergy and secular activists. With increasing economic standing, evangelicals also tended to acquire more of an interest in the policies of low taxation and limited government unceasingly advocated by the Republican party. By moving to cities, evangelicals came face to face with direct assaults on the social values dominant in their rural and small-town strongholds. As a result of this social transformation, evangelicals emerged in the 1970s with both greater capacity and disposition for political action.

But to explain why evangelicals were mobilized principally on the basis of traditional moral and social values, rather than economic appeals, reference to changes in objective economic achievement is not sufficient. For most observers, the critical factor in preparing the ground for the New Christian Right was change in subjective social status. According to the "status politics" model that has been used to explain different types of right-wing political action, moral crusades such as that mounted by the religious right represent a symbolic response by groups to declines in their social prestige (Lipset and Raab 1970, 1981). Joseph Gusfield described "status politics" in the following terms:

As his own claim to social respect and honor are diminished, the . . . citizen seeks for public acts through which he may reaffirm the dominance and prestige of his style of life. Converting the sinner to virtue is one way; law is another. Even if the law is not enforced or enforceable, the symbolic import of its passage is important to the reformer. It settles the controversies between those who represent clashing cultures. The public support of one conception of morality at the expense of another enhances the prestige and self-esteem of the victors and degrades the culture of the losers. (1963, 4–5)

The evangelicals, it has been argued, watched with dismay as society turned away from the values represented by traditional morality and opinion leaders appeared to give priority to the interests and aspirations of groups, such as blacks, who had long ranked below them in social esteem. Under this interpretation, resentment about declining social respect paid to devout members of the evangelical community prompted their support for movements pledged "to reestablish, through formal political processes, the social support that the group's values once commanded" (Crawford 1980, 149).

Challenging the assumption that evangelicals were necessarily losing social prestige, some observers have broadened the status-politics framework into a "politics of lifestyle concern." In this view, movements such as the New Christian Right, rather than trying to recapture lost prestige or social honor, have attempted to defend the values, customs, and habits that form the basis of their life-style (Conover 1983; Lorentzen 1980; Moen 1984; Page and Clelland 1978). Through early training and later participation in group life, evangelicals are exposed to a culture that emphasizes "adherence to traditional norms, respect for family and religious authority, asceticism and control of impulse" (Wood and Hughes 1984, 89). When social policies appeared to challenge this frame of reference by endorsing attacks on religion or encouraging self-indulgence and alternatives to the traditional family, it has been argued, evangelicals fought back by supporting policies more in tune with their cultural values.

The concerns of the evangelicals were not entirely symbolic. They criticized the federal government for taking over a number of tasks once reserved for the family (Moen 1989). Medicare was condemned for encouraging people to shirk family obligations, welfare benefits were alleged to encourage promiscuity, and high rates of taxation were blamed for forcing women from the household into the workplace. Of course, the long string of Supreme Court decisions restricting government action in support of religion did hamper the expression of evangelical faith in public schools. Although a conspiracy of "secular humanists" was an effective symbolic device rather than an empirical reality, there is undeniable evidence of a broadly secular orientation among strategically placed members of the American elite (McCloskey and Zaller 1984, 26). Evangelicals had something to worry about.

Whether couched in its narrow or broad form, status-politics theory asserts that the roots of evangelical political mobilization can be found in perceived social-group interests. That hypothesis has been examined carefully and remains the object of debate.[8] Several studies of moral conservatism have failed to find evidence of status discontent among advocates and the rank and file. Noting that these studies had not measured the degree to which moral conservatives actually felt deprived of social respect, Wald, Owen, and Hill (1989) assessed the relationship between perceived social respect and support for NCR goals and organizations among a sample of Protestant churchgoers. They found strong support for status politics in the acute sense of status deprivation felt by the most enthusiastic supporters of evangelical political action. To the extent that study is supported by additional research, it suggests that both objective and subjective social forces interacted to foster the New Christian Right.

Institutional Influences

The role of religious institutions was also important in this regard. The social transformation of evangelicals produced a major emphasis on what was called "church planting." The so-called super churches, like Jerry Falwell's Thomas Road Baptist Church, took on a wide range of functions and developed into religious equivalents of major corporations (Fitzgerald 1981). Less ambitious local churches also began to provide a wide array of services for their members. As the ministry became more professional, the seminaries produced clerical leaders who managed church entry into such fields as education, day-care, and counseling. The evolution of the churches from places of worship to social service centers brought them under the authority of government regulations affecting zoning, educational practices (curriculum content, teacher certification, desegregation mandates, tax-exempt status), day-care facilities, minimum-wage laws, and working conditions. The result was a series of classic confrontations between the state's interest in regulating the private provision of social services and the church's claims of immunity under the free-exercise clause. With such substantial investments, the churches could no longer afford a policy of political disengagement.

Whatever their motivation, evangelical clergy gradually took up more active political involvement than recorded previously. In studies conducted during the 1960s, scholars found that clergy from conservative Protestantism were much less likely than their liberal counterparts to take public stands on political concerns and were themselves less likely to participate in politics (Quinley 1974). The emphasis on converting sinners took precedence over changing laws. More recent research finds much lower participation differences among clergy from different denominations (Beatty and Walter 1987; Guth 1989b). The parishioners appear to be listening. Those from doctrinally conservative Protestant denominations do not report receiving less political direction than mainline Protestants or Catholics (Welch et al. 1990). As we would expect, the priorities of the communication differ, with conservative clergy stressing the profamily agenda while liberal ministers emphasize "peace and justice" issues like hunger and poverty. But the conservative clergy appear to have caught up with their mainline counterparts in the degree to which they preach about politics.

The rapid expansion of the "electronic church" was another manifestation of evangelical growth that stimulated political involvement (Hadden and Swann 1981). According to recent figures (Hadden 1984, 162–163; Rifkin 1979, chap. 5, 99–108), more than one thousand radio stations and sixty-five television stations are currently devoted exclusively to religious broadcasting. Three "Christian" television networks now broadcast around the clock, and several others offer similar programming for parts of the day; together these networks reach an audience estimated at 25 million people. Still more such activity can be expected with the growth of cable television coverage and the proliferation of low-power television stations. Because the airwaves are regulated by the Federal Communications Commission, religious broadcasters have a natural interest in government decision making.

The growth of evangelical institutions affected not only the interests but also the political capacity of the religious right. Social movements depend on access to potential supporters and to resources that can be pressed into service. Potentially powerful political forces in their own environment, local evangelical churches are also aligned with central organizations that can coordinate nationwide political action. Part of Moral Majority's strength was its direct access to local preachers through the network of churches affiliated with the Baptist Bible Fellowship (Liebman 1983). Television evangelists have direct access to viewers and the capacity to tap into mailing lists with millions of names. Not surprisingly in view of these resources, the major political movements targeting evangelicals were initiated by pastors with access to vast broadcasting empires. Jerry Falwell of Moral Majority had his "Old Time Gospel Hour," the Christian Voice was connected to the Reverend Pat Robertson's Christian Broadcasting Network, and the Roundtable's leading spokesman, James Robison, had a nationally syndicated program. The extent and effectiveness of their televised political appeals remains a subject of debate (Abelman and Pettey 1988; Tamney and Johnson 1983; Will and Williams 1986; Sirotnik, Heeren, and Lindsey n.d.).

Of course, reliance on broadcasting and national church alliances cannot guarantee success in political life. As some of the liberal clergy had already discovered, an evangelist who preaches politics instead of the Gospel may lose those in the audience who want religion to address their spiritual concerns. Moreover, constant demands for funds may produce decreasing returns from a weary audience. Competition among media ministers may undermine the unity required for effective political action. The local churches that serve as the base of operations for the New Religious Right, finally, may also fiercely resist attempts at central coordination, fragmenting the energy of the group and giving unwanted publicity to loose cannons such as the Moral Majority chapter head from California who publicly advocated the execution of homosexuals.[9]

Values

The third aspect of religion, comprising theology and values, has also played a part in stimulating the New Christian Right. The new willingness of evangelicals to apply their religious values to public policy has been especially puzzling to the social theorists who used to explain evangelical abstention from politics by citing religious values. How could a theology that once emphasized otherworldliness and personal salvation now become a basis for political activism? Of course, not all evangelicals approved of the new political activism; enough embraced it, however, to require an explanation.

Robert Wuthnow (1983) has suggested that in engaging in politics, the evangelicals were responding to changes in society that encouraged the application of religious values to public policy. At the national level, several trends blurred the traditional view of "morality" as a matter largely for individual behavior and thus raised new public concern about the ethical standards of public institutions. As evidence of the growing trend to approach public policy from an ethical viewpoint, Wuthnow cited "criticism of the Vietnam war as an act of public immorality, the various legislative actions taken in the aftermath of Watergate to institutionalize morality as a matter of official concern, and major Supreme Court decisions symbolically linking government with morality" (ibid., 176). Ironically, Jimmy Carter helped to point the way for evangelicals when he hinged his 1976 campaign on the need to restore trust, honesty, and morality to American public life. All these developments reflected growing recognition that government should not be totally independent of moral considerations and paved the way for morally based criticism of national policy.

Few groups were as receptive to this approach as the evangelicals. Contrary to their historical image, evangelicals have a long tradition of fighting back against perceived assaults by public authority on their favored social values. In the past, this tendency had surfaced mostly in local conflicts over issues such as liquor licensing, sex education, and pornography. In the 1970s, however, the challenge appeared to emanate from a national government that seemingly had loosened restraints in hundreds of ways. Faced with a Supreme Court that reduced limits on public expressions of sexuality to an administration that allowed homosexuals to meet with a presidential assistant, evangelicals felt their values under siege in the national arena.

The actions of secular authority not only offended traditional moral values—reason enough to act—but also seemed to threaten the ability of evangelicals to protect themselves and their families from corrupting influences. Encouraged by the politicizing of morality exhibited in reaction to civil rights, Vietnam, and Watergate, theological conservatives sought to apply the same moral outrage to social policy questions. And to prosecute the crusade, they could call on an increasingly affluent constituency through several organizational channels.

Civility and Consensus

Before considering the effects of this activity, it is worth examining a troubling issue posed by the activities of the New Christian Right. The emergence of the movement, particularly its aggressive and uncompromising political style, raised fears about religious bigotry and extremism. When religion motivates political action, there is always the danger that people will assume that their positions are ordained by God and will regard their opponents as sinful. Precisely such an attitude was revealed by the North Carolina congressman who accused his Southern Baptist opponent of challenging "the principles outlined in the Word of God" (Johnson 1986). Another favorite of the Christian Right, Rep. Mark Sijlander (R-Mich.), appealed to fundamentalist voters to help him "break the back of Satan" (cited in Diamond 1989, 71). Because she was "tired of having the devil's people run things," an Indiana woman told a reporter, she had volunteered for a campaign "to get some of God's people" in office.[10] Even though all three candidates lost their elections, the campaign tone was worrisome.[11]

A development that some took as evidence of that intolerance was the issuance of "moral report cards" by several of the New Christian Right organizations during campaigns (*Congressional Quarterly* 1980).[12] Like other interest groups that rate elected officials by their support for favored causes, the evangelical lobbies identified a key set of roll call votes and ranked candidates by their fidelity to the position endorsed by the group. The issues were identified as moral questions, and representatives who "failed" the test were targeted for defeat in literature distributed to churchgoers.

This action received substantial criticism from persons who could not discern a moral dimension in voting to cut spending on behavioral research from the budget of the National Science Foundation, to abolish the Department of Education, to require a balanced federal budget, or to prohibit school busing—to cite just a few of the issues that made up the various report cards or profamily voting indexes. Others resented the claim that there was only one "moral" position on such complicated issues as abortion and school prayer or denied that a representative's underlying attitude could accurately be discerned from just a single vote. Ironically, the "moral voting" test was failed by several of the most widely respected representatives in Congress, as well as most of the ordained clergy in the legislative branch. Even though the literature distributed to churchgoers did not expressly declare that officials who voted "wrong" were necessarily immoral in their own lives, the inference could easily be drawn from the accompanying claim that the nation's decline had stemmed from the failure of government leaders to adhere to the "godly principles" of the nation's Founders. In some local areas, candidates who had flunked the Christian Voice test claimed they were accused of immorality or "unchristian" voting (*Congressional Quarterly* 1980, 2624; Simon 1984, 89–90). (The flavor of the conflict is reflected in a Christian Voice flyer distributed in 1984; see Figure 7.1.) All in all, the ratings left hard feelings in Congress and may have contributed to the rough going that the New Right platform encountered after the election. The resentment was only partially redeemed when it became known that the highest-scoring group of congressmen included

Christian Voice's "Report Card" on Key 1984 Presidential Candidates

REPORT CARD :
Reagan vs. Mondale vs. Hart

Take the issues test. The following are the Presidential candidates' positions on issues important to Christian Voters. Match your position with the candidates'.

Issue	Ronald Reagan		Walter Mondale		Gary Hart		Your position	
	yes	no	yes	no	yes	no	yes	no
Prayer in School	✔		✔			✔		
Taxpayer-Funded Abortion		✔	✔		✔			
Gay Rights Amendment		✔	✔		✔			
Equal Rights Amendment		✔	✔		✔			
Unverifiable U.S.-Soviet Arms Agreement		✔	✔		✔			
Excessive Government Spending	✔		✔		✔			

Source: Christian Voice Moral Government Fund, Washington, D.C.: 1984.

a representative who was caught on videotape accepting a bribe, another who was convicted of tax evasion, and two who confessed to sexual misconduct. Nonetheless, the practice continued in 1988.

The responsibility for raising the temperature of the political atmosphere with strident appeals did not rest exclusively with the evangelical action groups. The opponents of the New Christian Right were not reluctant to indulge in some of the same tactics they condemned in the conservative movement. Although thoughtful and reasoned critiques of the NCR were presented, careful examination of the literature of groups such as People for the American Way or well-established organizations like the American Civil Liberties Union reveals examples of self-righteousness, distortion, oversimplification, and attempts to "monopolize the symbols of legitimacy" by staking exclusive claim to the flag, national traditions, and common American values (Hunter 1983, 162). As Hunter has pointed out, members of the evangelical movements are expressing their dissatisfaction with important changes in American society. If the methods and language of their advocacy have not always been moderate, it is also true that their claims have not always been treated with the respect and civility they deserve.

If the New Religious Right was reminiscent in some respects of past evangelical political involvement, it differed markedly in others. Largely absent have been the attacks on racial and religious minorities that had disfigured evangelical political crusades of the past. Moral Majority, in particular, reached out directly to Catholics, Jews, and blacks by describing itself as a political rather than a religious movement, by opening membership up to all persons, and by stressing issues that might build alliances across religious lines. Support for Israel was a constant theme in Moral Majority literature, and Falwell has repeatedly referred to the Judeo-Christian basis of the nation's heritage. In 1984 the Minnesota chapter of Moral Majority actually endorsed the reelection effort of a Jewish senator (Pressman 1984, 2317). The abortion issue, on which the New Christian Right has been as adamant and unyielding as any group in America, offered a potential bridge to Catholics, and the interpretation of abortion as a civil rights issue for the unborn represented an oblique appeal to blacks. Even feminists, who recoiled from the New Christian Right because of its opposition to the Equal Rights Amendment and general support for male authority in the family, were offered support in their fight against pornography (Duggan 1985). Occasional public expressions of anti-Semitism and anti-Catholicism from movement activists put some dents in this image of respectability and breadth of vision, however.

The New Christian Right as a Mass Movement

Sensitive to charges of improperly mixing religion with politics, the leaders of the New Christian Right vehemently denied that their organizations were narrow-minded or sectarian. By choosing names like Moral Majority and American Coalition for Traditional Values, the founders of those organizations invited support from a broad range of people. In their more expansive moments, New Christian Right activists insisted that they better represented the vast majority of the American public than political elites who denied the importance of religious values in public life. Thanks to the development of tools such as public opinion polls, some of these claims can be assessed. In this section, we attempt to determine the breadth of public support for the institutions and policies spearheaded by the Christian conservatives.

If we infer popular standing from the public reputation of the organizations or their standard-bearers, the New Christian Right must be adjudged spectacularly ineffective. National polls have revealed that the Reverend Jerry Falwell was one of the least popular figures on the national political scene and an electoral liability for candidates he endorsed; Falwell received "the highest negatives of anyone except Khomeini," said one political consultant in comparing Falwell to the then spiritual leader of Iran, and "was less warmly regarded than Jane Fonda, Senator Edward Kennedy, and 17 other public figures" listed in a Republican poll (cited in Sigelman, Wilcox, and Buell 1987, 879). The most careful estimates of membership in Falwell's organization, Moral Majority, disputed its founder's claim to have enrolled as many as 3 million members, finding only about .5 million instead (Hadden and Swann 1981, 164–165). That organization suffered a very negative public image among the relatively small share of the population that was familiar with it (Buell and Sigelman 1985). When asked to indicate their feelings about a range of politically active organizations during the 1980 and 1984 presidential campaigns, respondents put "evangelical groups, like the Moral Majority" near the bottom of the list (Perkins 1989). Using a composite measure, Sigelman, Wilcox, and Buell (1987) found only about 10 percent of the population supportive of NCR organizations whereas two-thirds to three-fourths were critical.

Things had not changed much by 1988 when Pat Robertson ranked at the bottom of the list of candidates for the GOP nomination. When Republican voters were asked to evaluate Robertson, many more offered negative than positive assessments (*Polling Report* 1988). Robertson's penchant for uttering "funny facts"—claims, for example, that George Bush had engineered a sex scandal involving a fellow televangelist or that Nancy Reagan had urged her husband to "go soft" on communism—further discredited his campaign.

During the civil rights movement, the cause of racial equality proved more popular than the organizations campaigning for it. In a similar manner, did the issue preference of the New Christian Right, if not the organizations themselves, engage the support of the public? One scholar (Simpson 1983) used poll data to estimate that as much as 70 percent of the adult population was receptive to the "sociomoral" platform advocated by the Christian Right. Some NCR positions, such as support for voluntary school prayer, commanded the blessing of a majority, while others alienated far more people than they attracted (see Figure 5.2). Because of variations in question wording and other survey features, there is no way to produce a definitive assessment of the level of public support for the platform of the Christian Right. Although demurring that their estimate was merely a rough indicator of public sentiment, Sigelman and Presser (1988, 334) revealed that only about 5 percent of the public supported the Moral Majority policy positions on abortion, sex education, the Equal Rights Amendment, and school prayer. Support for the core items making up the entire "profamily" agenda, limited to a minority of the population, has declined over the course of the 1970s and 1980s (Mueller 1983; Smith 1982; Yinger and Cutler 1982). In the face of New Right efforts to the contrary, the public has apparently become *more* liberal on issues like abortion, tolerance for homosexuality, and women's rights.

Jerry Falwell's critics used to adorn their cars with bumper stickers proclaiming that "The Moral Majority is neither." While it is beyond the scope of this inquiry to assess the morality of the New Christian Right, the evidence does paint it clearly as a minority movement. The profamily agenda and the organizations that propagate it have struck the most responsive chord precisely where they might be expected to make a strong appeal—to persons deeply attached to evangelical Protestant denominations and values (Barrett and Harris 1982; Buell and Sigelman 1985; Baker, Epstein, and Furth 1981; Brudney and Copeland 1984; Hertel and Hughes 1987; Kellstedt 1989c; Nemeth and Luidens 1989; Patel, Pilant, and Rose 1982, 1985; Shupe and Stacey 1983; Sigelman, Wilcox, and Buell 1987; Smidt 1989c; Tamney and Johnson 1983, 1988; Wilcox 1986, 1989a; Yinger and Cutler 1982; Wald and Lupfer 1983). As secularization theory suggests, the traditional values of orthodox Christianity appeal disproportionately to groups with the most limited exposure to modernizing institutions—respondents who are older, less educated, less affluent, women not employed outside the house, and residents of the South. When Pat Robertson campaigned in 1988, he drew both electoral and financial support from the same well of Protestant theological conservatism (Brody 1988; Green and Guth 1988; Smidt 1989b). As many studies have suggested, involvement in theologically conservative churches seems to breed a strong attachment to traditional moral values and a tacit willingness for clergy and church members to try to enshrine these values in public policy (Himmelstein 1986).

Even at that, evangelical Protestants must not be portrayed as a monolithic source of support for the New Christian Right. That mistake was made by journalists (see Yankelovich 1981, 5) and even by Pat Robertson, who confidently claimed "the seventy million evangelical Christians in this country" as his political base (cited in Reid 1987). The size of the "evangelical Christian" bloc, the target constituency for NCR mobilization, has been determined in two ways. The first method, used in Chapter 4, identifies "denominational" evangelicals by counting the number of persons affiliated with specific Protestant denominations (possibly combining them with "morally conservative" Mormons, Catholics, and Jews). The alternative, which produces an estimate of "doctrinal" evangelicals, uses survey questions to identify evangelicals by theological convictions. While the denominational strategy has its uses, particularly when good survey data are unavailable, most social scientists believe the doctrinal method more accurately captures the unique religious values and behavior displayed by evangelicals (Kellstedt 1989d; Wilcox 1986). Many use some variation on a three-part scale developed by the Gallup organization (Gallup 1981). In order to qualify as an evangelical under Gallup's formula, a person must affirm that they (1) have had a "born-again" experience or call themselves born-again Christians, (2) have encouraged other people to believe in Jesus Christ, and (3) believe in a literal interpretation of the Bible.

The persons who satisfy this standard or fit similar evangelical profiles still constitute an excessively generous estimate of the "evangelical" constituency. The "born again" measure, which has occasionally been used alone to identify evangelicals, is subject to dramatic shifts in agreement depending on how the question is worded. Examining two versions of the question asked in 1980, Smidt and Kellstedt (1987, table 1) found the "born again" share of the population to be 24 percent with one question, just under 49 percent with the other. Recent experiments with other variations show that three times as many survey respondents will claim to be born again in response to a generous as opposed to a demanding version of the question (Dixon, Levy, and Lowery 1988). Though the variation is less dramatic, it is also difficult to measure beliefs about the authority of the Bible. A significantly higher percentage of people are likely to accept one survey's measure of literalism, "The Bible is God's Word and all it says is true," than a statement such as "The Bible is the actual Word of God and is to be taken literally, word for word" (Smidt 1989d, 35). With flabby items and disagreement over how precisely to demarcate evangelicals, the evangelical share of the Christian population has been estimated as low as 12.5 percent and as high as 40.1 percent (Smidt and Kellstedt 1987, table 6). It seems that the pool of "evangelicals" derived from the standard survey-based definition includes many people with a suspect evangelical commitment.

Despite a popular tendency to lump together fundamentalists, born-again Christians, conservative Protestants, charismatics, and others as supporters of the "Christian Right," the evangelical community as a whole was surprisingly resistant to the appeals of organizations like Moral Majority. In a 1983 survey of registered voters with evangelical theological convictions, more than a quarter did not recognize Falwell and his organization; opinions were equally divided pro and con among those who did recognize the names (Rothenberg and Newport 1984, 100, 140). Remarkably, among a population heavily targeted by Moral Majority, that organization was less well-regarded than two liberal rivals long condemned as purveyors of secular humanism—the National Organization of Women and the National Education Association. Even when the sample was purged of blacks, Catholics, and those with minimal church involvement—groups less disposed to accept the NCR platform—the evangelical community hardly embraced the sociomoral platform associated with Moral Majority (Kellstedt 1989c). Though majorities of the sample approved the Christian Right agenda on school prayer, American support for Israel, and tuition tax credits, substantial majorities also took positions diametrically opposed to the leadership of the conservative Christian organizations on other issues. In supporting the distribution of birth control information in the schools, favoring passage of the Equal Rights Amendment, and rejecting the notion that acquired immune deficiency syndrome (AIDS) is a form of divine retribution for homosexuality, the evangelicals broke ranks with some of their spokesmen. On other issues on which the New Christian Right has conveyed clear preferences—supporting increases in defense spending, opposing a nuclear freeze, calling for restrictive abortion policy—evangelical opinion was split, with no single opinion clearly preferred over the alternatives.

Given this pattern, it will come as little surprise that Pat Robertson's presidential candidacy failed to win majority support among evangelical groups (Johnson, Tamney, and Burton 1989). Smidt (1989b) found that Robertson attracted less than a fifth of doctrinal evangelicals who voted in the southern presidential primaries on "Super Tuesday" and only a third of the Republicans in that religious group (see also Brody 1988). Evangelical ministers, the crucial link between the Robertson campaign and its target constituency, were much less enthusiastic than expected (Langenbach 1989). Only about 10 percent of his fellow ministers within the Southern Baptist Convention preferred Robertson for the Republican nomination (Guth 1989a).

Even within its core constituency, the evangelical community, the New Christian Right was a minority movement. Among evangelicals, which groups most strongly endorsed the conservative political style championed by Falwell and Robertson? To begin with, the Christian Right made relatively little headway among blacks and white Catholics, who together make up as much as one-third of the people defined as doctrinal evangelicals. As noted elsewhere, despite their social conservatism, blacks remain committed to the Democratic party and most of the liberal political agenda (Williams 1986). Catholic evangelicals and "prolife" advocates are also markedly more liberal than Protestant evangelicals, particularly on questions where church leaders have transmitted a "peace and justice" orientation (Leege and Welch forthcoming; Wilcox and Gomez 1990).

Within the remaining white evangelical community, conservative sentiments were most pronounced among two subgroups: fundamentalists and charismatics. Despite Falwell's wry definition of a fundamentalist as an evangelical who has gotten mad, the two labels refer to separate identities for many churchgoers. The fundamentalist label is most attractive to evangelicals who reject modern culture, insist on the importance of maintaining purity by separation from other faiths, and tend more to a literal understanding of the Bible. While all such estimates are hazardous, about one-third of the people who endorse evangelical theology describe themselves as fundamentalists (Smidt 1988). Such persons have been found to be considerably more conservative than nonfundamentalist evangelicals and have also enlisted much more wholeheartedly in the New Christian Right organizations (Green and Guth 1988; Jelen 1987; Smidt 1988; Wilcox 1987). Among ministers, for whom social issues are likely to be paramount, self-identified fundamentalists are three to four times as likely as nonfundamentalists to adopt conservative positions on a broad range of public issues (Beatty and Walter 1988). Fundamentalist clergy in the Southern Baptist Convention were about twice as likely as nonfundamentalists to prefer Pat Robertson over George Bush in 1988 (Guth 1989a). Among the fundamentalist laity, however, political attitudes are not radically different from the mainstream except on social issues (Hood and Morris 1985).

The charismatic movement within Christianity, formerly a lower-class phenomenon, spread across the American religious spectrum in the 1970s. While charismatics accept the doctrinal beliefs associated with evangelicalism, they also emphasize the "baptism of the Holy Spirit," based on events recorded in Acts 2, whereby they are infused with divine power by the Holy Ghost. The "indwelling of the Spirit" enables them to speak in tongues, heal by faith, and utter prophecies based on the Bible. These views are often regarded as heretical and even possibly satanic by more conventional evangelicals who assign exclusive religious authority to Scripture. The roughly one-third of doctrinal evangelical Protestants who accept the charismatic label are more conservative than their brethren on social morality issues (Smidt 1989e).[13] Pat Robertson, an evangelical who enlisted in the charismatic revival while a seminary student, drew his strongest support from ministers in charismatic denominations such as the Assemblies of God (Langenbach 1989). Charismatic self-identification was the single largest factor distinguishing donors to Robertson's political action committee from contributors to committees sponsored by other Republican candidates and organizations (Green and Guth 1988, 156), and it also differentiated Robertson from Bush supporters within Republican state parties (Smidt and Penning 1990) and in the electorate in "Super Tuesday" primaries (Wilcox 1990).

These findings should serve as a strong caution against attributing a single, unified political perspective to the remarkably diverse community of evangelical Protestants. Even excluding Catholics and black evangelicals, groups whose political priorities diverge sharply from the NCR platform, Wilcox (1989b, 408–410) found a large majority of white evangelicals to be either ignorant of Moral Majority, opposed to it on ideological grounds, or sympathetic to its views but committed to the Democratic party. This pattern is explicable once we recognize that the social issues that form the profamily platform are not the only questions on the national agenda. When the focus shifts to economic policy, foreign relations, or the environment, evangelicals are not nearly so cohesive, nor do they diverge so much from the attitude patterns of other religious groups. Like other groups of voters from a common religious tradition, evangelicals tend to divide along lines of class, region, gender, and the like when the issue does not relate to the profamily issue, and sometimes even when it does.

The diversity of evangelicalism accounts for the bitter criticism the New Christian Right drew from within. Some leaders of the fundamentalist wing, believing the only task of the churches was to win souls for Christ, continued to preach against political involvement. Critics like the Reverend Bob Jones denounced Falwell for endangering the souls of fundamentalists by forging political alliances with the unsaved. From the other wing of evangelicalism, Social Gospel advocates such as the Sojourners protested against an unholy alliance between the "prolife" forces on abortion and such "antilife" causes as militarism, capital punishment, apartheid, and social inequality.

The New Christian Right has enjoyed a less than overwhelming endorsement from the recognized leadership of the evangelical community. As Robert Booth Fowler (1982) documented, the most influential leaders of evangelical Protestantism had been moving toward a more moderate political position throughout the 1960s. They formed Evangelicals for Social Action to capitalize on the growing willingness of theological conservatives to support social reform. The most widely recognized spokesman for evangelical concerns in the United States today, the Reverend Billy Graham, is a case in point (Pierard 1983a; Stockton 1989). At the beginning of his career, Graham exhibited some of the political and social tendencies that were typical of fundamentalist Protestants. But over the course of the years, Graham moved toward the center of the political system by integrating his crusades, speaking out in favor of civil rights legislation, and, most recently, advocating strenuous efforts to improve relations with the Soviet Union and to diminish the nuclear arms race. Graham has repeatedly warned that any attempt to identify a particular political agenda with Christianity is likely to bring discredit on religion and to interfere with evangelization.

The Political Ramifications of the NCR

As an electoral movement, the New Christian Right adopted two major goals—to get evangelical Protestants to participate in politics and to support candidates who endorsed conservative programs and policies. Because most evangelicals lived in the Democratic South and had a reputation for political passivity, achieving either objective required changing ingrained patterns of behavior. Jerry Falwell quickly declared victory on both counts, claiming credit for registering 3 million evangelicals and mobilizing them in a bloc behind Republican nominees for national office.[14] The failure of the Pat Robertson campaign, in spite of ample financing and high name recognition among evangelicals, suggests the magnitude of the challenge and the limits to Falwell's claims.

In trying to overcome the evangelical tradition of low political involvement, the New Right groups have devoted considerable energy to persuading conservative Protestants that political action is compatible with the Scriptures. This effort *appears* to have paid off. Data from the 1960s and 1970s revealed that doctrinal evangelicals were appreciably less likely to vote than other citizens.[15] Since then, the absolute level of turnout among evangelicals has grown and the differential between evangelical and nonevangelical has narrowed (Smidt and Kellstedt 1987, table 31; Smidt 1987, 429). In 1980, paced by a turnout surge among white southerners, evangelicals actually voted at a higher rate than nonevangelicals. This pattern was not sustained in either 1984 or 1988, but the gaps were much smaller than in previous elections.

Tempting as it is to credit this participation increase to the Christian Right, the evidence does not warrant that conclusion. The long-term increase in evangelical turnout rates seems primarily a function of the modernization of the South. For evangelicals, as for other population groups, increases in socioeconomic standing go hand in hand with greater political interest and involvement. In the shorter term, the sharpest growth in the electoral activity of both doctrinal and denominational evangelicals was registered in 1976—before the New Christian Right was a national force—and evangelical turnout subsequently declined relative to nonevangelicals despite the extensive mobilization efforts in 1984 (Wilcox 1989b, 145–148).

What of the second objective, rallying evangelicals to the Republican side in presidential elections? Again, the patterns in the data suggest movement in this direction. Based on interviews with doctrinal evangelicals in surveys with comparable religious questions, Smidt and Kellstedt (1987, table 34) report that evangelicals moved in a more Republican direction from 1976 through 1984. Over the course of this period, they evolved from voting about 4 percent more Democratic than nonevangelicals in 1976 to become 7 percent more Republican in 1984. Again, the New Christian Right organizations can take relatively little credit for this pattern. First, the Republican preference was established *before* the New Christian Right organizations began their mobilizing efforts. Kellstedt and Noll's (1990, 360) analysis of denominational evangelicals shows that they had been more Republican than the rest of the nation as far back as 1956. The apparent increase in Republican voting in 1984 seems like a return to normal following abnormally high Democratic voting in response to the candidacy of a fellow evangelical in both 1976 and 1980. The NCR groups thus appear to have capitalized on an underlying transformation rather than to have created it. Second, and even more tellingly, the evangelicals who entered the electorate for the first time in 1980 were actually *more* likely to support the Democratic presidential candidate than were nonevangelicals or evangelicals who had voted before (Smidt 1983, table 8). This occurred despite the intense efforts by conservative evangelical groups to enlist new evangelical voters on behalf of Ronald Reagan.

How much of a difference did the NCR make in presidential elections? Given the general tenor of the findings reported thus far, the reader should not be surprised to find that neither denominational nor doctrinal evangelicals were distinctively more pro-Reagan in 1980 than their opposite numbers. Like most of the electorate, they treated the election largely as a referendum on Carter's performance as president, not a choice between divergent moral platforms (Himmelstein and McRae 1984; Hibbs 1982). Only among the small share of the electorate that felt close to evangelical groups like Moral Majority—a group composed disproportionately of fundamentalists—was Reagan's support substantially higher than the norm; some 86 percent of this group supported Reagan against 55 percent of the much larger group that did not feel close to evangelical groups in politics (Brudney and Copeland 1984, 1075). Because of its cohesiveness, this roughly 6 percent of the electorate contributed an estimated 10 percent of the Reagan vote.

The extraordinary level of religious mobilization in 1984 appears to have heightened the religious dimension of electoral choice (Copeland and Brudney 1988). As in 1980, denominational evangelicals were not significantly more pro-Reagan than voters from other denominations. But both doctrinal evangelicals and persons who identified with evangelical political action were appreciably more supportive of the Reagan candidacy in 1984.[16] The level of Reagan support among doctrinal evangelicals was 73 percent compared to 58 percent for nonevangelicals. The identifiers with evangelical groups in politics, who grew from 6 percent in 1980 to 16 percent in 1984, gave Reagan 78 percent of their votes, 21 percent more than persons who did not identify with evangelicals. Even though this group grew in size, relative declines in cohesion and turnout from 1980 actually reduced their contribution to the Reagan vote. Nonetheless, it seems that moral issues assumed a salience in voters' minds that had not been attained in 1980 (Kellstedt 1989b; Woodrum 1988).

How much of this was due to the Christian Right and how much to Ronald Reagan's unique persona remains to be seen. The first analyses from 1988, when Ronald Reagan did not head the Republican ticket, emphasize the continuing appeal of conservative Republicanism to evangelicals (Kellstedt 1989a; Smidt and Kellstedt 1990; Kellstedt, Kellstedt and Smidt 1990). Even though the election of 1988 was closer and the absolute level of Republican support among evangelicals was lower than in 1984, differences between evangelical and nonevangelical voters remained quite substantial. George Bush received approximately 70 percent of the votes cast by denominational evangelicals, 6 percent more than he received from mainline Protestants. Using doctrinal rather than denominational criteria, the gap in Bush support between evangelical and nonevangelical Protestants reached 14 percent in 1988, very close to the 1984 level. Many analysts now consider evangelicals a reliable element in the Republican coalition during presidential elections.

NCR-sponsored candidates for lower offices do not appear to have enjoyed similar success (Johnson, Tamney, and Burton 1989—but see A. Miller and Wattenberg 1984, 313). Anecdotal evidence supports the claim that evangelicals newly registered by Moral Majority were crucial in the primary defeat of a moderate Republican congressman from Alabama in 1980 (*Congressional Quarterly* 1980), but other congressional candidates strongly identified with the Christian Right have a poor electoral record (Benenson 1988). Conservative religious themes and organizations have contributed to the successful Senate campaigns of North Carolina's Jesse Helms. For his vociferous and unwavering support of the NCR platform in the Senate and on the campaign trail, Helms was designated "a national treasure" by Jerry Falwell. In a battle against a strong opponent in 1984, Helms benefited from a massive effort to register white voters in conservative churches. Countering Democratic efforts to place more blacks on the voter roles, the Helms campaign relied on an organization headed by the Moral Majority state chairman, a minister, to eke out a narrow victory (Johnson and Edsall 1984; Luebke 1985–1986). During the 1990 campaign, Helms renewed his "politics of values" by framing the campaign as a choice between "decent, God-fearing people" against an unholy coalition of "gays, radical feminists and arts people,"[17] the latter referring to supporters of federal funding for allegedly blasphemous and pornographic works of art. Helms's cultural conservatism helped him win the vote of more than two-thirds of white Protestants, well above his statewide percentage of the total vote.[18] Beyond Helms, it is difficult to identify any Senate campaign where the NCR itself was the critical factor (Lipset and Raab 1981; Zwier 1984).

After this generally skeptical assessment of the New Christian Right, it is important to emphasize that I mean only to challenge claims about the movement's potency and not to deny strong evidence of increased political conservatism among evangelical Protestants. Whether the NCR mattered or not, some evangelicals do appear to be undergoing change in the manner sought by conservative activists. Electoral data tell only part of the story; three other developments point to greater prospects for change. Although evangelicals as a whole do not appear to have shifted their loyalty from the Democrats to Republicans, such change has been significant among younger evangelicals in the South (Kellstedt 1989b, 1989e). As the young are often the carriers of new political alignments, this suggests that religion may have contributed to a subtle shift in political dynamics that will become fully apparent in years to come. Second, if partisan *identification* has been stable, evangelicals have been changing their partisan *affections*, a term signifying how positively or negatively a party is perceived. From being predominantly Democratic in affection in 1980, southern white evangelicals became primarily Republican in 1984 (Smidt 1989a). Changes in partisan identification and electoral choice may well follow in time.

Finally, the Republican party and its conservative agenda now command a high level of support among some key elements of the Southern Baptist Convention (SBC), the single largest denomination in evangelical Christianity (Blumenthal 1984, 23). Once believers in a strong wall of separation between church and state, church delegates had endorsed abortion as a right just two years before the Supreme Court decision of *Roe v. Wade* and had repeatedly endorsed Supreme Court rulings prohibiting organized prayer in public schools. Through its membership in the Baptist Joint Committee, the church had lobbied for the types of welfare policies consistent with a Social Gospel approach to Christianity. By contrast, the annual convention has now shifted into a much more activist mode, attacking nearly every policy the SBC once supported, and has withdrawn from the Baptist Joint Committee. A continuing survey of Southern Baptist pastors begun in 1980 shows dramatic change among the clergy in support for state action to reinforce traditional values and in commitment to the Republican party (Guth 1983a, 1983b, 1985, 1989b).

A Republican Dilemma?

Whatever its strengths and weaknesses as a mass movement, the New Christian Right has channeled many of its activists into Republican party organizations. Evangelical Protestants have flocked to local and state party caucuses, in some cases taking over from traditional leaders, and have claimed both a significant bloc of delegates and major platform influence at recent national conventions. In a tribute to the rapid gains made by conservative evangelicals, *Washington Post* reporter Thomas Edsall concluded, "The muscle of the Christian right in the GOP is roughly parallel to the power of the AFL-CIO or the NEA within the Democratic Party" (1985, 8).

Despite the prospect of attracting new partners to their coalition, longtime Republicans have not always welcomed the converts. Describing the Robertson forces as something like "the bar scene out of *Star Wars*" (cited in Hertzke 1989, 6), the Republican state chairman of

Michigan symbolized the negative reaction of many in the GOP establishment. His counterpart in Georgia declared that the Christian Rightists who took over that state's party had the attitudes "that brought you the burning of Joan of Arc, the Salem Witch trials and the Ayatollah Khomeini" (Gurwitt 1989, 54). Barry Goldwater, the patron saint of conservative Republicanism, protested aloud at the "bunch of kooks" whose platform for the Arizona state party declared the United States "a Christian nation" with a constitution "based upon the absolute laws of the Bible" (cited in Hertzke 1989, 5). Republican elites in several states were particularly aggrieved at the seizure of party power by newcomers who had only recently left the Democratic party.

To some extent, the resentment directed by party regulars against the evangelical newcomers is an inevitable by-product of a struggle for power. But it also reflects a cultural conflict, what one participant called "the God Squad versus the Regulars" (ibid., 7). The conservative Christian activists who have moved into Republican party circles bring different values, priorities, and styles. Compared to party regulars, they are substantially more religious and are religious in a different, more intense manner. While sharing the economic conservatism of the regulars, they attach much greater priority to social issues and take an extremely nationalistic line in foreign policy. They disdain political compromise, believe parties must stand clearly for issues, and see little virtue in harboring a diversity of viewpoints (Green and Guth 1988; Smidt and Penning 1988). This "purist," or "amateur," political style puts them at odds with party regulars who are more willing to bargain and negotiate if it advances the fortunes of the party. The evangelical activists tend to see the Republican party as a vehicle for implementing their social vision; the regulars view the party as a worthy end in itself.

The entry of the evangelical activists threatens both the internal harmony and larger electoral prospects of the Republican party. According to Rebecca E. Klatch (1988), social and economic conservatives disagree fundamentally over the individual and society, the role of the state, and the position of women. Unlike economic conservatives, who believe society will thrive when individuals are free to pursue self-interest, social conservatives entertain a model wherein "society brings the individual under the moral authority of God, the church, and the family, thereby restraining man's instincts and curbing individual self-interest" (ibid., 31). It follows that economic conservatives want to limit and dismantle the state while social conservatives want to use the state to achieve a different set of goals from those it has recently pursued under the influence of "secular humanism." Finally, according to Klatch, social conservatives assign priority to defending a traditional role for women as housewives and caregivers; they oppose day-care, liberalized abortion, and gay rights as threats to traditional sex roles. "Laissez-faire women, on the other hand," writes Klatch, "are pro-choice and support day care, as long as it remains in private hands; they firmly reject any government role in legislating sexuality or moral matters as an intrusion on individual liberty" (ibid., 34). It may prove difficult for the Republicans to contain two such contradictory worldviews within the same party.

The Republicans also face a strategic dilemma in their drive to secure a national majority. To get more evangelical voters into the Republican camp will require a consistent emphasis on social conservatism. That is the goal of the evangelical elites who have penetrated the inner circles of Republicanism. Yet to become the majority party at all levels of government, Republicans also have to appeal to a large bloc of non-evangelical voters. Ronald Reagan thrived primarily because his conservative economic policies appealed to many young voters and affluent members of the post–World War II "baby boom" generation. Such voters respond to economic conservatism *and* social liberalism (Ladd 1982, chap. 3; Warren E. Miller and Levitin 1976; Maddox and Lille 1984). They tend to take a libertarian line on social issues. The prospect of severe limits on abortion access, a key goal of the evangelicals, "could drive a stake through the heart of the Reagan coalition" by driving away the nonevangelicals (Schneider 1989, 2). Moreover, members of this target constituency want day-care facilities, environmental protection, spending on public education—issues that leave conservative evangelicals either indifferent or alienated. An emphasis on New Right concerns is thus likely to drive nonevangelicals away from the GOP (Broder 1984; Edsall, 1990). The tension between these two voter groups could be managed in 1984 and 1988 because the strong economy satisfied the nonevangelicals and the Christian Right approved the moral emphasis in the party platform. Without Ronald Reagan and with the prospect of a recession, the future may bring this latent conflict to the forefront of Republican politics.

The internal problems of the Republicans do not automatically spell recovery for the Democrats. After all, the growth in Republicanism among evangelicals comes at the expense of Democrats. Moreover, the growing concern about moral issues in politics also increases the tensions within the Democratic coalition. The Republican evangelical activists have something of a mirror image in the "secular left" of the Democratic party. This group, predominantly unattached to churches and distinguished by an almost militant commitment to free choice in personal behavior, has assumed a growing importance within the Democratic elite (Guth and Green 1986, 1990). The priorities of this important group do not square with the fundamental social conservatism of many core Democratic groups (*Times Mirror* 1988). By representing free choice in abortion, public expression, and other domains, the Democrats may appease their secular voters at the price of alienating their traditional base. In sum, neither party can be entirely cheerful about the political consequences of moral concern (Ladd 1989).

The Consequences for Public Policy

Because all this electoral activity has been aimed at changing public policy at the national level, it is appropriate to examine the success of Christian political action at that level. For the most part, the record has been one of failure. Despite the prodding of the evangelical groups, lobbying by church members, the vocal support of President Reagan, the presence of important allies in the House and Senate, and fear of electoral retribution, the major programs advocated by groups like Moral Majority were not enacted. The Senate voted down a constitutional amendment permitting organized school prayer and did not enact the tuition tax credit requested by supporters of religious schools. The third primary objective of the movement, prohibiting abortion, remains elusive. In the *Webster* decision of 1989 (profiled in Chapter 8), the Supreme Court accepted certain state restrictions on abortion but did not invalidate the *Roe v. Wade* precedent by returning complete control over abortion to the states. Even if the Court were to take that step, both pre-*Roe* practice and the responses to the *Webster* decision suggest that legal abortion would remain the rule in many communities. Moreover, it is not at all clear that the Christian Right can claim much credit for any restrictions imposed on abortion.

The symbolic nature of most of the New Christian Right's victories is exemplified by a 1985 Education Department regulation prohibiting local school districts from using certain federal funds to support courses in "secular humanism." As noted above, that term has come to symbolize the philosophy that many evangelical spokesmen regard as the root of American problems—that is, a belief in humanity as the supreme force in the universe. Because secular humanism has been identified as the foundation of such topics as biological evolution, prohibitions on prayer in public schools, and any number of other practices (Eidsmoe 1984, chap. 15), the ruling might seem to have been an important victory. However, the regulation left the concept undefined, and any attempt to specify it would almost certainly fail to pass judicial scrutiny (Barringer 1985). From "victories" such as this, the members of the religious right may have learned, as have other change-oriented persons before them, that the American political system has a genius for resisting external pressure.

Still, evangelical groups have affected national policies in ways short of changing public policy. As Matthew C. Moen has argued, the New Christian Right succeeded in obtaining passage of national legislation offering partial redress of its grievances (Moen 1989). In place of organized school prayer, it has received "equal access" for religious group meetings in class.[19] Abortion has not been prohibited, but federal funds no longer support it. The Equal Rights Amendment was defeated once and has a long way to go before it again approaches passage. The failures of the conservative religious groups to get all they want may even have fueled the drive for a new national constitutional convention. At the state and local levels, where they are often the best-organized groups, local chapters of New Christian Right organizations have carried some of their proposals into law (Pierard and Wright 1984).

Moen also noted that the efforts to challenge national policy on social issues has kept those controversies from falling off the national agenda. Finally, the emphasis in New Christian Right rhetoric on traditional values has encouraged politicians of all stripes to discuss those values in the public realm. As illustrated by Governor Mario Cuomo's keynote address to the 1984 Democratic National Convention, both parties have come to believe in the importance of appeals to moral concerns. Or perhaps more cynically, the presence of the New Christian Right may have " 'made politicians think about the moral quotient before casting their votes' " (cited in Moen 1989, 145).

The New Christian Right did not enter politics merely to restore discussion of values to the public agenda nor to attain symbolic victories. Judging by the ambitious standards they set for themselves—nothing less than to restructure American public policy in a Judeo-Christian framework—the leaders of national organizations fell far short of their goals. Once the source of dramatic initiatives in the areas of school prayer, abortion, and other social issues, the NCR was reduced by the late 1980s to fighting rearguard actions rather than taking legislative initiatives to change public policy (Moen 1989, chap. 11). With the departure of Ronald Reagan from the White House, the prospects for the future appeared bleak indeed.

To some degree, the Christian Right was the victim of its own excessive expectations. With its fragmented structure and multiple centers of power, the political system of the United States has long resisted radical attempts to reshape public policy. In that sense, the NCR was merely the latest reform group to confront the power of "immobilism" inherent in the American political system. The movement might have done better had it chosen to remain active primarily at the state and local levels, where it was incubated and generally faced fewer obstacles than on the national stage. Beyond this "strategic" mistake, the movement also suffered from "tactical" defects common to other religious groups that have entered political life—pursuing very broad mandates, ignoring legislative detail, claiming more public support than was warranted (Donnelly 1987). In addition, some advocates for the movement have blamed its legislative weakness on the lukewarm advocacy of the "pragmatists" who were said to dominate the Reagan administration. By these accounts, NCR leaders allowed the administration to devote far more energy to promoting economic changes than to promoting traditional social values.

Other commentators, including those inside the movement itself, have begun to suggest that the limits were largely self-inflicted. Deceived by poll reports into thinking that their agenda commanded overwhelming public support, evangelical activists frequently disdained "basic rules of politics, such as respect for opposing views, an emphasis on coalition-building and compromise, and careful rhetoric" (Atwood 1990, 45). Instead, they indulged in a number of acts and schemes—such as the biblical "scorecards" noted earlier—that deeply antagonized potential allies.

Although political newcomers commonly commit this type of mistake, the NCR may have been particularly prone to err in that way because of its distinctive theological inspiration. Thomas Atwood (1990), a Republican activist with the Pat Robertson campaign, identified several ways in which religious habits bred political problems for conservative evangelicals. Confident in their ability to determine God's will, they quickly claimed God's approval for certain political positions and candidates and rejected opposition to their proposals as disobedience to God's will. An insistence on purity of purpose and absolute standards, derived from evangelical doctrine, disposed NCR activists to reject small but attainable victories in favor of grandiose and implausible goals. Atwood also accused some evangelicals of "triumphalism," claiming they should rule by virtue of moral superiority, and of ascribing to the state the capacity for human redemption. While both approaches may rally the faithful, they hinder efforts to achieve broader public appeal. If the NCR is to overcome such problems, Atwood has counseled it to tone down its rhetoric, diminish its expectations, and settle for half a loaf. That may be a tall order if the tendencies toward excess are indeed rooted in doctrine.

With the decline or disappearance of many of the organizations that first spearheaded the NCR and the quick demise of the Pat Robertson presidential campaign, the movement now looks set to return to the type of "grass roots" efforts that first brought it national attention. Many Robertson activists have dispersed to the state and local ranks of the Republican party and groups like Moral Majority have been superseded by organizations such as Focus on the Family, Concerned Women for America, and Eagle Forum (Paige 1987; Diamond 1989). Pat Robertson himself has organized a new "Christian Coalition" which seeks to establish chapters at both the state level and in local communities. According to its director, the emphasis on grass-roots activism recognizes that "the real battles of concern to Christians are in neighborhoods, school boards, city councils and state legislatures" (*Church & State* 1990). Even without such supporting organizations, many conservative Christians have already redirected their efforts to the states and localities, working for goals as disparate as banning "obscene" lyrics in popular music, challenging sex education programs, and providing options to abortion (Morken 1990).[20] By concentrating on the lower levels of American political life and doing so without emphasizing their religious orientations, these activists represent an important new stage in evangelical political mobilization.

The success of the new strategy and tactics depends in large measure on the response of evangelical activists. Their active support cannot be taken for granted. Disappointed by the glacial pace of political change to date and difficult to mobilize on the basis of rather incremental policy changes, evangelicals may simply retreat from the political world into their "ghettoized Christian subculture" with its own bookstores, mass media, celebrities and institutions (Aikman 1988, 23). Alternatively, the evangelical constituency may itself be transformed as a consequence of its increasing exposure to modernity. As evangelicals partake more fully of American culture, they will be exposed to the same tensions, challenges, and opportunities that have changed the political orientations of other Americans. This may blunt the hard edges of evangelical activism.

With the New Christian Right, as with other political movements, things are not always as they seem to be. Its magnitude and impact have not been so immense as supporters have claimed nor so insignificant as opponents would like to believe. The NCR movement may be new, but it draws on well-established traditions of American life. Some observers have even interpreted the new Christian conservatism as an attempt to revitalize the civil religion discussed in Chapter 3. The idea of the United States as a redeemer nation and its people as "chosen" to lead humankind took a severe beating from the traumas of the 1960s and 1970s. These developments may have accelerated an ongoing shift in cultural values that undermined the moral consensus in American society (Anthony and Robbins 1983). Hence, in a 1975 book describing the status of civil religion, Robert Bellah referred to the "broken covenant." By insisting on official support of traditional moral values and of the view of the United States as a nation under divine judgment, the leaders of the New Christian Right have sounded themes with a strong civil religious orientation. As I argued when the concept of civil religion first came up in Chapter 3, that tradition has both noble and seamy aspects.

As the newest players in the game of national politics, the evangelical Protestants have attracted most of the attention of trend spotters. But the evangelicals have not been the only religious group to reassess traditional political loyalties. As the next chapter will make clear, Catholics have also undergone a profound political transition at the same time that mainline Protestant churches have appeared to lose enthusiasm for constant political engagement. Only black Protestants and Jews seem to have resisted pressures for political change.

NOTES

1. To the extent religion remained a force in politics, advocates of modernization theory expected the action to come primarily from "peace and justice" supporters on the Christian Left.

2. It is very difficult to find information about the political behavior of northern evangelicals after the 1920s. John Hammond's (1979) study of the revivalist ethos in Ohio and New York suggests that northern evangelicals strongly supported both restrictive social policies and the Republican party.

3. Unpublished studies by Damaske (1970), Freeman (1962), George (1971), and Reinhardt (1975) documented the political conservatism of evangelicals, but their findings did not influence mainstream electoral analysis.

4. "Spurred by White House Parley, TV Evangelists Spread Political Word," *New York Times*, Sept. 10, 1984, 1.

5. "Religion Is Powerful GOP Theme," *Washington Post*, Aug. 24, 1984, 8A.

6. Ibid.

7. Robertson's campaign was sustained by the Freedom Council, a Christian political-advocacy group set up under his direction in 1981. Charges that the finances of the Freedom Council were illegally mingled with CBN funds had not been resolved by the end of the campaign.

8. Critics like Moen (1988) argue that the "status politics" model does not fit groups with a broad agenda and concerns, such as tuition tax credits, which are tangible rather than symbolic. In my own judgment, the status-politics approach does not limit moral reform to symbolic acts and the issue of tuition tax credits can be interpreted as defending an institution (in this case, Christian schools) perceived as central to a threatened way of life. Some skeptics (Conover 1983) have converted status-politics theory to an economic model, an approach that does not do justice to its assumptions. Wesley E. Miller's (1985) finding of a steady level of status complaints in fundamentalist publications during the 1970s is damaging to the hypothesis only if status politics is advanced as the sole explanation for the Christian Right.

9. "Spurred by White House Parley, TV Evangelists Spread Political Word," *New York Times*, Sept. 10, 1984, 1; "The Moral Majority Finds Its Own Units May Need Guidance," *Wall Street Journal*, Feb. 12, 1981, 1, 17.

10. "Evangelist Gets Scant Support from GOP in House Campaign," *Wall Street Journal*, Oct. 23, 1986, 68.

11. John Smith, a mayoral candidate in Jacksonville, Florida, relied so heavily

on his Baptist church for campaign support that he became known locally as "John the Baptist."

12. "Evangelical Group Disagrees with 276 in Congress," *New York Times*, Nov. 2, 1980, 34.

13. The charismatic movement has attracted large numbers of Catholics and black Protestants. They are strikingly less traditionalist than white Protestant charismatics and much less committed to political action by religious groups (Smidt 1989e).

14. "The 'Arrival' of Jerry Falwell," *St. Petersburg Times*, Jan. 28, 1985, 1, 8A.

15. Unfortunately, the major social science opinion polls did not do a good job identifying evangelicals until 1980. Before then, denominational classifications were relatively crude and the surveys contained few if any questions about religious values. That makes it difficult to determine the magnitude of recent change.

16. Many conditions favored a Republican trend among evangelicals in 1984: the absence of economic and foreign policy issues that might normally have drawn evangelicals toward the Democrats, the Republican embrace of conservative social values on questions like abortion and school prayer versus the Democratic determination to keep contentious moral issues off the national agenda, and the Democratic nomination of a liberal, northeastern, Catholic woman for the vice-presidency.

17. "Unseating Helms: Rival Charts His Uphill Climb," *New York Times*, July 16, 1990, 1A, 12A; "In North Carolina's Senate Race, a Divisive TV Fight Over 'Values'," *New York Times*, Sept. 23, 1990, 1, 32; "Helms Kindled Anger in Campaign and May Have Set Tone for Others," *New York Times*, Nov. 8, 1990, 3B.

18. "The 1990 Elections," *New York Times*, Nov. 6, 1990, 8B.

19. Moen (1989, 114) demonstrates that many in the Christian Right viewed this proposal as a "sellout" of school prayer and were dragged along rather reluctantly.

20. David Shribman, "Religious Right Drops High-Profile Tactics, Works on Local Level," *Wall Street Journal*, Sept. 26, 1989, 1A, 19A.

REFERENCES

Abelman, Robert, and Gary Pettey. 1988. "How Political Is Religious Television?" *Journalism Quarterly* 65:313–319.

Aikman, David. 1988. "Washington Scorecard." *Christianity Today* (October), 22–23.

Allinsmith, Wesley, and Beverly Allinsmith. 1948. "Religious Affiliation and Politico-Economic Attitudes: A Study of Eight Major U.S. Religious Groups." *Public Opinion Quarterly* 12:377–389.

Anthony, Dick, and Thomas Robbins. 1983. "Spiritual Innovation and the Crisis of American Civil Religion." In *Religion and America*, edited by Mary Douglas and Steven M. Tipton, 229–248. Boston: Beacon.

Arrington, Theodore S., and Patricia A. Kyle. 1978. "Equal Rights Amendment Activists in North Carolina." *Signs* 3:666–680.

Atwood, Thomas C. 1990. "Through a Glass Darkly." *Policy Review* 5:44–53.

Baker, Ross K., Laurily K. Epstein, and Rodney D. Furth. 1981. "Matters of Life and

Death: Social, Political, and Religious Correlates of Attitudes on Abortion." *American Politics Quarterly* 9:89–102.

Baker, Tod A., Robert P. Steed, and Laurence W. Moreland, eds. 1983. *Religion and Politics in the South: Mass and Elite Perspectives.* New York: Praeger.

Barrett, Sharon W., and Richard J. Harris. 1982. "Recent Changes in Predictors of Abortion Attitudes." *Sociology and Social Research* 66:320–334.

Barringer, Felicity. 1985. "A Ban on Teaching 'Secular Humanism.'" *Washington Post Weekly Edition,* January 28, p. 32.

Beatty, Kathleen Murphy, and Oliver Walter. 1987. "A Group Theory of Religion and Politics: The Clergy as Group Leaders." *Western Political Quarterly* 42:129–146.

———. 1988. "Fundamentalists, Evangelicals and Politics." *American Politics Quarterly* 16:43–59.

Benenson, Bob. 1988. "Christian Right's Aspirants for Congress Find Their Language, Beliefs Scrutinized." *Congressional Quarterly Weekly Report,* May 14, pp. 1272–1273.

Bergstrom, Charles, and David Saperstein. 1984. "God and Politics." *Washington Post Weekly Edition,* September 10, p. 28.

Blumenthal, Sidney. 1984. "The Righteous Empire." *New Republic,* October 22, pp. 18–24.

Bogue, Donald J. 1959. *The Population of the United States.* New York: Free Press of Glencoe.

Boles, Janet K. 1979. *The Politics of the Equal Rights Amendment.* New York: Longman.

Brady, David W., and Kent L. Tedin. 1976. "Ladies in Pink: Religious and Political Ideology in the Anti-ERA Movement." *Social Science Quarterly* 56:564–575.

Broder, David S. 1984. "In Oregon, Voting for President Means Choosing the Lesser Evil." *Washington Post Weekly Edition,* September 24, p. 12.

Brody, Richard A. 1988. "Party Alignment of the Southern Christian Right: An Exploration of the *Washington Post* Pre-Primary Poll in South Carolina." Paper presented at the annual meeting of the American Political Science Association, Washington, D.C.

Brudney, Jeffrey L., and Gary W. Copeland. 1984. "Evangelicals as a Political Force: Reagan and the 1980 Religious Vote." *Social Science Quarterly* 65:1072–1079.

Bryant, Anita. 1977. *The Anita Bryant Story.* Old Tappan, N.J.: Revell.

Buell, Emmett H., and Lee Sigelman. 1985. "An Army That Meets Every Sunday? Popular Support for the Moral Majority in 1980." *Social Science Quarterly* 66:426–434.

Burner, David. 1967. *The Politics of Provincialism: The Democratic Party in Transition, 1918–1932.* New York: Norton.

Burnham, Walter Dean. 1968. "American Voting Behavior and the 1964 Election." *Midwest Journal of Political Science* 12:1–40.

Burris, Val. 1983. "Who Opposed the ERA? An Analysis of the Social Bases of Antifeminism." *Social Science Quarterly* 64:305–317.

Buzzard, Lynn. 1989. "The 'Coming-Out' of Evangelicals." In *Contemporary Evangelical Political Involvement: An Analysis and Assessment,* edited by Corwin E. Smidt, 133–146. Lanham, Md.: University Press of America.

Church & State. 1990. "The Christian Coalition: Ganging Up on the First Amendment." *Church & State* (April), 12.

Clabaugh, Gary K. 1974. *Thunder on the Right: The Protestant Fundamentalists*. Chicago: Nelson-Hall.

Congressional Quarterly. 1980. "Lobbying for Christ." *Congressional Quarterly Weekly Report*, September 6, pp. 2627–2634.

Conover, Pamela Johnston. 1983. "The Mobilization of the New Right: A Test of Various Explanations." *Western Political Quarterly* 36:632–649.

Conover, Pamela Johnston, and Virginia Gray. 1983. *Feminism and the New Right*. New York: Praeger.

Converse, Philip E. 1966. "Religion and Politics: The 1960 Election." In *Elections and the Political Order*, edited by Angus Campbell, Philip E. Converse, Warren E. Miller, and Donald Stokes, 96–124. New York: Wiley.

Copeland, Gary W., and Jeffrey L. Brudney. 1988. "Ronald Reagan and the Religious Vote: Trends, Continuities, and Discontinuities." Paper presented at the annual meeting of the American Political Science Association, Washington, D.C.

Craig, Wyn. 1987. *The Fiery Cross: The KKK in America*. New York: Simon and Schuster.

Crawford, Alan. 1981. *Thunder on the Right: The "New Right" and the Politics of Resentment*. New York: Pantheon.

Crespi, Irving. 1971. "Structural Sources of the George Wallace Candidacy." *Social Science Quarterly* 52:115–132.

Damaske, Frederick Hans. 1970. "Sects and Politics: The Political Attitudes and Behavior of Conservative-Evangelical and Neo-Fundamentalist Protestants." Ph.D. diss., University of Minnesota.

D'Antonio, Michael. 1989. *Fall From Grace: The Failed Crusade of the Christian Right*. New York: Farrar, Straus and Giroux.

Dawidowicz, Lucy S., and Leon J. Goldstein, eds. 1974. *Politics in a Pluralist Democracy: Studies of Voting in the 1960 Election*. Westport, Conn.: Greenwood.

Diamond, Sara. 1989. *Spiritual Warfare: The Politics of the Christian Right*. Boston: South End.

Dixon, Richard D., Diane E. Levy, and Roger C. Lowery. 1988. "Asking the 'Born-Again' Question." *Review of Religious Research* 30:33–39.

Donnelly, Brenda W. 1987. "The Social Protest of Christian and Nonreligious Groups: The Importance of Goal Choice." *Journal for the Scientific Study of Religion* 26:309–326.

Duggan, Lisa. 1985. "The War on Pornography Makes Strange Bedfellows." *Washington Post Weekly Edition*, September 16, pp. 24–25.

Edsall, Thomas B. 1985. "Pulpit Power: Converting the GOP." *Washington Post Weekly Edition*, July 8, pp. 8–9.

———. 1990. "Split Personality in the GOP." *Washington Post Weekly Edition*, July 23, p. 13.

Eidsmoe, John. 1984. *God and Caesar*. Westchester, Ill.: Crossway.

Fitzgerald, Frances. 1981. "A Disciplined, Charging Army." *New Yorker*, May 18, pp. 53–141.

Fowler, Robert Booth. 1982. *A New Engagement: Evangelical Political Thought, 1966–1976*. Grand Rapids, Mich.: Eerdmans.

Freeman, Donald M. 1962. "Religion and Southern Politics: A Study of the Political Behavior of Southern White Protestants." Ph.D. diss., University of North Carolina.

Gallup, George, Jr. 1981. "Divining the Devout: The Polls and Religious Belief."
   Public Opinion 4:20, 41.
George, John H. 1971. "The Collegiate Silent Majority: Social Class, Religion, and
   Politics." Ph.D. diss., University of Oklahoma.
Goff, Robert O. 1977. "The Washington County Schoolbook Controversy: The Po-
   litical Implications of a Social and Religious Conflict." Ph.D. diss., Catholic Uni-
   versity of America.
Green, John C., and James L. Guth. 1988. "The Christian Right in the Republican
   Party: The Case of Pat Robertson's Supporters." *Journal of Politics* 50:150–168.
Grupp, Frederick W., and William M. Newman. 1973. "Political Ideology and Re-
   ligious Preference: The John Birch Society and the Americans for Democratic
   Action." *Journal for the Scientific Study of Religion* 12:401–413.
Gurwitt, Rob. 1989. "The Christian Right Has Gained Political Power. Now What
   Does It Do?" *Governing* (October), 52–58.
Gusfield, Joseph. 1963. *Symbolic Crusade: Status Politics and the American Temperance
   Movement.* Urbana: University of Illinois Press.
Guth, James. 1983a. "Preachers and Politics: Varieties of Activism Among Southern
   Baptist Ministers." In *Religion and Politics in the South,* edited by Tod A. Baker,
   Robert P. Steed, and Laurence W. Moreland, 161–183. New York: Praeger.
———. 1983b. "Southern Baptist Clergy: Vanguard of the Christian Right?" In *The
   New Christian Right,* edited by Robert C. Liebman and Robert Wuthnow, 117–130.
   New York: Aldine.
———. 1985. "The Christian Right Revisited: Partisan Realignment Among Southern Baptist Ministers." Paper delivered at the annual meeting of the Midwest
   Political Science Association, Chicago.
———. 1989a. "A New Turn for the Christian Right? Robertson's Support from the
   Southern Baptist Ministry." Paper delivered at the annual meeting of the American Association for the Advancement of Science, San Francisco.
———. 1989b. "Pastoral Politics in the 1988 Election." Paper delivered at the annual
   meeting of the American Political Science Association, Atlanta.
Guth, James L., and John C. Green. 1986. "Faith and Politics: Religion and Ideology
   Among Political Contributors." *American Politics Quarterly* 14:186–200.
———. 1990. "Politics in a New Key: Religiosity and Participation Among Political
   Activists." *Western Political Quarterly* 43:153–179.
Hadden, Jeffrey. 1984. "Televangelism and the Future of American Politics." In *New
   Christian Politics,* edited by David G. Bromley and Anson Shupe, 151–165. Macon,
   Ga.: Mercer University Press.
Hadden, Jeffrey K., and Charles Swann. 1981. *Prime Time Preachers.* Reading, Mass.:
   Addison Wesley.
Hammond, John L. 1979. *The Politics of Benevolence: Revival Religion and American Voting
   Behavior.* Norwood, N.J.: Ablex.
Hertel, Bradley R., and Michael Hughes. 1987. "Religious Affiliation, Attendance,
   and Support for 'Pro-Family' Issues in the United States." *Social Forces* 65:858–
   882.
Hertzke, Allen D. 1989. "Pat Robertson's Crusade and the GOP: A Strategic Anal-
   ysis." Paper delivered at the annual meeting of the Midwest Political Science As-
   sociation, Chicago.

Hibbs, Douglas A., Jr. 1982. "President Reagan's Mandate from the 1980 Elections: A Shift to the Right?" *American Politics Quarterly* 10:387–420.

Hill, Samuel S., and Dennis E. Owen. 1982. *The New Religious Political Right in America.* Nashville, Tenn.: Abingdon.

Himmelstein, Jerome. 1986. "The Social Bases of Antifeminism: Religious Networks and Culture." *Journal for the Scientific Study of Religion* 25:1–15.

Himmelstein, Jerome L., and James A. McRae, Jr. 1984. "Social Conservatism, New Republicans, and the 1980 Election." *Public Opinion Quarterly* 48:592–605.

Hood, Ralph W., Jr., and Ronald J. Morris. 1985. "Boundary Maintenance, Social-Political Views, and Presidential Preference Among High and Low Fundamentalists." *Review of Religious Research* 27:134–145.

Hunter, James Davison. 1983. "The Liberal Reaction." In *The New Christian Right*, edited by Robert C. Liebman and Robert Wuthnow, 150–167. New York: Aldine.

Jelen, Ted G. 1987. "The Effects of Religious Separatism on White Protestants in the 1984 Presidential Election." *Sociological Analysis* 48:30–45.

Jenkinson, Edward B. 1979. *Censors in the Classroom.* New York: Avon.

Johnson, Haynes. 1986. "The Ambassador for Christ Race." *Washington Post Weekly Edition*, October 13, p. 24.

Johnson, Haynes, and Thomas B. Edsall. 1984. "North Carolina's Three Rs: Race, Religion, and Registration." *Washington Post Weekly Edition*, October 15, pp.12–13.

Johnson, Stephen D., and Joseph B. Tamney. 1985. "The Christian Right and the 1984 Presidential Election." *Review of Religious Research* 27:124–134.

Johnson, Stephen D., Joseph B. Tamney, and Ronald Burton. 1989. "Pat Robertson: Who Supported His Candidacy for President?" *Journal for the Scientific Study of Religion* 28:387–399.

———. 1990. "Factors Influencing Vote for a Christian Right Candidate." *Review of Religious Research* 31:291–304.

Jones, Ethel B. 1983. "ERA Voting: Labor Force Attachment, Marriage and Religion." *Journal of Legal Studies* 12:157–168.

Jorstad, Erling. 1981. *Evangelicals in the White House: The Cultural Maturation of Born-Again Christianity, 1960–1981.* Nashville, Tenn.: Abingdon.

Kellstedt, Lyman A. 1989a. "Evangelical Religion and Political Behavior: A Validation Effort." Paper delivered at the annual meeting of the Society for the Scientific Study of Religion, Salt Lake City.

———. 1989b. "Evangelicals and Political Realignment." In *Contemporary Evangelical Political Involvement: An Analysis and Assessment*, ed. Corwin E. Smidt, 99–118. Lanham, Md.: University Press of America.

———. 1989c. "The Fallwell Issue Agenda: Sources of Support Among White Protestant Evangelicals." In *Research in the Social Scientific Study of Religion*, edited by Monte L. Lynn and David O. Moberg, 109–132. Greenwich, Conn.: JAI.

———. 1989d. "The Meaning and Measurement of Evangelicalism: Problems and Prospects." In *Religion and Political Behavior in the United States*, edited by Ted G. Jelen, 3–22. New York: Praeger.

———. 1989e. "Religion and Partisan Realignment." Paper delivered at the annual meeting of the Midwest Political Science Association, Chicago.

Kellstedt, Lyman, Paul Kellstedt, and Corwin Smidt. 1990. "Evangelicals and Mainline Protestants in the 1988 Presidential Election." Paper presented at the annual meeting of the American Political Science Association, San Francisco.

Kellstedt, Lyman A., and Mark A. Noll. 1990. "Religion, Voting for President, and Party Identification, 1948–1984." In *Religion and American Politics*, edited by Mark A. Noll, 355–379. New York: Oxford University Press.

Klatch, Rebecca E. 1988. "The New Right and Its Women." *Society* (March–April), 30–38.

Kleppner, Paul. 1979. *The Third Electoral System*. Chapel Hill: University of North Carolina Press.

Knoke, David. 1976. *Change and Continuity in American Politics: The Social Bases of Political Parties*. Baltimore: Johns Hopkins University Press.

Ladd, Everett Carll, Jr. 1982. *Where Have All the Voters Gone?* 2d edition. New York: Norton.

––––––. 1989. "Trouble for Both Parties." *Public Opinion* (May–June), 3–8.

Ladd, Everett Carll, Jr., and Charles D. Hadley. 1975. *Transformations of the American Party System*. New York: Norton.

Langenbach, Lisa. 1989. "Evangelical Elites and Political Action: The Pat Robertson Presidential Candidacy." *Journal of Political and Military Sociology* 17:291–304.

Lazerwitz, Bernard. 1961. "A Comparison of Major United States Religious Groups." *Journal of the American Statistical Association* 56:568–579.

Leege, David C., and Michael R. Welch. Forthcoming. "Dual Reference Groups and Political Orientations: An Examination of Evangelically Oriented Catholics." *American Journal of Political Science*.

Leuchtenburg, William E. 1958. *The Perils of Prosperity, 1914–1932*. Chicago: University of Chicago Press.

Levine, Lawrence W. 1975. *Defender of the Faith: William Jennings Bryan, The Last Decade, 1915–1925*. New York: Oxford University Press.

Liebman, Robert C. 1983. "Mobilizing the Moral Majority." In *The New Christian Right*, edited by Robert C. Liebman and Robert Wuthnow, 50–73. New York: Aldine.

Lipset, Seymour Martin. 1960. *Political Man*. Garden City, N.Y.: Doubleday Anchor.

Lipset, Seymour Martin, and Earl Raab. 1970. *The Politics of Unreason*. New York: Harper and Row.

––––––. 1981. "The Election and the Evangelicals." *Commentary* (March), 25–31.

Lorentzen, Louise J. 1980. "Evangelical Life-Style Concerns Expressed in Political Action." *Sociological Analysis* 41:144–154.

Luebke, Paul. 1985–1986. "Grass-Roots Organizing: The Hidden Side of the 1984 Helms Campaign." *Election Politics* 3:30–33.

McCloskey, Herbert, and John Zaller. 1984. *The American Ethos*. Cambridge: Harvard University Press.

Maddox, William S., and Stuart A. Lilie. 1984. *Beyond Liberal and Conservative*. Washington, D.C.: Cato Institute.

Menendez, Albert J. 1977. *Religion at the Polls*. Philadelphia: Westminster.

Miller, Arthur H., and Martin P. Wattenberg. 1984. "Politics from the Pulpit: Religiosity and the 1980 Elections." *Public Opinion Quarterly* 48:301–317.

Miller, Warren E., and Teresa E. Levitin. 1976. *Leadership and Change: Presidential Elections from 1952–1976*. Cambridge, Mass.: Winthrop.

Miller, Warren E., Arthur H. Miller, and Edward J. Schneider. 1980. *American National Election Studies Data Sourcebook, 1952–1978*. Cambridge: Harvard University Press.

Miller, Wesley E. 1985. "The New Christian Right and Fundamentalist Discontent: The Politics of Lifestyle Concern Hypothesis Revisited." *Sociological Focus* 18:325–336.

Moen, Matthew C. 1989. *The Christian Right and Congress*. Tuscaloosa: University of Alabama Press.

———. 1984. "School Prayer and the Politics of Life-Style Concern." *Social Science Quarterly* 65:1065–1071.

———. 1988. "Status Politics and the Political Agenda of the Christian Right." *Sociological Quarterly* 29:429–437.

Morken, Hubert. 1990. "Religious Lobbying at the State Level: Case Studies in a Continuing Role for the New Religious Right." Paper presented at the annual meeting of the American Political Science Association, San Francisco.

Mueller, Carol. 1983. "In Search of a Constituency for the 'New Religious Right.'" *Public Opinion Quarterly* 47:213–229.

Mueller, Carol, and Thomas Dimieri. 1982. "The Structure of Belief Systems Among Contending ERA Activists." *Social Forces* 60:657–675.

Nemeth, Roger J., and Donald A. Luidens. 1989. "The New Christian Right and Mainline Protestantism: The Case of the Reformed Church in America." *Sociological Analysis* 49:343–352.

Oldendick, Robert, and Stephen E. Bennett. 1978. "The Wallace Factor: Constancy and Cooptation." *American Politics Quarterly* 6:469–484.

Orum, Anthony M., and Edward W. McCrane. 1970. "Class, Tradition, and Partisan Alignments in a Southern Urban Electorate." *Journal of Politics* 32:156–176.

Page, Ann, and Donald Clelland. 1978. "The Kanawha County Textbook Controversy: A Study in Alienation and Lifestyle Concern." *Social Forces* 57:265–281.

Paige, Connie. 1987. "Watch on the Right: The Amazing Rise of Beverly LaHaye." *Ms.* (February), 24–28.

Patel, Kant, Denny Pilant, and Gary L. Rose. 1982. "Born-Again Christians in the Bible Belt." *American Politics Quarterly* 10:255–272.

———. 1985. "Christian Conservatism." *Journal of Political Science* 12:17–30.

Perkins, Jerry. 1989. "The Moral Majority as a Political Reference in the 1980 and 1984 Elections." In *Religion and Political Behavior in the United States*, edited by Ted G. Jelen, 157–168. New York: Praeger.

Phillips, Kevin P. 1982. *Post-Conservative America*. New York: Vintage.

Pierard, Richard V. 1983a. "From Evangelical Exclusiveness to Ecumenical Openness: Billy Graham and Socio-Political Issues." *Journal of Ecumenical Studies* 20:425–446.

———. 1983b. "Reagan and the Evangelicals: The Making of a Love Affair." *Christian Century* 100:1182–1185.

———. 1985. "Religion and the 1984 Election Campaign." *Review of Religious Research* 27:98–114.

Pierard, Richard V., and James L. Wright. 1984. "No Hoosier Hospitality for Humanism: The Moral Majority in Indiana." In *New Christian Politics*, edited by David G. Bromley and Anson Shupe, 195–212. Macon, Ga.: Mercer University Press.

Polling Report. 1988. "Campaign Update." *Polling Report,* Feb. 8, p. 6.

Pool, Ithiel de Sola, Robert P. Abelson, and Samuel Popkin. 1965. *Candidates, Issues, and Strategies.* Cambridge: MIT Press.

Pope, Liston. 1953. "Religion and the Class Structure." In *Class, Status, and Power,* edited by Reinhard Bendix and Seymour Martin Lipset, 316–323. New York: Free Press of Glencoe.

Pressman, Steven. 1984. "Religious Right: Trying to Link Poll Power and Lobby Muscle." *Congressional Quarterly Weekly Report,* September 22, pp. 2315–2319.

Public Opinion. 1985. "Southern Whites: The Great Conversion." *Public Opinion* 7:34.

Quinley, Harold E. 1974. *The Prophetic Clergy: Social Activism Among Protestant Ministers.* New York: Wiley Interscience.

Reagan, Ronald. 1984. "Religion and Politics Are Necessarily Related." *Church & State* 37:9–11.

Reid, T. R. 1987. "Robertson's Christian Soldiers Are Marching to a Political Fray." *Washington Post Weekly Edition,* October 12, p. 16.

Reinhardt, Robert Melvin. 1975. "The Political Behavior of West Virginia Protestant Fundamentalist Sectarians." Ph.D. diss., University of West Virginia.

Ribuffo, Leo. 1983. *The Old Christian Right.* Philadelphia: Temple University Press.

Richburg, Keith R. 1986. "Public Schools and the Politics of Curriculum." *Washington Post Weekly Edition,* January 20, pp. 14–15.

Rifkin, Jeremy, with Ted Howard. 1979. *The Emerging Order: God in the Age of Scarcity.* New York: Ballantine.

Roof, Wade Clark, and William McKinney. 1987. *American Mainline Religion: Its Changing Shape and Future.* New Brunswick, N.J.: Rutgers University Press.

Rothenberg, Stuart, and Frank Newport. 1984. *The Evangelical Voter.* Washington, D.C.: Free Congress Research and Education Foundation.

Schneider, William. 1984. "An Uncertain Consensus." *National Journal,* November 10, pp. 2130–2132.

———. 1989. "Trouble for the GOP." *Public Opinion* (May–June), 2, 59–60.

Shriver, Peggy. 1981. *The Bible Vote.* New York: Pilgrim.

Shupe, Anson, and William Stacey. 1983. "The Moral Majority Constituency." In *The New Christian Right,* edited by Robert C. Liebman and Robert Wuthnow, 104–117. New York: Aldine.

Sigelman, Lee, and Stanley Presser. 1988. "Measuring Public Support for the New Christian Right: The Perils of Point Estimation." *Public Opinion Quarterly* 52:325–337.

Sigelman, Lee, Clyde Wilcox, and Emmett H. Buell, Jr. 1987. "An Unchanging Minority: Popular Support for the Moral Majority, 1980 and 1984." *Social Science Quarterly* 68:876–884.

Silk, Mark. 1988. *Spiritual Politics: Religion and America Since World War II.* Simon and Schuster, 160.

Simon, Paul. 1984. *The Glass House.* New York: Continuum.

Simpson, John H. 1983. "Moral Issues and Status Politics." In *The New Christian Right,* edited by Robert C. Liebman and Robert Wuthnow, 188–207. New York: Aldine.

Sirotnik, Barbara, John Heeren, and Donald B. Lindsey. N.d. "The Impact of the

Prime Time Preacher's Political Views on Television Audiences: An Experiment." Unpublished paper, California State University, San Bernardino.

Smidt, Corwin. 1983. "Born-Again Politics: The Political Behavior of Christians in the South and Non-South." In *Religion and Politics in the South*, edited by Tod A. Baker, Robert P. Steed, and Laurence W. Moreland, 27–56. New York: Praeger.

———. 1987. "Evangelicals and the 1984 Election: Continuity or Change?" *American Politics Quarterly* 15:419–444.

———. 1988. "Evangelicals Within Contemporary American Politics: Differentiating Between Fundamentalist and Non-Fundamentalist Evangelicals." *Western Political Quarterly* 41:601–620.

———. 1989a. "Change and Stability Among Southern Evangelicals." In *Religion in American Politics*, edited by Charles W. Dunn, 147–160. Washington, D.C.: CQ Press.

———. 1989b. "Evangelicals and Initial Presidential Candidate Preferences in 1988: An Analysis of the Super-Tuesday Primaries." Paper presented at the annual meeting of the American Association for the Advancement of Science, San Francisco.

———. 1989c. "Evangelicals and the New Christian Right: Coherence Versus Diversity in the Issue Stands of Evangelicals." In *Contemporary Evangelical Political Involvement: An Analysis and Assessment*, edited by Corwin E. Smidt, 75–98. Lanham, Md.: University Press of America.

———. 1989d. "Identifying Evangelical Respondents: An Analysis of 'Born-Again' and Bible Questions Used Across Different Surveys." In *Religion and Political Behavior in the United States*, edited by Ted G. Jelen, 23–44. New York: Praeger.

———. 1989e. "'Praise the Lord' Politics: A Comparative Analysis of the Social Characteristics and Political Views of American Evangelical and Charismatic Christians." *Sociological Analysis* 50:53–72.

Smidt, Corwin, and Lyman Kellstedt. 1987. "Evangelicalism and Survey Research: Interpretive Problems and Substantive Findings." In *The Bible, Politics, and Democracy*, edited by Richard John Neuhaus, 81–102. Grand Rapids, Mich.: Eerdmans.

Smidt, Corwin, and Paul Kellstedt. 1990. "Evangelicals in the Post-Reagan Era: An Analysis of Evangelical Voters in the 1988 Presidential Election." Paper presented at the Citadel Conference on Southern Politics, Charleston, S.C.

Smidt, Corwin E., and James M. Penning. 1990. "A Party Divided: A Comparison of Robertson and Bush Delegates to the 1988 Michigan Republican State Convention." *Polity* 23:127–138.

Smith, Tom W. 1982. "General Liberalism and Social Change in Post–World War II America: A Summary of Trends." *Social Indicators Research* 10:1–28.

Spring, Beth. 1984. "Some Christian Leaders Want Further Political Activism." *Christianity Today*, November 9, pp. 46–49.

Stockton, Ron R. 1989. "The Evangelical Phenomenon: A Falwell-Graham Typology." In *Contemporary Evangelical Political Involvement: An Analysis and Assessment*, edited by Corwin E. Smidt, 45–74. Lanham, Md.: University Press of America.

Tamney, Joseph, and Stephen D. Johnson. 1983. "The Moral Majority in Middletown." *Journal for the Scientific Study of Religion* 22:145–157.

————. 1988. "Explaining Support for the Moral Majority." *Sociological Forum* 3:234–255.

Tedin, Kent L. 1978. "Religious Preference and Pro/Anti-Activism on the Equal Rights Amendment Issue." *Pacific Sociological Review* 21:55–66.

Tedin, Kent L., David W. Brady, Mary E. Buxton, Barbara M. German, and Judy E. Thompson. 1977. "Social Background and Political Differences Between Pro- and Anti-ERA Activists." *American Political Quarterly* 5:395–408.

Times Mirror. 1988. "The People, the Press and Politics: Post-Election Typology Survey." Los Angeles: Times Mirror.

Wald, Kenneth D. Forthcoming. "Ministering to the Nation: The Campaigns of Jesse Jackson and Pat Robertson." In *Nominating the President 1988,* edited by Emmett Buell and Lee Sigelman. Knoxville: University of Tennessee Press.

————. 1990. "The New Christian Right in American Politics: Mobilization Amidst Modernization." In *Religious Resurgence and Politics in the Contemporary World,* edited by Emile Sahliyeh. Albany: State University of New York Press.

Wald, Kenneth D., and Michael B. Lupfer. 1983. "Religion and Political Attitudes in the Urban South." In *Religion and Politics in the South: Mass and Elite Perspectives,* edited by Tod A. Baker, Robert P. Steed, and Laurence W. Moreland, 84–100. New York: Praeger.

Wald, Kenneth D., Dennis E. Owen, and Samuel S. Hill, Jr. 1989. "Evangelical Politics and Status Issues." *Journal for the Scientific Study of Religion* 28:1–16.

Warner, R. Stephen. 1979. "Theoretical Barriers to the Understanding of Evangelical Christianity." *Sociological Analysis* 40:1–9.

Welch, Michael R., Lyman A. Kellstedt, David C. Leege, and Kenneth D. Wald. 1990. "Are the Sheep Hearing the Shepherds? Pastoral Cues, Congregational Responses and Political Communication Processes." Unpublished paper, University of Notre Dame.

Wilcox, Clyde. 1986. "Fundamentalists and Politics: An Analysis of the Effects of Differing Operational Definitions." *Journal of Politics* 48:1041–1051.

————. 1987. "Religious Orientations and Political Attitudes: Variations Within the New Christian Right." *American Politics Quarterly* 15:274–296.

————. 1989a. "Evangelicals and the Moral Majority." *Journal for the Scientific Study of Religion* 28:400–414.

————. 1989b. "The New Christian Right and the Mobilization of the Evangelicals." In *Religion and Political Behavior in the United States,* edited by Ted G. Jelen, 139–156. New York: Praeger.

————. 1990. "Religion and the Preacher Vote in the South: Sources of Support for Jackson and Robertson in Southern Primaries." Paper presented at the Citadel Conference on Southern Politics, Charleston, S.C.

Wilcox, Clyde, and Leopoldo Gomez. 1990. "The Christian Right and the Pro-Life Movement: An Analysis of the Sources of Political Support." *Review of Religious Research* 31:380–389.

Will, Jeffrey, and Rhys Williams. 1986. "Political Ideology and Political Action in the New Christian Right." *Sociological Analysis* 47:160–168.

Williams, Linda F. 1986. "Blacks and the Religious Right Have Few Common Interests." *Focus* 14:6–7.

Wohlenberg, Ernest H. 1980. "Correlates of Equal Rights Amendment Ratification." *Social Science Quarterly* 60:676–684.

Wood, Michael, and Michael Hughes. 1984. "The Moral Basis of Moral Reform: Status Discontent Vs. Cultural Socialization as Explanations of Anti-Pornography Social Movement Adherence." *American Sociological Review* 49:86–99.

Woodrum, Eric. 1988. "Moral Conservatism and the 1984 Presidential Election." *Journal for the Scientific Study of Religion* 27:192–210.

Wuthnow, Robert. 1983. "The Political Rebirth of American Evangelicals." In *The New Christian Right*, edited by Robert C. Liebman and Robert Wuthnow, 168–187. New York: Aldine.

Yankelovich, Daniel. 1981. "Stepchildren of the Moral Majority." *Psychology Today* (November), 5–10.

Yinger, J. Milton, and Stephen J. Cutler. 1982. "The Moral Majority Viewed Sociologically." *Sociological Focus* 15:289–306.

Zwier, Robert. 1984. "The New Christian Right and the 1980 Elections." In *New Christian Politics*, edited by David G. Bromley and Anson Shupe, 173–184. Macon, Ga.: Mercer University Press.

8. Continuity and Change Outside the Evangelical Camp

The really big story is that amid the clamor of invisible armies and righteous empires, there is a noticeable silence in the way most Americans bring their values and beliefs to bear upon the democratic process.
—Wade Clark Roof, *Wall Street Journal*, February 24, 1988

The past few years have been marked by great ferment in the relationship between religion and American political life. As previous chapters have demonstrated, religious issues and controversies have assumed much greater importance in political debate than they had commanded previously. With public attention so concentrated on attempts to forge the evangelical Protestants into a cohesive voting bloc, it has been easy to lose sight of the constant pressures for political change also faced by the majority of Americans affiliated with nonevangelical churches. Like the evangelicals, the other major religious groups in America have been encouraged to modify their traditional political patterns and to increase their involvement in public affairs. The response of the various nonevangelical groups to a changing political environment is the subject of this chapter.

After a period of dramatic internal change, the Catholic church has shed its predictable conservatism, especially on foreign and military policy, to adopt a new role as gadfly and activist on a wide range of issues. Although Catholic thought has generally moved to the left, the church fathers have maintained a staunchly conservative outlook on the issue of abortion. In the process, members of the Catholic clergy have largely replaced the ministers from mainline Protestantism as the leading political activists among the clergy. The mainline denominations in American Protestantism, once the driving force for many social reform campaigns, seem to have pulled back somewhat from active engagement in the political realm. The patterns of black politics have shifted the least,

279

with Protestant clergy continuing to play a leading role as spokespersons for the minority community. And Jews, though still a mainstay of the liberal coalition, have had occasion to reassess their traditional alliances.

In examining the new political tendencies of American religious groups, I will emphasize the role of religious leaders. In many religious communities, the clergy take the lead in defining institutional interests and applying theology to public issues. If social change alters the perspective of church members, the impact will usually register first with the ministry. Hence my discussion of trends in the political behavior of religious groups would be incomplete without close attention to those exhibited by members of the clergy. At the same time, it is important to recognize that religious leaders do not control the political perspectives of church members. Rather, in their attempt to shape the political outlook of coreligionists, ministers compete for influence with secular politicians, the media, and many other organized groups. The political attitudes of congregants are also shaped by personal experiences and the perspectives derived from living in a variety of social contexts that cannot be manipulated by the church. In each religious group under study here, even the most centralized and hierarchical, some discrepancy between the attitudes of the religious elite and the views from the pews is inevitable.

Catholicism: The Conservative Political Heritage

For persons whose impression of Catholic politics was formed during the 1980s, it must be hard to imagine just how radically the situation has changed in a short time. During the past decade, the church came to public attention because of its opposition to many of the policies pursued by the Reagan administration. The bishops issued critical pastoral letters on nuclear strategy and the economy, priests and nuns participated enthusiastically in a mass movement against nuclear weapons, and members of the church spearheaded opposition to American policy in Central America. By contrast, for most of the twentieth century, the Catholic church in the United States was closely associated with conservative political causes. Although that political tradition has not been extinguished—as testified to by the national prominence of Catholic conservatives like Patrick Buchanan, Phyllis Schlafly, William F. Buckley, and Henry Hyde—it must compete for Catholic allegiance with a liberal tradition represented by Mario Cuomo and Edward Kennedy. As we saw in Chapter 4, Catholic attitudes on most issues now cluster around the middle of the American political spectrum (Penning 1986). This leftward shift among Catholics has been every bit as substantial as the more publicized right-wing movement of the Protestant evangelicals.

The traditional pattern of Catholic politics in the United States was epitomized by the career of Francis Cardinal Spellman, from 1939 to 1967 the archbishop of New York. As head of the major Catholic center in the United States and a person of considerable persuasive ability, he imposed a distinctly conservative tilt to the church's effort to influence the public realm (Cooney 1984). Intensely anti-Communist, suspicious of the civil rights and labor movements, and a strong advocate of government efforts to prohibit public displays of "immorality," Spellman forged strong links between the church and leaders of secular conservative movements. Under his influence, the Catholic hierarchy enthusiastically endorsed the active involvement of the United States in military conflicts wherever communism was thought to be a threat. From Spain in the 1930s through Vietnam in the 1960s, Spellman consistently favored a policy that has been satirized by the phrase "Pass the Lord and praise the ammunition."

Although it is difficult to sort out cause and effect, an exhaustive review of polling data by Seymour Martin Lipset (1964) concluded that Spellman's views on world affairs were echoed by rank-and-file members of the church. Two major ultranationalistic mass movements of the twentieth century, the Coughlinite and McCarthy crusades, were led by Catholics and drew somewhat more support from Roman Catholics than from other religious groups.[1] The John Birch Society, a right-wing organization that gained notoriety in the 1960s, also drew greater backing from Catholics than from the population at large. Because all these movements enjoyed substantial support from Protestants and were opposed by some Catholics, their special appeal to Catholics should not be exaggerated (Crosby 1978). Nonetheless, when compared with the rest of the population, Catholics exhibited greater readiness to support American military involvement around the globe.

The militaristic tendency was apparent among young Catholics who participated in a number of studies about attitudes toward the use of force in international politics (Klineberg 1950, 175; Eckert and Mills 1935). In a 1952 survey of almost three thousand students on eleven university campuses, Peter Blau (1953) found that devout Catholics scored higher than other religious groups on a scale measuring emphasis on power (rather than cooperation) in world affairs. When a similar study was conducted in 1967 by Connors, Leonard, and Burnham (1968), the same pattern was noted. Among approximately one thousand students from four eastern colleges, Catholics exhibited the most warlike attitudes. In both studies, which controlled for social characteristics associated with religion, the disposition to support the use of force was greatest among Catholics who were most deeply attached to the church and exposed to Catholic institutions (but see Starr [1975] for evidence that religious involvement was not important).

The strong conservatism evinced by American Catholics during the time of Spellman's reign as the "American pope" can be explained by group interests, social standing, and theology. In many of the countries where communism sought to gain power, the Catholic church had been a dominant social force and often a political factor of immense significance. As such, communism represented not just a set of economic arrangements, but also a fundamental threat to the established power of Catholic institutions. The outspoken antireligiousness of Communist leaders and the active persecution of the church wherever communism had come to power further inflamed Catholic opinion, thus giving Catholics a tangible reason to oppose the expansion of communism. This concern helped to build early Catholic support for the American military effort in Vietnam. The dispatches from the National Catholic News Service made it seem "as though the big story in Vietnam is how the war affects Catholic missionaries, Catholic institutions, Catholic programs, Catholic political personalities, Catholic villages, Catholic soldiers, Catholic anything" (Deedy 1968, 126).

Social factors also contributed to the tendency of Catholic spokesmen "to identify their Americanism with their Catholicism" (Dohen 1967, 175). The Irish, who dominated the American Catholic hierarchy, brought to the United States a tradition of blending nationalism with religion. This tendency was reinforced by the insecure social status of the Catholic immigrants in America. As the historian Richard Hofstadter (1965) speculated in an essay first published during the 1950s, immigration may create status problems that can be resolved by expressing love of country in extreme ways. During the period of mass immigration, militant native-stock Protestants had impugned the "Americanism" of Catholic immigrants, leaving the victims with a strong desire to prove their worthiness. Even immigrants who embraced their new country with full and unconditional loyalty might also have been "troubled by the thought that since their forebears have already abandoned one country, one allegiance, their own national allegiance might be considered fickle" (Hofstadter 1965, 59). To reassure themselves and others that this reputation for disloyalty was not warranted, Hofstadter suggested, Catholic immigrants and their descendants flocked to patriotic societies and veterans' groups, eager to display extreme vigilance through acts of superpatriotism. From this viewpoint, the fervent anticommunism of Catholics represented an opportunity to assert their oneness with American values. Like other theories that attribute deeply felt political attitudes to personal insecurities, this application of the status-politics framework has been controversial.

The conservatism of American Catholics has also been attributed to theology. Although it differs radically on matters of church organization, Catholicism shares with Protestantism a creed that stresses human sinfulness. Unlike Protestantism, however, Catholicism traditionally resorted to prayer, rather than political action, as the way to address social evil. Frustrated by the indifference of Catholic leaders to the poverty of an industrial city, a Socialist pioneer in early twentieth-century Great Britain decried the otherworldly basis of Catholic social doctrine:

Rome never forgot the individual and was sensitive to every change in his condition or prospects. But she took little account of this perishing life, and her regard for the human body was very much that of the mediaeval ascetic or Jesuit priest. The soul alone persists and endures. The salvation of the soul is, then, the great end of life and all saviours. Nothing else matters. The people's children suffered and had suffered more cruelly during this century and the last, than ever before. No matter. The stake and the rack have a place in the scheme of salvation. The insanitary area may also cure heretics, may discipline fruitfully even the children of Mother Church. (McMillan 1927, 88)

According to this perspective, otherworldliness was responsible for a basic indifference to questions of social reform, be it domestic or international, and diminished the attractiveness of left-wing ideologies to Catholics.[2] The Catholic emphasis on authority and hierarchy may have further disposed American Catholics to support national leaders who undertook military intervention in the name of national security.

On the basis of such explanations, Catholics acquired a reputation for extreme political conservatism that has been hard to shake—even in the face of polls showing that Catholics now occupy the middle of the American political spectrum (see Chapter 4). That reputation was never entirely warranted, even in the heyday of anticommunism during the 1950s. Catholic politicians like Alfred E. Smith and Robert F. Wagner, who served as New York's governor and senator, respectively, helped to lay the foundations for the welfare system in the United States (O'Brien 1968). During the period that Cardinal Spellman tried to steer Catholics in the New York diocese to conservative causes, a Catholic woman named Dorothy Day founded the Catholic Worker movement in an attempt to identify the church with progressive views on issues like poverty, labor, social justice, civil liberties, and international disarmament (Piehl 1982). Catholic theologians, too, were steadily moving away from traditional beliefs about the rigid separation between heaven and earth, forging a new concern with social ethics (Curran 1982).

Even if they dismissed the signs of liberalization as unrepresentative of mainstream Catholic thought, political analysts could not overlook hard evidence of Catholic support for the Democratic party. Yet rather than acknowledge that this partisan tradition indicated the potential for Catholic liberalism, most scholars attempted to explain away the Democratic affiliation with the same economic self-interest argument used to account for the Democratic affiliation of southern evangelicals. By addressing the economic problems of the working class, they argued, Franklin D. Roosevelt had safeguarded the immediate interests of most American Catholics. Out of gratitude for his policies and for his appointments of Catholics to public jobs, Roosevelt and his immediate successors enjoyed continuing electoral support from the Catholic voter. But as the memory of the New Deal eroded and issues of foreign policy and civil rights replaced economic security on the Catholic political agenda, the "natural" conservatism of American Catholics once again came into play. During the late 1960s, when conservative political activists hoped to replace the New Deal coalition with a right-wing majority more to their liking, Catholics were perceived as the most likely converts and became the target of special appeals. Despite these efforts, the subsequent political movement of Catholics has not been toward a wholehearted embrace of conservatism but, at least among the clergy, toward a more liberal posture on most major national issues.

The Transformation of Catholic Attitudes

If the conservatism of traditional Catholic politics had been due to communal isolation and immigrant culture, the social transformation of Catholic life was bound to produce new departures in political action. Indeed, during the decades after World War II, Catholics in America experienced dramatic upward mobility. Even when allowance is given for the enormous variation among individual Catholics, the community as a whole enjoyed substantial increases in economic status, social acceptance, and the acquisition of politically relevant skills and resources.[3] Having "left the ghetto" (Hanna 1979, 22) economically and psychologically, Catholics were primed to assume a larger role in national political life. The direction of that new energy was principally determined by events in Rome.

What changed the Catholic church in America—or what gave official approval to trends that might have been developing independently—was a meeting of the world's bishops called in 1962 by Pope John XXIII. Known as Vatican II, or the Ecumenical Council, this historic meeting of church fathers revolutionized church liturgy and ritual. Most important from a political standpoint was that the leaders of the Catholic church called on the members to apply their Christian values to the problems of the world. In documents condemning the sinfulness of poverty, war, injustice, and other social ills, the church put its authority squarely behind the worldwide movement for social change. This profound shift of mood, coinciding with the assumption of the presidency by an energetic and vigorous Catholic, prompted an enthusiastic response from the American Catholic community (Hanna 1979, chap. 2). In developments that did not always meet with the approval of the older and more conservative bishops or of many Catholic laypeople, many young priests and nuns enrolled in the civil rights and antipoverty movements.

The enthusiasm for political change among Catholic leaders might not have survived into the 1980s without a corresponding transformation in the organization of the American church (Hanna 1985; Kennedy 1985). Under the impact of Vatican II, the American bishops established the United States Catholic Conference to speak with one voice about public issues. Absorbing several older institutions, the newly established organization developed departments specializing in domestic antipoverty efforts, campaigns for Third World economic development, and the promotion of world peace and social justice. This action-oriented church bureaucracy was increasingly staffed by professionals with substantial secular training and a commitment to broad-ranging social reforms. As Mary Hanna (1985, 15) notes, the reform impulse has persisted to the present day because it was embodied in new institutions that "push the Church as a whole and the bishops toward action on social and political questions." A new breed of bishops, large in number because a mandatory retirement age produced more openings than normal in the hierarchy, has proved highly receptive to the Vatican II outlook. Although the differences between the current and pre—Vatican II bishops can easily be overstated (see the data in Kennedy 1985, chap. 2), contemporary leaders of the Catholic church, like the parishioners, experienced a much more cosmopolitan upbringing than their predecessors. Young enough to have absorbed the liberalism of the 1960s and more familiar with secular environments, they have imparted a much more liberal cast to Catholic social and political thought.

Another influence that propelled the American Catholic elite in new directions during the 1970s was the movement known as "liberation theology." In response to the papal call for a renewed emphasis on social justice, some Latin American bishops and many clergy abandoned the traditional alliance between the church and the ruling classes of the region. Instead of defending the status quo, liberation theologians argued, the church should join the poor in resisting large landowners and their allies in military governments. Many priests and lay Catholics acted on this belief by forming a "church of the people" that engaged oppressive regimes in direct political, economic and military challenges. Liberation theology imparted a willingness to challenge the power of the state in pursuit of the prophetic mission of the church. This example stimulated many American Catholics (and Protestants) similarly to reconsider the role of their church in struggles between rich and poor.

The liberalization of American Catholic attitudes did not occur overnight, nor was it always clear that the church was moving in that direction. The most dramatic evidence of the new mood came in Catholic reactions to the war in Vietnam. As it did for so many other Americans, the Vietnam War eventually prompted many Catholics to rethink their traditional support for American military involvement around the globe. At the extreme wing of the antiwar movement, a Catholic was the first young man to be imprisoned for publicly destroying his draft card, and a pair of Jesuit priests, Daniel and Phillip Berrigan, became leaders of a campaign of civil disobedience launched to protest American military action in Vietnam (Meconis 1979). Among the young men who fled to Canada rather than serve as conscientious objectors, Catholics were apparently represented to a disproportionate degree (Surrey 1982). Despite these passionate expressions of antiwar feeling, most Catholics did not abandon their strong support for military action during the early years of the war. In Gallup polls taken between 1965 and 1967, Catholics were more supportive than Protestants of American military participation by about 10 percent (calculated from data in Mueller 1973, 143). Whereas many Protestant and Jewish spokesmen condemned American participation in the war, the Catholic bishops issued a statement that concluded "It is reasonable to argue that our presence in Vietnam is justified" (reprinted in Drinan 1970, 192). Cardinal Spellman was perhaps the most enthusiastic supporter of military action in American religious circles.

But as the war dragged on into the late 1960s, Catholic support gradually eroded. In 1968 the bishops issued a new pastoral letter that was notably less enthusiastic than its 1966 predecessor (ibid., 195). While raising more questions than answers, the new statement called on Catholics to judge the legitimacy of American participation in Vietnam by the "just war" principle—a doctrine that deems military action appropriate only if all other methods have failed to achieve an equitable settlement and if the use of force is proportional to the goal of the war. Recognizing that Catholics differed among themselves over whether the Vietnam conflict passed the test of a just war, the bishops pointedly refrained from reaching a judgment. One Catholic clergyman who decided that Vietnam violated the standard set by the just war doctrine, Father Robert Drinan of Boston, ran for a seat in the U.S. Congress on an antiwar platform and became the first priest elected to the House in many years. By 1971, the bishops moved explicitly into the antiwar camp, passing a resolution calling for an immediate halt to American military participation in Southeast Asia. Consistent with this new "dovish" emphasis, they also took a strong position in favor of amnesty for draft evaders and war resisters and expressed opposition to the use of conscription outside the context of a genuine national emergency. As the hierarchy moved toward positions taken up earlier by the religious leadership of mainline Protestantism and Judaism, the Catholic lay population also developed attitudes toward the Vietnam War that were indistinguishable from the rest of the American public (Mueller 1973, 143).

Since those watershed years, the American bishops have consistently called for conciliation and negotiation in preference to military action in world affairs. In Latin America, for example, the Catholic church has spearheaded opposition to U.S. financial and military assistance to governments threatened by leftist insurgents. As noted earlier, Catholics have played a key role in providing illegal sanctuary for refugees from the strife in Central America. Through acts of civil disobedience ranging from nonpayment of income taxes to assaults on military property, individual Catholics, including members of the clergy, have protested efforts by the U.S. government to take the side of conservative forces in that region. In addition, missionaries from the Maryknoll order have worked throughout Latin America to promote social change through programs of land reform, social welfare benefits, and the like.[4]

In 1983, when the bishops issued a well-publicized letter on nuclear weapons, the American hierarchy bid a final farewell to the Spellman era (Mornion 1983; Dwyer 1984). Entitled *The Challenge of Peace: God's Promise and Our Response,* the lengthy letter was intended to educate Catholics about church doctrine on war and violence in world affairs. It expanded on many of the themes that first appeared in the Vietnam-era statements, emphasizing the relevance of the just war standard and the need for individual Catholics to reach their own, independent judgments rather than accept governmental decisions as inherently worthy of support. Catholics were also told that although military service was a worthy endeavor when motivated by a generous love of country, the church fathers supported persons whose conscience prompted them to refuse to bear arms or to otherwise defend themselves with tools of violence. On the issue of nuclear weapons, the major focus of the statement, the bishops declared that the idea of deterring war by matching the weaponry of an opponent—a cornerstone of American nuclear strategy—was an inadequate basis for long-term peace on earth. Indeed, because deterrence was credible only if it rested on a willingness actually to use nuclear weapons, some bishops found the entire concept immoral. Noting that nuclear weapons could almost never be used in a manner that satisfied Catholic standards for a just war, they called on governments to accelerate efforts to achieve disarmament.

As abstract expressions, these statements could be endorsed in principle by nearly all public officials, even those identified as conservative on the issue of nuclear policy. But the letter provoked controversy because it challenged the Reagan administration policy on several counts. Specifically, the bishops called on the U.S. government to undertake some exploratory, independent initiatives of weapons reduction; to set up a regular schedule of summit meetings with the leaders of adversary governments; to tighten controls on the export of nuclear materials with potential military uses; and, in an effort to promote research and teaching on the peaceful resolution of conflicts, to establish a national peace academy. Each of these actions had previously been rejected by administration policymakers. Moreover, the bishops condemned as "morally reprehensible in its hypocrisy" Reagan's policy of supporting repressive governments when he thought that the likely alternative would be even less desirable. By noting that the United States shared responsibility for the conditions that generated world tension and had not always behaved honorably in global affairs, the bishops further took on the president who had publicly attributed global disorder to the "evil empire" of the Soviet Union. For the first time in American history, the Catholic hierarchy had lined up against a president on questions of fundamental military policy.

Did the hierarchy carry the parishioners? Although some conservative Catholics denounced the letter as naive or inappropriate, it apparently stimulated the Catholic rank and file to reconsider their positions on questions of peace and war. As Andrew Greeley (1985) first pointed out, Catholic opinion on military spending underwent a dramatic shift after the issuance of the pastoral letter in 1983. As Figure 8.1 shows, Protestant and Catholic attitudes on U.S. military spending were very similar in 1983. Although Catholics were, even then, more likely than Protestants to believe that the United States was overspending for military purposes, the group differences were small enough to be attributable to chance. But in 1984, Catholics shifted dramatically into the "too much" category and opened up substantial differences between themselves and Protestants. By comparison with both their 1983 attitudes and the 1984 Protestant preferences, Catholics in 1984 had

Figure 8.1 Catholic Versus Protestant Attitudes on Defense Spending, 1983 and 1984 (Source: General Social Surveys, 1983, 1984). Respondents were asked if they thought the United States was spending "too much money, too little money, or about the right amount" in a series of program areas. In 1983, the subject of military spending was introduced with the phrase "the military, armaments, and defense." In 1984, about one-third of the respondents were asked about "national defense" and another third about "strengthening national defense"; the remaining third were asked the question as it had been posed in 1983. Because the distribution of responses was similar using all three question forms, they were combined as one for analysis.

moved significantly toward the view that the United States was devoting too many resources to military purposes. Coupled with evidence that Catholic attitudes on other issues had not changed much or moved further away from Protestant opinion, this finding made a strong case for attributing the transformation to the bishops' pastoral letter on nuclear weapons. To bolster that interpretation, a study in one midwestern city found that Catholics were substantially more likely than Protestants to know of their church's position on nuclear weapons and that knowledge of the hierarchy's position produced greater approval for a "freeze" on the further construction and deployment of nuclear warheads (Tamney and Johnson 1985). Gallup surveys also found sharp growth in Catholic support for the nuclear freeze after *The Challenge of Peace* was issued (Gallup and Castelli 1987, 83).

Subsequent research has qualified Greeley's interpretation by pointing out the apparently short-lived nature of the change induced by *The Challenge of Peace*. In 1985, Catholic opposition to military spending dropped while polls recorded a rise in the proportion of Protestants who thought the United States was spending too much on defense. As a result, the opinions of the two groups converged and have remained together in subsequent polls. Even more damaging to the reputation of the pastoral was the report from a 1987 poll that only 29 percent of Catholics claimed they were familiar with the bishops' message on nuclear weapons (Davidson 1989). When that subgroup was asked to evaluate the document, only 57 percent said they approved its contents. If just 17 percent of the entire Catholic community knew *and* supported the pastoral a mere four years after it was issued in a blaze of publicity, then its long-term impact is dubious.

Nonetheless, considering the many barriers between the bishops and the Catholic population, the magnitude of the change the pastoral produced is more impressive than its rapid decay (Wald 1989). In the first place, the message of the pastoral seems to have penetrated Catholic opinion despite a formidable range of obstacles that include inattention, selective perception, distortion, and other devices by which people screen out new information that challenges old beliefs. Second, even if Catholic attitudes ceased to be distinct from Protestant opinion after 1984, this may merely reflect the delayed impact of the pastoral on Protestant opinion (cf. Curry 1984; Bernbaum 1984). In any case, both communities remained significantly less enthusiastic about defense spending after 1984 than they had been in 1983. Finally, as Allen Hertzke (1989) has argued, the bishops weighed in at a critical moment in the public debate on nuclear policy. At a time when the Reagan administration derided arms control to concentrate instead on a major buildup of American military strength, the public deliberations leading up to the pastoral letter gave moral support to the emerging "nuclear freeze" movement. The conservative reputation of the bishops enhanced the impact of their message, adding to the other forces that eventually persuaded the Reagan administration to move to the negotiating table. In these terms, *The Challenge of Peace* stands out as a remarkably effective political intervention by a modern religious group.

The leftward shift on international politics was accompanied by a growing concern among Catholic clergy about questions of economic policy. Rather than speak of this concern as a break with tradition, it is more accurate to describe it as renewed emphasis upon a traditional theme in Catholic social thought. In its modern statements on economic questions, the papacy had never wholeheartedly endorsed the doctrine of capitalism and had criticized the system for its undue emphasis on competition and individualism. Reflecting that skepticism about the merits of unrestricted market economies, the American bishops had in 1919 issued a "Program of Social Reconstruction" that called for major changes in economic arrangements. With the adoption of many of these proposals by the New Deal and the general affluence that marked the post–World War II era, the issue of domestic economic justice dropped to a lower place on the Catholic agenda.

Like many other issues related to social justice, it regained primacy as part of the heightened social consciousness that accompanied the Vietnam War protests. In the 1966 statement on Vietnam, the bishops had hinted that the ultimate source of world tension was to be found in social conditions like hunger, poverty, and unemployment. With each successive statement on national or international conflict, this theme grew stronger. The church became more active in the economic arena, concentrating resources to combat poverty and giving strong support to Cesar Chavez, a Catholic activist, first to organize farmworkers and then to boycott corporations that undermined contracts between agricultural producers and the union (Ortiz 1984). From this experience and their own firsthand experience with the poverty in inner-city parishes, the bishops developed a strong interest in economic policy. At the same 1980 conference that authorized the pastoral message on nuclear war, the bishops began preliminary work on a formal letter on economic questions.

The pastoral was issued late in 1986 under the title *Economic Justice for All*. The first draft, released for comment late in 1984, drew intensive coverage from the national news media (Weber and Anderson 1985). The letter made news because it emphasized the prevalence of economic inequality, denounced such suffering in biblical terms, and attributed economic problems to the American economic and political system. Putting the church on the side of the poor and underprivileged, the bishops endorsed proposals for a substantial increase in the minimum wage, statutory limits on personal income and wealth, federally mandated welfare standards, federal support for new job programs, and pay scales that reflected the intrinsic worth of a job as well as market considerations. A chapter on agricultural policy called for massive emergency aid to farms and rural banks damaged by defaulted loans. Many of the specific proposals embedded in the report had already been rejected by the Reagan administration. Even though the draft was not released until after the 1984 presidential election so that it would not be taken as a criticism of President Reagan's policies, its recommendations collided with the administration's announced commitment to reduce governmental involvement in the domestic economy.[5]

The bishops faced considerable difficulty in swinging Catholic opinion to their side on this issue.[6] A group of conservative Catholics, including business leaders, public officials, and scholars, published a letter of their own before the bishops' pastoral got into print.[7] Described by one reporter as "a strong celebration of the capitalist system and the individual entrepreneur, not the government, as the true benefactors of the poor and jobless,"[8] the letter from the Lay Commission on Catholic Social Teaching and the U.S. Economy, as the group called itself, argued that the political freedom accompanying free enterprise economies promotes the living standards of all citizens. Just as the bishops' draft can too easily be treated as an endorsement of Socialist economics, the unofficial response can be unfairly caricatured as a brief for laissez-faire policies. In fact, the commission praised labor unions and recognized that the profit motive is not sufficient to care for the entire interests of humanity and may introduce significant evils that call for government response. Still, the issuance of such a missive indicated that influential Catholics were not unanimously in favor of the bishops' economic proposals, and other reports have suggested that the official statement was greeted unenthusiastically by the rank and file (Davidson 1989; Tamney, Burton, and Johnson 1988).

The greater impact of the pastoral letter on nuclear war compared to the economic message underscores the importance of process, timing, and content in church political action. The credibility of the nuclear letter was enhanced by the careful and public deliberations that preceded it. The letter on war and peace was framed and issued at a time of grave public concern over the possibility of nuclear war; the economic letter, by contrast, emerged when the economy seemed buoyant and the extent of problems like homelessness and unemployment were not fully recognized. Furthermore, war and peace is the kind of issue that more readily lends itself to sudden shifts of opinion. Calls for reducing military spending can be simple and powerful, appealing both to altruism and self-interest. By contrast, calls for higher rates of taxation and redistribution of resources may strike at the very economic system that provided advantages to many Catholics. As such, they will inspire greater resistance.

Abortion: The Catholic Response

During the same period that the Catholic religious elite was rethinking its traditional positions on a wide range of political issues, the church also gained public attention as a major force resisting the liberalization of abortion laws in the United States.[9] That stance was derived from Catholic doctrine defining the fetus as a form of human life that should enjoy a nearly absolute right to existence. From that perspective, abortion, along with any other deliberate interference with the gestation of a fertilized human egg, constitutes the moral equivalent of murder (Callahan 1970, chap. 12).

Although the abortion debate reached the national agenda only in 1973, when the U.S. Supreme Court issued its momentous decision striking down most existing state laws, the lines of the conflict had been drawn much earlier. Responding to a worldwide liberalization of abortion laws, Pope Paul VI had reiterated Catholic opposition to any termination of pregnancy in his 1968 encyclical on birth control, *Humanae Vitae*. When church law was revised in 1971, abortion was added to the list of crimes that mandated excommunication. As the states began to loosen restrictions on abortion in the 1960s, often at the urging of physicians and lawyers, Catholics took the lead in the so-called Right to Life organizations formed to oppose the new trends. Late in 1972, the American bishops created a committee to publicize the church's position and to coordinate its antiabortion activities.

In *Roe v. Wade*, the Supreme Court argued that a constitutional right to privacy prohibited states from limiting abortion during the first three months of pregnancy. Concerns for maternal health could justify medical regulations in the second trimester, and the government's interest in encouraging "normal childbirth" permitted restrictive policies in the last three months. The decision wiped out state laws that forbade abortion without regard to circumstance or timing. Armed with a record of public opposition to what the advocates of liberalization called abortion reform and the network to organize parishioners, the Catholic church was well placed to provide leadership when the *Roe v. Wade* decision brought the issue to national prominence.

The attack on liberalized abortion laws was waged on several fronts. Shortly after the decision was announced, the bishops created a lobbying organization, the National Committee for a Human Life Amendment, whose goal was to reverse the Supreme Court decision by passage of a constitutional amendment extending legal protection to the fetus. When the Senate Judiciary Committee held hearings on proposed antiabortion amendments in 1974, four Catholic bishops appeared among the many clergy who testified on the issue. When the Senate Judiciary Committee deadlocked over the issue, failing to send any of the nearly sixty proposed amendments to a vote on the Senate floor, abortion opponents decided to press the attack through a variety of interim measures. While keeping as their ultimate objective a constitutional amendment prohibiting abortion, antiabortion forces focused on the more immediate goal of limiting the availability of abortion by restricting funding at the state and national levels and by adopting administrative regulations to deter women from using abortion facilities.

Like other groups that seek to wield influence in the legislative process, the opponents of abortion have attempted to accumulate power through the development of grass-roots electoral organization. Although they have intervened in presidential politics, even to the extent of sponsoring a symbolic campaign for the Democratic presidential nomination, their major focus has been on electing antiabortion candidates to state and congressional office. The full extent of church involvement in these actions was spelled out in the highly detailed *Pastoral Plan for Pro-Life Activities* issued in 1975 by the bishops. The bishops' plan called for the development in each congressional district of an identifiable, tightly knit, and well-organized "prolife" unit (Jaffe, Lindheim, and Lee 1981, 75) that would provide financial assistance, campaign workers, and publicity to antiabortion candidates. The plan envisioned close ties between the secular "right to life" organizations and the Catholic parish. In practice, the church has supplied the movement with physical, financial, and human resources, leading some critics to the conclusion that the right-to-life movement is largely an expression of the Catholic hierarchy (Merton 1981; Jaffe, Lindheim, and Lee 1981, 76–83; Paige 1983). Although academic researchers have expressed skepticism about the electoral impact of the abortion issue in national elections (Traugott and Vinovskis 1980; Granberg and Burlison 1983; Granberg 1987; Vinovskis 1979; Bolce 1988), the antiabortion movement has gained a reputation for political clout that has prompted many lawmakers to pay it careful heed (Margolis and Neary 1980).

As the prospect of amending the Constitution faded, the opponents of abortion confronted the Supreme Court with a variety of laws testing the limits of the *Roe* decision. In several states and localities, legislative bodies tried to qualify the Court's ruling by imposing preconditions on women seeking abortions—permission of the spouse or parents, mandatory waiting periods—or by setting medical requirements intended to make the operation impractical. Some localities adopted zoning regulations to prevent the operation of abortion facilities and required that physicians warn prospective patients to expect serious physical and psychological aftereffects. The Supreme Court struck down most of these restrictive features as religiously motivated laws with no overriding secular purpose (Friedman 1983).

Other laws and regulations received Court approval, however. Most important, the Court upheld the legality of a ban on the use of Medicaid funds for abortion under most circumstances and permitted publicly funded hospitals to refuse to perform elective abortions. Given the green light in the Medicaid decision, Congress has put similar antiabortion restrictions on military benefits, District of Columbia appropriations, federal employee health insurance, and the foreign assistance program (Cohodas 1983, 1692). In addition, thirty states have prohibited their health-care contributions from being used to support elective abortion.[10] Consistent with President Reagan's vocal condemnation of elective abortion (Reagan 1984), his administration championed most of these efforts and extended them to the international sphere. On the domestic front, the administration joined the efforts of antiabortion groups to eliminate federal support for birth control activities that had proceeded under Title X of the Public Health Act. George Bush endorsed these efforts during the 1988 presidential campaign and pledged his efforts to overturn the *Roe* decision.

With the replacement of three justices from the majority faction in *Roe* by conservative appointees, many observers expected that decision to be overturned during the 1988–1989 session of the Supreme Court. When it finally issued its ruling in the case known as *Webster v. Reproductive Health Services,* the Court severely qualified the guarantees extended in 1973 but did not invalidate the earlier decision. Specifically, the five justices in the *Webster* majority gave Missouri the right to forbid public employees and facilities from conducting discretionary abortions or counseling in favor of it and to insist the physicians must determine whether the fetus is "viable" outside the womb before performing abortions on women who are twenty or more weeks pregnant. More generally, the decision signaled the Court's willingness to consider new state restrictions on the availability of abortion. In two such cases during the 1989–1990 term, the Court acted in the spirit of *Webster* by upholding parental notification laws for abortion seekers under the age of eighteen. Assuming the survival of the *Roe* principle granting liberal access to abortion—a hazardous prospect given the continuing changes on the Court—the prospect is for a steady stream of cases resembling the piecemeal decision-making process in the school prayer issue.

Abortion: A Catholic Issue?

Can abortion be considered a Catholic issue? To some extent, the answer depends on whether the church—both the hierarchy and the laity—is wholeheartedly united around an antiabortion stance. At the level of religious elites, there is no question that the Catholic bishops have invested enormous energy and passion in the abortion issue, assigning it priority over many other concerns. Even though the church's position on the issue has not produced the same level of dissent as its policy against artificial contraceptives, visible signs of disagreement within the Catholic community have cropped up. A small group of scholars and members of various religious orders, organized in "Catholics for Free Choice," has publicly argued that church teaching is in fact compatible with the public availability of abortion under some circumstances (Kissling 1985).[11] Roughly one-third of the parish priests interviewed in a *New York Times*/CBS News poll supported that view, against the remaining two-thirds who endorsed official church teaching against abortion under any circumstances.[12] The two-to-one margin in favor of the bishops' position constitutes a strong consensus but falls short of unanimity.

But do the parishioners accept the guidance of the church on abortion? On many public questions that impinge on personal behavior, including the use of artificial birth control methods, the Catholic laity clearly does not welcome the counsel of its clergy (Leege 1987). Similarly, as the bishops' decision to engage actively in public relations confirms, the hierarchy does not enjoy unanimous support from the Catholic community when it speaks in its name about abortion. In the most active form of disagreement, many Catholic women have utilized the freedom brought by *Roe v. Wade* to obtain legal elective abortions.[13] Less dramatically (see Figure 4.9), Catholics have split over the question of abortion policy, with sizable minorities favoring a liberalized policy in cases of rape, probable birth defects, or serious threat to maternal health. That was in fact the single most common preference among lay Catholics surveyed along with parish priests in 1987 and it actually commanded majority support from parish-affiliated Catholics in another study (Leege and Gremillion 1986).[14] The laity similarly believed that a "good Catholic" could reject church teaching on abortion and strongly disapproved of church efforts to change national abortion policy directly or by pressuring Catholic officials. If describing abortion as a Catholic issue implies unanimity of opinion, then the label does not fit.

Abortion still might be considered a Catholic issue if it is uniquely salient to members of that faith. More so than other groups, the *Roe* decision stimulated Catholics to adopt antiabortion positions and the church unquestionably took the lead in mobilizing opposition and resistance (Franklin and Kosaki 1989; Hofman 1986). Yet even in this sphere, Catholics cannot be depicted accurately as the sole source of opposition to liberalized access, and in fact are not the most intransigent opponents of abortion; that status fell to evangelical Protestants, white and black alike (see Figure 4.9). Religious behavior and doctrine, not denominational affiliation, most strongly relate to abortion attitudes (Harris and Mills 1985). The most radical forms of attack on abortion— sit-ins, acts of civil disobedience, and clinic bombings—have primarily been the province of fundamentalist Protestants.

If opposition to abortion is not a Catholic monopoly nor a position accepted by all members of the church, neither is support for *Roe v. Wade* a wholly secular phenomenon. While public leadership of the pro-choice movement has been associated with feminist organizations like the National Organization of Women and the family-planning advocate, Planned Parenthood, several Protestant and Jewish groups have worked to resist restrictive abortion policy (Rainey 1985). The Religious Council for Abortion Rights (RCAR), a Washington-based umbrella group with more than thirty institutional members, has gained a reputation for effective lobbying in Congress. It has recently branched out to monitor abortion-related activity in the administrative agencies and has tried to raise public support for the principle of free choice in reproductive decisions. RCAR does not take a theological position on the abortion issue but rather emphasizes the diversity among American faiths over the status of the fetus as a human being. With such divergent views, the organization argues, extending legal protection to the fetus amounts to enshrining one theological view—the Catholic doctrine—as law. The alleged Catholic basis for antiabortion legislation is then cited as a violation of the antiestablishment clause of the First Amendment. From this legal perspective, which has yet to gain constitutional standing by a Supreme Court decision, *Roe v. Wade* is treated as a positive contribution to the level of religious freedom in America.

Although abortion cannot be reduced to an exclusive Catholic issue, the most active opponents of liberalization have indeed been recruited from the Catholic community. Several studies of the antiabortion movement have identified the typical activist (outside the South) as a Catholic housewife of limited education, much of it obtained in church-affiliated schools. Deeply devout and a regular churchgoer, she was likely to come from a large family and to be the mother of several children (Granberg 1981b, 1982a, 1982b; Luker 1984). According to a study of California right to lifers conducted by sociologist Kristin Luker (1984), these women overcame a background of political inactivity out of anger at a Supreme Court decision that seemed to strike directly at their fundamental values about motherhood, the role of women, and the purpose of sex. Assuming that men and women differ in nature, the former best suited for the role of public work and the latter for raising children, the women chose to forgo opportunities for attaining professional skills in favor of stressing their role as caregivers to children and husband. Luker points out that liberalized abortion laws undermine that set of values in three respects:

First, it is intrinsically wrong because it takes a human life and what makes women special is their ability to nourish life. Second, it is wrong because *by giving women control over their fertility,* it breaks up an intricate set of social relationships between men and women that has traditionally surrounded (and in the ideal case protected) women and children. Third and finally, abortion is wrong because it fosters and supports a world view that deemphasizes (and therefore *downgrades*) the traditional role of men and women. Because these roles have been satisfying ones for pro-life people and because they believe this emotional and social division of labor is both "appropriate and natural," the act of abortion is wrong because it plays havoc with this arrangement of the world. (1984, 161–162)

The supporters of liberalized abortion have proved to be almost the complete opposite of these traditionalist Catholics in social condition and outlook. On the evidence available from this type of intensive interview and from sample surveys, the apparent Catholic versus non-Catholic dimension to the abortion debate is part of a broader conflict over the place of traditional values and sexual norms in society (Jelen 1984; Wagenaar and Bartos 1977; J. Legge 1985). Liberalized abortion is particularly abhorrent to persons enmeshed in traditional social settings and imbued with conservative norms—many, but not all, of whom are Catholic—and acceptable to persons who have been part of modernizing institutions. The conflict is less a denominational fight or a battle between religion and irreligion than a dispute between differing styles of religious belief.

Since abortion touches on such fundamental differences in how some people view the world and their own place in it, it should not be surprising that the debate has unleashed so much passionate energy. The tension has been particularly acute for Catholics in public office. Traditionalist Catholics, whose views were formed in the pre–Vatican II era, have tended to justify opposition to abortion in terms of a universal doctrine of the sanctity of life that need not be restricted to Catholics. But other Catholic officials, including those sympathetic to liberalized abortion on social grounds or representatives of constituencies with mixed attitudes, have not found it easy to stake out an acceptable position. If they were to honor their Catholic background by opposing the free availability of abortion, they could be criticized for representing Catholic interests—a charge that historically has handicapped Catholics seeking public office in the United States. Yet coming down on the side of liberalized abortion would endanger their ability to draw Catholic electoral support.

The Catholic officials who have supported liberalization have justified their position by claiming that their primary responsibility as public officials is to uphold decisions legitimately promulgated by the Supreme Court. Just how fiercely church officials have reacted to this claim was illustrated in 1984, when Representative Geraldine Ferraro, a devout Catholic, received the Democratic nomination for vice-president. Though personally opposed to abortion, she had voted against curbs on the use of federal funds to prohibit elective abortion and indicated that her votes on abortion policy would not be influenced by her private faith. This position drew a rebuke from the head of the U.S. Catholic Conference, Bishop James Malone of Youngstown, Ohio, who criticized attempts by candidates to distinguish between private and public morality.[15] More pointedly, the newly installed archbishop of New York, John Cardinal O'Connor, wondered aloud during a television interview how Catholics could vote in good conscience for a candidate who did not pledge to support restrictive abortion policies. The steady drumbeat of criticism directed at Ferraro and the appearance of several bishops at Reagan campaign rallies came close to an endorsement of the Republican ticket (Dickenson 1984).[16] Recognizing an opportunity to make inroads on the traditional allegiance of Catholics to the Democratic party, Republican spokesmen called attention to the bishops' criticism of prochoice Catholics and emphasized that the GOP platform more closely mirrored the church's teachings on abortion.

By seeming to endorse a candidate in a partisan election, the church hierarchy came in for its own share of criticism from political leaders (Califano 1984). While endorsing the church's right to speak out on issues with a moral dimension, leading Catholic Democrats asserted that the clergy had overstepped the proper "wall of separation" between church and state. Senator Edward Kennedy publicly asserted the impropriety of church attempts to impose a restrictive abortion policy on the nation:

Where decisions are inherently individual ones or in cases where we are deeply divided about whether they are, people of faith should not invoke the power of the state to decide what everyone can believe or think or read or do. In such cases—cases like abortion or prayer or prohibition or sexual identity—the proper role of religion is to appeal to the free conscience of each person, not the coercive rule of secular law.[17]

In his defense of Ferraro and other Catholic politicians who opposed restrictive abortion policies, New York governor Mario Cuomo revived the notion of "civil peace" first enunciated in the 1950s by the Catholic theologian John Courtney Murray. In a religiously diverse society like the United States, Murray had argued, attempts by one religious group to prohibit what it regards as evil practices might endanger the harmony of the social order. Hence, he reasoned, it is better to tolerate such evil rather than undermine a society that has permitted such a wide degree of freedom to Catholics and other religious minorities (Wolf 1968, chap. 1). By insisting on the need for an abortion policy that did not enjoy national consensus, Cuomo argued, the Catholic church might well encourage other religious groups to press for policies that endangered religious liberty.

The Catholic public official lives the political truth most Catholics through most of American history have accepted and insisted on: the truth that to assure our freedom we must allow others the same freedom, even if occasionally it produces conduct by them which we would hold to be sinful. We know that the price of seeking to force our beliefs on others is that they might someday force theirs on us.[18]

Thus, according to Cuomo, Catholics should not threaten the peace of society and the freedom accorded to religion by using the state to impose policies deeply offensive to many people. He conceded that the church had every right to condemn abortion and to work for conditions that would eliminate its necessity but, echoing Senator Kennedy, he believed it should attempt to implement its views by appealing to the consciences of individuals.

As the campaign progressed, the church leadership appeared to draw back from the implied attack on Ferraro and other Catholic politicians who had supported *Roe v. Wade*. In a statement issued on behalf of his fellow members of the U.S. Catholic Conference, Bishop James Malone emphasized that the church had no intention of supporting candidates for office and insisted that abortion was one issue among many that Catholics should use to judge potential officeholders.[19] In the end, nearly 60 percent of Catholic voters supported the Republican ticket in 1984, and the defections from the Democratic party appeared to have been highest among those Catholics the most deeply involved in parish life.

That the Democratic ticket fared so poorly among Catholics, even with a Catholic on the ballot, indicated the potential of abortion to disrupt traditional alliances.[20]

Despite Bishop Malone's attempt to defuse tension, the 1984 debate revealed a church leadership deeply divided over tactics. For some bishops, abortion is still the paramount moral issue of the day and a candidate's position on that single issue remains a litmus test of acceptability.[21] The other camp, represented by Joseph Cardinal Bernadin of Chicago, has taken the position that abortion should be part of a "seamless garment" of issues, including nuclear war, human rights, capital punishment, and poverty, all involving threats to human life. The call for "a consistent ethic of life" has even produced an ecumenical political action committee, "JustLife," that funds congressional candidates who favor "economic justice, reducing and eliminating abortion, and reversing the nuclear arms race" (Hayes and Sider 1988, 2).

Despite the apparent support of the pope, those who subscribe to the "seamless garment" approach face an uphill battle to restructure Catholic opinion along new lines. Research reveals that abortion opponents are not noted for their opposition to capital punishment, military spending, and the use of force in world affairs—all positions that the bishops have treated as expressions of the prolife ethic. Neither, despite the prolife implications, are antiabortionists more favorable than supporters of liberalization to increased spending on health, gun control laws, or the mandatory use of seat belts (Granberg 1981a; Granberg and Granberg 1981; Sawyer 1982; Cleghorn 1986; Johnson and Tamney 1988). What distinguishes the prolife activists—aside from resistance to abortion, euthanasia, and suicide—is conservative preferences on social issues relating to traditional sex roles. To date, most "prolife" Catholics compartmentalize this sentiment rather than extend the principle to other areas of public policy.

Standing apart from the traditional lines of political debate, the abortion dispute constitutes an exception to the recent trend of liberalized thinking among the clergy and laity. But because its leaders have been so vocal about the issue, the antiabortion movement has sometimes obscured the trend in Catholic politics—even from Catholic parishioners themselves. During the next few years, the church hierarchy will have to decide on the priority to be given abortion relative to the other issues on the national agenda. Should the bishops opt unreservedly for the package of policies under the prolife theme, they will still have to counter a widespread public impression that abortion is their sole concern.

The Political Traditions of Mainline Protestants

Unlike evangelical Protestants or Roman Catholics, mainline Protestants had established a strong and active presence in American political life well before the 1970s. In fact, at the national level the members of the mainline denominations have dominated the most influential positions in the American political system. Most presidents have been members of a mainline Protestant church; especially strongly represented have been Episcopalians and Presbyterians (Kane 1974, 325). For most of the twentieth century, Catholics and Protestants from an evangelical background were rarely considered serious candidates for the nation's highest elective position. Although Congress has been more accessible to members of other religious groups, the churches associated with mainline Protestantism have also claimed a far greater share of the membership in that body than size alone would warrant (Gaustad 1968, 125–128; Menendez 1977, 219–220).

The political predominance of mainline Protestants has largely stemmed from their high socioeconomic status. Although any large religious community inevitably contains persons of diverse social background, taken as a group, the members of mainline churches have enjoyed a higher socioeconomic standing than have members of the other major religious families in the United States. As a result, they have tended to support the social system from which they have derived substantial benefits. In the twentieth century, when national political conflict has been organized around the issue of governmental responsibility for social welfare and regulation of economic activity, individuals affiliated with the mainline denominations have for the most part sided with conservative political forces. As noted in Chapter 4, members of this religious tradition have shown some of the highest levels of Republican support and economic conservatism.

The conservative orientation of the membership has frequently collided with a more liberal outlook among church leaders. Clergy from the mainline Protestant denominations have periodically given birth to movements that cast a skeptical eye on prevailing social and economic arrangements. In this "Social Gospel" tradition, the distinctive feature of reform sentiment has been a belief that God's spirit pervades the world. Rather than seeing God as aloof to human social patterns, the liberal theological tradition has insisted that God is immanent, or present, in human life. Consequently, love of one's neighbor, not personal holiness, should be the principal ethical concern of Christianity (Gilkey 1968). According to this perspective, the will of God is associated with particular schemes for social reform, so it falls to the Christian, as a religious duty, to strive to bring about change in human social conditions. The clergy have usually been the most active carriers of this particular vision (Garrett 1973). As noted in Chapter 6, the Washington offices of the mainline Protestant churches have also represented this view in their recent lobbying.

At the beginning of the twentieth century, when the Social Gospel movement was particularly strong, it contributed to the split in American Christianity between the mainline denominations and their evangelical and fundamentalist adversaries. Although the conflict was rooted in a number of sources, the traditionalists who appropriated the evangelical label objected to the tendency among modernist theologians to equate Christianity with support for social reform. Though the evangelicals were not indifferent to social problems, they emphasized the priority of spiritual communion between God and individuals. Hence, they interpreted social problems as the outgrowth of individual moral failings and supported solutions such as conversion or spiritual rebirth. As pointed out in the previous chapter, the evangelical wing eventually found itself cast in the role of defending traditional social values against the onslaught of modern forces and largely retreated from the national political arena after repeated defeats during the 1920s.

Even though members of what became known as the mainline wing were divided internally over the proper definition of Christianity, much of the clergy moved into the Social Gospel camp. Their enthusiasm for social reform waxed and waned with national political circumstances (Carter 1954; May 1963; Meyer 1961). Enthusiasm was high in the period before World War I, low in the decade after, and high again during the presidency of Franklin D. Roosevelt. Interest in social problems dropped to the bottom of the church agenda during the prosperous years of the post–World War II era, when many churches concentrated their energies on building new facilities for their suburban congregants. By the late 1950s, the Protestant churches from the mainline denominations were the target of strong attacks for their supposed indifference to social problems.

Few of the critics could have imagined just how sharply the situation would change in a short time. During the 1960s, social reform moved back to the top of the Protestant agenda. In the churches, a "new breed" of social action–oriented clergy jumped enthusiastically into a variety of progressive causes (Cox 1968). Members of the new breed were found leading rent strikes, organizing pickets around city hall, serving in community action organizations, financing low-cost housing projects, and helping welfare recipients form unions to better press their claims on reluctant government bureaucracies. At the same time that such action flourished in isolated communities, national attention was drawn to the Protestant clergy's participation in civil rights demonstrations and their leadership role in organizations that opposed American involvement in the Vietnam War.

In a 1968 survey of parish ministers in California, taken when political activism was at its height, political scientist Harold Quinley (1974) reported on the extent of clergy involvement in three social movements—a campaign to defend California's "fair housing" ordinance from a repeal effort, to support efforts to unionize migrant farm workers, and to oppose the Vietnam War. Among the 1,580 clergy who responded to Quinley's survey, the rate of activism was pronounced— though uneven—across the three issue areas. On the fair housing campaign, a civil rights issue that attracted the highest level of activism, a clear majority of the Protestant ministers took public action in the form of sermons, petitions, or other public statements conveying support for maintenance of the ordinance. For Methodist, Congregationalist, Episcopalian, and Presbyterian clergy, who most enthusiastically endorsed the social reform ministry, antirepeal activity also included prayers about the issue, organization of study or advocacy groups in the church, service on public committees, and the writing of letters to public officials. Roughly one-fourth of the ministers took similar high-profile stances on the Vietnam War, including a substantial number who attended protest meetings, belonged to antiwar organizations, or participated in public marches. The plight of farmworkers drew somewhat lower rates of involvement but still gained attention and support from a sizable share of the sample.

The impression of a united bloc of liberal clergy was further reinforced by their high visibility in some of the most dramatic protests of the era. In a number of southern communities where conflict over desegregation of public schools raised social tension to a fever pitch, clergymen played a key role on the front lines, frequently exposing themselves to intimidation and violent assaults from segregationists (Campbell and Pettigrew 1959, 3–4). Shortly before the 1965 Selma to Montgomery march to secure voting rights, the civil rights movement gained another martyr in the Reverend James Reeb of Boston. A Unitarian minister who had answered the call of Martin Luther King, Jr., for ministerial involvement, Reeb died from a savage beating inflicted by opponents of the planned march. Other ministers similarly risked their lives in boarding buses bound for the South during the "Freedom Summer" campaigns. In expressing their opposition to racial segregation and, later, to American policy in Vietnam, some clergy departed from conventional political activity to perform acts of civil disobedience or even violence. The nation grew accustomed to pictures of clergymen being led off to jail for participation in illegal sit-ins or other such activities.

It is important to keep in mind, however, that a great many ministers did not conform to this description of social action. In their study of the Little Rock (Arkansas) school desegregation crisis of 1957–1958, Campbell and Pettigrew (1959) stressed that most ministers from the mainline churches, while not supporting school segregation, kept their distance from the controversy engulfing their community. Similarly, if Quinley's study of California ministers held true nationwide, many clergy apparently kept their Sunday sermons free of any sustained commentary on the divisive political and social issues of the 1960s (Stark et al. 1971, chap. 5). Neither would it be accurate to conclude that the politically active mainline clergy uniformly supported the liberal side on these issues; some members of Quinley's sample reported undertaking activities in favor of repealing the housing ordinance, defending American military involvement in Southeast Asia, or resisting the unionization campaign on the farms. Similarly, several community surveys revealed that substantial numbers of mainline ministers continued to preach the traditional Protestant perspective, emphasizing personal piety as the best response to social problems (Koller and Retzer 1980; Nelsen 1975). Such conservative activism was rare, however. Quinley and others (Tygart 1977) note two strong trends in the data: first, the level of clergy activism was highest among the theological liberals; and second, the bulk of activists did in fact work on what was defined as the liberal side on the three issues.

In attempting to account for the different levels of political activism among mainline clergy, scholars have stressed both individual and structural factors. As individuals, the activist clergy were more likely than their inactive counterparts to have received advanced education from secular institutions and to have been raised in urban areas (Ammerman 1981). These traits reflect exposure to agents of modernization that probably undermined a traditional conception of religion and encouraged clergy to view their task in much broader terms. Indeed, according to the research of sociologist Hart Nelsen (1975; Nelson, Yokley, and Madron 1973), activists and nonactivists exhibited very different understandings about the role of religion in society and adjusted their ministerial priorities accordingly. Using postal surveys, Nelsen discovered that clergymen who regarded themselves principally as spiritual leaders, personal counselors, church administrators, or educators tended to embrace conservative political ideas and to preach the traditional moral concerns about individual rectitude. The activists were recruited from the ranks of clergy who defined their principal responsibility as community problem solving. Believing they were meant to address a wide range of problems that could not necessarily be solved by personal piety, these clergy were more likely to sermonize on social problems and to favor direct political involvement as a solution.

These differences in role orientation were reinforced by participation in supportive social networks. Protestant parish ministers were more likely to engage in civil rights activity—even in the face of congregational resistance—when they belonged to national denominations that issued clear directives in support of the civil rights movement (Wood 1981). It was equally important for activists to find a local haven to sustain their liberal activities. In her study of civil rights involvement among Protestant ministers in Tuscaloosa, Alabama, Nancy Ammerman (1981) found that geographical proximity to a university campus and a perception of procivil rights attitudes in the local community were important factors drawing clergymen into public activism. Ministers could apparently draw emotional and intellectual support from these sources to offset the hostility their actions might arouse among parishioners and fellow ministers.

Mainline Activism: Sources and Reactions

To understand why the "new breed" clergy emerged when it did, it is important to consider the social, creedal, and institutional aspects of mainline Protestantism. I noted earlier that changes in the national political climate drew both evangelicals and Catholics more fully into the political arena. The same factors had some influence on the mainline Protestants. The political issues that engaged clergy during the activist era—civil rights, Vietnam, social justice—touched on profound moral values at the core of Christian thought. As Quinley (1974, 3) put it, "The churches could hardly preach Christian brotherhood and love for one's fellow man and at the same time remain silent on such issues as civil rights and the war in Vietnam." But the explanatory power of this theological explanation is limited by awareness that Protestant clergy had historically kept silent in the face of social conflicts no less harmful to the spirit of brotherhood and love for one's fellow man and that many ministers did refrain from speaking out publicly even in the turbulent 1960s. Another explanation of the clergy's decision to speak out points to a perceived need to preserve the institutional strength of the church and the social influence of the ministry. According to this theory, the liberal Protestant churches saw an emphasis on social action as a bridge to the well-educated and modernized members of their parishes. The demand for relevance was particularly urgent at a time of radical challenge to Christian orthodoxy, when a scientific worldview had undermined some traditional elements of belief and Americans seemed disposed to experiment with Eastern religions. Unless the churches could seem "relevant" to contemporary social problems, in other words, they would lose their appeal to young people and progressive thinkers. For the clergy, who had been criticized earlier for silence on pressing moral matters, participation in social movements may have presented an opportunity to maintain a leadership role in society, through aggressive championing of liberal causes. This interpretation of the clergy's motivation amounts to yet another application of the "status politics" framework.[22]

If the causes of activism among the clergy were debatable, the immediate effect was clear-cut. In church after church, the activist clergy ran headlong into the status quo sentiments of more conservative congregants (Quinley 1974; Hadden 1969). In what another author described as a "gathering storm," the clergy encountered substantial resistance to their attempts to speak for the church on controversial public issues. By majorities ranging from 55 percent on the farm worker issue to 83 percent on the fair housing referendum, the clergy in the California sample reported encountering opposition from at least some members of their congregation. On the race relations campaign, about one-third indicated conflict with the church board, and one in ten said their position had produced efforts to remove them from the pulpit. The Vietnam issue and the farm worker dispute incited conflicts of similar intensity, although with lower rates of opposition.

Faced with this resistance from congregations who apparently preferred a priority on worship and spirituality, many clergy sought safe havens in appointments outside the local parish. Accordingly, the liberal ministers took refuge in campus ministries, denominational "social action" bureaucracies, the seminaries, and other environments that were more supportive of political activity by church leaders. Freed from accountability to a conservative constituency, ministers in these positions supplied a disproportionate share of the activist clergy (Hadden and Rymph 1971). To this day, nonparish environments continue to harbor many politically liberal clergymen and clergywomen who would probably find it difficult to coexist with typical members of their denomination (IEA and Roper Center 1982). Other reform-minded members of the clergy and seminary students, weary of the constant battles within the church, simply opted to leave the ministry for opportunities in secular agencies.

Those who remain in the pulpit have continued to press for a liberal and activist social agenda. In a 1988 poll of Protestant ministers, clergy from mainline denominations gave greater emphasis than their evangelical counterparts to the social reform mission of the church and assigned less importance than evangelicals to missionary activities (Guth 1989). Compared with Baptists, ministers from the Presbyterian Church and the Disciples of Christ reported giving more attention to social problems in sermons and sponsoring more church study groups. Many mainline churches were also active in the nuclear freeze movement and in programs to combat homelessness. As in the 1960s, they preach to congregations with many members who do not welcome the "intrusion" of politics in religion (see Welch et al. 1990, table 3).

The problems faced by the progressive clergy stem in large measure from the social perspectives of church members. As Wade C. Roof (1978) has demonstrated in his study of North Carolina Episcopalians, the social basis of contemporary Christianity has shifted because of the declining plausibility of religious doctrine to persons most deeply affected by modernization. Traditional religious teachings have the greatest appeal for persons with limited exposure to education, urbanization, and impersonal bureaucracies. Such persons who are deeply anchored in their local communities tend to exhibit a narrow perspective on the world and to defend vigorously those traditional social values that have lost favor among the progressive clergy. As a consequence, even liberal denominations with many new-breed clergymen and clergywomen drew their church members and activists disproportionately from theological and political conservatives. It is *not* the case, as Roof stressed, that theological conservatism brings about traditional attitudes on social and political issues. Rather, he contended, traditional religious values are the most plausible to persons whose limited exposure to the outside world had safeguarded them from the challenge of modern social thought.

In a religious marketplace in which churches compete for membership, the individual Protestant faces a wide choice of potential churches with which to affiliate. From the late 1960s through the current period, membership trends have run against the mainline denominations and in favor of the evangelical confessions. Some observers have interpreted the erosion of mainline membership in terms of parishioner resistance to the social activism characteristic of liberal Protestantism. What people want from their churches, declared Dean Kelley (1977) of the National Council of Churches, is comfort rather than challenge. When the liberal ministers nonetheless insisted on social reform as the first priority, Kelley and others maintained, the members voted with their feet, deserting in favor of evangelical churches that spoke to the personal needs and fears of Christians. The mainline clergy seem to have ended up with the worst of both worlds: too action-oriented to suit the preferences of many congregants, and too conventional to maintain the faith of their young, affluent, well-educated constituents.

Patterns of Retrenchment

Faced with pressure from parishioners and church boards, the mainline churches have adopted a lower profile and curtailed some of their social and political activities. Much conservative criticism had come to focus on the National Council of Churches (NCC), an ecumenical organization of mainline denominations that spearheaded church social action during the 1960s (Pratt 1972). In response to declines in membership and complaints about the appropriateness and representativeness of NCC activity, affiliated churches began to reduce their contributions to NCC and other interfaith organizations. The organizations, in turn, cut back on staff and social action.[23] In response, the general secretary of the Council announced plans to increase the voice of member churches in the decision-making process and to give greater emphasis to worship and spiritual matters. While the Council has not stopped issuing statements critical of prevailing social arrangements, it has given more attention to traditional religious issues such as the extent of sex and violence in popular media. These steps have not eliminated suspicion of the NCC among many parishioners from member denominations.

Within the individual churches themselves, similar patterns have been evident. In response to the eroding membership base, churches have given renewed attention to worship and other traditional activities. To make more effective use of limited resources, smaller denominations joined together in merged confessions. Already, various branches of Lutherans and Presbyterians have joined in new churches, and nine other denominations, with more than 20 million members, have been considering a new union.[24] Because endorsement of controversial social and political policies might threaten the harmony of these new unions, the denominations have been reluctant to tread too deeply into the realm of public action. In contrast to their previous willingness to enter the political arena, the mainline churches have been conspicuously silent during the last few presidential elections.

As both a symbol and source of the political retreat, eighteen clergymen issued "An Appeal for Theological Affirmation" at the conclusion of a meeting in Hartford, Connecticut, in January 1975. Although the signers included Catholics and evangelicals, most were from mainline churches, and the instigators had strong liberal credentials as civil rights activists and leaders of organizations that had opposed American involvement in Vietnam. Widely interpreted as a call for withdrawal from the social activism of the 1960s, the "Hartford Appeal" condemned a number of fashionable doctrines as "false and debilitating to the Church's life and work." The signers insisted that the essence of Christianity could not be reduced to modern movements for social reform, whether left- or right-wing, and reaffirmed traditional beliefs about the primacy of God and the need for individual redemption (Berger and Neuhaus 1976).

In all facets of the mainline church, then, the recent period has been marked by political retrenchment. The new breed, who never represented more than a minority force within a largely conservative tradition, succeeded for a time in altering the image of liberal Protestantism but eventually succumbed to pressures for a lower profile. Though individuals continue to press for liberal political causes, the family of mainline Protestants has let the leading role go by default to the newly energized evangelicals and Roman Catholics.

Black Protestants: The Perpetuation of Liberalism

The discussion of political trends among evangelical Protestants, Roman Catholics, and mainline Protestants has emphasized change—from inaction to mobilization for the first two groups, and a shift in the opposite direction for the mainline Protestants. But for the two remaining religious groups, Jews and black Protestants, the operative word has been "stability." Although neither group was unmoved by the events of the 1970s, they have remained the most reliable pillars of national support for liberal candidates and causes.

That blacks have stayed on the political left is hardly surprising. As an identifiable minority group, the object of continuing discrimination, subject to the highest rates of unemployment and the lowest levels of economic security, the black community has remained overwhelmingly in favor of an activist government. In the 1980s, Republican attacks on many programs and policies that blacks ardently supported cemented blacks' ties to the Democratic party. In polls from the 1984 and 1988 national elections, blacks surpassed all other groups in their level of commitment to the Democratic party and their electoral support for Democratic nominees at all levels of office. The commitment of blacks to public spending on social welfare programs remains strong (see Figure 4.5).

At first glance, it seems that blacks manage to combine two loyalties often characterized as opposites—traditional religion and political liberalism. The extent of black political liberalism has already been documented; blacks are also distinguished by strong adherence to evangelical doctrine, intense religiosity, and high levels of church commitment. Do these qualities, normally associated with a conservative stance on many so-called life-style issues, fail to influence blacks in the same manner? Not entirely. Recall from Chapter 4 the strong social conservatism exhibited by blacks on a number of social issues. Compared to many white religious groups, black Protestants were much less enthusiastic about abortion for either health or social reasons and were much more reluctant to extend civil liberties to groups outside the mainstream. Such differences have been confirmed in other studies and shown to extend to related issues such as school prayer (Seltzer and Smith 1985; Combs and Welch 1982; Secret, Johnson, and Welch 1986). Religious beliefs largely account for black opposition to abortion (Wilcox 1990a).

But on other issues that have been linked to the profamily agenda, black religiosity either fails to instill moral conservatism or actually promotes liberal views. Susan Marshall (1990) found for example that church attendance, correlated strongly with opposition to the Equal Rights Amendment among white women, had no impact on the attitude of black women to the same object. Religious identification and private devotionalism appear to encourage whites to accept the "priestly" version of civil religion that sanctifies the nation; they have precisely the opposite effect on blacks (Woodrum and Bell 1989). Among whites, as we learned in the previous chapter, charismatic identification, personal religiosity, and high levels of church attendance were associated with greater levels of support for the conservative presidential candidacy of Pat Robertson. Among blacks sampled in Washington, D.C., these qualities were related to support for Jesse Jackson, a candidate whose platform was the polar opposite of Robertson's (Wilcox 1990b).

The solution to this apparent puzzle may be the rich, multifaceted evangelicalism conveyed in black churches that has the potential to encourage either liberal or conservative political tendencies. One component of black evangelical theology emphasizes the innate sinfulness

of humankind and the consequent importance of family values in restraining immorality. Social traditionalism may encourage blacks, as it
does whites, to favor restrictions on abortion and to oppose limitations
on school prayer. Yet black Protestantism also contains a strong prophetic component, a response to centuries of oppression. Portraying Jesus primarily as a force for liberation, this aspect of black theology
makes religion a spur to social justice. The prophetic element guides
religious blacks to a critical stance regarding the United States and attracts them to the candidacy of a Jesse Jackson.

The political response of blacks seems to depend on which aspect of
theology is evoked by a particular public issue. Because white women
see the Equal Rights Amendment primarily as a challenge to traditional
sex roles, evangelical religious commitment inspires opposition to the
proposal. For blacks, however, the amendment apparently connotes the
salient value of equality and legal protection against discrimination. As
such, blacks who are imbued with a strong religious commitment are
more sympathetic to the proposal. On the issues of paramount concern
for most black Americans—economic security and civil rights—religious commitment is likely to reinforce the liberal thrust of that community.

The Infrastructure of Black Politics

More surprising than the persistence of liberalism has been the continued presence of members of the black clergy in political leadership
roles. Through the Southern Christian Leadership Conference (SCLC)
and local ministerial alliances, the Reverend Martin Luther King, Jr.,
and like-minded black clergymen provided vital organizational resources and strategy for the civil rights movement in the late 1950s and
early 1960s. In a fascinating reconstruction of the early days of the civil
rights campaign, Aldon Morris (1981, 1984) has demonstrated the critical role of black ministers and churches in training and recruiting volunteers, communicating with supporters, and providing havens for the
early sit-ins, boycotts, and mass marches. Even those southern blacks
who were outside the centers of organized resistance to segregation recognized ministers as the natural leaders of political activism (Matthews
and Prothro 1966, 180–185). The same pattern held in the early 1970s,
according to a national survey of black adults conducted by political

scientist Hanes Walton (1985, 47–49). When asked to identify the major influences on their thinking, respondents identified the "black church" and "black minister" more frequently than any other institution or organization.

But with time and changes in the political and social situation of blacks, the political leadership of ministers came to be challenged by new elites. The first signs of competition for leadership emerged when the civil rights movement entered what was described as its "black power" phase. Disappointed with the limited consequences of the civil rights legislation passed into law in 1964 and 1965, younger activists from outside the churches called on blacks to pursue more aggressive action to achieve social, economic, and political progress. As part of their appeal to black nationalist sentiment, the more militant leaders frequently denounced the clergy of the major black denominations for a supposed unwillingness to challenge the white power structure. To the extent that the black power movement was church-related, its center of gravity was located in nontraditional religious faith rather than in the mainstream black churches. The religious group most critical of Christianity, the Black Muslims, called for a complete separation of blacks from the white community and developed a theology that identified the white man as the incarnation of the devil. Although these non-Christians have never come close to displacing the traditional denominations, the assassination of Martin Luther King, Jr., robbed the civil rights movement of the most prominent leader with a distinctly Christian orientation to political action.

The black power revolt represented dissatisfaction with the limited progress of the civil rights movement under the leadership of the mainline clergy. Ironically, however, the very successes of the movement also produced a rival set of claimants for community leadership. With some relaxation of segregation and expanded educational opportunities, limited numbers of blacks were able to move into formerly white-dominated voluntary associations specializing in policy areas such as health, employment, education, and social welfare. With professional training, administrative skills, and political sophistication, such experts assumed some of the political and social responsibilities previously monopolized by the ministers (Wilson 1965, 297–300). The growing corps of blacks in government positions—another consequence of the civil rights movement—further accentuated the transition away from clergy domination. Today, the typical black candidate for public office, be the position elective, appointive, or administrative, is most likely to emerge not from the clergy but from the sector of black professionals trained in law, business, public administration, or another field outside the church (Cole 1976, 43; Smith 1981, 210). Unlike the leadership of the black power revolt, however, the black professionals and public officials have remained closely tied to the mainstream churches (Salamon 1973, 628–629; Fenno 1978, 113–124).

Despite the emergence of a secular leadership class, the clergy have continued to provide major political leaders of the black community. In Congress, the Reverend Walter Fauntroy of Washington, D.C., has been one of the leading spokesmen for the concerns of the black community. A Philadelphia preacher, the Reverend William Gray, was elected as assistant majority leader of the House Democrats. This followed his successful leadership of the House Budget Committee.[25] Andrew Young, an ordained minister who was King's assistant in the SCLC, resigned a House seat to accept the cabinet-level position of ambassador to the United Nations during the Carter administration and later became mayor of Atlanta. In social action, too, black ministers have continued to provide the lead. As of 1982, the three top officials in the National Association for the Advancement of Colored People (NAACP), the oldest civil rights organization in the United States, were Protestant ministers ("The Black Church" 1982, 5), as were the founders and leaders of the urban job-training organizations such as the Chicago-based "People United to Save Humanity" (PUSH) and the Opportunities Industrialization Commission (OIC) in Philadelphia. The founder of OIC, the Reverend Leon Sullivan, has also been instrumental in forging American opposition to the white minority regime in South Africa. At the local level, too, ministers have continued to play an important political role even with the advent of the new black leadership class (Hadley 1987).

Black ministers have been able to play such a strategic role because they command the resources of the strongest institution in black life. The roots of the church run deep enough to make it the natural focus of organized activity in the black community and to enable it to withstand competition from secular organizations. As a typical example, the minister of the Shiloh Baptist Church in the nation's capital presides over a community outreach program that provides more than ninety separate services to neighborhood residents and over five thousand parishioners.[26] The church has hosted most of the leading lights of the civil rights movement and has been visited in the recent past by such major national political leaders as Senator Edward Kennedy and President Ronald Reagan. In other urban centers, there have been church-based organizations such as the East Brooklyn Churches (EBC), described by an observer as "a powerful, politically independent, dues-paying organization that can turn out 7,000 people for a rally, register 10,000 new voters in a year and persuade politicians to put up new street signs [and] inspect local grocery stores" (Hornblower 1985). The EBC was instrumental in the building of low-cost housing that has restored to viability parts of Brooklyn that were once written off as terminally blighted.

From the perspective of organizational theory, leaders of the church enjoy (1) regular opportunities to communicate their views on issues to members of the community, (2) immense prestige and credibility, and (3) control over a network of social agencies that meet human needs. Such resources can easily be turned to political advantage. When black politics was restricted by law and custom, the black church could still provide a basis for some limited bargaining with the white political elite. In Chicago during the turn of the century, a bishop of the local African Methodist Episcopal church used his pulpit, personal influence, and administrative control over an extensive system of welfare activities to mold blacks into a cohesive voting bloc. In exchange for supporting a victorious white mayoral candidate, the clergyman was able to obtain new public facilities in the black community and some patronage positions in municipal government for congregants (Katznelson 1976, 92–93).

To judge by the role of black churches in more recent Chicago elections, the stakes may have changed but the methods have not. With the prospect of electing a black to the mayor's office, the churches played a crucial role in a dramatic voter registration drive late in 1982 (Kleppner 1985, 145–150). One prominent black minister bluntly told his parishioners that nonregistrants were not welcome in the congregation. A voter registration card was the price of access to the free food distributed by one of the major Baptist churches in the black community. Under the slogan "Praise the Lord and Register," the black churches committed themselves wholeheartedly to serving as registration centers. Because of the massive increase in black voter enrollment and high turnout among the newly registered, the black candidate, Harold Washington, won the Chicago mayoral election in 1983. The churches have provided similar support for successful black mayoral candidates in Philadelphia and Birmingham.

When public office-holding came to be a realistic possibility, the political options of black clergymen expanded well beyond the limits of the segregation era. In fact, securing public office has frequently come to be viewed as an extension of the pastoral role. As one black minister with congressional experience told another who was considering running for office, "Congress will not be difficult. It is essentially pastoring, ministering to the folks in your district" (Hall 1985, 13). Combined with a gospel of social action, these institutional and social forces have provided a powerful impetus to organized political action.

The presidential campaigns of Jesse Jackson reinforced the trend by providing the clergy-activist with a national platform. An associate of Martin Luther King, Jr., Jackson had concentrated on black economic development during the 1970s. In Chicago, he founded the PUSH organization (People United to Save Humanity), which eventually spread throughout the United States. The PUSH philosophy encourages blacks to cultivate conservative social values (self-help, strong discipline, drug avoidance) in the pursuit of what most conservative whites must surely regard as radical social, economic, and political objectives. True to his background in the civil rights movement, Jackson has not shied away from the use of boycotts, demonstrations, and sit-ins to protest alleged discrimination. Although failing to win either the 1984 or 1988 Democratic presidential nominations, he succeeded in mobilizing impressive political support.

Jackson's campaign was deeply rooted in the black churches (Hertzke 1988; Wald forthcoming). They provided the forum in which his candidacies were first explored and the base for voter registration drives essential to its success. Churches also served as the key organizational units of the campaign and generated most of the activists and money to fuel the cause. The religious dimension of Jackson's campaign was most apparent to whites in the candidate's religious language and appeals. Jackson's entire platform rested on a belief in the kinship of humankind through its common link to God; in this view, poverty, racism, and sexism are not merely social problems but sins against the divine spark in all people. He portrayed political action in messianic terms, constantly invoking biblical metaphors and turning an attack on drug use into something resembling a religious crusade. The Jackson platform bore strong traces of both the Social Gospel and liberation theology.

There is every reason to believe that the church will continue as the vanguard of political action for black Protestants. This does not mean that all black clergy should be expected to play a leadership role in political life. Like its white Protestant counterpart, the black religious community contains ministers who firmly believe that political mobilization ought to be a secondary concern lest it detract the church from the paramount task of saving souls. Even in the heyday of the civil rights movement, the SCLC was regarded with suspicion by some leaders of major black confessions, and many preachers refrained from taking aggressive or challenging political stances (Hamilton 1972, chap. 5; Paris 1978).

In terms of social traits such as youth and education, the most politically active ministers of black churches closely resemble their white counterparts in the new-breed clergy of the mainline Protestants (Berenson, Elifson, and Tollerson 1976). But because the laity of the largest and most active black churches recognizes a need for an activist government to promote social change, black clergymen face much less resistance to social and political activism.

Scholars continue to debate the impact of strong religious feeling on the development of black politics. Advocates of the so-called opiate interpretation insist that religion has primarily been a conservative force, its otherworldly nature encouraging blacks to wait for justice in heaven rather than to pursue it here on earth. At the other extreme, the contrasting "inspiration" view contends that "it was precisely through the Biblical story, the Negro Spiritual, and the event of Christian worship that black people knew the existence of being bound together in the persecuted family of a righteous God who destined them someday to break the bonds of oppression" (Gayraud Wilmore, cited in Johnson 1986, 311). The coexistence of conservative and radical themes in black theology, noted earlier in this chapter, may provide support for each interpretation under appropriate circumstances. Indeed, research on the role of religion during the civil rights movement disagreed as to whether ministerial leadership and religious consciousness helped or hindered the development of black political consciousness (Marx 1967, chap. 4; Hunt and Hunt 1977; Nelsen, Madron, and Yokley 1975).

In the modern period, the evidence suggests that religion contributes to political assertiveness in the black community. Blacks who are active in churches are more likely to vote even when taking into account their socioeconomic status and other related factors (F. Harris 1990). Churches apparently teach black congregants to identify with the black community and this sense of group solidarity, in turn, encourages blacks to pursue collective political remedies for their problems (Allen, Dawson and Brown 1989; Wilcox and Gomez 1990). As with all generalizations, this conclusion has limits. It is quite likely that participation in some religious groups, particularly those pentecostal sects that stress turning inward, does inhibit political commitment among blacks. But whether the impact is toward political engagement or withdrawal, there can be little doubt that the black religious tradition will continue to shape the form of modern black political action.

Jews and American Political Trends

Given their relatively small numbers, Jews might not seem to warrant special attention in a general volume about religion in American politics. But several aspects of Jewish political behavior have prompted scholars to pay close attention to this particular community. To begin with, Jews are extremely active in American political life. They are represented well beyond their numerical share of the population as candidates and officials, campaign activists, political contributors, members of interest groups, and—not least—as regular voters in primary and general elections. Their high rate of voting, coupled with geographic concentration in large and competitive states, makes them especially important in presidential elections. The nature, as well as the amount, of Jewish activism also stands out. Collectively an affluent religious group, Jews nonetheless hold liberal political views that seem contrary to their economic self-interest. In fact, unlike non-Jews who typically become much more Republican as their income increases, Jewish voters do not "vote their pocketbooks" to the same degree (Fisher 1989, 43). While most religious groups define themselves in terms of theological beliefs or prescribed codes of behavior, many Jews actually regarded liberalism as the very essence of Judaism itself (Sklare and Greenblum 1967, chap. 10; Liebman and Cohen 1990, 97).

In Chapter 4, we noted several explanations for the strength of Jewish liberalism. The popular theory that liberalism was somehow implicit in Jewish theology, first advanced by Lawrence Fuchs (1956), has been undercut by repeated findings that the most religiously observant Jews are also the most politically conservative (Cohen 1983, 143–153; Penn and Schoen 1988, 25; Lazerwitz, Winter, and Dashefsky 1988). If their liberalism is not mandated by creed and seems counter to group interest, then social standing probably seems the best explanation. Scholars generally attribute Jewish political preferences to the community's sense of itself as a potential target of hostility from the non-Jewish majority. Despite attaining objective levels of prominence undreamed of by earlier generations, American Jews still feel vulnerable to persecution and anti-Semitism (Liebman and Cohen 1990, 42–50). Why should a sense of social marginality attract American Jews to the left side of the political spectrum? From history, Jews learned that the left historically favored the cause of minorities, and liberalism is still seen as more sympathetic to minority groups than the political alternatives. Even if they do not benefit directly from the social programs sponsored by liberals, Jews regard such programs as a safeguard against the social tensions that breed religious bigotry (Fein 1988). The superiority of social situation over creed theories is clinched by the markedly less liberal orientation of Israeli Jews, a majority in their own land (ibid., chap. 5).

Since the 1960s, some observers have predicted that urban unrest, affirmative action, and concern for the fate of Israel would eventually drive Jews out of the Democratic coalition and into alliance with conservative forces. One powerful impetus to political change was the upsurge in conflict between Jews and blacks. Before the "black power" movement, when the civil rights campaign concentrated principally on attacking formal barriers to equality, Jews were the single most ardent supporters of the movement in the white community. Aside from membership and leadership roles in interracial civil rights organizations, Jews made up a massively disproportionate share of the young white students who went South as volunteers for desegregation (Liebman 1979, 68). White politicians who developed a reputation as civil rights activists enjoyed nearly unanimous electoral support from Jewish voters; those who became symbols of white resistance, such as George Wallace of Alabama, looked elsewhere for support.

Once the civil rights movement moved to northern cities and came to focus on de facto expressions of racism, however, the two communities began to divide.[27] Tensions arose over demands by the advocates of black power for "community control" of ghetto life. As the immigrant group that had preceded blacks to the city, Jews still occupied an important place in private businesses and public institutions in the central city. Hence, though directed at whites in general, demands for black ownership of businesses, black-only leadership in civil rights groups and increased black representation in public employment challenged Jews in particular. The bitter expressions of hostility from some protagonists on both sides conveyed the impression of a fundamental estrangement rooted in a rising tide of black anti-Semitism and Jewish racism.

In New York, the city with the largest concentration of Jews, these clashes became particularly intense. Attacks on Jewish-owned businesses during ghetto riots and conflicts between blacks and Jews in the public schools brought national publicity. Relationships eventually deteriorated to the point that a Brooklyn-born rabbi, Meier Kahane, formed the Jewish Defense League (JDL) to patrol inner-city neighborhoods with sizable concentrations of Jews. By offering armed protection to Jews who felt threatened by crime and anti-Semitic attacks, the JDL bore a strong resemblance to the most militant black organizations in the ghetto. Condemned by many Jewish leaders as a thinly disguised appeal to racist sentiment, the JDL nonetheless played on fears of racial violence widespread in the Jewish community.

On a more general level, tensions arose over the development of "affirmative action" programs in public employment, graduate and professional school admission, and other important sectors. The principle of affirmative action is that past discrimination against blacks or any other group can most effectively and justly be overcome by giving temporary preference to black applicants in competition for channels to upward mobility. The legitimacy of the principle and its application to concrete situations have generated considerable conflict within the liberal community. The doctrine goes well beyond the traditional understanding of "equality" into realms that have been described by unfriendly observers as "reverse discrimination" or "affirmative discrimination." Some of the most trenchant criticisms of the new policy came from Jews who regarded the programs as tantamount to setting up governmentally approved "quotas" for access to social advancement. Since such quotas had once been used to exclude Jews from careers in prestigious and remunerative occupations, their proposed introduction for purposes of spurring black advancement called forth strong opposition from much of the Jewish community. When the Supreme Court considered cases about the constitutionality of specific affirmative action programs, the major Jewish organizations that had once joined black plaintiffs in discrimination cases usually weighed in on the side challenging the new schemes.

Once the closest of allies, the two groups began to trade charges of racism and anti-Semitism. Blacks attributed the deteriorating relationship to Jewish unwillingness to admit their legitimate claims for jobs, housing, and political power, whereas Jews tended to blame racial agitation and black envy of Jewish achievement. In retrospect, the clash seems to have been a predictable outcome of the process of ethnic succession in American cities, more intense but otherwise quite like the earlier battles between white ethnic groups on the urban frontier. Even at the height of the conflict in New York, a specially commissioned public opinion poll revealed an underlying harmony between blacks and Jews (L. Harris and Swanson 1970, chap. 2). According to the poll, Jews were more likely than white Catholics and no less likely than white Protestants to acknowledge that blacks suffered discrimination, and only blacks shared the Jewish perception that the latter were still victims of discrimination in the city.

The Jewish commitment to liberalism was thought to have been further undermined by the issue of Israel. As noted earlier, the Jewish community was galvanized by the outbreak of the Six-Day War in 1967 between Israel and its Arab neighbors, which immeasurably strengthened the commitment of American Jews to the Zionist cause. As American Jews increased their support for the Jewish homeland in the Middle East, many self-identified liberals moved the other way by showing greater sympathy for the claims of Palestinian nationalists. Jews who had once championed the United Nations and given verbal support to some national liberation movements watched with dismay as the 1975 General Assembly declared Zionism to be a form of racism and equated Israelis with white South Africans as colonial oppressors.

During the administration of President Jimmy Carter, the Israeli issue fused with concern over black attitudes to the Jewish community (Feuerlicht 1983, chap. 6; for an earlier tie, see Carson 1984). At the United Nations, Ambassador Andrew Young had forged strong ties with

some of the Third World representatives who had been the most vociferous critics of American support for Israel. In August 1979, it was revealed that Young had held a meeting with a representative of the
Palestine Liberation Organization (PLO), the umbrella group of Palestinian nationalism. Since the United States had an official policy to boycott the PLO until it granted recognition to Israel, Young's meeting was
condemned by Israel and by leaders of American Jewish organizations.
Under pressure from the State Department, Young eventually resigned.
Blacks were angry about the apparent Jewish attack on their most influential advocate in the administration and felt that Young had been
singled out for retribution. The Jews were outraged at the sympathy that
blacks had shown to an organization that advocated violence in order
to achieve Palestinian aims.[28] In 1980, Jewish voters appeared to repay
the Carter administration for its alleged pro-Arab tilt by giving President
Carter less than a clear majority of their vote in his reelection bid. Although Israel was not the only reason for the decline in Jewish support
for the Democratic ticket, it surely contributed in a major way.

These various tensions prompted a small group of Jewish intellectuals
to argue that it was time for a permanent change in alliance. In journals
like *Commentary* and *Public Interest*, "neoconservatives" like Irving Kris-
tol urged Jews to reconsider their traditional attachment to liberalism.
Jewish interests, it was argued, were most likely to be served by the
conservative policies of the Republican administration that took office
in 1981. In national defense, for example, Jews were told that Israel
would benefit from the massive rearmament undertaken by the Defense
Department. The administration's hostility to affirmative action programs fell well within the Jewish opposition to the use of quotas to
increase black representation in the public sector and other places. Similarly, some of the neoconservatives encouraged Jews to vote their
pocketbooks by supporting the anti-inflation and tax-cutting programs
launched by the Reagan White House.

The attempt to move Jews out of the Democratic camp received an
unexpected push from the presidential campaigns of the Reverend Jesse
Jackson. During a public appearance in 1984, Jackson was overheard
to refer to Jews as "Hymies" and New York City as "Hymietown." Although Jackson apologized for his offensive language, bad feelings were
revived as the public learned more about his ties with Minister Louis
Farrakhan, the head of a Black Muslim sect known as the Nation of

Islam (Cohen 1989). By meeting with Libyan leader Col. Muammar Qaddafi and referring to Judaism as either a "gutter" or "dirty" religion, Farrakhan revived all the Jewish fears about the growth of black anti-Semitism. Jackson's insistence on condemning Farrakhan's remarks but not the man himself did not placate Jewish anger.[29] Neither were Jews endeared to a candidate so clearly sympathetic toward Palestinian nationalism. Though Jackson endorsed the existence of Israel and called for secure borders, Jews were more persuaded by the photograph of him in the physical embrace of PLO leader Yasir Arafat and the candidate's (unsuccessful) efforts to pass a platform plank endorsing an independent Palestinian state. Usually much more supportive of black candidates than other white voters, Jews rejected Jackson because they regarded him as antagonistic.[30] The Republicans spared no effort to tie the Democratic presidential nominees to Jackson's position on the Middle East and to publicize his alleged anti-Semitism (Madison 1984; Edsall and Peterson 1988).[31]

Despite predictions that Jewish liberalism would decay under the combined onslaught of all these factors, both the data presented in Chapter 4 and the findings of other studies show Jews still much more likely than others to favor liberal policies on a wide range of public issues (Lerner, Nagai, and Rothman 1989; Fisher 1985; Lipstadt, Pruitt, and Woocher 1984; Cohen 1989). This liberalism has continued to translate into very high levels of Jewish support for Democratic congressional and gubernatorial candidates. In 1986, Jews typically preferred Democrats to Republicans by margins of three or four to one (Sussman 1986; Singer 1987). Despite fond hopes that 1980 signaled a permanent conversion to Republicanism in presidential elections, Jews soon returned to their traditional preferences. Depending on which poll is consulted, the Democratic nominees in 1984 and 1988 carried somewhere between two-thirds and three-fourths of the Jewish vote. The gap in Democratic support between Jews and non-Jews, which had dropped to only 14 percent in 1980, returned to the same mid-20 percent range it had reached during the 1950s (Fisher 1989, 43).

The failure of Jews to respond to Republican overtures evidently meant that Jewish voters were more worried about the new political prominence of the evangelical Protestants than about the conflicts with black leaders. In support of this interpretation, a 1984 *Los Angeles Times* poll revealed that Jewish voters were actually more hostile to the Reverend Jerry Falwell, who had actually courted them on behalf of the Reagan campaign, than to Jesse Jackson (Schneider 1985, 58). And while 58 percent of Falwell's Jewish critics supported Walter Mondale, a whopping 78 percent of the anti-Jackson Jews stayed with the Democratic ticket on election day. Why do Jews react so much more negatively to a white Protestant preacher who supported Israel unreservedly than to a black Protestant preacher who flirted with the Arab cause? According to political scientist Seymour Martin Lipset (1985, 23), "The answer would seem to lie in the millennia-old history of European Jewry as a minority, persecuted and discriminated against by conservative religious and secular establishments." The evangelical Protestants are associated in the Jewish mind both with the policies of "Christian government" and with skepticism about the value of government support for welfare. Neither association endeared Jews to the Republican ticket in 1984 or 1988.

Jews today are cohesive but certainly not unanimous in their preferences for liberal issues and candidates. There are signs of willingness by some members of the community to reconsider their traditional ties. Younger Jews, though still much more Democratic than their non-Jewish counterparts, are more sympathetic to Republican candidates than their grandparents (Fisher 1989). Pro-Israeli political action committees donate roughly one-third of their funds to Republican candidates (Malbin 1986). But still, in all, Jews remain politically where they have been for more than half a century—well to the left of the American population.

Strong ties bound religion and politics in the 1980s. Yet it has also been demonstrated in this and the previous chapter that religious groups have reacted quite differently to national political trends. They have not all responded to the same issues nor responded similarly to common developments. While some of the uniqueness reflects group tradition and the pull of traditional loyalty, equal weight must be given to factors rooted in creedal, social, and institutional traits.

The larger consequences of the relationship for the health of the body politic—the important question of whether religious involvement is good or bad for the political system—will be taken up in the concluding chapter.

NOTES

1. Charles E. Coughlin was a Detroit priest who had become a national celebrity with his radio broadcasts in the 1920s. During the 1930s, his broadcasts combined economic radicalism with attacks on Jews, communists, and the "New Deal" of Franklin D. Roosevelt. A U.S. senator from Wisconsin, Joseph McCarthy drew fame for his attacks on alleged communist penetration of the United States government in the late 1940s and early 1950s.

2. Some commentators have speculated that American Catholics drew their fatalism from the peasant culture of the Italian and Irish countrysides. If urbanized and cosmopolitan European Catholics had predominated among American immigrants, the story of Catholic social values would probably have read very differently.

3. This upward mobility was true mostly for Catholic natives who were at least the third generation of their family in America. For more recent immigrants, especially Hispanic Catholics from Mexico and Puerto Rico, economic conditions and social integration were much less advanced.

4. "Activism Affirmed by Catholic Order," *New York Times*, Dec. 10, 1984, 5A.

5. As Michael Novak (1984) acknowledged, the bishops also strongly endorsed such capitalist practices and motivations as tax incentives, small business, multinational corporations, and policies designed to promote entrepreneurial activity.

6. "Catholic Bishops' Pastoral Draft Jolts Community," *Washington Post*, Nov. 19, 1984, 8A.

7. "Catholic Group Extols Capitalism as Bishops Ready Economic Study," *New York Times*, Nov. 7, 1984, 1, 21.

8. "In Celebration of Creative Capitalism in Society," *New York Times*, Nov. 7, 1984, 21.

9. Terms such as "liberal" and "conservative" do not fit well on issues such as abortion. In describing support for legalized abortion as "liberal" and opposition as "conservative," I do not mean to suggest that there is anything intrinsically liberal about supporting abortion as a right or anything inherently conservative about a restrictive policy. My use of these terms refers to liberal or conservative access to abortion.

10. Despite attempts to raise the cost of abortions beyond the ability to pay, specialized clinics emerged to perform a mounting number of abortions annually. During the 1980s, roughly 30 percent of pregnancies were terminated by abortion in the United States.

11. "Fifty-five Scholars Say Church's Abortion Stand Is Not Monolithic," *New York Times*, Sept. 15, 1984, 29. As evidence of the hierarchy's sensitivity on the issue, however, the clergy who signed a public advertisement promoting a prochoice perspective were forced to relent or resign from their orders.

12. "Poll Shows Most Priests Want the Right to Marry," *New York Times*, Sept. 11, 1987, 1.

13. An elaborate study in Hawaii, which had liberalized abortion laws well before most of the nation, showed that Catholic women made extensive use of elective abortion but were also less likely than pregnant women from other denominations to terminate pregnancy artificially (Leon and Steinhoff 1975). A 1987 national survey

disclosed that Catholic women were just as likely as other women to obtain abortions. Among the subgroups of white non-Hispanic Catholic women, however, the abortion rate was half the national average (Henshaw and Silverman 1988).

14. "Poll Shows Most Priests Want the Right to Marry," *New York Times*, Sept. 11, 1987, 1.

15. "Bishop: Politicians Can't Separate Moral Views from Public Policy," *Gainesville Sun*, Aug. 11, 1984.

16. "Catholic Activism: Reasons and Risks," *Gainesville Sun*, Sept. 23, 1984, 5B.

17. "Excerpts from Speech by Kennedy," *New York Times*, Sept. 11, 1984, 10.

18. "Excerpts from Cuomo Talk on Religion and Public Morality," *New York Times*, Sept. 14, 1984, 13.

19. "Text of Bishops' Statement on Role of the Church in Politics," *New York Times*, Oct. 14, 1984, 1A.

20. There were similar results in 1972 when George McGovern's liberalism on abortion was one of the factors reducing Catholic support for the Democratic ticket even though the vice-presidential nominee, R. Sargent Shriver, was a member of the church.

21. "Key Portions of Archbishop's Speech on Abortion and Politics," *New York Times*, Oct. 16, 1984, 14.

22. Interestingly, the historian Richard Hofstadter (1955, 148–152) offered a similar explanation to account for the initial surge of mainline activism during the Progressive era.

23. "The Sporadic Activism of U.S. Churches," *New York Times*, Jan. 11, 1976, 20 (sect. 4).

24. "Mainline Churches Kept Fairly Quiet During Campaigns," *Miami Herald*, Dec. 28, 1984, 1E, 5E.

25. Prior to Gray's election, former representatives Adam Clayton Powell and Charles Diggs probably represented the pinnacle of black power in the House. Both were ministers of large, influential churches.

26. "D.C.'s Shiloh Baptist Is a Symbol of Black Political Activism," *Gainesville Sun*, Sept. 1, 1984, 1C.

27. De facto segregation occurs not because of law but because of segregation in other areas of life.

28. Whatever the views of black leaders toward Israel, black Americans remained favorably disposed to that country and preferred it to its Arab enemies (Gilboa 1987, 275–277).

29. For black reaction to the Farrakhan movement, see the special polls of a national black sample in Simon Wiesenthal Center (1986).

30. "Tally Breaks Sharply Along Racial Lines," *Los Angeles Times*, Apr. 20, 1988, 1.

31. "Platform Shows Foreign Policy Shift to Win Jewish, Ethnic Votes for GOP," *Wall Street Journal*, Aug. 16, 1988, 54.

REFERENCES

Allen, Richard L., Michael C. Dawson, and Ronald Brown. 1989. "A Schema-Based Approach to Modelling an African-American Racial Belief System." *American Political Science Review* 83:421–442.

Ammerman, Nancy T. 1981. "The Civil Rights Movement and the Clergy in a Southern Community." *Sociological Analysis* 41:339–350.

Berenson, William, Kirk W. Elifson, and Tandy Tollerson III. 1976. "Preachers in Politics: A Study of Political Activism Among the Black Ministry." *Journal of Black Studies* 6:373–392.

Berger, Peter, and Richard John Neuhaus, eds. 1976. *Against the World, for the World.* New York: Seabury.

Bernbaum, John A., ed. 1984. *Perspectives on Peacemaking.* Ventura, Calif.: Regal.

"The Black Church." 1982. *Crisis* 89:5–50.

Blau, Peter M. 1953. "Orientation of College Students Toward International Relations." *American Journal of Sociology* 59:205–214.

Bolce, Louis. 1988. "Abortion and Presidential Elections: The Impact of Public Perceptions of Party and Candidate Positions." *Presidential Studies Quarterly* 28:815–829.

Califano, Joseph, Jr. 1984. "Moral Leadership Is Not Partisanship." *Washington Post Weekly Edition,* September 3, p. 28.

Callahan, Daniel, ed. 1970. *Abortion: Law, Choice and Morality.* New York: Macmillan.

Campbell, Ernest Q., and Thomas F. Pettigrew. 1959. *Christians in Racial Crisis.* Washington, D.C.: Public Affairs Press.

Carson, Claybourne, Jr. 1984. "Blacks and Jews in the Civil Rights Movement." In *Jews in Black Perspectives: A Dialogue,* edited by Joseph Washington, 113–131. Rutherford, N.J.: Farleigh Dickinson Press.

Carter, Paul A. 1954. *The Decline and Revival of the Social Gospel.* Ithaca: Cornell University Press.

Cleghorn, J. Stephen. 1986. "Respect for Life: Research Notes on Cardinal Bernardin's 'Seamless Garment'." *Review of Religious Research* 28:129–141.

Cohen, Steven M. 1983. *American Modernity and Jewish Identity.* New York: Tavistock.

———. 1989. *The Dimensions of American Jewish Liberalism.* New York: American Jewish Committee.

Cohodas, Nadine. 1983. "Campaign to Overturn Ban on Abortion Funding Begun." *Congressional Quarterly Weekly Report,* August 20, pp. 1689–1693.

Cole, Leonard. 1976. *Blacks in Power.* Princeton, N.J.: Princeton University Press.

Combs, Michael, and Susan Welch. 1982. "Blacks, Whites, and Attitudes Toward Abortion." *Public Opinion Quarterly* 46:510–520.

Connors, John F., Richard C. Leonard, and Kenneth E. Burnham. 1968. "Religion, Church Attitudes, Religious Education, and Student Attitudes to War." *Sociological Analysis* 29:211–219.

Cooney, John. 1984. *The American Pope.* New York: Times Books.

Cox, Harvey. 1968. "The 'New Breed' in American Churches: Sources of Social Activism in American Religion." In *Religion in America,* edited by William G. McLoughlin and Robert N. Bellah, 368–383. Boston: Beacon.

Crosby, Donald F. 1978. *God, Church and Flag: Senator Joseph R. McCarthy and the Catholic Church, 1950–1957.* Chapel Hill: University of North Carolina Press.

Curran, Charles E. 1982. *American Catholic Social Ethics: Twentieth Century Approaches.* Notre Dame, Ind.: University of Notre Dame Press.

Curry, Dean C., ed. 1984. *Evangelicals and the Bishops' Pastoral Letter.* Grand Rapids, Mich.: Eerdmans.

Davidson, James D. 1989. "The Pastoral Letters on Peace and the Economy: A New Approach to Church Teachings." In *Catholic Laity in a Changing Church*, edited by Dean Hoge and William V. D'Antonio, 121–131. Kansas City, Mo.: Sheed and Ward.

Deedy, John G., Jr. 1968. "The Catholic Press and Vietnam." In *American Catholics and Vietnam*, edited by Thomas E. Quigley. Grand Rapids, Mich.: Eerdmans.

Dickenson, James R. 1984. "Almighty Politics." *Washington Post Weekly Edition*, October 1, p. 11.

Dohen, Dorothy. 1967. *Nationalism and American Catholicism*. New York: Sheed and Ward.

Drinan, Robert F., S.J. 1970. *Vietnam and Armageddon*. New York: Sheed and Ward.

Dwyer, Judith A., ed. 1984. *The Catholic Bishops and Nuclear War*. Washington, D.C.: Georgetown University Press.

Eckert, Ruth E., and Henry C. Mills. 1935. "International Attitudes and Related Academic and Social Factors." *Journal of Educational Sociology* 9:142–153.

Edsall, Thomas B., and Bill Peterson. 1988. "Testing the Ties Between Jews and the Democratic Party." *Washington Post Weekly Edition*, October 31, pp. 14–15.

Fein, Leonard. 1988. *Where Are We? The Inner Life of America's Jews*. New York: Harper and Row.

Fenno, Richard F. 1978. *Home Style*. Boston: Little, Brown.

Feuerlicht, Roberta Strauss. 1983. *The Fate of the Jews: A People Torn Between Israeli Power and Jewish Ethics*. New York: Times Books.

Fisher, Alan M. 1985. "The Jewish Vote in 1982: A Good Look, A Good Predictor." *Jewish Social Studies* 47:281–294.

———. 1989. "Where the Jewish Vote Is Going." *Moment* 14:41–43.

Franklin, Charles E., and Liane C. Kosaki. 1989. "Republican Schoolmaster: The U.S. Supreme Court, Public Opinion, and Abortion." *American Political Science Review* 83:751–777.

Friedman, Lawrence M. 1983. "The Conflict Over Constitutional Legitimacy." In *The Abortion Dispute and the American System*, edited by Gilbert Y. Steiner, 13–29. Washington, D.C.: Brookings.

Fuchs, Lawrence H. 1956. *The Political Behavior of American Jews*. Glencoe, Ill.: Free Press.

Gallup, George, Jr., and Jim Castelli. 1987. *The American Catholic People*. Garden City, N.Y.: Doubleday.

Garrett, William R. 1973. "Politicized Clergy: A Sociological Interpretation of the 'New Breed'." *Journal for the Scientific Study of Religion* 12:383–397.

Gaustad, Edwin S. 1968. "America's Institution of Faith." In *Religion in America*, edited by William G. McLoughlin and Robert N. Bellah, 111–133. Boston: Beacon.

Gilboa, Eytan. 1987. *American Public Opinion Toward Israel and the Arab-Israeli Conflict*. Lexington, Mass.: D.C. Heath.

Gilkey, Langdon. 1968. "Social and Intellectual Sources of Contemporary Protestant Theology in America." In *Religion in America*, edited by William G. McLoughlin and Robert N. Bellah, 137–166. Boston: Beacon.

Granberg, Donald. 1981a. "The Abortion Activists." *Family Planning Perspectives* 13:157–163.

————. 1981b. "Comparison of Members of Pro- and Anti-Abortion Organizations in Missouri." *Social Biology* 28:239–252.

————. 1982a. "Comparison of Pro-Choice and Pro-Life Activists: Their Values, Attitudes, and Beliefs." *Population and Environment* 5:75–94.

————. 1982b. "Family Size Preferences and Sexual Permissiveness as Factors Differentiating Abortion Activists." *Social Psychology Quarterly* 45:15–23.

————. 1987. "The Abortion Issue in the 1984 Elections." *Family Planning Perspectives* 19:59–62.

Granberg, Donald, and James Burlison. 1983. "The Abortion Issue in the 1980 Elections." *Family Planning Perspectives* 15:231–238.

Granberg, Donald, and Beth Wellman Granberg. 1981. "Pro-Life Versus Pro-Choice: Another Look at the Abortion Controversy in the U.S." *Sociology and Social Research* 65:424–433.

Greeley, Andrew M. 1985. *American Catholics Since the Council: An Unauthorized Report*. Chicago: Thomas More.

Grupp, Frederick W., and William M. Newman. 1973. "Political Ideology and Religious Preference: The John Birch Society and the Americans for Democratic Action." *Journal for the Scientific Study of Religion* 12:401–413.

Guth, James L. 1989. "Pastoral Politics in the 1988 Election." Paper presented at the annual meeting of the American Political Science Association, Atlanta.

Hadden, Jeffrey. 1969. *Gathering Storm in the Churches*. Garden City, N.Y.: Doubleday Anchor.

Hadden, Jeffrey K., and Raymond C. Rymph. 1971. "The Marching Ministers." In *Religion in Radical Transition*, edited by Jeffrey K. Hadden, 99–110. New Brunswick, N.J.: Transaction.

Hadley, Charles D. 1987. "The Transformation of the Role of Black Ministers and Black Political Organizations in Louisiana Politics." In *Blacks in Southern Politics*, edited by Laurence W. Moreland, Robert P. Steed, and Tod A. Baker, 133–146. New York: Praeger.

Hall, Carla. 1985. "How a Philadelphia Preacher Won Converts to His Budget Gospel." *Washington Post Weekly Edition*, June 10, pp. 12–13.

Hamilton, Charles V. 1972. *The Black Preacher in America*. New York: William Morrow.

Hanna, Mary T. 1979. *Catholics and American Politics*. Cambridge: Harvard University Press.

————. 1985. "The Catholic Bishops' Pastoral Letter on Poverty." Paper delivered at the annual meeting of the American Political Science Association, New Orleans.

Harris, Frederick C. 1990. "Religion Among Blacks: A Political Mobilizer, Not 'Opiate'." Paper presented at the annual meeting of the Midwest Political Science Association, Chicago.

Harris, Louis, and Bert E. Swanson. 1970. *Black-Jewish Relations in New York City*. New York: Praeger.

Harris, Richard J., and Edward W. Mills. 1985. "Religion, Values and Attitudes to Abortion." *Journal for the Scientific Study of Religion* 24:137–154.

Hayes, Kathleen, and Ron Sider, eds. 1988. *JustLife / 88: A 1988 Election Study Guide for Justice, Life, and Peace*. Philadelphia: JustLife Education Fund and William B. Eerdmans.

Henshaw, Stanley K., and Jane Silverman. 1988. "The Characteristics and Previous

Contraceptive Use of U.S. Abortion Patients." *Family Planning Perspectives* 20:158–168.

Hertzke, Allen D. 1988. "Jackson, Robertson and the Politics of Community: Religious Mobilization and the 1988 Presidential Campaign." Paper presented at the annual meeting of the International Political Science Association, Washington, D.C.

———. 1989. "The Peace Pastoral: Context and Influence." Paper presented to the conference, "The Challenge of Peace: The Catholic Church in Public Debate," Catholic University of America, October 27–28, Washington, D.C.

Hofman, Brenda D. 1986. "Political Theology: The Role of Organized Religion in the Anti-Abortion Movement." *Journal of Church and State* 28:225–248.

Hofstadter, Richard. 1955. *The Age of Reform*. New York: Vintage.

———. 1965. *The Paranoid Style in American Politics*. New York: Vintage.

Hornblower, Margot. 1985. "Now a Suburb Grows in Brooklyn—And Without Federal Help." *Washington Post Weekly Edition*, July 29, pp. 31–32.

Hunt, Larry L., and Janet G. Hunt. 1977. "Black Religion as Both Opiate and Inspiration of Civil Rights Militance: Putting Marx's Data to the Test." *Social Forces* 56:1–14.

IEA and Roper Center. 1982. "Theology Faculty Survey." *This World* 1:27–108.

Jaffe, Frederick S., Barbara Lindheim, and Philip R. Lee, eds. 1981. *Abortion Politics: Private Morality and Public Policy*. New York: McGraw-Hill.

Jelen, Ted G. 1984. "Respect for Life, Sexual Morality, and Opposition to Abortion." *Review of Religious Research* 25:220–231.

Johnson, Stephen D. 1986. "The Role of the Black Church in Black Civil Rights Movements." In *The Political Role of Religion in the United States*, edited by Stephen D. Johnson and Joseph B. Tamney, 307–324. Boulder: Westview.

Johnson, Stephen D., and Joseph B. Tamney. 1988. "Factors Related to Inconsistent Life-Views." *Review of Religious Research* 30:40–46.

Kane, Joseph N. 1974. *Facts About the Presidents*. New York: H. H. Wilson.

Katznelson, Ira. 1976. *Black Men, White Cities*. Chicago: University of Chicago Press.

Kelley, Dean M. 1977. *Why Conservative Churches Are Growing*. Second edition. San Francisco: Harper and Row.

Kennedy, Eugene. 1985. *Reimagining American Catholicism*. New York: Vintage.

Kissling, Frances. 1985. "The Catholics Who Support Choice." *Washington Post Weekly Edition*, September 2, p. 28.

Kleppner, Paul. 1985. *Chicago Divided: The Making of a Black Mayor*. DeKalb, Ill.: Northern Illinois University Press.

Klineberg, Otto. 1950. *Tensions Affecting International Understanding: A Survey of Research*. New York: Social Science Research Council.

Koller, Norman B., and Joseph D. Retzer. 1980. "The Sounds of Silence Revisited." *Sociological Analysis* 41:155–161.

Lazerwitz, Bernard, J. Allen Winter, and Arnold Dashefsky. 1988. "Localism, Religiosity, Orthodoxy and Liberalism: The Case of Jews in the United States." *Social Forces* 67:229–242.

Leege, David C. 1987. "Catholics and the Civic Order: Parish Participation, Politics, and Civic Participation." Report no. 11, Notre Dame Study of Catholic Parish Life. Notre Dame, Ind.: University of Notre Dame.

Leege, David C., and Joseph Gremillion. 1986. "The People, Their Pastors, and the Church: Viewpoints on Church Policies and Positions." Report no. 7, Notre Dame Study of Catholic Parish Life. Notre Dame, Ind.: University of Notre Dame.

Legge, Jerome S. 1985. "Self-Interest Versus Symbolic Politics: The Formulation of Attitudes Toward Abortion Policy." Paper presented at the annual meeting of the Southern Political Science Association, Nashville, Tennessee.

Leon, Joseph J., and Patricia G. Steinhoff. 1975. "Catholics' Use of Abortion." *Sociological Analysis* 36:125–136.

Lerner, Robert, Althea K. Nagai, and Stanley Rothman. 1989. "Marginality and Liberalism Among Jewish Elites." *Public Opinion Quarterly* 53:330–352.

Liebman, Arthur. 1979. *Jews and the Left.* New York: Wiley Interscience.

Liebman, Charles S., and Steven M. Cohen. 1990. *Two Worlds of Judaism: The Israeli and American Experiences.* New Haven, Conn.: Yale University Press.

Lipset, Seymour Martin. 1964. "Three Decades of the Radical Right: Coughlinites, McCarthyites, and Birchers." In *The Radical Right,* edited by Daniel Bell, 373–446. Garden City, N.Y.: Doubleday Anchor.

———. 1985. "Most Jews Are Still Both Democratic and Liberal." *Washington Post Weekly Edition,* January 14, 22–23.

Lipstadt, Deborah, Charles Pruitt, and Jonathan Woocher. 1984. "What They Think: The 1984 American Jewish Young Leadership Survey." *Moment* 9:13–17.

Luker, Kristin. 1984. *Abortion and the Politics of Motherhood.* Berkeley and Los Angeles: University of California Press.

McMillan, Margaret. 1927. *The Life of Rachel McMillan.* London: J. M. Dent.

Madison, Christopher. 1984. "Mondale Walks Tightrope to Hold Black Support Without Risking Jewish Vote." *National Journal,* September 8, pp. 1654–1658.

Malbin, Michael. 1986. "Jewish PACs: A New Force in Jewish Political Action." *Jerusalem Newsletter,* no. 90.

Margolis, Michael, and Kevin Neary. 1980. "Pressure Politics Revisited: The Anti-Abortion Campaign." *Policy Studies Journal* 8:698–716.

Marshall, Susan E. 1990. "Equity Issues and Black-White Differences in Women's ERA Support." *Social Science Quarterly* 71:299–314.

Marx, Gary T. 1967. *Protest and Prejudice: A Study of Belief in the Black Community.* New York: Harper and Row.

Matthews, Donald R., and James W. Prothro. 1966. *Negroes and the New Southern Politics.* New York: Harcourt, Brace and World.

May, Henry F. 1963. *Protestant Churches and Industrial America.* New York: Octagon.

Meconis, Charles A. 1979. *With Clumsy Grace: The American Catholic Left, 1961–1975.* New York: Seabury.

Menendez, Albert J. 1977. *Religion at the Polls.* Philadelphia: Westminster.

Merton, Andrew H. 1981. *Enemies of Choice: The Right-to-Life Movement and Its Threat to Abortion.* Boston: Beacon.

Meyer, Donald B. 1961. *The Protestant Search for Political Realism, 1919–1941.* Berkeley and Los Angeles: University of California Press.

Mornion, Philip J., ed. 1983. *Catholics and Nuclear War.* New York: Crossroads.

Morris, Aldon. 1984. *The Origins of the Civil Rights Movement.* New York: Free Press.

———. 1981. "Black Southern Student Sit-In Movement: An Analysis of Internal Organization." *American Sociological Review* 46:744–767.

Mueller, John E. 1973. *Wars, Presidents, and Public Opinion*. New York: Free Press.

Nelsen, Hart M. 1975. "Why Do Pastors Preach on Social Issues?" *Theology Today* 32:56–73.

Nelsen, Hart M., Thomas Madron, and Raytha L. Yokley. 1975. "Black Religion's Promethean Motif: Orthodoxy and Militancy." *American Journal of Sociology* 81: 139–148.

Nelsen, Hart M., Raytha L. Yokley, and Thomas W. Madron. 1973. "Ministerial Roles and Social Actionist Stance: Protestant Clergy and Protest in the Sixties." *American Sociological Review* 38:375–386.

Novak, Michael. 1984. "The Bishops and the Poor." *Washington Post Weekly Edition*, November 26, p. 29.

O'Brien, David J. 1968. *American Catholics and Social Reform: The New Deal Years*. New York: Oxford University Press.

Ortiz, Isidro. 1984. "Chicano Urban Politics and the Politics of Reform in the Seventies." *Western Political Quarterly* 37:564–577.

Paige, Connie. 1983. *The Right to Lifers*. New York: Summit.

Paris, Peter J. 1978. *Black Leaders in Conflict*. New York: Pilgrim.

Penn, Mark J., and Douglas E. Schoen. 1988. "Prospects for the Jewish Vote in 1988." *Election Politics* 5:24–26.

Penning, James. 1986. "Changing Partisanship and Issue Stands Among American Catholics." *Sociological Analysis* 47:29–49.

Piehl, Mel. 1982. *Breaking Bread: The Catholic Worker and the Origin of Catholic Radicalism in America*. Philadelphia: Temple University Press.

Pratt, Henry J. 1972. *The Liberalization of American Protestantism*. Detroit: Wayne State University Press.

Quinley, Harold E. 1974. *The Prophetic Clergy: Social Activism Among Protestant Ministers*. New York: Wiley Interscience.

Rainey, Jane G. 1985. "Religious Involvement in the Pro-Choice Movement: Challenging Some Stereotypes of the Abortion Debate." Paper delivered at the annual meeting of the American Political Science Association, New Orleans.

Reagan, Ronald. 1984. *Abortion and the Conscience of the Nation*. Nashville, Tenn.: Thomas Nelson.

Roof, Wade Clark. 1978. *Community and Commitment: Religious Plausibility in a Liberal Protestant Church*. New York: Elsevier.

Salamon, Lester M. 1973. "Leadership and Modernization: The Emerging Black Political Elite in the American South." *Journal of Politics* 35:615–646.

Sawyer, Darwin O. 1982. "Public Attitudes Toward Life and Death." *Public Opinion Quarterly* 46:521–533.

Schneider, William. 1985. "The Jewish Vote in 1984: Elements in a Controversy." *Public Opinion* 7:18–19, 58.

Secret, Philip E., James B. Johnson, and Susan Welch. 1986. "Racial Differences in Attitudes Toward the Supreme Court's Decision on Prayer in the Public Schools." *Social Science Quarterly* 67:877–886.

Seltzer, Richard, and Robert C. Smith. 1985. "Race and Ideology: A Research Note Measuring Liberalism and Conservatism in Black America." *Phylon* 46:98–105.

Simon Wiesenthal Center. 1986. "The Farrakhan Phenomenon." *Response* 13: 2–3.

Singer, David. 1987. *American Jews as Voters: The 1986 Elections.* New York: American Jewish Committee.

Sklare, Marshall, and Joseph Greenblum. 1967. *Jewish Identity on the Suburban Frontier.* New York: Basic.

Smith, Robert C. 1981. "The Black Congressional Delegation." *Western Political Quarterly* 34:203–221.

Stark, Rodney, Bruce D. Foster, Charles Y. Glock, and Harold E. Quinley. 1971. *Wayward Shepherds.* New York: Harper and Row.

Starr, Jerrold. 1975. "Religious Preference, Religiosity, and Opposition to War." *Sociological Analysis* 36:323–334.

Surrey, David S. 1982. *Choice of Conscience: Vietnam Era Military and Draft Resisters in Canada.* New York: Praeger.

Sussman, Barry. 1986. "Jews Voted Strongly Democratic." *Washington Post Weekly Edition,* November 24, p. 37.

Tamney, Joseph B., Ronald Burton, and Stephen Johnson. 1988. "Christianity, Social Class, and the Catholic Bishops' Economic Policy." *Sociological Analysis* 49:78–96.

Tamney, Joseph B., and Stephen D. Johnson. 1985. "Christianity and the Nuclear Issue." *Sociological Analysis* 46:321–328.

Traugott, Michael W., and Maris A. Vinovskis. 1980. "Abortion and the 1978 Congressional Elections." *Family Planning Perspectives* 12:238–246.

Tygart, Clarence E. 1977. "The Role of Theology Among Other 'Belief' Variables for Clergy Civil Rights Activism." *Review of Religious Research* 18:271–278.

Vinovskis, Maris A. 1979. "Abortion and the Presidential Election of 1976: A Multivariate Analysis of Voting Behavior." *Michigan Law Review* 7:1750–1771.

Wagenaar, Theodore C., and Patricia E. Bartos. 1977. "Orthodoxy and Attitudes of Clergymen Towards Homosexuality and Abortion." *Review of Religious Research* 18:114–125.

Wald, Kenneth D. 1989. "From the Word of God to the Voice of God: The Impact of the Peace Pastoral on Public Opinion." Paper presented at the conference, "The Challenge of Peace: The Catholic Church in Public Debate," Catholic University of America, October 27–28, Washington, D.C.

———. "Ministering to the Nation: The Campaigns of Jesse Jackson and Pat Robertson." In *Nominating the President 1988,* edited by Emmett H. Buell and Lee S. Sigelman. Knoxville, Tenn.: University of Tennessee Press, forthcoming.

Walton, Hanes, Jr. 1985. *Invisible Politics: Black Political Behavior.* Albany: State University of New York Press.

Weber, Paul J., and John L. Anderson. 1985. "The Impact of the Bishops' Pastoral on the Primary and Secondary Media." Paper delivered at the annual meeting of the American Political Science Association, New Orleans.

Welch, Michael R., Lyman A. Kellstedt, David C. Leege, and Kenneth D. Wald. 1990. "Are the Sheep Hearing the Shepherds? Pastoral Cues, Congregational Responses and Political Communication Processes." Paper delivered at the annual meeting of the American Political Science Association, San Francisco.

Wilcox, Clyde. 1990a. "Race, Religion, Region and Abortion Attitudes." *Sociological Analysis,* forthcoming.

————. 1990b. "Religious Sources of Politicization Among Blacks in Washington, D.C." *Journal for the Scientific Study of Religion,* forthcoming.

Wilcox, Clyde, and Leopoldo Gomez. 1990. "Religion, Group Identification and Politics Among American Blacks." *Sociological Analysis* 51 (Fall 1990): 271–285.

Wilson, James Q. 1965. *Negro Politics: The Search for Leadership.* New York: Free Press.

Wolf, Donald J., S.J. 1968. *Toward Consensus: Catholic-Protestant Interpretations of Church and State.* Garden City, N.Y.: Doubleday Anchor.

Wood, James R. 1981. *Leadership in Voluntary Organizations: The Controversy Over Social Action in Protestant Churches.* New Brunswick, N.J.: Rutgers University Press.

Woodrum, Eric, and Arnold Bell. 1989. "Race, Politics, and Religion in Civil Religion Among Blacks." *Sociological Analysis* 4:353–367.

9. Religion and American Political Life

The challenge of practical politics is to combine the passion of religion with the civil tolerance of democratic pluralism.

—Clarke E. Cochran, *Religion in Public and Private Life*

Viewed against the backdrop of history, the recent rise in political activism among some religious groups is not a departure from national tradition but only the renewal of a long-standing pattern in American political life. As previous chapters have documented, religion—in the guise of sacred values, institutions, and social groups—has operated at several levels of politics. Religion was present at the creation of the American political system, and was one of several elements contributing to the design of governmental institutions and to the core of beliefs that grew into the national political culture. The place of religion in a pluralistic society has generated a seemingly endless supply of legal disputes about the proper relationship between church and state. Religious affiliation has long been a potent influence on mass partisan loyalties and has been a factor inspiring the positions taken by political elites on a wide range of pressing national issues. If the past few years are any indication, religion has retained a potency that will keep it among the social forces likely to fuel political conflict.

What may not be clear are the political and social consequences that result from the interaction between the spheres of religion and politics. By referring to "consequences," I do *not* mean either the impact of political activism on religion nor the effect of religious intervention on the disposition of particular policies. Both are legitimate issues that have been examined elsewhere in the book. Rather, this chapter's theme is the effect of religious activism on the general tenor of political life in the United States. Specifically, I will assess the benefits and costs to democracy and the functioning of the political system of the religious presence in public life. My conclusion, that religion in politics is neither an unvarying source of good nor a consistent evil influence, is unlikely to please either the most ardent advocates of a "Christian America" or secularists who want to keep religion safely outside the public arena. It is consistent, however, with the historical record, which has shown that religion has the capacity both to ennoble and to corrupt political life.

The Case Against Religious Influence in Politics

Even if they were to lower their profile, religious groups would still be important actors in American political life. Does this reality bode good or evil for the future of politics in the United States? The question is not merely academic, for although certain forms of religious influence cannot be controlled, the government has some limited power to encourage or discourage organized political involvement by the churches (Kelley 1982, 64–83, 111–128, 151–164). To cite one important example, the tax-free status of churches is conditional on their refraining from endorsing candidates or devoting more than a certain percentage of resources to lobbying and political action. Currently interpreted to give churches substantial leeway for public involvement, the laws could be tightened to make it more difficult for clergy to engage in political action or to use their congregations as a base for movements with public goals.[1] Considering the strong public sentiment for keeping the churches "out of politics," such a restrictive policy might enjoy broad support. That makes it even more important to assess the pros and cons of active political involvement by churches and religiously inspired activists.

The rise of religious activism in politics has been a source of concern and apprehension to many observers, including those who are sympathetic to religion as an institution (see, for example, Maguire 1982). At the heart of that concern lies the fear that religious controversy in politics will lead to extremism and polarization, infecting the body politic with unhealthy doses of fanaticism and ill will. Carried to extremes, critics have contended, the entry of religious issues into the public agenda may produce violence, undermining the very foundations of democratic politics.

Why should religion have such dire consequences for the stability of government? Many commentators have insisted that democratic government depends on a willingness to negotiate, to bargain, to approach politics in the spirit of compromise. Some issues naturally lend themselves to this type of treatment. Conflicts over money—demands for pay raises, proposals to increase taxes, competition for federal funding— are inherently subject to bargaining, because financial benefits are divisible in terms of dollars. Economic conflicts can usually be managed within the framework of a stable political system. But when conflicts take on an either/or dimension, the impediments to compromise can prompt antagonists to subvert the political system by resorting to armed violence. On one occasion in American history when such an all-or-nothing issue—slavery—dominated the national agenda, the result was a complete breakdown of the political system and a bloody civil war.

Like slavery, religious issues may challenge the normal system of governance. Policy debates with such a moral dimension do not readily lend themselves to compromise solutions. If you regard abortion as murder and I see it as a neutral medical procedure, it will be hard to find a middle ground that either one of us will accept as a legitimate public policy. Revealing precisely that type of unyielding outlook, a Louisiana state representative recently described the legislative conflict over abortion in his state as just the latest episode of an eternal battle between good and evil. Perhaps that attitude explains why bombing attacks against abortion clinics are concentrated in states where opponents of abortion have failed to restrict the practice (Nice 1988). The same kind of problem arises in the context of debates over prayer in public schools, the rights of homosexuals, traditional sex roles, and other policy areas in which religious groups have been active. Without realistic hope for a compromise solution that is minimally acceptable to all sides, such issues are likely to fester and breed support for extremist action.

A related problem raised by critics of church activism involves the potential impact of religious values on the *style* of political activists. As religious issues do not easily admit to compromise solutions, so, too, religious values may produce rigidity, dogmatism, authoritarianism, and contempt for alternative points of view. Such destructive traits, far from being accidental, may actually be the normal consequence of religious commitment (Liebman 1988, chap. 3). One aspect of religious faith that encourages extremism, its claim to possess the truth, inspires believers with unshakable confidence in the rightness and inevitability of their efforts. Religion also provides standards of truth and justice; believers may push relentlessly to bring all of society under these ideals.

Finally, because "religious adherence becomes a criteria
people can be evaluated" (ibid., 40), people of stron
respect the motives and values of their political oppor

Carried to extremes, these qualities can poison the
sphere and endanger social stability. A person who believes tha.
she is acting under God's direct command may be prone to regard compromise as a betrayal of divine intention. Activists who believe that God
is on their side are likely to perceive their opponents as not merely mis-
guided or confused but as evil and malevolent. Once political opponents
are denuded of their human qualities and transformed into symbols of
iniquity, conduct toward them may turn barbarous. In this connection,
one wonders what political lessons the students at a Christian school
in Florida must have drawn when their principal burned the Soviet flag
at a school assembly.

This apprehension about the potentially destabilizing effects of religious values on political conflict has been reinforced by the experience
of other countries. Sadly, the world does not lack examples of inquisi-
tions, crusades, and massacres resulting from the fusion of religious passion with secular authority. In the contemporary era, there have been
troubling reports from Iran about the pathetic eagerness of children to
offer themselves up as virtual human sacrifices in a "holy war" for Islam
(Hansen 1984). The political consequences of religiously oriented politics is also evident in the carnage of Northern Ireland, Lebanon, India,
and other trouble spots around the globe. Closer to home, there has
been the appalling example of mass suicide in Jonestown and the disturbing reports about the rise of "Christian" paramilitary cults in the
depressed farmbelt country.[2] From time to time—but always too
often—we read newspaper accounts about churches or congregations
that evolve into totalitarian cults, practicing horror in the name of God,
and undermining social harmony.

On a less dramatic level, a systematic study of seventeen Western nations with strong electoral traditions confirmed the dangers of a strong
religious presence in party politics (Rose and Urwin 1969). In approximately half the countries, the principal line of electoral conflict was
defined by religious affiliation or practice; the remaining nine nations
lacked a strong religious dimension to party competition. According to
Rose and Urwin, the countries with the strongest religious divisions had
experienced much more strain, violence, and political instability than

ad the nations whose politics were largely free of religious controversy. In some cases, religious conflict in the former group had even contributed to the collapse of governmental systems and the emergence of antidemocratic politics. The correlation between the strength of "ethnocultural" cleavages and political instability appears to have persisted to the present day (Powell 1982, 44–47).

Do these findings necessarily apply to the United States? Does the entry of religious groups in the political arena threaten the stability of the political system? Reasonable people can disagree over the answer to this question, but there can be no denying that some of the symptoms attributed to religiously based politics have appeared in American life. To demonstrate the basis for that conclusion and to show how the problem is not restricted to any one side of the religious spectrum, I offer accounts of two experiences that helped bring me to an awareness of the possible costs of recent trends in religious-political interaction.

In the summer of 1980, while supervising the work of two student interns at the Republican National Convention in Detroit, I happened to encounter a Texas delegate in a hotel lobby. Stopping and pointing to the large pro-ERA button on my lapel, she challenged me to justify my support for an amendment that, she declared, would undoubtedly lead to incest. Astonished by the question, I asked her how the constitutional amendment could possibly encourage incest. Instead of answering, she looked me coldly in the eye, scowled and asked if I was a Christian. When I answered no, she announced loudly that there was no point in talking any further, pointedly turned her back on me, and strode away angrily—as if escaping a leper.

About five years later, I was attending a national conference of political scientists in Chicago when I fell into conversation with a distinguished colleague from another university. In the course of discussing my work on this book, I tried to make a case for some of the positive consequences of religious involvement in American political life. For every example of an ignoble or repressive movement that she brought up, I countered with an example that I thought illustrated religion at its best. As I was defending Moral Majority from a charge of bigotry, she suddenly exploded with the ferocious declaration, "I *hate* religion and politics!" After an awkward pause, the conversation moved to another, safer, topic.

What these two anecdotes convey, aside from my own puzzling abil-

ity to provoke outbursts in otherwise calm people, is the degree of passion that religion can inspire in political life. It does not bode well for
political discourse when a political activist declares publicly that there
is no point in discussing a policy issue with an interested onlooker. And
literally to turn one's back on another person, as the Texas delegate did
to me, is the first step in a process that can lead to treating a fellow
human being as a mortal enemy. Similarly, two professional political
scientists ought to be able to discuss a recent development in national
life without one of them expressing hatred for the argument of another.
In both cases, the strength of convictions about matters of deep personal
concern destroyed calm and reasoned debate. Though neither the Texas
delegate nor the political scientist would be likely to throw bombs, their
actions gave me a glimpse of the thought process that might lead to the
kind of behavior that disfigures countries such as Lebanon and Northern
Ireland. As no academic research ever could, they brought home to me
the danger of public conflicts about matters of conscience and moral
outlook.

Even though it lacks the dramatic impact of a personal encounter,
academic research can offer guidance on the question of whether such
experiences are typical. Aside from anecdote, is there persuasive evidence that strong religious convictions (of whatever kind) promote rigidity and dogmatism, the elements of an antidemocratic outlook? Many
social scientists have interpreted the weight of evidence to support a link
between the intensity of religious belief and various indicators of an
antidemocratic orientation. That conclusion has been based on comparison of the expressed political and social attitudes of people with
different reported levels of exposure to religious influence.

The link between religious attachment and political intolerance was
supported by one of the first major academic surveys of American attitudes toward civil liberties (Stouffer 1966). Using a format that would
be widely imitated in subsequent research, the investigator gauged tolerance in 1954 by asking members of a national sample if they would
support various forms of freedom for unpopular groups—Socialists,
Communists, and atheists. The results indicated that general attachment to religion was associated with low levels of support for basic civil
liberties. Specifically, a high level of tolerance characterized 28 percent
of respondents who had attended church in the month before the survey
but a substantially higher 36 percent of the people who were not

churchgoers (ibid., 142). The difference held up with controls for social factors related to religion that might independently reduce political tolerance. Stouffer also discovered that some kinds of religion were less conducive to tolerance than others (ibid., 143–144). At one extreme, only 21 percent of Southern Protestants fell into the "most tolerant" category whereas 73 percent of Jewish respondents were so classified. Northern Catholics and Protestants, who scored about the same on the tolerance scale, held a position midway between the extremes.

In the three decades since Stouffer's findings were first published, they have been repeatedly confirmed by other researchers. The General Social Survey has included questions about the willingness to extend civil liberties to five relatively unpopular groups: advocates of racism, communism, atheism, militarism, and homosexuality. Religious group differences during the 1980s produced essentially the same patterns observed in 1954 (see Figure 4.7). The nonaffiliated were substantially more likely than persons attached to religion to score high on a scale of support for civil liberties. Among religious groups, the same ordering reported by Stouffer was in evidence: low tolerance among evangelical Protestants (black and white alike), intermediate support for civil liberties by Catholics and mainline Protestants, the highest commitment to democratic norms among Jews. These findings have also been extended to other antidemocratic orientations. Thus, researchers have found that hostility to blacks, Jews, and other minority groups has most often been expressed by adherents of theologically conservative churches and has been least common in persons outside the churches.

In some cases, religiously based intolerance goes beyond attitudes into behavior. A recent survey of attempts to censor instructional material in Florida found fundamentalists active in these efforts and most complaints, whatever the source, echoed the rhetoric heard in New Christian Right circles (Scheurer 1990). An even more ominous symbol of religiously based political intolerance, the "Christian Reconstructionist" movement, has exerted some influence on leaders of the New Christian Right. Leaders of this fringe movement propose a radical reconstruction of American society on the basis of their reading of Old Testament law (Clapp 1987). The blueprint includes severe punishment for assorted "deviants"—"homosexuals, incorrigible children, adulterers, blasphemers, astrologers" as well as Sabbath breakers and practitioners of witchcraft—the reimposition of slavery, and the abolition of democracy. The assurances by activists that these changes will be introduced by popular consensus hardly makes reconstructionism a democratic movement.

The initial explanations for the intolerance of fundamentalism concentrated on the social or organizational components of traditional religion. Stouffer attributed the connection to the religiously threatening nature of nonconformity, that is, the direct challenge that atheism and communism posed to religious belief. Advocates of the social explanation linked intolerance to the limited education, social isolation, and parochial life-styles of fundamentalist churchgoers. Both explanations suggest that intolerance is not inherent in religion but largely a product of circumstances. If religious traditionalists did not feel directly threatened by political dissenters or broadened their perspectives through modernization, they would show more tolerance for views and groups outside the mainstream.

Less comforting is another possibility we have already entertained—that intolerance might be built into religious commitment. Amid mounting empirical evidence connecting particular types of religious attachment with antidemocratic orientations, researchers began to look for explanations of the relationship in the creedal aspects of religion—either what people believed or the manner in which they believed it. Milton Rokeach (1971) called attention to the mixed nature of religious messages—their dual emphasis on the oneness of humankind and the rigid separation between true believers and heathen. He argued that the latter tendency frequently overwhelmed the benevolent impulse at the root of religious traditions. Other investigators, influenced by Rokeach's work on styles of thinking, hypothesized that conventional religion attracted people who could not accept doubt, ambiguity, or challenges to their belief systems, and who were prone to reject people who did not share their attitudes or outlooks (Budner 1962, 38–40; Raschke 1973). Finding that the intolerance of fundamentalists and pentecostals could not be explained wholly by low socioeconomic standing, hostility to specific groups, or the strength of religious commitment, Wilcox and Jelen (1990) attributed narrow-mindedness primarily to doctrine. Persuaded they already have the truth, true believers see nothing valuable about hearing dissenting views. Wald, Owen, and Hill (1989) found that supporters of the New Christian Right were rooted in environments emphasizing obedience and attaching considerable ideological value to maintaining authority. This tendency to ascribe intolerance to the very nature of religious commitment can be captured in the conclusion of an influential study by Nunn and his colleagues (1978, 140): "Traditional Christians, who participate actively in their churches and who find themselves with limited resources to comprehend and affect the larger world, closely link God and political authority and are also likely to see political nonconformity as the work of the Devil."

Assessing the Evidence

These results paint a disturbing portrait of the capacity for democratic thinking and action among deeply religious people and lead to concern about the implications of their increasing involvement in political life. Dogmatism, close-mindedness, and intolerance are not traits that promote civility or the free exchange of ideas. If such traits are pronounced among religious activists and their opponents, there is a solid basis for concern about the increasing politicization of religious issues. In my view, however, the evidence supporting a link between religiosity and the propensity to intolerance is not strong enough to warrant alarm.

In the first place, studies on the relationship between religious commitment and various forms of antidemocratic orientations have not uniformly pointed to a strong connection. In his careful review of relevant research published during the 1960s, Wuthnow (1973, 122) found that religious commitment was positively related to social conservatism in only about one-half of the reported analyses; more commonly, the variables were unrelated or negatively associated.[3] Wuthnow further demonstrated substantial methodological deficiencies in many of the studies that contributed to the conventional wisdom. Typical weaknesses included a lack of appropriate controls for external influences, the use of unrepresentative samples, and reliance on overly simple measures of complex political and religious orientations. An additional flaw has recently been noted in studies that have purported to measure the impact of religious affiliation on political tolerance. Even though they have claimed to measure general orientations toward civil liberties, most studies have commonly asked respondents about their willingness to extend constitutional rights to left-wing groups or other organizations perceived as especially threatening to Christian values. When the target groups have included those that threaten the values of liberal religious groups, the interdenominational differences in tolerance narrow appreciably even if they do not disappear altogether (Sullivan, Piereson, and Marcus 1982, 137–139; Beatty and Walter 1984, 322–327). Even with such elaborations, however, persons outside the churches seem substantially more tolerant of opposing viewpoints than church members (Smidt and Penning 1982).

A second problem has been the reliance of all such studies on attitudes rather than on behavior. People do not always act consistently with their expressed beliefs. The crisis that enveloped the American Civil Liberties Union (ACLU) over the Skokie case in 1977 showed that the attitude-behavior gap can be especially large in the realm of civil liberties. In Skokie, a Chicago suburb with a high concentration of Jewish refugees from the Nazi Holocaust, local authorities tried to block a planned march by members of a Nazi organization. When the ACLU provided support for the Nazis' legal challenge to the Skokie ordinance—an action for which there was ample precedent in its history—the organization lost thousands of members and a vital proportion of financial resources. Even for supporters of an organization whose sole purpose was the defense of civil liberties, it was easier to express tolerance in the abstract than in practice (Gibson and Anderson 1985). The higher levels of tolerance expressed by the nonreligious might erode under similar pressure—as, indeed, religious activists have charged.[4]

Moreover, those who have viewed religious commitment as a source of antidemocratic sentiment have not always distinguished among different types of commitment. Most studies have simply examined the attitude differences between church members and nonaffiliates, or between different denominations, or, in a few cases, between churchgoers of varying frequency. These are poor approximations of what might well turn out to be the real source of variation in the linkage between religious commitment and tolerance—differences in the manner in which people absorb religious values. In a pioneering survey of democratic attitudes in the United States, researchers from the University of California stressed that people hold their religious values in different ways (Adorno et al. 1950, chap. 18). For example, some attend church only out of a sense of duty to parental expectations or because it conforms to social practice in their community. They find in religion support for their way of life and sanctification of the social order—but nothing of a prophetic vision that might challenge them to change their behavior or act more sensitively to others. What is missing from such conventional or nominal religiosity is deeply rooted acceptance of the nobler values associated with major religious traditions—love, charity, compassion, and forgiveness. Some adherents do not hear these messages either because they are not physically present often enough or, more likely, because they do not try to listen to what is being said or implied. But other persons who take religion seriously—meaning that they embrace the ethical messages transmitted by a religious tradition—internalize that tradition and assign the highest priority to acting righteously. Before condemning individuals for falling short of biblical standards, they are likely to recall the admonition to hate the sin but love the sinner. Hence, the authors predicted:

The more "human" and concrete a person's relation to religion, the more human his approach to those who "do not belong" is likely to be: their sufferings remind the religious subjectivist of the idea of martyrdom inseparably bound up with his thinking about Christ. (Adorno et al. 1950, 731)

In a moving illustration of precisely that style of deep commitment, the psychiatrist Robert Coles (1985) reported about six-year-old Ruby. The first black child to integrate a New Orleans school in 1960, she had to march every day past a howling and vicious mob threatening her life:

As she walked by the mob, sometimes a hundred or so strong, protected by federal marshals on her way to a sadly deserted classroom, she said, "Please, dear God, forgive those folks, because they don't know what they're doing." She'd heard in Sunday school that Jesus had once reached out similarly and she was trying to follow suit.

That type of religious commitment—which is precisely what is meant by "taking religion seriously"—could very likely militate against the arrogance that threatens democratic interchange.

This argument about a link between "genuine" religious commitment and thoughtful, reasoned behavior has attracted some research support. Gordon Allport (1958, 421–422) reported an intriguing study in which standard prejudice scales were administered to Catholic and Baptist laymen. The process of selecting respondents was designed to produce persons who exhibited diverse styles of religiosity—commitment to the essence of the faith versus commitment for social or professional reasons. These different styles of commitment were labeled, respectively, as "intrinsic" and "extrinsic" orientations to religion. The Catholic participants were selected by a knowledgeable parishioner who was asked to recommend some church members who were deeply influenced by faith and others who participated for secular advantages. In an attempt to match this distinction between "devout" and "institutional" church members, the Protestant participants were recruited from regular and irregular attenders at Bible class. In both cases, "the most devout, more personally absorbed in the religion, were far less prejudiced than the others."

The negative association between "intrinsic" religious commitment and prejudice has been found to hold in larger and more systematic studies (Gorsuch and Aleshire 1974; Studlar 1978; Wilson and Bagley 1973). The findings point to a curvilinear pattern: broad-mindedness is endorsed by people on the extremes of religious commitment—those outside the churches and those most deeply involved in religious groups—and the association between religion and various forms of prejudice is manifested by people who are only moderately involved with churches.[5] Recent work by H. Wesley Perkins (1983, 1985) has further rehabilitated strong religious commitment by linking it empirically to social compassion and concern for inequality, as well as to lower levels of racial prejudice. There is further support for this approach in recent work by C. Daniel Batson. Batson refined Allport's "intrinsic" category by introducing a third form of religious commitment, the "quest" dimension. In this "mature" form of religiosity, faith encourages believers to accept complexity, criticize and doubt their own motivations, and keep an open mind as they search for truth. This third style of attachment is designed to distinguish between intrinsics whose commitment to orthodoxy makes them intolerant and highly committed persons who do not demand from their faith "black and white" answers to all of life's dilemmas. Persons with high scores on the "quest" scale turn out to be less prejudiced (Batson et al. 1986) and to employ more sophisticated standards of moral judgment (Sapp and Jones 1986).

Hence, it seems reasonable to maintain that religion versus irreligion is not the crucial dimension underlying political attitudes but that religious people differ politically based on the nature and motivation of their religiosity. Specifically, some forms of religious commitment, far from threatening democracy, may reinforce constructive tendencies in public life. Unfortunately, I have not yet found any studies that examine directly the relationship between political tolerance and styles of religious commitment. In the closest such research project, support for unquestioning loyalty to the president was positively related to religious orthodoxy, high levels of ritual involvement, and strong belief in God but was negatively associated with the incidence of private prayer (Schoenfeld 1985). The author interpreted his findings in a manner consistent with the hypothesis suggested here, finding the more "priestly" aspects of religion conducive to support for political authority, but the spontaneous, unstructured, and unmediated act of prayer imparting a healthy sense of skepticism about public officials. Until more direct studies become available, it will remain arguable that intense religious commitment—measured in qualitative rather than quantitative terms—actually promotes healthy democratic orientations.

Finally, I am comforted by the belief that political participation may actually teach religious activists to moderate their style and tame their expectations. There is fairly consistent evidence that political activists are more tolerant than nonparticipants.[6] Although it has not yet been shown that political participation actually *causes* more tolerant outlooks, a logical case can be made for such a relationship. From the perspective of social learning theory, political participation should bring the individual into contact with others who value the opportunity to influence policy through democratic means. This experience might enhance the individual's respect for a system that facilitates such opportunities. The only evidence relevant to the argument has been provided by Guth and Green's (1984) mail survey of financial contributors to various party and ideological political action committees (PACs). Contributors to religiously oriented PACs and antiabortion electoral efforts were not less tolerant than the sample as a whole or than some mainstream groups. In fact, the (admittedly) small number of "religiously" conservative activists were more supportive of political liberties than were many "secular" conservative givers—contributors to antitax, gun ownership, libertarian, and Republican causes. Though far from proving the assertion about the moderating influence of political involvement, such fragmentary findings give hope that religious extremists will learn the rules of the game as a consequence of participation in conventional political action.

For all these reasons, some observers have retreated from earlier predictions about the baleful effect of religious activism on the political system. Of course, people tend to find what they are looking for, so I want to point with caution at some signs that the American political system can indeed accommodate religiously inspired campaigns for candidates or issues. The essence of the argument is that while such issues may strain the system by making compromise difficult and attracting the attention of persons with passionate commitments, the system can cope with this situation. To some extent, such activity may even enhance the vitality of political life.

The abortion issue provides perhaps the best illustration of how the political system adapts to the pressure applied by deeply committed activists. Advocates on both sides of the issue will usually admit that the rhetoric used to advance the cause does not elevate the tone of political discourse. The debate has often been conducted in harsh and uncompromising language in which phrases such as "baby killer" and "Nazi" are used in place of thought. Such a style of argument is more likely to open wounds than to persuade. In Congress, too, the opposing sides have sometimes used their power to deny free expression to the "enemy." When the prochoice wing was ascendant in the Senate, proposed constitutional amendments did not receive the amount of floor debate they warranted; later, the prolife wing used its majority status to support some dubious assaults on congressional procedures. The issue has also intruded on governmental decision making in areas that appear to be far removed from any substantive relationship to abortion. The fear about abortion's disruptive potential has certainly been intensified by the alarming outbreaks of violence on the fringes of the antiabortion movement. Taken together, those trends have persuaded some observers, such as former senator Barry Goldwater, that the abortion debate might threaten "the perpetuation of our form of government."

Despite such fears, careful study suggests that most of the abortion-related activity has stayed well within the bounds of democratic norms (Steiner 1983). Despite the excesses alluded to, most leaders have seemed committed to defusing the issue, channeling it in ways that do not threaten the political process. Without abandoning their beliefs, some staunch supporters of abortion restriction have nevertheless forgone the use of certain weapons out of a concern for the larger health of the political system. Senator Mark Hatfield, the chair of the Senate Appropriations Committee, has resisted attempts to attach antiabortion bills to appropriations legislation, and Senator Jake Garn, a leader of the antiabortion movement in Congress, resigned from the advisory board of a prolife political action committee because of its decision to target several incumbents for defeat solely because they voted against restrictive policies on abortion. In both cases, techniques that might have advanced the cause were rejected because their use seemed to undermine procedural norms that contributed to effective governance. The prochoice coalition has also demonstrated concern for the maintenance of accepted procedure by approving several prolife nominees for federal jobs.

It is noteworthy that despite its bitterly divisive nature, the abortion issue has engendered a willingness to compromise. The advocates of restriction by constitutional amendment have seemingly withdrawn from a position of favoring only an absolute prohibition on abortion to one that would permit abortion under certain conditions. Supporters of liberalized policies might not appreciate the magnitude of these compromises nor their divisive impact on prolife activists, but they do in fact constitute a significant revision of earlier positions, indicating the willingness of antiabortion forces to adapt to political realities.

The search for compromise is also apparent in the courts and the legislative branch. Ever since *Roe v. Wade*, the Supreme Court has steered a middle course by rejecting the extreme options of allowing abortion on demand or returning to the pre-1973 situation. Instead, the Court has granted its approval to some limitations on access to abortion while continuing to uphold the principle of abortion as a constitutionally protected right of privacy. Similarly, Congress has moved the issue to the familiar terrain of the budgetary process, debating whether federal funds should be used to pay for abortion. This conflict follows a well-established precedent of using control over appropriations as a means for settling policy debates. In both the legislative and judicial arenas, the debate has focused on bargainable questions of implementation of the law.

To go one step further, it can be argued that the abortion debate has actually invigorated public life in the United States. This argument challenges the standards of democracy used by critics of religiously inspired political activism. Those who have criticized the place of such passionate issues on the public agenda sometimes have argued from a conception of democracy that treats mass involvement in policy making as suspect or potentially dangerous to governmental stability. Critics of mass participation point to the outbreak of violence associated with religious controversies in such diverse societies as India, Lebanon, and Northern Ireland. Based on such examples, some commentators contend that high-energy issues like abortion may promote an excess of public excitement and involvement, leading to a surge of high hopes followed by disillusionment when the system yields an ambiguous compromise. Rather than treating active citizen participation as a requirement of the democratic process, these "revisionist" democrats have tended to approach it as a threat to the stability of democratic governance. Correspondingly, far from deploring apathy and limited citizen action, they see them as useful for diminishing the intensity of political conflict. Without the oversight of intense activists, they argue, political elites should have the opportunity to forge policy in a more orderly and manageable atmosphere.

But this particular view of democracy is not the only conceivable model available from the history of political thought. Another view defines the continuous and active involvement of the people in public decision making as the key characteristic of a democratic system (Pateman 1970; Tesh 1984). In this view, issues like abortion enhance democracy by forcing ordinary men and women to take a stand on issues of public significance and by encouraging them to act on their beliefs in the public realm. In the process of advocacy, mobilization, and negotiation, citizens learn the skills necessary to maintain a democratic political system. If it is possible that mass involvement will disturb existing arrangements, it should also strengthen belief in principles that support a democratic political system. The rise of the abortion issue challenges not democracy per se, but rather a particular conception of democracy that keeps important issues off the agenda, or limits their focus, or leaves decision making to political elites. Groups motivated by passionate conviction on issues like abortion "try to politicize that which had been private, to broaden that which had been narrow, and to bring ordinary citizens into that which had been the province of professionals" (Tesh 1984, 44). That may not be orderly—but perhaps orderliness is not an appropriate standard for democratic politics.

The Case for Religion in Politics

In the last section, I evaluated the case against religious activism in politics and found it wanting. Though the rise of religiously based political issues may present challenges to the capacity of a democratic political system, the American political process seems adequate to the task. Now it is time to consider the positive claims for religion in politics.

Earlier in this book, I reported the belief of some scholars that religion contributed to the development of democratic values and the acceptance of democratic practices in the United States.[7] Some observers have gone well beyond that statement, debatable as it is, to make an even larger claim for religion. They argue that religion is an *essential* support for a democratic political orientation and warn that the decay of religious values or their exclusion from policy debate will weaken the health of the American political system. While acknowledging that problems accompany political debate over moral values, they have asserted that the absence of faith from the political realm is far more dangerous to democracy than is an excess of passion.

Whatever its role in the past, how might religion today be expected to sustain democratic political institutions? According to some advocates, the dominant religions in the United States uphold beliefs that are essential to the maintenance of democratic values. Consider the notion of "human rights," a fundamental element of American political culture. On what basis can we assert that human beings, simply because they are human beings, are entitled to the various liberties spelled out in the U.S. Constitution? Although the idea of human rights is so deeply embedded in American thought that it almost seems "natural," it has usually been justified in religious terms. The religious traditions that have dominated American life commonly assert the equality of human beings before God. By virtue of humankind's common link to God, it is declared, all people deserve to be treated with a minimum of decency and respect. The Bill of Rights, supported by public opinion, embodies a religiously grounded teaching.

Other elements in the American creed have been said to originate in some conception of a divine presence. The political scientist Ernest Griffith once attempted to list the beliefs essential to the survival of democracy and to show how each one depended on the Judeo-Christian heritage:

1. Love for and belief in freedom: best based upon belief in the sacredness of the individual as a child of God.

2. Active and constructive participation in community life: best based upon the obligation of the Christian, the Jew, and other believers to accept responsibilities, cooperating with and working for their brother men [sic].

3. Integrity in discussion: best based upon the inner light of truth being primary in a world God meant to be righteous.

4. The freely assumed obligation of economic groups to serve society: best based upon the Christian insight into the nature of society as set forth, for example, by the parable of the body and its members.

5. Leadership and office holding regarded as public trusts: best based upon or inspired by the example and teachings of religious prophets, such as Jesus, who accepted such a service "to the death."

6. Attitudes assuring that passion will be channeled into constructive ends: best based upon religious faiths that unite an obligation to love and serve with a recognition of the primacy of individual personality.

7. Friendliness and cooperation among nations: best based upon the vision of world brotherhood derived from a faith that we are all children of a common Heavenly Father. (1956, 113)

In this view, religion provides the standards for judgment that are necessary to give meaning to concepts such as fairness, justice, goodness, and dignity.

The bald claim that religion is essential to maintain democratic values immediately inspires two critical questions. First: is religion the only basis for supporting the democratic outlook, or are other secular systems of belief capable of performing the same task? If alternatives are available, then religion can hardly be treated as essential to the survival of democratic government. But even if religious values do undergird freedom, that does not necessarily suggest that religious groups should enter the political arena. Hence the second question: should religion fulfill its public function only by speaking to the consciences of individuals or by entering the political arena more directly?

To maintain that religion is the only basis for morality, a position that President Reagan appeared to endorse during the 1984 campaign, is to ignore the existence of secular philosophies that also support respect for human rights and liberties. In fact, the research of many political scientists has suggested that the health of democracy depends less on public opinion of any sort than on favorable social and economic conditions (Lipset 1960, chap. 2). Nonetheless, advocates of religion have argued that it supplies a more powerful rationale for democracy than does any competing system of thought. In particular, they have claimed, religion—and religion alone—has the capacity to impart a sacred character to democratic values, to make them objects of faith that can resist all threats. By grounding a respect for human dignity in a force beyond human comprehension, like a transcendent God, the values rise above debate and are protected from the whims of public opinion or the challenges of competing philosophies. Only religion can provide a standard of judgment that transcends human authority. In the United States, the major religious groups thus contribute to the preservation of a democratic order by making support for political liberty an article of faith.

But does this necessarily mean that religious groups should enter the political order? Can't they contribute to the defense of democratic values without becoming embroiled in political activity and partisan debate? The advocates of a strong religious presence have answered these questions by pointing to the danger of a rigid separation between private conscience and public activity. When religious groups refrain from taking stands on controversial public issues, they may give the impression that religion speaks only to the concerns of private life. If religion is rigidly confined to the sphere of private morality, it has been argued, society runs the risk of enacting public policy without regard for moral consequences. It is important that religious claims enjoy a legitimate status in political debate, if only to guard against the danger of amoral government actions. This argument recalls the emphasis on the prophetic role of the churches, a familiar theme in the American civil religion discussed in Chapter 3.

Religious groups thus perform the important task of reminding us that public decisions inescapably involve and reflect values. Without such reminders, political conservatives have warned us, society might be willing to sacrifice the aged and the ill in the name of "efficiency" or some other standard.[8] Liberals have relied just as much on transcendent values when they demanded protection for the poor and oppressed, even at the cost of economic growth. The values operating in these examples—respect for life and compassion—will carry greater force in public consciousness when they are defended with the same resources as are competing secular values. The political activity of religious groups can thus be seen as necessary for the defense of moral judgment in public policy making. Even in a society where religious commitment is widespread, the churches have a duty to insist on its application to the problems of the day. Contentious though that might be, the alternative is even less satisfactory for the health of society.

In the modern world, Richard J. Neuhaus has argued tirelessly, religion supplies a counterweight to the greatest threat faced by democracy—a slide into totalitarianism. In a passage worth quoting at length, Neuhaus summarized the importance of religion in keeping government under popular control:

Once religion is reduced to nothing more than privatized conscience, the public square has only two actors in it—the state and the individual. Religion as a mediating structure—a community that generates and transmits moral values—is no longer available. Whether in Hitler's Third Reich or in today's sundry states professing Marxist-Leninism, the chief attack is not upon individual religious belief. Individual religious belief can be dismissed scornfully as superstition, for it finally poses little threat to the power of the state. No, the chief attack is upon the *institutions* that bear and promulgate belief in a transcendent reality by which the state can be called to judgment. Such institutions threaten the totalitarian proposition that everything is to be within the state, nothing is to be outside the state. (1984, 82)

If that analysis is correct, the church alone stands between the individual and the government, preventing the latter from swallowing up the former.

In truth, world history has supplied notable examples of religious values inspiring stubborn resistance to governments that demand complete obedience. Although the German churches as a group did not cover themselves with glory during the rise of nazism, some of the most courageous resisters to Hitler were motivated by belief in divinely inspired values transcending the norms of national loyalty. In the 1980s, the Catholic church preached on behalf of the autonomy of individuals against both leftist governments—as in Poland and Nicaragua—and right-wing regimes in countries like El Salvador and the Philippines. The contemporary movements mentioned previously in this book—Sanctuary, the nuclear freeze, antidraft activity, refusal to pay taxes for military programs—seem to draw disproportionately from Catholics attuned to the message that emanated from the Second Vatican Council. In all such cases, religion can provide a sense of perspective that may prompt the individual to challenge the authority of the state. By forcefully reminding individuals that their behavior must conform to higher standards, a religious tradition can promote disobedience to the excessive demands of government or other authority figures.

Religious values may guard against totalitarian sympathies in yet another manner. One great source of evil behavior is certainty, the unshakable conviction that the individual possesses some higher truth. Armed with certainty about the "one true master race" or the "inevitable destiny" of communism, human beings have committed some of the greatest crimes in history. Doubt is a potential antidote to such monstrousness because it activates the conscience. A person who is *not* wholly certain may question the rightness or appropriateness of behavior—including his or her own actions.

Christianity may engender doubt by its insistence on the fallenness of humankind. The doctrine of original sin teaches that humans are depraved and cannot be certain even of the righteousness of their own behavior. Sustained by this assumption, the Founders of the United States devised a governmental system that would make it difficult for would-be tyrants to accumulate enough power to overwhelm democratic institutions. One who assumes that humans are imperfect may counsel against the type of utopianism that has occasionally disfigured the world. While doubt can lead to confusion and paralysis, it may also prompt a pause that enables people to rethink the possible consequences of a particular course of action. In that way, the doctrine of original sin may serve as a hedge against extremism (Marty 1980; Niebuhr 1944).

Each facet of religion may contribute to the protection of a democratic political system. Religious *values* can supply a basis for rejecting the claims of the state by giving precedence to sacred obligations. For example, slavery and other systems of oppression have been condemned by some church leaders as incompatible with the dictates of religion and the content of the Bible. Religious *institutions* transmit the beliefs that can stand as a buffer between individuals and the state. They expose congregants to standards of right and wrong and may preach about how best to apply values to concrete situations. And when the individual is deeply attached to a religious *community,* he or she may prove more resistant to recruitment by political causes that threaten human rights. People bonded to others by social ties are probably less susceptible to the allure of totalitarian movements than are social isolates (Kornhauser 1959).

I believe that the foregoing argument provides the strongest case for an active religious presence in all aspects of society, including the political arena. Like the case against religious activism in politics, it is best treated as a hypothesis. Note that I described religion's impact on democracy in terms that emphasized potential—*can, may, might,* and *could.* Those terms were used because they convey the conditional impact of religion. To put it bluntly, although religion may enhance freedom in many respects, it can also undermine it. According to one eminent historian (Muller 1963), the record of religion with regard to human freedom is remarkably mixed. As has just been pointed out, religious values have in some instances supported the spirit and practice of democratic government. Yet the concept of democracy arose with the Greeks, well before the beginning of the Judeo-Christian era, and the church has often been a bulwark of resistance to the spread of democratic values. In a conclusion that dramatically calls attention to the coexistence of democratic and antidemocratic impulses in Western religion, Muller concluded that "Christianity did more to promote the growth of freedom than did any other of the higher religions . . . while it also opposed freedom of thought, speech, and conscience more fiercely than did any other religion except Mohammedanism" (ibid., 3).

If religion is to fulfill its promise as a bulwark against tyranny, it must encourage its followers to resist rulers who demand actions that are inconsistent with religious values. The evidence on that point does not suggest that religious commitment necessarily works to produce more reasoned behavior. The ambivalent relationship between religion and support for constituted authority was revealed in a disturbing study conducted by two psychologists from Atlanta (Bock and Warren 1972). They built on the famous experiments devised by another psychologist, Stanley Milgram (1974), who put laboratory subjects in a situation where an authority figure encouraged them to help with an experiment that involved inflicting pain on other subjects. Specifically, the participants were ordered to administer what they thought were electrical shocks to fellow subjects who had been unsuccessful in what was portrayed as a learning experiment. Milgram's finding that most persons obeyed the commands—even in the face of loud protests from the purported victim of the shocks—raised fundamental questions about what human qualities accounted for refusal to go along with destructive behavior.

The scenario devised by Milgram seemed an excellent opportunity to investigate one issue not carefully considered in his original experiments, the role of religious values in distinguishing between compliance and acceptance. The Atlanta psychologists thus recruited thirty college students, measured their religious values and commitment, and then put them through what amounted to a facsimile of the original Milgram experiments. In findings that will recall the studies of prejudice described earlier in the chapter, Bock and Warren discovered a strong but nonlinear relationship between religious commitment and willingness to inflict pain on others. Those with low or high levels of attachment to religion were substantially more likely than persons of moderate attachment to resist the instructions to administer shocks. To explain this finding, the investigators suggested that the nature of religious commitment—rather than its amount—was a critical factor in the subjects' decision to comply or refuse:

In the Judeo-Christian tradition, a high value is placed on a strong, well-defined response to "the will of God." In fact, a decisive response even if negative is to be preferred over neutrality. The Biblical position is that the man who is undecided about basic religious issues is unable to be decisive when confronted by an ethical dilemma. His tendency is to forfeit his choice to any impinging power. On the other hand, having taken a definite religious stance, one is in a position to act in accord with conscience. (1972, 190)

If the findings of this study can be assumed to hold for the general population in real-world settings—both untested assumptions—then they should diminish our confidence that religious commitment will automatically inspire resistance to tyranny. Once again, it depends on the quality of religious commitment that brings people into the public sphere. People who appear to have internalized the ethical principles of religion—along with those who have minimal contact with religious institutions—will probably prove most likely to resist orders that conflict with widely accepted ethical principles. Based on the limited experimental data, those whose religious commitment is moderate do not seem endowed with a tendency to challenge rulers who demand that citizens abdicate conscience.

As we saw in Chapter 7, white evangelical Protestants have greatly increased their political involvement during the past few years. Critical observers have argued that the style of religious commitment exemplified by some of the evangelical activists possesses dangerous authoritarian tendencies. This charge has been more often made than substantiated, in part because of weakness in the empirical measurement of "authoritarianism."[9] Lacking better evidence, there are signs that some of the politically minded evangelical leaders do not practice democracy very actively in the institutions they control. Thus, the dynamic evangelical churches that have provided leadership for the New Christian Right conform to fairly rigid and hierarchical authority patterns that give members very little experience of democratic decision making to carry with them into the public arena (Fitzgerald 1981). At the Christian university he founded and continues to lead, the Reverend Jerry Falwell has provided a code of conduct that is similarly weighted toward authority (Baker 1985). Under the rules, students at Liberty Baptist may not participate in unauthorized demonstrations, are obliged to attend church, and may be expelled for participation in demonstrations or petition drives not approved by university authorities. Students are thus asked to waive a number of rights guaranteed under the Constitution, including protection against warrantless searches of their rooms. Again, we cannot know for certain if these practices are widespread in evangelical Protestantism or common among all types of religions; nor is it guaranteed that adherents of such churches draw lessons about governance from religious institutions or that such lessons would carry over to the behavior of church members in other settings. Nonetheless, these tendencies should dissuade observers from asserting too confidently that religious commitment in politics necessarily acts as a brake on totalitarian tendencies.

What, then, can we finally conclude about the impact of religion on democracy in the contemporary situation? There is little alternative but to conclude that religion may sometimes sustain democratic values and sometimes undermine them. The source of the paradox is simply that religious values are ambiguous with regard to politics. They contain messages that can lead persons of common faith in different directions. The multiple political uses of religious ideas have been demonstrated repeatedly in specific policy conflicts. In the period leading up to the Civil War, Northerners and Southerners alike found ample justification for slavery and abolition in the same religious document. During the Prohibition era in this century, learned clergymen argued earnestly about the message of the Scriptures with regard to intoxicating beverages. The problem arises today even in the unlikely context of environmental policy, a subject of conflicting biblical images. Just as some interpret God's intention that people should have dominion "over all the earth" (Gen. 1:26) as a call to exploit the environment in the interests of human happiness, others cite the Twenty-fourth Psalm, "The Earth is the Lord's," to promote reverence for the natural environment and support a preservationist ethic (Blackburn 1972). The problem is no less vexing at the general level of democracy. Jesus' call in Matt. 22:21 to "render therefore unto Caesar the things which are Caesar's; and unto God the things that are God's," does not define precisely what it is that humanity owes to state and to church. Depending on how responsibility is allocated between God and Caesar, that biblical injunction may be interpreted as a call to revolution or, at the other extreme, as a plea for servility.

The problem of limited guidance even extends to such fundamental questions as the best form of human government. The doctrine of original sin is interpreted by some theologians as a call to caution, an injunction against committing evil in the name of higher values. As such, it may promote a belief in the wisdom of limited government. Yet it has also been used as an argument against the human capacity for self-government. If mortals are prone to greed, jealousy, rapaciousness, envy, pride, and other expressions of sinfulness, then they are simply not worthy of basic rights or opportunities to exercise their free will in politics. Even today, people of faith continue to argue if the Bible is capitalistic or socialistic, supportive of abortion or not, militaristic or pacifistic. The most careful students of religious thought simply cannot agree on the precise relevance of Christian doctrine to specific issues or if Christianity is inherently conducive to democracy or dictatorship (Wolin 1956). I submit that the obstacle is not deficient understanding, but the mixed political messages contained in the major religious creeds.

Given the ambiguity of religious texts and teachings, the mixed historical record, and the empirical evidence cited earlier in the chapter, it would be foolhardy to assert that religious faith necessarily upholds democratic values. In some contexts and for some types of people, it may enhance freedom. Or it may encourage particular types of freedom while enforcing conformity in other realms of human endeavor. It seems to matter less if people are religious than how they hold their religious values and attempt to apply them in concrete situations. An upsurge in religiously based political activity is neither to be welcomed uncritically nor condemned out of hand.

It seems appropriate to end this work by stressing that science cannot establish whether religious claims are true or false. But science, especially social science, can attempt to discover the consequences of religious values, institutions, and communities for the political system. This book has attempted to describe how religion interacts with the political system in one country and has explained why some patterns recur. Because of the limitations of previous research and the inherent tentativeness of science, I have emphasized the provisional status of my conclusions. More and better research might clarify the patterns of religious influence in politics, and might even provide a basis on which to offer confident predictions about the future of the relationship between the two domains. The impact of religion on American political life is surely important enough to warrant the effort.

NOTES

1. In that regard, a Supreme Court that put stricter limits on religious action by the churches might have responded more favorably to the unsuccessful federal lawsuit filed by critics of the Roman Catholic church. Charging that the church's intense antiabortion activism made it a political group, the prochoice critics demanded that the Internal Revenue Service withdraw tax-exempt status from the Roman Catholic church.

2. "Racist Aryan Nation Group Inducts New Disciples," *New York Times*, Oct. 20, 1985, 31.

3. Lest it be thought that conservative preferences are antidemocratic sentiments, let me emphasize that most of the scales Wuthnow examined really measured what has aptly been called "pseudo-conservatism," surface agreement with right-wing goals but usually involving means that most conservatives would reject. What passes for mass conservatism often lacks the subtlety and respect for democratic means that characterizes the conservative intellectual tradition (McClosky 1958).

4. From a social-learning perspective, the differences of expression might only reflect the greater familiarity of nonaffiliates with democratic norms and their ability to recognize the socially desirable response (McClosky and Zaller 1984).

5. Wade Clark Roof (1974) has suggested that the apparent prejudice of churchgoers is principally an outgrowth of their localistic orientation, a consequence of their limited exposure to agents of modernity.

6. In an interesting study that compared different types of activists, Sharon Presley (1985) showed that party activists tended to be recruited from conventional religious backgrounds, whereas political resisters reported either no religious affiliation or membership in an unconventional church. As the resisters included persons who had committed acts of civil disobedience or otherwise exposed themselves to legal sanctions, the results suggested that membership in mainstream churches is

associated with adherence to democratic norms and that defiance of legally constituted authority is more common among persons outside the established churches.

7. The same argument has been made about countries undergoing modernization. In such societies, religious values may contribute to a democratic outlook and
help to draw citizens into political action (Smith 1970). As I noted in Chapter 2,
active involvement in a church may serve to encourage the development of political
skills and promote electoral participation.

8. Opponents of liberalized abortion make just such an argument when they
contend that the prochoice position is grounded in values that lead to disrespect for
human life and dignity. Supporters of liberalized abortion would respond that forcing
women to bear unwanted children is a greater denial of respect for human life and
dignity. Hence, the abortion debate is a conflict between different interpretations of
what is right rather than a clash between advocates of morality versus amorality.

9. Specifically, the scales that purport to measure unquestioning support for authority and related signs of intellectual rigidity are loaded with items that tap support
for traditional religious values. Thus, a five-point scale purporting to measure "conventionality," a construct associated with authoritarianism, included participation
in church activities and a belief in the truth of religion as elements of a conventional
outlook (Raden 1982). Worse yet, another study labeled respondents as "religious
dogmatists" if they agreed with such statements as "Regular attendance of services
is a necessary part of religion" or "Parents should make every effort to ensure that
their children develop strong religious convictions" (Fagan and Breed 1970). When
authoritarianism is thus equated with attachment to traditional religion, it is not
possible to determine if the two concepts are actually linked.

REFERENCES

Adorno, T. W., Else Frenkel-Brunswik, Daniel J. Levinson, and R. Nevitt Sanford.
    1950. *The Authoritarian Personality.* New York: Harper and Brothers.
Allport, Gordon W. 1958. *The Nature of Prejudice.* Abridged edition. Garden City, N.Y.:
    Doubleday Anchor.
Baker, Donald. 1985. "It's Not Exactly 'Animal House'." *Washington Post Weekly Edi-
    tion,* May 27, pp. 7–8.
Batson, C. Daniel, et al. 1986. "Religious Orientation and Overt and Covert Racial
    Prejudice." *Journal of Personality and Social Psychology* 50:175–181.
Beatty, Kathleen Murphy, and Oliver Walter. 1984. "Religious Preference and Prac-
    tice: Reevaluating Their Impact on Political Tolerance." *Public Opinion Quarterly*
    48:318–329.
Blackburn, Joyce. 1972. *The Earth Is the Lord's.* Waco, Tex.: Word.
Bock, David C., and Neil Clark Warren. 1972. "Religious Belief as a Factor in Obe-
    dience to Destructive Commands." *Review of Religious Research* 13:185–191.
Budner, Stanley. 1962. "Intolerance of Ambiguity as a Personality Variable." *Journal
    of Personality* 30:29–50.
Clapp, Rodney. 1987. "Democracy as Heresy." *Christianity Today,* February 20,
    pp. 17–23.
Cochran, Clarke E. 1990. *Religion in Public and Private Life.* New York: Routledge, 168.

Coles, Robert. 1985. "Out of the Mouths of Babes: When Ethics and Reality Collide." *Washington Post Weekly Edition,* September 2, p. 24.

Fagan, John, and George Breed. 1970. "A Good, Short Measure of Religious Dogmatism." *Psychological Reports* 26:533–534.

Fitzgerald, Frances. 1981. "A Disciplined, Charging Army." *New Yorker,* May 18, pp. 53–141.

Gibson, James L., and Arthur J. Anderson. 1985. "The Political Implications of Elite and Mass Tolerance." *Political Behavior* 7:118–146.

Gorsuch, Richard L., and Daniel Aleshire. 1974. "Christian Faith and Ethnic Prejudice: A Review and Interpretation of Research." *Journal for the Scientific Study of Religion* 13:281–307.

Griffith, Ernest S., John Plamenatz, and J. Roland Pennock. 1956. "Cultural Prerequisites to a Successfully Functioning Democracy." *American Political Science Review* 50:101–137.

Guth, James L., and John C. Green. 1984. "Political Activists and Civil Liberties: The Case of Party and PAC Contributors." Paper presented at the annual meeting of the Midwest Political Science Association, Chicago.

Hansen, Karsten. 1984. "Where the Martyrs Come Running." *Manchester Guardian Weekly,* March 25, p. 9.

Kelley, Dean M., ed. 1982. *Government Intervention in Religious Affairs.* New York: Pilgrim.

Kornhauser, William. 1959. *The Politics of Mass Society.* Glencoe, Ill.: Free Press.

Liebman, Charles S. 1988. *Deceptive Images.* New Brunswick, N.J.: Transaction.

Lipset, Seymour Martin. 1960. *Political Man.* Garden City, N.Y.: Doubleday Anchor.

McClosky, Herbert. 1958. "Conservatism and Personality." *American Political Science Review* 52:27–45.

McClosky, Herbert, and John Zaller. 1984. *The American Ethos: Public Attitudes Toward Capitalism and Democracy.* Cambridge: Harvard University Press.

Maguire, Daniel C. 1982. *The New Subversives: Anti-Americanism of the Religious Right.* New York: Continuum.

Marty, William R. 1980. "The Search for Realism in Politics and Ethics: Reflections by a Political Scientist on a Christian Perspective." *Logos* 1:93–124.

Milgram, Stanley. 1974. *Obedience to Authority.* New York: Harper and Row.

Muller, Herbert J. 1963. *Religion and Freedom in the Modern World.* Chicago: University of Chicago Press.

Neuhaus, Richard John. 1984. *The Naked Public Square.* Grand Rapids, Mich.: Eerdmans.

Nice, David C. 1988. "Abortion Clinic Bombings as Political Violence." *American Journal of Political Science* 32:178–195.

Niebuhr, Reinhold. 1944. *The Children of Light and the Children of Darkness.* New York: Scribner's.

Nunn, Clyde Z., Harry J. Crockett, Jr., and J. Allen Williams, Jr. 1978. *Tolerance for Nonconformity.* San Francisco: Jossey-Bass.

Pateman, Carole. 1970. *Participation and Democratic Theory.* Cambridge, Eng.: Cambridge University Press.

Perkins, H. Wesley. 1983. "Organized Religion as Opiate or Prophetic Stimulant: A

Study of American and English Assessments of Social Justice in Two Urban Settings." *Review of Religious Research* 24:206–224.

———. 1985. "A Research Note on Religiosity as Opiate or Prophetic Stimulant Among Students in England and the United States." *Review of Religious Research* 26:269–280.

Powell, G. Bingham, Jr. 1982. *Contemporary Democracies*. Cambridge: Harvard University Press.

Presley, Sharon. 1985. "Moral Judgment and Attitudes Toward Authority in Political Resisters." Paper presented at the annual meeting of the Midwest Political Science Association, Chicago.

Raden, David. 1982. "Dogmatism and Conventionality." *Psychological Reports* 50: 1020–1022.

Raschke, Vernon. 1973. "Dogmatism and Committed and Consensual Religiosity." *Journal for the Scientific Study of Religion* 12:339–344.

Rokeach, Milton. 1971. "Paradoxes of Religious Belief." In *Religion in Radical Transition*, edited by Jeffrey K. Hadden, 15–24. New Brunswick, N.J.: Transaction.

Roof, Wade Clark. 1974. "Religious Orthodoxy and Minority Prejudice: Causal Relationship or Reflection of Localistic World View?" *American Journal of Sociology* 80:643–664.

Rose, Richard, and Derek Urwin. 1969. "Social Cohesion, Political Parties, and Strains in Regimes." *Comparative Political Studies* 2:7–67.

Sapp, Gary L., and Logan Jones. 1986. "Religious Orientation and Moral Judgment." *Journal for the Scientific Study of Religion* 25:208–214.

Scheurer, Daniel. 1990. "The New Christian Right and Instructional Materials in the Public Schools of Florida." Ph.D. diss., College of Education, University of Florida, Gainesville.

Schoenfeld, Eugen. 1985. "Religion and Loyalty to the Political Elite: The Case of the Presidency." *Review of Religious Research* 27:178–188.

Smidt, Corwin D., and James M. Penning. 1982. "Religious Commitment, Political Conservatism, and Political and Social Tolerance in the United States: A Longitudinal Analysis." *Sociological Analysis* 43:231–246.

Smith, Donald Eugene. 1970. *Religion and Political Development*. Boston: Little, Brown.

Steiner, Gilbert Y., ed. 1983. *The Abortion Dispute and the American System*. Washington, D.C.: Brookings.

Stouffer, Samuel. 1966. *Communism, Conformity, and Civil Liberties*. New York: John Wiley.

Studlar, Donley. 1978. "Religion and White Racial Attitudes in Britain." *Ethnic and Racial Studies* 1:306–315.

Sullivan, John L., James Piereson, and George E. Marcus. 1982. *Political Tolerance and American Democracy*. Chicago: University of Chicago Press.

Tesh, Sylvia. 1984. "In Support of 'Single-Issue' Politics." *Political Science Quarterly* 99:27–44.

Wald, Kenneth D., Dennis E. Owen, and Samuel S. Hill, Jr. 1989. "Habits of the Mind? The Problem of Authority in the New Christian Right." In *Religion and Political Behavior in the United States*, edited by Ted G. Jelen, 93–108. New York: Greenwood.

Wilcox, Clyde, and Ted Jelen. 1990. "Evangelicals and Political Tolerance." *American Politics Quarterly* 18:25–46.

Wilson, Glenn D., and Christopher Bagley. 1973. "Religion, Racism, and Conservatism." In *The Psychology of Conservatism*, edited by Glenn Wilson, 117–128. New York: Academic.

Wolin, Sheldon. 1956. "Politics and Religion: Luther's Simplistic Imperative." *American Political Science Review* 50:24–42.

Wuthnow, Robert. 1973. "Religious Commitment and Conservatism: In Search of an Elusive Relationship." In *Religion in Sociological Perspective*, edited by Charles Y. Glock, 117–132. Belmont, Calif.: Wadsworth.

Index

Index